TOBRUK

'THIS IS HALLOWED GROUND
FOR HERE LIE
THOSE WHO DIED
FOR THEIR COUNTRY'

— Inscription at the Tobruk War Cemetery

This history has been written for
Jim Gauton, Charlie Jones, Louis Angel,
Jock Leggat, George Maers, Sidney Eisbruck,
Jim Pearce and all the other Rats of Tobruk,
wherever they may be.

'... men over whose bones great men clambered into
the history books'.
— Wolf Heckman

TOBRUK

The Great Siege
Reassessed

FRANK HARRISON

With very best wishes

FRANK HARRISON.

2000.

**ARMS AND
ARMOUR**

Arms and Armour Press
A Cassell Imprint
Wellington House, 125 Strand, London WC2R 0BB

Distributed in the USA by Sterling Publishing Co. Inc.,
387 Park Avenue South, New York, NY 10016-8810.

First published in 1996
This paperback edition 1997

British Library Cataloguing-in-Publication Data:
a catalogue record for this book is available from
the British Library

ISBN 1-85409-452-1

Designed and edited by DAG Publications Ltd.
Designed by David Gibbons; edited by Michael Boxall;
Printed and bound in Great Britain by
MPG Books Ltd, Bodmin, Cornwall

CONTENTS

LIST OF MAPS

ACKNOWLEDGEMENTS

I wish to thank many people whose kindness, interest and help have assisted in the production of this history. Research centres which have allowed me to study their collections and to use copyright material and photographs are: The Public Record Office at Kew, where I was able to read the War Diaries of all the units involved and cables between Middle East Command and the War Cabinet, and also to study the maps used in Tobruk during the siege; The Imperial War Museum, where I read the Afrika Korps War Diaries and was able to peruse hundreds of photographs; The Tank Museum, where I read reports of actions, and inspected photographs; The Liddell Hart Military Archives at King's College, where I read letters from Rommel to his wife, Lucy, and son, Manfred, and also letters between Liddell Hart, the Rommels and several German Generals; and The Royal Signals Museum, where I sat again in an ACV and saw the wireless set I used in the Tobruk Tanks. I am especially grateful to Paul Kemp of the Imperial War Museum for his assistance with photographs. I thank the Australian War Memorial for allowing me to use the photograph of Jack Edmondson, VC.

The following publishers have kindly allowed me to quote from the works listed: B. T. Batsford Ltd, London (*The Life and Death of the Africa Korps* by Ronald Lewin, 1977); Oxford University Press (*Sidi Resegh Battles* by J. A. Hagar Hamilton, 1957, and *Infantry Brigadier* by Major General Sir H. Kippenberger, 1949). I also thank Sir Bernard Fergusson for allowing me to use two verses from the poem in his history, *The Wild Green Earth*.

I am indebted to Major General Rea Leakey, who allowed me to read and quote from his memoirs, and to Major General A. H. Lascelles who both met and wrote to me about his time spent as Brigade Major of the Tobruk Tanks. I thank the following other Rats of Tobruk for their interest and help; F. G. Barrett (KDG), Phillip Bell (3rd Hussars), Bill Cargill (Black Watch), K. A. Dickens (Leicesters), Don McTier, DCM (RTR), Jim

Pearce (R Signals), Henry Ritchie (RA) and Reg Stringer (RAF). I thank especially, Ken Rumbold (RAF), who is the Federal Secretary of ROTA, and Jack Warner (R Signals) for allowing me to use photographs from their collections.

Others to whom I owe a debt are Clare Coad, who translated Afrika Korps documents for me; Frank May (RAF) of the Djebel Association for his advice, Ted Harrison who arranged for me to use the library at Leeds University; Frances Harrison and Tony Shermoen, who arranged for me to use translations of German texts at Berkley University; Judith Harrison, who arranged library access in Calgary, and Marie and Bernard Harrison, who hosted my many safaris to the London research centres. I thank my sons, Tony and Mark, for helping me through the torments of word processing, and I thank Mary, my wife, for her toleration of the dawn-to-dusk hours I spent writing this book, and my vagueness at those times when I was still shaking the sand out of my shoes. Most of all, though, I thank those men to whom this work is dedicated, my comrades who stood and fought at Tobruk, many of whom still sleep there.

At the going down of the desert sun...

INTRODUCTION

As the sub-title suggests, this book offers a reassessment of the longest siege in British military history. Two infantry divisions were involved, one Australian, the other British. The Australian 9th Division successfully defended the fortress of Tobruk against Rommel's Afrika Korps and its Italian Allies during the first six months of the siege, and won fame by so doing. It has a second claim to historical renown – together with its supporting British artillery and tanks it inflicted the first defeat upon German Arms in the Second World War. These military triumphs won by the division have been acclaimed, and rightly so.

The British 70th Division took over the defence of the fortress when the Australian division was withdrawn by sea. During the battles of 'Crusader' in late 1941, the plan was for Eighth Army to advance from the Egyptian frontier and link with a sortie made from the fortress by this division and its supporting armour and artillery (TOBFORCE). This would have cut off the Axis troops in north-east Cyrenaica, including almost the whole of the Afrika Korps, and would have allowed Eighth Army the use of Tobruk's port as a supply depot. TOBFORCE made the break-out from the fortress as ordered, fighting its way through the ring of investing enemy posts in a series of battles that were as bloody as any fought in all the Western Desert campaigns, and it created the required corridor. When Rommel repulsed Eighth Army's attempts to make the link, TOBFORCE clung to the corridor it had made, and although under constant attack from all sides did not give up one inch of the ground it had won. Indeed, it extended that corridor by seizing El Duda ridge, and finally making the link with the New Zealand 2nd Division. When that division was also driven from the field, TOBFORCE still clung to its corridor, and its defeat of 21st Panzer Division's final attempt to retake El Duda heralded the collapse of the German front in 1941 and Rommel's withdrawal from Cyrenaica.

At the time, TOBFORCE had been expected to take a subsidiary role in 'Crusader', and this is how the action has since been treated by military historians. Yet of all the planned battles of that benighted operation, the creation and holding of the Tobruk corridor was the only one to succeed. Alas, Britain's 70th Division received little credit for its bravery. It won no acclaim, it was broken up at the whim of Wingate, vanished into the Burmese jungle with him, and disappeared from history.

Why is it that one division was lauded, the other ignored? Could it be because the first belonged to the Australian Imperial Army, whose nation recognises its heroes, while the second was composed of British county and regional regiments which have always been taken for granted by its nation? This reassessment has been written in an attempt to redress the balance, to place the British 70th Division where it belongs – on the plinth alongside Australian 9th Division, as joint heroes of the siege and break-out at Tobruk.

The besieged troops could not have held out without the support of the Royal Navy, and to a lesser extent, the Royal Air Force. For eight months the Royal Navy kept a garrison of more than 25,000 men supplied in the essentials of life and warfare. When the time came to make the exchange of the two infantry divisions, it completed the exercise with a minimum loss of life. These duties were carried out without demur, but at great cost in men and ships. The passage from Alexandria to Tobruk became known as 'The Suicide Run', the ships and crews being exposed to unceasing attack from the air, not only during the voyage but even more so when they were inside Tobruk harbour, and also to the U-boat threat. The Royal Air Force presence was limited to a few Lysanders and Hurricanes operating from primitive airfields inside the perimeter. They faced impossible odds, with enemy aircraft in far greater numbers attacking from several airfields in the vicinity. After a brave, and costly fight, the survivors were withdrawn from the garrison. They departed with honour, having won the admiration of those who had watched their uneven struggle.

Both of these magnificent supporting efforts illuminate the first two parts of this book.

Of all the military figures which paraded across that forbidding stage, two stand supreme, one on each side of the opposing divide. One was

Montgomery, the ultimate victor. The other was Rommel, Commander of Panzergruppe Afrika, that mythical warrior who bestrode the Western Desert before the arrival of Montgomery. It is no exaggeration to say that this man became a legend in his own lifetime, and that the myth which surrounded his exploits was manufactured as much by the admiration and fear he brought to the ordinary soldier on the opposing side, as by the Berlin media. Not too long ago, the sons of Montgomery and Rommel stood together in the north-west of England, taking the salute at the march-past of the Africa Star Association's commemoration of the 50th Anniversary of El Alamein. The respect in which these veterans held his murdered father was then extended to the son. Some perhaps saw the ghosts of those two leaders alongside their sons, many perhaps echoed a much earlier thought...

'If only we'd had Rommel leading us...'

Rommel and Tobruk were insolubly linked. He suffered his first defeat there. He suffered his second defeat there. It became for him the Jewel in the Crown of Cyrenaica and he determined to possess that jewel. Eventually he did so, but not in 1941 when he most needed it. It seems proper that any work on the siege should recognise this link, and that in a work of reassessment the recognition should be made in an appraisal of Rommel's strategy, tactics, successes and failures during 1941, the year of his arrival in the desert and of his obsession to take Tobruk. This book has therefore been divided into three parts.

Part One tells of the work of the Australian 9th Division, supported by British armour and artillery, and under the command of the Australian General Morshead. This phase saw the repelling of two major attacks on the garrison, and the development of aggressive patrolling beyond the perimeter. These are described in detail. The phase ended with the withdrawal of the Australian Division and its replacement by the British 70th Division, the Polish Carpathian Brigade and a Czech battalion.

Part Two describes that change-over and the preparations made for the break-out by the British division. It then tells the story of the sixteen days of the break-out in full and previously unrelated detail, using a diary format.

Part Three asks the questions about Rommel and offers answers. How justified was the myth that grew around the man? Was he the fearless and chivalrous leader who might at any moment burst out from the desert at the head of his panzers to confound his enemy? Was he the master of manoeuvre, the brilliant exploiter of the mistakes of his opponents, the tactician supreme, the Desert Fox of myth?

This history is a blend of military action and human response. In war games, counters are moved through the various moments of attack and retreat. In real war it is the human who moves and often falls. In order to prevent this account becoming simply another movement of counters, a human perspective has been introduced which embraces the leaders and the led. It is intended to put flesh on to figures rather than to intrude into the military story.

The verses at the head of each chapter in Part One are from the poem 'Tobruk' written while the author was in a prisoner-of-war camp in Italy. They are in sequence, and complete the poem.

PART ONE: SIEGE
The Story of Australian 9th Division

DESERT DUST

Infinite the stars,
   Finite, the soldier.
Shine on him, let him
   Grow older, grow older.

Timeless the air,
   Youthful, the soldier.
Fill his lungs, let him
   Grow older, grow older.

Ageless the sand,
   Infant, the soldier.
Particled ... drifting.
No older, no older.

ONE

We clung to the escarpment,
   shoulder of Africa,
stealing a moment of its long life.
   We knew its stars,
heard its piards.

The Calling of Names

The first name called was Jones, and I thought it's the British Army, it's bound to be alphabetical and that lets me out. Thank God for that!

Jones, Charles Toc, Signalman out of Edmonton in far-away Canada, come to England to join the Royal Navy in which his father had served, but, frustrated in that effort, taking to khaki and ending up in front of a wireless set in a 3rd Armoured Brigade HQ tank. I didn't know about his Canadian background as I sat on the steps of the Scuola Benito Mussolini in the port of Tobruk, scuffing my heels in the sand which lay like a blanket over their angled edges. I was sweating. I wasn't interested in backgrounds, I had one ear cocked ready to catch the next name, the other ear was occupied by a sudden burst of thunder in the west, the far too near to me, west.

What did I know about Jones, Charles Toc? Twice he had come to my attention during the time in which I had been with what I had been ordered to think of as my second family. One summer's afternoon of my few English days in its paternalistic fold we had emerged from out of the dark wood below Thursley where our tanks lay hidden, and had climbed through Surrey's shining fields to the small church in that village, where a wedding was to take place. Charlie Jones played the male lead. The female lead was his cousin, an East End of London girl, and they were being married by our Anglican padre against the wishes of her parents. One week later, after a honeymoon of two days in the village pub (which was all that our whip-round would allow), the new Mrs Jones was back in the East End and we were out of our green and pleasant land and climbing the rougher, colder hills of the heaving Atlantic. The sun of that afternoon was – is still – strong in the memory, a treasured last glow of social sanity.

The second occasion occurred on a beach in Durban. One of the boys – and we were all little more than that – had overdone the dressing-up bit in the hope of attracting a daughter of that entrancing southern city. He was paying the price; ridicule is cruel among young males, especially among young military males. He was suffering, and Charlie, who was anything but cruel, turned cruelty into humour. He peeled to the bone and posed next to the lad so that someone could take a photograph of this sartorial contrast. If that photograph is still in existence somewhere and suggesting that Charlie was an extrovert, it is an example of how circumstances can distort, because in fact Charlie was as deeply quiet as the spruce forests of his northern home.

The thunder rolled again. Sweat spurted again. I was acutely aware that below us in the harbour the SS *Balmora* was getting up steam to take us back to Egypt; that the thunder was less than twenty miles away and had nothing to do with climatic conditions, and that if the Sergeant didn't quicken up this little act of betrayal we might not make it down to that ship before it reversed away from the quayside. Oh yes, a neat little act of betrayal was taking place and we all knew it. Four men were being sacrificed to the greater good of a couple of dozen others. A fair-enough trade you might say, unless you happened to be one of the four.

The second name called was Leggat, Christian name unknown because since he spoke Glaswegian, 'Jock' had always sufficed. I was less interested in his name than in its initial letter. It confirmed that the British Army was behaving true to form, it was indeed alphabet bound, and I was as good as on the *Balmora*.

What did I know about Leggat? That he was a regular soldier like most of the squadron and, poor devil, would remain in the Army beyond any horizon I wished to contemplate. That he was not the most cheerful of men and nature had not helped here, giving him a pair of eyebrows which could indicate the coming of bad weather, real or metaphorical, better than any dispersal of mercury. Until a few days before this little gathering he had played no part in my life; I had known him as an 'oldie' with a reputation for finding things which were not always lost. Then one of his findings had proved providential to me. Standing in the dirt at the side of a desert track after quitting my relic of a tank, I was wondering just how big Germans were and how often they sharpened their bayonets, when through the dust rolled an Italian water truck. Leggat was driving it. He drove it down the twisting track of the precipice above Derna, through the flames which were devouring that little town and up the other side, minutes before the track was blown. He drove it through the fire-fight that was being waged across the airfield and whoever was doing the fighting paused in astonishment to allow us to pass. Leggat was that kind of a man, a pragmatist who was determined to get back to Glasgow whatever might happen to the rest of the Army, and to get back as quickly and as whole as he could. Jock's eyebrows did not register great approval at hearing his name read out.

The third name called was Gauton, and that destroyed the myth of military consistency. But hope springs eternal, Jones, Leggat and Gauton did not possess a single stripe between them and surely any detachment being left behind as HQ Signals to a tank brigade, no matter how truncated this latter might be, must have someone with formal authority in charge. So I reasoned, forgetting that through the long days and longer nights of the recent retreat, formal authority had been more noticeable by its absence than its presence. That, with a rapidity that could only be admired, it had disappeared over the horizon at the very first sound of Panzer Mk III engines.

Back then to Gauton, James Warwick. A Territorial Army signalman from Manchester and a quiet, introverted lad who was physically strong and verbally dismissive. He had been posted to the brigade in the same detachment as myself but there had been no social intercourse between us, we were not yet on the same wave-length.

And the last name when it eventually came? Harrison of course. Wartime only Signalman Harrison, out of Preston in the beautiful county of Lancashire, could forget about the *Balmora* and start to consider himself a citizen of Tobruk. Easter was almost upon us and I suppose betrayal was in season, but it might have helped if someone – our CO for example – had taken us to one side and told us that we had been selected because of some expertise that we had shown during the recent desperate days, but Layzell was elsewhere, and all around us men were fastening haversack buckles and avoiding our eyes. I didn't have a haversack to buckle; mine was last seen on fire on the back of an armoured car south of Mersa Brega. I obviously didn't have a second family either, there was no shaking of hands, no wishing of luck. We four abandonees tramped out to a waiting truck and I never saw any of my erstwhile brothers again.

We took the Derna Road out from town. We didn't speak much, we were in shock I suppose. Half an hour earlier we had thought ourselves on the way back to shampoos in Alexandria, and eggies-on-bread and Shafto's Cinema. Now we were heading for quite a different theatre. We were also in silent and shared depression; not all that long ago we had been conquering heroes singing our way to Tripoli past snaking miles of Italian prisoners. For weeks the exhilaration of victory had been our psychological diet, now we had the shameful taste of retreat on our tongues and it was not wholesome.

Shock and despair; unpleasant companions to take with us as we left the tarmac of the Via Balbia and began to churn through the sand towards the Solaro escarpment – no wonder we were silent. Then came a rude interruption. A truck overtook us, smothering us with its dust. It was open like our own and it was filled with infantrymen. They were wearing tin hats and had their rifles propped up beside them, they were singing and they didn't seem to be giving a damn, not for the dust and not for the crashing of the truck springs and certainly not for the thunder claps coming from out of the west. They broke their singing to curse us with strange oaths and to bless us with stranger signs, and then they were gone with their cloud of dust, in search of our common enemy. They were Australians of course, sons of the southern sun, and something strange happened at that moment, which I have never forgotten. I quite lost my sense of despair. I realised that whatever I was being asked to face I could not be in better company to meet it.

An incredibly hard man

Our common enemy. Who was he? In one word, Rommel, although we didn't know the name at that time. One man does not make an army, but not since Napoleon had a military commander been such a symbol of leadership and battlefield victory over superior forces as this man. He was to intrude into the lives not only of his own men and the Italians, but into the lives of every one of the scores of thousands of British and Dominion troops who fought in Africa. His days may have been numbered even then, but has a single man on either side of the warring divide escaped the lasting effects of that intrusion?

A Württemberger, and lacking the soldierly spoon of Prussianism in his mouth at birth, he had not been favoured by the *Reichswehr*, even though his First World War medals included the Pour Le Mérite. It was not until he came to the notice of Hitler through his best-seller, *Infanterie Greift An* (*The Infantry Attacks*) that he began his rise through the ranks. He asked Hitler for, and was given, command of a panzer division for the attack on the Western Front, where he proved a master of *Blitzkrieg*. He told his wife that time and again he had found that the day went to the side that was first to plaster its opponents with fire. That, and surprise, were his techniques, but if he lacked fire-power there were also bluff and bravery. 'Let it be clear' he said. 'There is no such thing as a Direction Front, but only a Direction Enemy.'[1] He was first across the Meuse and the Seine – personally. He forced the Highland Division into surrender at St-Valéry. He drove right across France to seize Cherbourg. His division captured 100,000 men and masses of *matériel*. He had wished for an immediate invasion of Britain and would probably have been among the first ashore had it taken place. He was already in the history books. He had clambered over many bones.

Our common enemy came to be personified in this one man.

What was he doing in Libya, the African Province of an Italian Dictator? Officially he was there to provide a blocking force to prevent the loss of the province to the British. Unofficially, he was there to seize the Nile Delta. The historically-pathetic Mussolini had sent a huge army across the border into Egypt, intending to add that country to his African empire. A much smaller, but more mobile and determined British Army had outflanked it, defeated it in a series of battles along the Libyan coast, and had finally destroyed what was left of it among the sand dunes of Beda Fomm. With a defenceless Tripoli in its sights, this British army had been halted in its tracks by political necessity, had been emasculated, its most experienced elements dispatched to Greece and Ethiopia, and only a rump left behind to defend the gains so recently made.

Meanwhile, strategic considerations had forced Hitler to intervene. If the British reached Tripoli, the whole of the western seaboard of the Mediterranean would be at risk, and British aircraft would dominate that sector of the great lake. Hitler decided to send a blocking force to save Tripoli. He then changed the nature of this force to allow offensive reconnaissance. It was to be a mechanised force with air support and commanded by an 'incredibly hard man'.

The highly mechanised force was the Afrika Korps, consisting of two armoured divisions, 15th Panzer Division (hereinafter PZ15) under command of General Major von Prittwitz, and 5th Light Division (5LT) under General Streich. The first of these had an infantry background and little experience in armoured warfare; the second was formed around parts of 3rd Panzer Division with the addition of 5th Panzer Regiment (PZR5). Fliegerkorps X (FLX), a strong combination of Stuka bombers and Messerschmitt fighters, was to be in support, and operate from airfields in Sicily. The vanguard division 5LT was to leave immediately for Tripoli and PZ15 would follow in May. And the incredibly hard man? Who other than Erwin Rommel, now promoted to Lieutenant-General.

Rommel was appointed on 6 February 1941. His timetable is instructive of the dynamism of the man, not to mention his psychological and physical intensity.

6 FEBRUARY: at conference with Hitler and Field Marshal von Brauchitsch, appointed Commander Deutsches Afrika Korps (DAK)

7 FEBRUARY: flies to Rome for conference with Italian Comando Supremo

8 FEBRUARY: flies to Sicily and orders FLX to attack in force in Cyrenaica

10 FEBRUARY: flies to Libya and meets General Gariboldi, Commander of the Italian forces, who was his nominal superior

13 FEBRUARY: flies over the Sirte Desert and is fired on by British forward troops

14 FEBRUARY: addresses the officers of 5LT in Tripoli

15 FEBRUARY: parades 5LT through Tripoli and out to the desert front.

This dynamism was brought to bear on the troops now under his command. Within 48 hours of arriving in Tripoli, Reconnaissance Battalion 3 (RB3) was in operation at Sirte, 300 miles east of that port. Within eleven days of his appointment he had its armoured cars probing the front of the emasculated British force, and in one of the ironical situations in which military history seems to abound, the first enemy he met in Libya was the last he had encountered in continental Europe. On that occasion, 3rd Armoured Brigade had escaped his clutches by taking to the boats at Cherbourg. Its fate had merely been postponed.

Clearly, Rommel was not a man to allow scorpions to nestle in his boots. Authorised to make a reconnaissance in force in the El Agheila region, he turned this into a full-scale attack, driving his men around and through the British troops and chasing these in front of him like jumped-on desert rabbits. Rommel took to the air to speed his advance. He flew over his men in a Fieseler Storch, dropped scribbled orders on to their heads, and threatened to land and harry them whenever they slowed. And when the current of military energy flagged as fatigue threatened to overcome his warriors, there was always his voice coming at any hour of day or night to galvanise it. Oberstleutnant Ponath, CO of 8 Machine Gun Battalion (8MG), wrote in his diary how Rommel appeared at 4.30

a.m. and ... 'bellows and chases us forward out of touch with the Battalion across the stony desert'.

Did Churchill really ask Wavell if he was waiting for the tortoise to stick out his head far enough before cutting it off? Some tortoise! Nor was Rommel a desert fox, the label subsequently pinned on him in recognition of his manipulation of opposing generals and his masterly use of the desert terrain. Rommel was a wolf, not a fox, and as we rode in our truck towards Solaro he was to our south, taking his first look in the direction of the fortress, licking his lips at the thought of the booty it was about to release to him when he blew down its walls.

What did this ravenous wolf have with him to reduce those walls? Tanks of course, 150 of them in 5LT, about half of which were variants of Pz Kpfw III (Mk III) and Pz Kpfw IV (Mk IV) cruiser tanks. The former had originally fired a 37mm gun, but this had been upped to 50mm, and the latter fired a 75mm gun. The 37mm was a long-barrelled gun; the 50mm gun had a shorter barrel, which was extended in later models, and Mk III panzers were intended primarily for mobile warfare. The 75mm was a stubby, anti-positional gun, which could also be effective against armour but only at closer range. Both marks carried a crew of five and could fire either armour-piercing or high-explosive shells. The remainder of his tanks were Pz Kpfw II (Mk II) light tanks carrying a crew of three, firing a 20mm gun, and mainly, but not exclusively, used for reconnaissance.

Most of his reconnaissance troops were mounted in either the four-wheeled Sd Kfz 222 or the eight-wheeled Sd Kfz 231 armoured cars, which both carried a 20mm gun. These had thinner skins than his tanks, but were monsters in comparison with the ancient British Marmon Herrington armoured cars. The machine-gun battalions were on motorcycles, whose side-cars carried the Mauser MG34 machine-gun.

Rommel's infantry were mounted, and armed with MG34s and KAR rifles, both of which fired 7.92mm cartridges, and MP40 machine-pistols and Luger pistols, both of which fired 9mm rounds. Among his artillery were 105mm howitzers whose shells weighed 32 pounds. During their early days in the desert his anti-tank gunners used the PaK36 which fired both armour-piercing or high-explosive 37mm shells (equivalent to the 2pdr shell used by the British tanks and anti-tank guns). They were not effective against the Matilda tank and would soon be replaced by the PaK38 which fired a 50mm shell, and proved to be an excellent anti-tank gun. Rommel also had eight mobile 88mm anti-aircraft guns, that superb weapon which was shortly to depress its barrel and as a result, to dominate the desert battlefields. Among other weapons his anti-aircraft gunners had the four-barrelled Vierling which fired a 20mm shell.

Such was his weaponry. He would continually add to it anything belonging to his opponents which he won in action and which could be of use, but for the present, a glance shows that much of what he arrived with was standardised. Most importantly – unlike the British cruiser and I tanks – the German Mk III and Mk IV were of the same family and able to act in complementary fashion and in concert. All of it was the equal of, and often superior to, its equivalent in the possession of his opponents, and, most importantly, he had the right men to use it and commanders of quality leading those men.

We had already suffered our first lesson at the hands of this man, but we had much more to learn on the afternoon when the truck carrying us pulled up under the shaded lip of the Solaro escarpment and we climbed out. The gunfire in the west had stopped and it was strangely quiet. Rommel had just lost the first of those commanders of quality.

TWO

Behind us the town trembled,
a crumpled icing.
Its walls read 'V il Re!' and
'This way to Sydney'.

The arrival of the Rats

Rats are supposed to leave a sinking ship. The Rats of Tobruk (so named by William Joyce of Haw Haw notoriety) were doing the opposite. During the past week they had stampeded in from Derna on the west side of that town, and straggled in from the desert to the south-west. They had come through the frontier wire from Egypt. They had driven along Mussolini's Via Balbia and the Senussis' Trigh Capuzzo. They had sailed up the coast from Alexandria and Mersa Matruh. All tracks and sea lanes had led to Tobruk, it seemed, and there were Rats dropping in from the air too, in the mad scramble to put together some obstacle which might hold up the military steamroller that was threatening to crush its way through Cyrenaica.

The major infantry force, the Australian 9th Division, had been holding positions around Benghazi, and its advanced units were farther south at Mersa Brega when Rommel launched his attack. It was a curate's egg of a division. Two of its brigades, 20th and 26th, had been detached from Australian 7th Division. It had no history as a division, it claimed no cohesive or recognisable character other than the nationality of its members. When it arrived back in Tobruk from the Benghazi front it found a fourth Australian infantry brigade waiting there. This was 18th Brigade, which had been stationed in Britain and then in Palestine. Leslie Morshead, who had been the commander of this brigade, was now the general in command of 9th Division.

One of the division's battalions, 2/13th, had fought a delaying action at Bir el Reghem to allow the remainder to fall back on Tobruk, thus becoming the first Australians to confront the Germans during the Second World War, and this battalion and its commander, Lieutenant-Colonel (Bull) Burrows, would also be the last Australians to fight during the siege. Most had done nothing more warlike than attack Jebel Akhdar's recalcitrant rock in the hope of creating a defensive line. The division was then forced to leave this line or be cut off, because Rommel had kicked open the back door into Cyrenaica and was outflanking it. It had retired into the perimeter on 9 April, its last battalion, 2/48th, coming in during the early hours of the following morning. The Australians were not the only infantry presence: there were also 18th Indian Cavalry Regiment, which was serving as infantry, and 1st Battalion Northumberland Fusiliers (1NF), those musicians of the heavy machine-guns, whose 'Vickers Variations' were to become a feature of Tobruk's days – and nights.

What else had arrived to strengthen this obstacle to the hard man's advance? Guns were the number one priority. Mercifully, which is the last word that should be applied to them, the three Field Regiments of Artillery that had been at the front had managed to extricate themselves from the chaos of the retreat and to make their differing ways into the fortress.[2] First

22

Regiment, Royal Horse Artillery (1RHA), which had been leap-frogging with what was left of 3rd Armoured Brigade all the way back from Mersa Brega, made a final jump that brought their precious 25-pounder guns on to the escarpment outside the perimeter. A final salvo of defiance launched in 'great eagerness and zest' against their pursuers, and then in they came. In also from the western desert and bringing their guns came 104RHA and 51st Field Regiment (51FRG). The thunder in the west to which we had been listening had been the latter regiment's guns thwarting Rommel's first attempt to seize the port.

In far-away Egypt there had been an urgent round-up of anything that could fire and anyone who could fire it. The Notts Hussars (107RHA) had been on firing practice at Tahag Camp in the Delta when the crisis erupted. They were called back to base in the early hours of 4 April; by dawn on the 5th they had been brought up to War Establishment, and at 0730 hrs they began their 700-mile journey to the port. Their colonel and adjutant sped ahead, and arrived at Tobruk on 9 April. They spent anxious hours hoping that their guns would not be intercepted by the enemy armoured vehicles which were reported to be across the desert tracks to the east of Tobruk, but the guns rolled in at 2200 hrs, having completed the long journey in four days. The crews were reported to be in good heart and eager for their first contact with the enemy.

Anti-aircraft units came in between 6 and 12 April. They included HQ 14th Light AA Brigade and its three batteries, 39, 40 and 57 Lt AA. Part of this brigade had been rushed up by sea with little in the way of weaponry, and it was given a mix of guns that had been captured from the Italians and stored inside the fortress. The 235th Heavy AA Brigade (235HAA), composed of 152, 153 and 235 Batteries, had taken roost on the cliffs above the harbour and were digging in their big guns. The last little group of gunners to get inside the fortress was especially welcome. Third RHA and Australian 3rd Anti-Tank Battalion (3AA/T), both firing 2pdr anti-tank guns, had fought their way out of the German encirclement at Mechili together with Indian 3rd Motorised Division. They came inside the perimeter on 9 April, under cover of the worst dust storm for years, bringing with them 40 precious guns including several 2pdr anti-tank guns mounted on *portées*.[3] And 3RHA came in with a boast

... 'they like to think of themselves as Tank Hunters'. Within the week they were to prove it.

Most importantly, so far as we four were personally concerned, a few tanks had arrived. They belonged to B, C and HQ Sqns, 1st Royal Tank Regiment (1RTR), the regiment that had shared with the Matilda tanks of 7RTR in the destruction of Graziani's army only three months before. A record exists of the hurry in which they were rushed to the fortress. Captain Rea Leakey of C Squadron had gone on leave to Alexandria, leaving that squadron behind at Ismailia, where it was practising landing its tanks from boats in preparation for an attack on the island of Rhodes. He and a friend were sailing in Alexandria harbour with two nurses, all four in swimming costume, when Leakey saw a man from his regiment who should have been in the Canal Zone many miles away walking along the quayside towards an old merchant ship, the *Thurland Castle*. The astonished Leakey watched the trooper climb the gangway on to the ship, and then decided he should check on what the man was doing so far from his regiment. He sailed his little boat across to the *Thurland Castle* and found himself looking up at a ship's rail packed with the grinning, approving and envious faces of the men of his squadron. At that moment the face of his CO joined the others but did not appear to be quite so approving. 'Get back to Cairo immediately, Leakey!' he ordered. 'Pick up the truck we've left for you and follow us to Tobruk! Get going now, you haven't a moment to spare.'

Leakey said a sad farewell to his nurse, dashed to Cairo, picked up the truck and raced westwards through night and day in a wheel-sharing exercise. He was stopped on the Egyptian side of Bardia by an MP who told him that the road to Tobruk had been cut, but he insisted on carrying on, and reached the eastern entrance to the fortress just ahead of some German armoured cars which were approaching from the south. 'Come in, you Pommy Bastards,' was his greeting. He drove straight to the harbour and found that the ship had beaten him to the port and was being unloaded. The tanks were far from battle-readiness, the guns of some were still in crates and covered with grease, and several were without wireless sets, but their crews had been working on them ever since they left Alexandria. They had been warned that they might be going straight into action on landing, and so they did – almost.[4] Meanwhile a secondary drama was taking place. Major George Hynes was watching the eleven cruiser and sixteen light tanks being winched ashore by the *Thurland Castle*'s derrick with a little more concern than the other spectators. Just before the regiment sailed for Tobruk he had drawn a lot of imprest cash in order to pay his squadron, and not wanting to carry it on his person, he had divided it up into several portions, which he had hidden under the seats of various tanks and vehicles. The rush to get the tanks ashore and away from the quayside had caused him to forget all about it.[5]

To these 22 tanks of 1RTR were added four Matilda tanks and their crews from 4RTR which had come on the same ship, and a handful of tanks that had been in the town's workshops. This motley of ancient A9 and A10s, and the odd A13s, plus the light tanks and the Matildas, was being formed into a resurrected 3rd Armoured Brigade, but with none of that ill-fated unit's senior officers. We four had been shanghaied from the SS *Balmora* at the very last moment when it was realised that this brigade had nothing in the way of HQ communications.

Nor was it only soldiers and their guns and tanks that had gathered for this last stand. In from El Adem had come 258 Wing, bringing its handful of Lysanders of 6 Squadron and a dozen or so Hurricanes of 73 Squadron from Sidi Bouamoud. The former settled on the western airfield on the Derna side and the latter on the El Gubbi airfield south of the town. And of course the sailors moved in too, taking over the biggest building on the waterfront for their Admiralty House – whenever could the Navy be kept out of a scrap – or the best billets?

Such had been the race to give the garrison some teeth with which to bite Churchill's tortoise. Thirty thousand men inside the perimeter wire staring south into the desert, where a rapidly increasing enemy force was beginning to congregate and look to the north in the hope of a glint of sea. All come to this desolate part of God's earth, whose only justification for human presence lay in the curved blue water of its bay; whose only apology for the slaughter which would soon take place there would be that this was honourable slaughter and would not include women and children.

THREE

From the bay,
  nipped finger of Mare Nostrum,
brave sea-runners blamed us.
    Stuka struck.
Sad in their scrapyard.

The shotgun inside the house

If we had a wolf on the prowl outside the door, we also had a double-bar-relled shotgun loaded and awaiting him inside the house. On 6 April a high-powered meeting had taken place in Cairo. Present were Cabinet Minister Anthony Eden; Generals Wavell and Dill; Admiral Cunningham, and Air Chief Marshal Sir Arthur Longmore. Before them was a cable which Churchill had sent to Wavell ordering him to hold the fortress to the death. They took the decision to do just this, and they appointed General Lavarack, then CO of Australian 7th Division, to become Commander-in-Chief of Cyrenaica Command (CYRCOM). At that time it was hoped that a mobile force could be maintained outside the fortress and that this would both harass and hinder the German advance. This mobile group comprising 11th Hussars and 4RHA was commanded by Brigadier Gott, and was standing off to the south-east in the vicinity of El Adem airfield.

On 7 April, Wavell and Lavarack flew to Tobruk where they had a meeting with Morshead. They installed a command arrangement to cover the situation: Lavarack in overall command would also oversee 18th Brigade and the external force, and Morshead would take respon-sibility for holding the town and its perimeter. Both commands would share HQs within the fortress. Wavell asked the two Australian generals to hold the town for eight weeks to give him time to assemble a force in Egypt that would be powerful enough to deal with Rommel.

This command arrangement was dissolved on 10 April when Rom-mel's men closed the coast road to the east of Tobruk, thus cutting off the town, and also moved on to El Adem airfield. Gott's force was too small to create any significant harassment and it was withdrawn to the frontier. Lavarack sailed out of the port four days later in order to operate his command from the frontier, and Morshead was left in complete charge of the defence of Fortress Tobruk. The first thing he did was call together his commanders and tell them ... 'There'll be no Dunkirk here. If we should have to get out we'll fight our way out. There is to be no surrender and no retreat.'[6] His commanders realised that he meant every word of this.

Morshead was the loaded shotgun.

If Rommel were the epitome of the German professional soldier, Morshead was his mirror-image among the democratic amateur fighting men. First a schoolmaster, then a business man, he had shown that he could rise to the top in environments which did not depend upon the flying bullet or the clicking of heels, but he had also shown that when pushed to it he could face the bullet and silence the clicking. He had also shown that he did not need all that much pushing. In the First World War he had left his Australian schoolroom to fight his way up the hill at Anzac Beach on the first day of that bloody landing. When the Australians withdrew from Gallipoli he took his battalion into the trenches in Flanders. The men of his new division were aware that whatever he might ask them to face, he had already faced himself.

When I first saw him I could not believe that this man was either an Australian or a fighting general; he was too trim to be kin to the army of toughs I was surrounded by, too, dare I say 'prim', to be a leader of fighting men. Then I heard the name these toughs had given to him, 'Ming The Merciless', and in their voices when they spoke it was the nearest thing to awe that an Australian will allow.

Prowling and hungry wolf outside, loaded shotgun inside, or, to switch the metaphor from hunting to fisticuffs, we were about to witness and be part of a heavyweight contest not only of opposites but also of opposing tactics. The Undefeated Blitzkrieg Boy from Germany against the No Dunkirk Here Bloke from Down-Under, and to the winner, not a Lonsdale Belt but the Jewel in the Crown of Cyrenaica.

The Jewel in the Crown

What was this Jewel in the Crown over which these two men were about to fight to the death? There was the harbour, some 2¼ miles in length

27

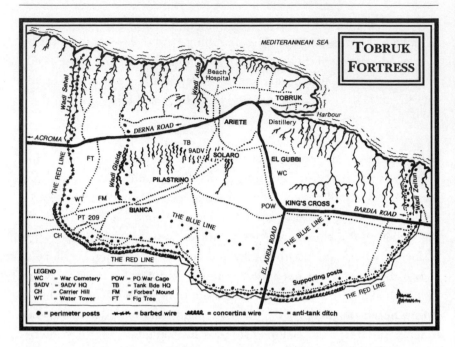

and a mile wide, which offered the best, and almost only, harbouring facilities in the 800 miles between Tripoli and the Egyptian frontier. It had several jetties and a basin deep enough to take ships as large as the *San Giorgio*, the burned-out Italian cruiser, then beached at the northern end of the harbour. With the port in his possession Rommel would be able to land reinforcements and supplies within 80 miles of that frontier, and thus spare his vehicles the wastage in time, fuel and wear-and-tear of the long drive from Tripoli to the battle front.

The harbour then was the major prize, but there were others. British supplies stockpiled inside the fortress included large quantities of motor fuel, that element so essential to desert mobility. There were the town's distilleries and wells which would provide that even more essential fluid for the human contingent. There were the armaments and vehicles held by the defending forces, and Rommel had already shown that he was not averse to his army driving into Cairo in British trucks; indeed, at this time he himself was travelling in a captured British Armoured Command Vehicle (ACV), which he called his 'Mammoth'. There were the British guns and a quarter of a million artillery shells stockpiled in readiness to feed them. Such were the material gains awaiting him, but there was perhaps an even greater psychological lure – entry into the pantheon of those who had successfully stormed the Land of the Pharaohs, that ancient cockpit of war: Alexander and Pompey, Caesar, Mark Antony, Napoleon, and now perhaps – Erwin Rommel. Only the men who crouched in their gun-pits behind the perimeter wire stood in his way. They must be removed, either from the earth or from further action, but certainly from across his line of communication.

All these prizes lay inside a semi-circle of land facing out to the desert with the town and its harbour almost at the centre of the base-line. The town itself was a couple of streets of white houses, a church, a barracks and a school. It was an Italian creation, intended to service the harbour and to house the colonial administrators and military families who governed this part of Mussolini's recently acquired African empire. The streets curved around the northern bend of the bay and straggled down to the several quays which the Italians had built to service their ships.

Each side of the semi-circle ends in deep and rugged wadis which run down to the sea: on the west Wadi Sehel, on the east Wadis Zeitun and Belgassem. These natural barriers served as the anchors of the defensive perimeter. Two major escarpments rise like steps within the semi-circle, each varying from 50 to 100 feet or more in height and leading on to a fairly flat plateau. A third step intrudes on the southern edge, curves away, and loops back to the south-west. Beyond lies the desert, flat to its shimmering horizon, which plays tricks on the eyes during the heat of the afternoon, except on those days when the dust arises. There is no horizon then, there is nothing beyond the stinging end of the individual nose.

The road system was of two qualitative levels. The Via Balbia was an Italian-built, tarmac road which skirted the coast along the whole length of the Libyan coastline. That section of it which entered the perimeter on the western side and ran into the town was known to us as the Derna Road. It made its exit from the town in a southerly direction and then branched, one arm going directly east and out of the perimeter in the direction of Bardia, the other going directly south to El Adem, the Italian airfield a few miles outside the fortress. The arm going east was known as the Bardia Road, that going south as the El Adem Road. The junction of the two became known as King's Cross. The second qualitative level comprised a series of tracks of little more than crushed or packed rock created out of topography or convenience. These wound out of the town and climbed the gaps in the escarpments to wander off to all parts of the perimeter.

The first of the escarpments from the coastline was the Solaro Escarpment, so known because Fort Solaro stood above it on the track leading from the town to Fort Pilastrino, which stood above the second escarpment. Pilastrino covered an important network of tracks, one leading out to Maccia Bianca and Forbes' Mound, another to Pt 209 and Ras El Medauur, a third south to the perimeter and a fourth, east to King's Cross. Each of these sites was to become important during the fighting which was about to erupt, but Pt 209 was of special significance because it was on the only hill of any height in the area and gave a commanding view of the western approaches to the town. Any attack on the fortress from the west or south-west would come through Pilastrino, any attack from the south or south-east would come via King's Cross.

Most of the outlying area was formed of great slabs of rock littered with disintegrated chunks and thinly spread with dust, rather than sand. In some of the wadis there was reputed to be grass but I never saw any. Scrub, yes, prickly and up to the knees in places, but not grass. Nor was the dust allowed to rest anywhere for more than a few hours, the climatic combination of great and quickly cooling land mass on one side, wide expanse of water on the other, and a thirsty sun perpetually overhead resulted in an unceasing restlessness in the air. Almost every afternoon brought its *khamsin*, and each *khamsin* its *ghiblis*. Somewhere not too far south of us must have been the heartland of the desert winds. We could scarcely make our afternoon brew without having one of its children drop in on us, and they had usually picked up as much heat and dust as they could *en route*, thus converting themselves into a rasp. Our faces were sand-papered as well as sun-scorched. It was a harsh environment.

The Red Line and the Blue Line
The perimeter defence line stretched a distance of sixteen miles. It began on the western coast at Wadi Sehel, bulged out in the south-west to take in Pt 209 and Ras El Medauur, thus covering this important hill,

and then curved south and east to end at Wadi Zeitun. Its distance from the town varied between eight and nine miles. It was marked out by a combination of wire and anti-tank trench for much of its length, the wire being a fence of two strands, each five feet in height. The anti-tank trench was neither continuous nor uniform in its effectiveness and in the south-west it was particularly poor.

This line was defended by a series of concrete posts which the Italian builders had set below ground level. There were 128 of them in two rows, the first forming the arc of defence, the second in close support of this arc. Posts in both rows were grouped for the purposes of control and administration, there being sixteen such groups. All the posts were linked by telephone, which also connected them with Fortress HQ. This was situated in a series of tunnels and underground chambers that had been blasted into the foot of the steep wall of the Solaro Escarpment.

Each front row post was surrounded by an anti-tank ditch and wire, and was sited so that its weapons could take advantage of the dog-legs created in the wire. Individual posts covered a circle some 90 yards in diameter and consisted of three circular firing pits connected by crawl trenches and with rough sleeping-quarters. The pits and trenches had concrete walls but no overhead covering apart from camouflage.

All the posts were numbered and had a letter prefix. Numbering began on the western side with the prefix S as far as Ras El Medauur. From here to the Bardia Road they carried the prefix R, and from the Bardia Road to the eastern coast, the prefix Z. Thus a post might be S3, R45 or Z82. This gave immediate reference as to locality.

The two lines of perimeter posts formed the 'Red Line'. Construction of a second line (Blue) was begun immediately, to follow the curve of the Red Line but two miles nearer the town. Eventually, some of the heavier weaponry, including mortars, was moved into this line. As time went by, practically the entire zone between the two lines was sown with mines as part of Morshead's defence-in-depth strategy, but mining at the onset of the siege was limited to what had been done by the previous inhabitants as protection for the Red Line. Finally, there was a Green Line but this existed more in theory than in practice. It was intended as a last line to be defended by tanks in the event of evacuation by sea. It was a switch line running along the northern edge of El Gubbi airfield and with Forts Ariete and Solaro as key positions. El Gubbi was little more than a level stretch of ground from which the rocks had been removed. A mobile caravan served as its control unit for the aircraft using the 'field'.[7]

In any attack against such an elongated defence line the advantage must lie with the attacker; he is able to assemble his spearhead at a single point and bring all of his fire power to that point – the *schwerpunkt* beloved of German commanders. The defender must spread his force thinly in order to man the entire perimeter, and must locate his fire power so that it can punish an attack from whichever angle this may come. In any such attack, therefore, it will be a small part of the garrison that is called upon to resist, while the remainder can do little other than listen and pray, if they are of that inclination. The defending commander must organise those troops not actually manning the defensive perimeter and who are to some extent mobile, into an aggressive reserve whose role is the limiting of any penetration of the line, and the restoring of the original positions by counter-attack. His tank and artillery elements will play a major part in this reaction to attack, but he will need to keep infantry in reserve for counter-attack purposes, no matter how thinly this may leave the outer line.

Morshead's defence arrangements

Such were the classic siege problems facing Morshead on 11 April, but there was also the problem of shortage of time. The defences were in a neglected state, much of the outer wire was down, mines had been lifted, loose sand had invaded the anti-tank ditch. The infantry had to sort themselves out in the line, familiarise themselves with a quite different environment from that which they had been experiencing, set up communication links, restore the line's defensive capabilities and hope that Rommel would allow them a few hours in which to do these things before descending upon them.[8]

Morshead's defence arrangements fell almost naturally into a three-layer system. The defence of the perimeter was entrusted to the three brigades of 9th Div, with 18th Brigade held in reserve. The western section was manned by the three battalions of 26th Brigade, but with the dismounted 18th Indian Cavalry covering the coastal sector at Wadi Sehel.

The central section covering the El Adem Road was manned by the three battalions of 20th Brigade, and the eastern side covering the Bardia Road by the three battalions of 24th Brigade, assisted by a scratch battalion made up from Australian Army Service Corps personnel. Each of these brigades had two of its three battalions in the front-line posts of the Red Line supported by one anti-tank company, and its third battalion in the supporting posts. A final group in the forward area was composed of 100 men of the King's Dragoon Guards. They had become available because of that regiment's loss of eighteen of its armoured cars during the recent retreat, and they had been put under the command of 2/23rd, who had given them the responsibility of protecting 2,700 yards of the perimeter covering the Lysander airfield near the Derna Road.

This disposal allowed Morshead an average of twelve men to each perimeter post, which was half the number used by the original Italian occupants. The discrepancy was compensated by increasing the fire power of each post, this being made possible by the liberal dispersal of captured Italian machine-guns and anti-tank guns. Further fire power was provided by the heavy machine-guns of NFs, two companies being with 26th Brigade and the remainder with 20th Brigade.

The second defensive zone was the hinterland of the Blue Line, where the artillery and armoured components of the garrison were placed in readiness to react to attack anywhere along the perimeter. Apart from the regiment of field guns attached to 2/12th, 9th Division had been sent into the desert without its artillery and had to rely on British guns for support. It was fortunate in the quality that was available. There were three regiments of Royal Horse Artillery: 1RHA, 104RHA and 107RHA which were each firing 25pdrs, and 51FRG with 18pdrs and 4.5in howitzers.[9] The 25pdrs of 1RHA and 107RHA were under command of 20th Brigade, those of 104RHA under 24th Brigade and the guns of 51FRG under 26th Brigade. This placed 72 field guns at the disposal of the Australian division. These were so situated that fire from 40 of them could be brought to bear on any sector without them having to be moved.

Defending the perimeter and the field guns against air attack were two Light AA regiments, 13th and 14th, and the Australian 8th Lt AA Regiment. These were firing a mix of guns, mostly captured Italian Bredas.[10]

At the onset of the siege the armoured element was a very mixed bag. It retained the title '3rd Armoured Brigade' but its colloquial title became 'The Tobruk Tanks'. Its human elements included personnel from 1st, 4th, 5th and 6th Tank Corps Regiments, and men of the 3rd Hussars and King's Dragoon Guards (KDGs). On 11 April the tank personnel were divided between twenty cruiser tanks, rather less than that number of light tanks, and the four Matilda ('I') Tanks. The Hussars were mounted in light tanks, and KDG crews were manning those armoured cars that had survived the retreat. The senior Tank Corps officer available, Lieutenant-Colonel Drew of 5RTR, had assumed command and had arranged his armour as follows:

> Two squadrons, each with two troops of light tanks manned by 3rd Hussars, and two troops of A13 tanks manned by 5RTR
>
> Two squadrons each with two troops of A13s all manned by 1RTR
>
> Two mounted infantry companies formed of 5RTR and one of 3rd Hussar personnel, each of these companies consisting of 30 men armed with two Bren guns, one Boys Rifle, and rifles.

Those KDGs who remained under Drew's command were ordered to patrol the two airfields and keep watch on the movement of enemy transport along the desert track south of the perimeter. The tank squadrons were dispersed in the wadis of the escarpments, and Brigade HQ was located in the vicinity of HQ 9th Div below the Solaro Escarpment. These arrangements illustrate the urgency of the situation on that day, and the expectation of a fight to the finish, in which all hands would be involved.

The third defensive zone was the town and its environs. This zone included the harbour and distilleries, and the fighting units here were guarding town and harbour against attacks from the air. They were the three batteries of 4th Heavy AA Brigade, namely 152HAA, 153HAA and 235HAA. Their guns were sited on the cliffs behind and above the town or to the immediate west and south of it. At the beginning of the siege they were firing a mix of 3.7in and 102mm guns, and shared a total of only sixteen heavy guns. A single Light battery (40th) which accompanied them had Bofors guns dispersed in single gun stations around the harbour. Its role was to shoot down those attacking planes which braved the harbour barrage as they bottomed out of their dive. A final gunnery component was the Notts Yeomanry. This regiment was facing away from the perimeter and had the task of preventing an attack from the sea.[11]

The last group of fighting men, but by no means the least, were the pilots of the Hurricanes of 73 Squadron and Lysanders of 6 Squadron. On 7 April, all RAF personnel except pilots, ground staff and IO 73 Sqn had been ordered to Buq Buq, but this order was revoked and they returned, to play an important part in the early days of the siege.[12] Among the crew of the Hurricanes were six Free French fighter pilots who had joined 73 Sqn from 274 Sqn.

So much for the fighting units, but there were many who, while not carrying rifles or manning other weapons, would be just as much in the fight while going about their more mundane work. These included Signalmen, Engineers, Ordnance Corps personnel, the Pioneer Corps working the harbour, RASC men manning the supply dumps, RAF ground crew and yes, the Military Police. A most important element was that manning the hospitals. The Australian 4th General Hospital was based in buildings on the edge of the town and also on a beach to the north. Its field dressing stations were located as follows:

24th Bde was served by 2/11 Field Ambulance Dressing Station near El Adem Road.

20th Bde was served by 2/8 FADS at Fort Solaro.

26th Bde was served by 2/3 FADS in Wadi Auda.

In retrospect it seems amazing that all the organisation required to install what was an army of bits and pieces into a novel situation and at the same time to make it ready to meet immediate assault, manifested itself so quickly. The answer lies in Morshead's good fortune in finding men of ability on hand at every level of action from Beachmaster to Quartermaster, from AA Controller to Tank Commander. They proved to be men who needed only delegation to set them to work, men who were not prone to panic under pressure nor likely to cover their ears under bombardment. The first days of siege demonstrated this. Where there might have been wide-spread confusion there was instead a quick settling down to work and the fitting together of a jig-saw into a recognisable and functional pattern. As any veteran of the desert campaigns knows, this was the exception rather than the rule, and ultimate credit for this must go to

Morshead, but his subordinate commanders should not be forgotten and are listed in Appendix 1. Meanwhile, all of us, leaders and led, looked out into the desert and wondered how long it would be before dust clouds on the horizon announced Rommel's first attempt to break us. We didn't realise that it had already taken place and had failed.

FOUR

We did not go there often.
We stayed near our holes,
looked out on the desert.

A Brigadier's ears, eyes, hands and memory

Our Commander was Henry Dinham Drew, OBE, MC. He was (for us) an old soldier. Seconded to the Machine Gun Corps from the Devonshire Regiment in 1915, he had served with them in France, was wounded twice and won the Military Cross. After that war he was seconded to the Tank Corps, his subsequent travels taking him to armoured car companies in Palestine, Egypt and India, so that he already had the sniff of sand in his nostrils as well as of gun smoke. In 1940 he took 5RTR to France as part of 3rd Armoured Brigade. Following that calamity he took this regiment to Egypt and then into Libya again, still as part of 3rd Armd Bde, and into another calamity. He watched his last half-dozen tanks go up in flames when trying to fight their way out of encirclement outside Derna, and had thus had the misfortune to be on the wrong end of a beating from the Germans on two different continents within nine months. Asked by Morshead to command a rag-bag of run-down armoured fighting vehicles against the same foe, he should have been a rather depressed and anxious man when he spoke to us at the ACV, which a couple of Middlesex Yeomanry drivers had managed to get back into the fortress and which was serving as his HQ. He gave no sign of either. 'Work my signals for me,' was all he asked. 'I want one wireless set on 24 hour watch taking reports from the armoured car patrols, we'll arrange the rest as and where we need it.' These were the only orders we received during the first six months of the siege – all our other arrangements were left in our own hands. For men who had been accustomed to having everything, even their diets, ordered for them, it was a novel but most welcome change.

The wireless operator at the HQ of an armoured brigade had three duties to perform. First and foremost was the operating of his No 9 Set as the command source for the three battalions making up the brigade. He had to maintain the net, that line of communication between the brigadier using this set and those sets being used by the commanders of the battalions. This was not always as simple as it may seem, given the problem of intervening hills and escarpments, the static from dust storms and enemy interference of a more lethal kind. There were often frantic seconds of searching the air waves and re-tuning that only the operator knew about, the trick being to appear in control whatever the problem. It was a mark of some success that our retention of the net was taken for granted by Drew and the other brigadiers who followed him.

The second requirement was to so work the set that the brigadier felt that he was sharing a conversation with the man on the other end of the link. He had an on-off switch to his microphone but the transmitting switch on the set itself had to be thrown each time the speaker changed. The relationship between the brigadier and his wireless operator worked best when an unspoken understanding grew between the two. This needed a good reading of the brigadier's speech and other habits, of his inclinations, and sometimes, of his tantrums by the operator, who worked as the brigadier's third hand so to speak.

The third important task was to record, not only the time of receipt or dispatch of signals but also their content. If it were a keyed message (WT) recording was fairly simple because there was a standard form which was filled in letter by letter as the message came in, or was given whole to the operator for transmitting. If communication were by voice (RT) it was more difficult, and there had to be a quick scribbling of each bit of the conversation and a subsequent re-write to make sense of this personal shorthand. These records were passed to the IO, who used them to write up the brigade's War Diary. Often the brigadier would ask for them to refresh his memory or to check on what exactly he had ordered. Thus the operator had to serve as ears, eyes, third hand and memory for the brigadier.

Brigadier Willison, with whom I would later share such a relationship, summed it up fairly well when he wrote ' ... When this moving office (the ACV) settled down for the night after a strenuous day's fighting, the Brigadier, acting as Duty Officer, was lying on the floor of the van, waiting to be kicked into activity by the wireless operator should anything arise.'[15] I would not in fact have kicked him because he was quite fiery and not above jumping to his feet and kicking me back, but there were moments when he said things to me which indicated that special relationship.

Most of the work done at Brigade HQ took place inside the ACV. This was a large steel-plated truck inside which was a table which the brigadier shared with his brigade major. A seat at the other side of this table was for the use of the Intelligence Officer. In the rear half of the vehicle were two wireless sets, one for use as the forward link for whichever superior authority the tank brigade happened to be working under, the other serving as the command link for the three tank regiments making up the brigade.[14] In the early days of the siege only one was in use. This was the set in communication with the armoured car patrols which kept watch over the two airfields and also mounted a 24-hour watch on traffic passing along the Trigh Capuzzo, a desert track to the south of Tobruk. Communication with HQ 9th Div was either by runner or by telephone line, the ACV being stationed in close proximity to the entrance to the tunnels in which this was located. The Signals Officer would normally inhabit the rear of the truck, but since we did not possess any such object we had this space to ourselves. The sets had spare earphones and microphones on long leads for the brigadier or the officer on watch to use.

This arrangement meant that the operator on duty was privy to everything that went on within the ACV; a silent (and unconsulted) witness at the centre of tactical discussion, battle planning and the battle itself. Given this immediacy with whatever action was in being, he was, if interested, second only to the brigadier and brigade major in awareness of what was taking place.

The beginning of a minor epic

Knowing what Drew wished of us, we now had to make the necessary arrangements. This meant drawing up a roster to cover a 24-hour watch on the set. Leggat decided that since none of us had formal authority, it was up to him as senior soldier (in length of service) to do this. Not unnaturally, his rota strongly favoured a son of Glasgow, who needed time off to exercise his assumed command. Jim Gauton caught my eye and we were at once in agreement; we asked Charlie Jones to see if he could produce a more equitable rota, and he did. The shifts began as 2-hourly sessions but we later changed this to four hours. I had the honour of opening communications by introducing myself to the operator in a KDG armoured car, patrolling somewhere out on the perimeter wire. For the next eight months four men, none of whom held any formal authority, would run the Tobruk Tanks' communications, a task normally demanding a full squadron of signalmen headed by a major. A minor, if unrecorded, epic in Royal Signals history was thus begun.

FIVE

At dawn
  the sun leapt into our days,
hot with hunger for our sweat.
    Salt rose at the joints, while along the wire
guns reveilled.

Hurrying to Suez

The gunfire which had so worried me when I was being snatched from the deck of the *Balmora* had been signalling Rommel's first attack on the fortress. It was a hurried attack whose premise seemed to be that whatever troops might be inside the garrison must be queuing to get away in the ships which his reconnaissance aircraft had reported to be entering the harbour. Perhaps Dunkirk (in which Rommel had been peripherally involved) had left too big an impression on the German's psyche so that it had become a yardstick of British unwillingness to fight. He was certainly not yet in a position to make a full-scale attack on the garrison; his triumphant but tired troops were scattered along the desert tracks between Mechili and Derna, and Generals Streich, CO 5LT, and Olbrich, CO PZR8, were talking the heresy of rest and servicing before they could launch an attack. Rest was the last thing on Rommel's mind.

The most advanced German troops were Ponath's Machine-Gun Battalion 8 (MGB8), von Wechmar's Reconnaissance Battalion 3 (RB3) and part of 605 Anti-Tank Regiment, which were all in the Derna area. Rommel sent these forward towards Tobruk under command of Oberst von Schwerin, a young officer who had given up command of an élite regiment in order to serve under Rommel in Africa. General Kircheim, who had originally arrived in Africa as the representative of the Army High Command, had been drafted into action by Rommel at the onset of his initial attack, given the Brescia Division and sent to attack Benghazi. He was now ordered to move forward and set up guns in a position which would bring Tobruk harbour under attack and thus prevent those ships from carrying out an evacuation. The unfortunate Kircheim did not get very far; he was caught in an RAF strafing attack, was wounded, and had to be evacuated. Rommel now needed a replacement in a hurry and one almost fell from the sky into his arms. Heinrich von Prittwitz und Graffron, CO of PZ15, flew into Tripoli ahead of his division and immediately motored up to Derna. Rommel saw him there, conscripted him, and sent him forward to lead the first assault on the port.

Von Prittwitz was ordered to launch the attack from the west on the following morning (10 April), under cover of a diversion to be made in the south-west by the Brescia Division and Trento Division's artillery. Von Prittwitz has been described as 'a go-getter' and even more of a Junker than Rommel.[15] A remark was passed between the two men, different sources ascribe it to either, but it was to the effect that if one battalion had been enough to take Derna, the force which von Prittwitz was being given should be sufficient to take Tobruk.[16]

Rommel wanted his armour to take part in the attack. He over-rode the protests of Streich and flew to Mechili where he ordered Olbrich to get his panzers on to the Via Balbia by dawn to support it. In the meantime von Prittwitz went forward to take command of the attacking force. He was exhausted after his long and hurried journey, and when he caught up with von Schwerin, he bedded down for the night. Rommel appeared at dawn, rousted him out of his bedroll, accused him of giving the British time to do another Dunkirk and chased him forward. Meanwhile, Ponath had reached to within sixteen kilometres of the town when he came to a bridge that crossed a wadi. They approached the bridge only to see it blown up in their faces by Lieutenant Bamgarten of Australian 2/3rd Field Company. At the same moment they came under concentrated fire from the guns of 51FRG; some guns belonging to the recently formed and unofficial Bush Artillery, and the machine-guns of the NFs. A battle developed across the wadi and continued for much of the day. It ended when the gunners withdrew into the fortress, having lost three men killed and 30 wounded. The Germans had also suffered. At the height of the battle von Prittwitz had appeared, leading several of von Schwerin's armoured cars. He took them in a charge down the highway and immediately came under intense attack. Three of the cars were set on fire and von Prittwitz suffered a direct hit from an anti-tank shell and was killed. The attack had been a hurried fiasco in which neither Brescia nor Trento played their allotted parts. Rommel was culpable. He had treated his opponents with contempt by launching the attack without anything in the way of reconnaissance or preparation and before he had the full potential of the force available to him at hand. He had sent the assault troops in along a highway on which the British gunners had had time to range their guns, and if there were any element of the British Army in the western desert of which it was unwise to be contemptuous it was the Royal Artillery. Von Prittwitz had paid the price of that contempt. The episode was summed up briefly in one of the last entries in Ponath's personal diary: 'Forward it goes, irresistibly (his 5th Coy of 8MGB). At Km.16 bridge blows up just in front of our point. Simultaneously strong enemy artillery fire ... General Prittwitz killed.'[17] Thus von Prittwitz achieved the dubious triple honour of being the first German to be killed at Tobruk, the first man in PZ15 to be killed and the first, but by no means the last, of Rommel's desert generals to suffer that fate.

It would not be correct to describe this as a serious attack or as a major rebuff for the attackers. It was an over-optimistic, under-prepared, minor effort which collapsed after the death of a commander who had been goaded into attacking without having time or opportunity to do any

41

real commanding. Why did Rommel insist upon the attack going in in such an unbalanced way? The question is worth pursuing because the answer to it may well illuminate much that was to happen in the months ahead at the dictate of this man. His brief from OKW had authorised *limited* reconnaissance in force. On 19 March von Brauchitsch had made it quite clear at a meeting with Rommel that a limited offensive to recapture Benghazi might be permitted *but only after PZ15 had arrived from Germany in May* (author's italics). Rommel had turned the reconnaissance into a major attack and had taken Benghazi by the beginning of April. On 2 April he had received a signal from his nominal superior, the Italian General Gariboldi: 'From information received I learn that your advance is still going on. This is in contravention of my directives. I ask you to await my arrival before continuing your advance.'[18]

Thus his advance was already in contravention of his orders from both the Italian and German High Commands. That this was deliberate is borne out by other sources. Before the initial reconnaissance in force began he had told his aide, Heinz Schmidt, newly arrived from the collapsing Ethiopian Front: 'We shall reach the Nile, make a right turn, and win back everything.'[19] The word 'everything' is important; perhaps he meant Ethiopia, and this would indicate that Rommel foresaw himself as controlling all the eastern side of Africa after the capture of Egypt. Perhaps he was consoling Schmidt, but that is hardly in keeping, either with Rommel's behaviour towards his subordinates or with their relationship at this early stage.

Two entries in 5LT's War Diary for 10 April continue Rommel's defiance of orders from on high. The first, written in the early morning reads: 'Our objective which is to be made known to all troops is: THE SUEZ CANAL. Encirclement of Tobruk is to be completed at all costs and at utmost speed. The main body under Prittwitz is to attack from the west.' This tied the von Prittwitz attack to the encirclement of the fortress so that none of the forces in the town would escape. The second entry, written at 1300 hrs, states: 'According to reports received at AK HQ [Rommel's Afrika Korps HQ] the British at this time had no reserves or any forces fit for action which might oppose an attack on Egypt. Accordingly, the intention of AK was to continue rapid advance to [the] east in order to defeat piecemeal such British reserves as might be hurried forward and before [the] enemy could transfer stronger forces from Abyssinia or Greece.'

Here are stated specific strategic objectives and intentions. Taken together with the comment made to Schmidt, they demonstrate Rommel's intention to carry out his own will regardless of contrary orders from on high. All his actions and words show the man's utter determination to seize the Nile Delta and its cities, and to dispense with the two stumbling blocks threatening that intention, the limitations being placed upon him by higher authority, and the defenders of the town just down the Via Balbia. His great haste to take Tobruk owed as much to his desire to circumvent interference from his superiors as it did to other compulsions – indeed, this desire was generating its own compulsion. Is a dog that bites through his leash in order to sink his teeth into the postman's leg impulsive or would utterly determined be a better description?

Rommel – a man in a hurry

Rommel was to the south of the fortress on the Acroma Track when he heard that von Prittwitz had been killed. This track leaves the Via Balbia on the western side of Tobruk, circles south-east to El Adem, much of it within sight of the perimeter, then continues eastwards to link up with the Via Balbia on the far side of the fortress, thus making a desert by-pass around the town. He had sent Major Knabe's motor-cycle detachment along it with orders to put a block on the Bardia Road exit. He was searching for other German units which he might hurry to strengthen that block, so that he could send von Wechmar on to the frontier. Streich and Olbrich met him on the track and angry words were exchanged between Rommel and Streich over the death of von Prittwitz. Rommel's reaction to this news of the failure of the impetuous attack was to say: 'We probably tried too much with too little. Anyhow, we are in a better position now.'[20]

So much for the unfortunate von Prittwitz.

Rommel then sent MGB2 to the Bardia Road block to release Wechmar, who was to drive on to Bardia and seize that coastal town. He ordered Knabe to dash to Sollum with a mixed force of infantry, and block the escape routes into Egypt.[21] The encirclement of Tobruk thus completed, and with troops on their way to invest the frontier, he now returned his attention to Tobruk. He made a personal survey of the perimeter in search of a suitable break-in point. This was all that was done in the way of reconnaissance, and as a result of it he decided on a location which would give his panzers quick access to King's Cross. Control of the crossroads there would place the town and the remaining perimeter defences at his mercy. He then ordered Streich to make the attack on the following day. Here was a man in the greatest possible hurry.

SIX

Days were always damaged.
Dust, becoming footloose at the shelling
clouded us in loneliness,
and we thought of England's rain.

The Easter Battles: Day One, 11 April 1941

These began that afternoon with a frontal assault in which Streich sent panzers and infantry against the perimeter in the southern sector. The infantry were once again Ponath's machine-gun regiment, and they had the support of anti-tank gunners of PZ15, who had arrived as advance party for their division. The panzers belonged to PZR5, the armoured element of 5LT. The infantry advanced first and the panzers led by Olbrich followed shortly afterwards on Ponath's right. The posts under threat were held by men of Australian 20th Brigade under command of Brigadier Murray, who were defending a 10-mile stretch covering both sides of the El Adem Road. Murray had 2/17th and 2/13th Bns in the line and 2/15th in reserve. It was upon these men, never before tested in such absolutes, that the choice of kill or be killed was about to fall.

Most inappropriately, the afternoon chosen by Rommel happened to be Good Friday, a day recognised by all these battling nations as one on which to commemorate *the* supreme sacrifice in the cause of peace; indeed, the timing matched almost exactly the moment of that historic sacrifice. Such considerations were far from the minds of the defenders in the posts who probably didn't even know what day of the week it was. They had already been subjected to Stuka attacks and now the guns of

Major Hetch's 18th AA Regiment were trying to make them keep their heads below their gun-pit parapets while Ponath led his men forward. Peering over the sandbags from their firing steps in the posts, the Australians watched as the enemy infantry approached. They sited their weapons and waited for the order to fire, these civilians in military dress, and perhaps wondered whether, when the moment came, they would be up to squeezing the triggers their sweaty fingers were stroking. They need not have worried on that account; when the order did come, the fingers obeyed, and the men of 2/17th received their baptism into this most awful of religions. At the same time they began a campaign which was to simmer and boil through the next eight months, and would end with their being undefeated and their division entering the pages of military history as one of the very great.

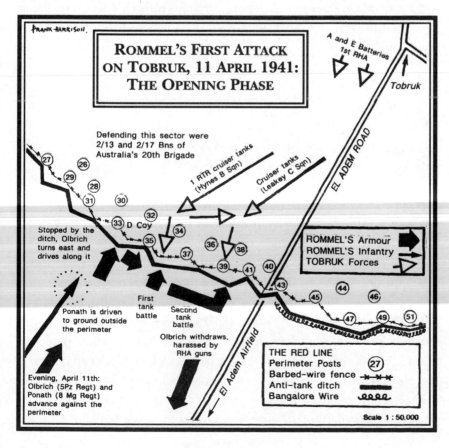

FRANK HARRISON.

ROMMEL'S FIRST ATTACK ON TOBRUK, 11 APRIL 1941: THE OPENING PHASE

A and E Batteries 1st RHA

Tobruk

Defending this sector were 2/13 and 2/17 Bns of Australia's 20th Brigade

1 RTR cruiser tanks (Hynes B Sqn)

Cruiser tanks (Leakey C Sqn)

EL ADEM ROAD

Stopped by the ditch, Olbrich turns east and drives along it

D Coy

ROMMEL'S Armour
ROMMEL'S Infantry
TOBRUK Forces

Ponath is driven to ground outside the perimeter

First tank battle

Second tank battle

Olbrich withdraws, harassed by RHA guns

El Adem Airfield

Evening, April 11th: Olbrich (5Pz Regt) and Ponath (8 Mg Regt) advance against the perimeter

THE RED LINE
Perimeter Posts   27
Barbed-wire fence
Anti-tank ditch
Bangalore Wire

Scale 1 : 50,000

Ponath's men went to ground and stayed there. They knew now that they weren't going to simply walk into the fortress. There was a pause while the two sides searched for each other with small-arms and machine-gun fire. Then the men in the posts heard the loud rumble of engines and, peering through the haze, saw the pig-shaped panzers floating towards them as if on pillows of dust. But pigs don't spit fire. For a moment or two the prospect for the men in the posts, who did not have any anti-tank guns, looked less than promising. Then the panzers met the anti-tank ditch and they had not been warned about this. The frustrated Olbrich was forced to halt his tanks. Then he turned eastwards and began to move in a line parallel to the ditch, searching for a way across.

Word of the assault flashed back from the posts under attack to Murray at his Brigade HQ in one of the supporting posts, and from Murray to 9th Div HQ in the caves at Solaro. Drew was informed that ten enemy tanks had broken into area 406423 and was ordered to intervene. He immediately sent 1RTR to locate these tanks and destroy them. Hynes and his temporary squadron of five cruiser and eight light tanks were south of Pilastrino, some of the drivers still sitting unwittingly on small fortunes. This was the nearest force to the area under attack, and he set off in search of the intruders, keeping his tanks to the west of the El Adem Road so that his gunners would have the advantage of the sun at their backs and in the eyes of the enemy.

When the turret is down a tank commander's vision is limited to a periscope and it is for this reason that most of them on both sides chose to advance with the turret open and their heads and shoulders out, and only to close down when action was imminent. This was how Hynes' men travelled that afternoon, tank commanders squinting to the east for the first sight of the enemy, drivers listening to their Tannoy earphones for orders, gunners and loaders with a round already 'up the spout' for a quick first shot. They saw nothing. Hynes reported all clear at the reported site and moved towards the El Adem Road. Before he could reach it he saw the enemy, not the ten panzers which had been reported but 30 or more. They were close to, but had not yet penetrated the perimeter. Hynes dropped down into the tank and closed the turret. Olbrich accepted the challenge and advanced along both sides of the road. A brief exchange of fire took place across the ditch and the British claimed three hits without suffering anything serious themselves. The panzers then withdrew to area 408421 where they came under fire from British batteries shooting from near King's Cross. These guns were being directed by FOO Captain Goschen, RHA, who was in one of the perimeter posts. His was a name which would be heard more than once in the coming months.

By this time Leakey had arrived on the scene commanding C Sqn tanks, and the combined British force moved in search of more action. They had just reached the El Adem Road when they saw ten panzers advancing towards the ditch about a mile to the south. As soon as they came within range the British tanks opened fire, this second tank battle of the afternoon taking place across the ditch in the area 410421. This time Hynes did not get off so lightly, his tank being hit in the suspension and immobilised. Its gun was still capable of firing and so the crew stayed inside and continued to fight. They were not allowed to do so for long, the tank suffering three hits in rapid succession. The first hit wounded the loader, the second caused an explosion among the tank's ammunition and the three men in the turret all suffered burns before they could evacuate. The third penetrated one of the sub-turrets and killed Trooper Knapton. He was the first British tank man to die during the siege.

After a quick check had shown that Knapton was dead, Hynes and the rest of his crew ran to the nearest friendly tank (commanded by Lieutenant Bangham) and scrambled on to it. They could have made a more fortunate choice; before they were properly aboard, it too was set on fire and both crews had to run for shelter in one of the perimeter posts.

This battle lasted for thirty minutes until Olbrich, unable to get across a ditch he hadn't known existed and unwilling to remain milling about under fire from the British artillery, quite properly withdrew. He left behind a Mk III panzer, two Italian Mk 13 tanks and a CV3, all barely 300 yards from the perimeter they had come to storm.

Meanwhile, to the west of these actions Ponath's men had watched their tank support disappear and were now out on a limb. They tried to dig in but found this impossible in ground where bare rock prevailed, and they were reduced to scraping hollows and buttressing these with whatever they could find in the way of slabs of stone. For the remainder of that day they had to lie in these makeshift sangars, unable to raise their heads and waiting for the sanctuary of nightfall. Peace of a sort returned for what was left of that Good Friday afternoon.

In the evening several Hurricanes took off from El Gubbi to strafe Ponáth's position. The pilots did not like this work, their War Diary entry on the previous day complaining that too many planes were being lost during such attacks. As if to support this claim, two of the aircraft came to grief; Sergeant Willis was killed and Sergeant Gudson (one of six Free French pilots who had joined 73 Sqn only two days before) was shot down. Other pilots were caught in a dust storm which blew up after they had taken off and blotted out their landing strip. Sergeant Marshall, who already had twelve enemy planes to his credit, made a safe touch-down at Mersa Matruh, but Flight Lieutenant Ball, DFC, failed to find a landing ground and was lost. So far then, Streich's attack had cost the garrison two tanks and three planes, as well as some of their crews – but not the fortress.

Enemy action was resumed after dark, but this time it was of a different type. Pioneers of Engineer Bn 200 moved in on the ditch; these were crack German troops whose speciality was the penetration of defence works, and they set about this task. But Murray had not been idle. Interception patrols had been sent out by both 2/13th and 2/17th. The latter found its section of ditch clear, but the men from 2/13th came upon this group of Pioneers. These took to their heels, abandoning enough in the way of materials and weaponry to indicate what was in Rommel's mind. Thus began a history of Australian infantry patrolling which was to be unsurpassed by any other army in any theatre of war. The night which witnessed this also saw how hard they could work. They sowed thousands of mines along the front of the battalion under threat.

Day Two, 12 April

Dawn found Ponath's panzergrenadiers established in a position 400 yards out from the perimeter and firing on posts held by 2/17th. A more serious threat was the gathering of enemy vehicles some 3,000 yards away on the approach from El Adem, but this was taking place in a hollow where it could not be observed by the defenders. Morshead determined that whatever was taking place there should not go undisturbed. He had his gunners plaster the area, and in the afternoon a flight of RAF bombers came up from Egypt, circled the depression and dropped their bombs on it. The Luftwaffe was in action too, making several low flights over the perimeter seeking weaknesses in the anti-tank ditch which the panzers might exploit. This should not have been necessary, because proper reconnaissance on the ground would have revealed the fact that in this sector, stretches of the anti-tank ditch were no more than 18 inches deep.

Meanwhile, matters were anything but peaceful at Rommel's desert HQ. Olbrich had been berated for giving up the previous day's attack so easily. Streich too suffered the lash of Rommel's tongue. He was ordered to make a new attack on the following night; this time Streich would lead the attack and he was told: 'I expect this attack to be made with the utmost resolution under your personal leadership'.[22] And in order to ensure that the utmost resolution was used, Rommel's aide, Schmidt, was to accompany Streich.

Day Three, 13 April

The day began with panzers operating over a front of some ten miles, astride the El Adem Road and reaching over to the west side of the perimeter. This wide dispersal of action had the twin functions of concealing what was going on in the depression and also of planting doubt in Morshead's mind as to where the next point of attack would be. Ponath and his men were still in their holes outside the perimeter. By now they had been in action continuously for fourteen days, during which they had spearheaded Rommel's advance, seized Derna, fought the von Prittwitz battle and taken two generals prisoner, one of whom was General O'Connor, conqueror of the Italian Army. Ponath must have been desperately in need of rest, but this was the last thing he would be allowed by Rommel, who appeared to get along without it himself. Indeed, Ponath was made to crawl from his exposed position to receive new orders and then to make the dangerous return journey. And his new orders? He and his men were to attempt what Olbrich had failed to do; under cover of darkness they were to get over the ditch and across the wire, and open a gap through which the panzers could advance. It is not difficult to imagine the reaction of his exhausted men to this news.

Morshead was not deceived. Enemy infantry had been observed de-bussing 3,000–4,000 yards south of and facing 2/17th's position. They had then been led forward in small groups until they were within 500 yards of the perimeter posts. Major Loder-Symonds of 1RHA was in R32 acting as FOO, and he brought his guns into action against them. They were forced to fall back and then regroup about 1,500 yards away from the perimeter. Morshead had by now decided that the attack was going to come in at this point and he committed his guns and tanks accordingly. Four RHA batteries were ordered to dig-in their 25pdrs in area 410424 where they would be covering the approach to the town from the threatened sector. The *portées* of 3RHA and the anti-tank guns of 3AA-T were brought out of reserve and moved close to King's Cross. Six of 3RHA's anti-tank guns were sent forward to the threatened posts where they were received gratefully by men who had expected to be facing panzers with only their rifles. Drew was ordered to have his cruiser tanks ready to meet an attack in the vicinity of El Adem Road. After that, Morshead could only wait and see, together with the men of 20th Brigade, who were standing-to on the firing steps of their concrete holes. The first phase of the Easter Battles was over, the second was about to erupt.

SEVEN

But at night we were all rats,
each in his hole,
girls on the wall,
their eyes bright upon us.

Rommel's Easter attack: the break-in

The assault proper began at 1700 hrs on 13 April under Rommel's personal command, when a heavy concentration of artillery fire from the Italian guns of General Gratti and the German guns of Hetch rained down on R31 and R32. It was followed by an infantry attack in the vicinity of R33 which was driven back by small-arms fire. This post had now been located by the attackers, however, and for more than an hour it was

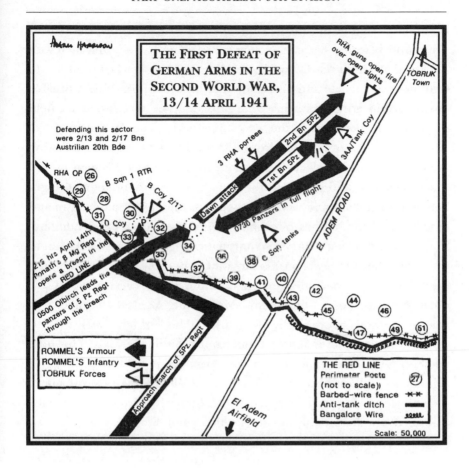

subjected to a barrage which included mortar fire. The men in R32 then saw trucks containing enemy infantry and towing guns crossing their front. Captain Balfe was in command of that post and he took up where Loder-Symonds had left off, bringing all four batteries of 1RHA into action. He thus became the first Australian infantry officer to act as FOO for RHA guns.

By this time, Ponath's panzergrenadiers and some of the pioneers of Engineer Bn 200 had reached the perimeter and were at work trying to nullify the defences and open up a breach through which the panzers might pass. They were heard by Lieutenant Mackell and his men who were guarding R33, and the lieutenant ordered small-arms fire against them. This immediately brought heavy retaliatory fire and Mackell, realising that a significant enemy presence was in his vicinity, decided to drive it off before it became entrenched. Taking half-a-dozen men with him, one of whom was Corporal Jack Edmondson, Mackell went out to find the invaders. He and his patrol were in fact approaching a sizeable enemy group armed with machine-guns, mortars and two small field pieces which they were in the act of digging in. The Australian patrol advanced under cover of fire from R33 until they were within throwing range of the enemy. Mackell then gave the command, his men hurled their grenades and charged forward. The first hand-to-hand fight between Australians and German troops was under way, and a grim and bloody stabbing of bodies, or bashing of heads it proved to be. Edmondson, a big and strong man whose only patrolling before this had been in the protection of sheep on his far-away farm, now became a fighting giant. He put two machine-guns out of action with his grenades and bayoneted at least one of the enemy. Meanwhile, Mackell's bayonet had stuck in the body of one of the Germans, and his legs were being held by this man while another attacked him from behind. He shouted for help and Edmondson, who had already been wounded in the throat and stomach but was still on his feet, responded. He killed one of the Germans, then a second, and then a third. The remainder fled from such ferocity, leaving many dead or dying in the ditch. But Edmondson, too, had fallen. His comrades carried him back to R33 where he died soon after arrival. He was awarded a posthumous Victoria Cross in recognition of his '... resolution, leadership and extraordinary resolve'.[23] His was the first VC to be won by an Australian during the war.

Nonsensical stories have been written about what happened on that night ... of shadows flitting about and leaving behind enemies with their throats cut; of Australians singing 'It's a long way to Tipperary' as they mowed down the infiltrating enemy. The truth lies more in the silent desperation of the Mackell–Edmondson struggle, it has no need of literary embellishment.

The probing between the posts continued until Ponath eventually led his group of panzergrenadiers across the ditch, got in behind R33, and established a bridgehead. He moved some men into a stone house to the north of the post,[24] and others constructed sangars for use as gun-pits.

He was soon able to bring machine-gun fire against R33 and its western neighbouring post R31, and under this covering fire his engineers began to make the gap for the panzers.[25] By 0500 hrs Olbrich was able to order the panzers of PZR5's 2nd Bn to advance into the fortress. They went astray, found themselves too far to the east and had to detour to the left until they found the gap. They passed through it and, carrying infantry on their backs, moved past Balfe and his men who were in R32. The defenders in the post kept their heads down and allowed them to pass unhindered. The German infantry then dismounted and the panzers advanced until they reached a defile about half a mile inside the wire, where they stopped, to wait either for the dawn, or for Streich to arrive. This was to prove a costly mistake.

Rommel had commanded the assault until Ponath's party was established inside the perimeter and the gap had been made. He then handed command over to Streich, and there may have been an element of 'That's how it should have been done in the first place' in Rommel's demeanour when he did so. Streich and Schmidt went forward to lead the panzer attack on the town, followed by the tank in which they intended to ride. Streich had the only map of the area that they had been able to lay hands on, but he made the same mistake as the panzers had, and before he could rectify this his small party found itself under the noses of infantrymen manning one of the perimeter posts. These promptly pinned the German commander down, and by the time he managed to extricate himself the battle was over.

When it became clear that penetrations into the fortress had been made in his part of the defences, Murray brought up B Coy of 2/17th and placed it at the rear of R32 as a covering force. Morshead was also aware by now that many enemy tanks were inside his defences and their intended route was fairly obvious to him. He decided to take them head on, using his guns, and the arrangements he had already made supported this decision. A/E Battery of 1RHA was dug in astride the projected enemy route of advance. The other batteries of that regiment were also in the King's Cross area and had their FOOs in R26. He now brought forward his anti-tank *portées* and positioned these on what would become the enemy's flank of attack. Drew was instructed to send the two squadrons of 1RTR to 415423, an area west of the El Adem Road, where they would have the advantage of higher ground. They moved up on to the escarpment and reached the vicinity of the POW cage, not far from the crossroads, and here they divided, B Sqn moving east towards R40 while C Sqn covered the western side of this part of the sector. They were fortunate; had they moved a little later they might well have bumped into Olbrich in the middle of the gully.

Here come the panzers!

Dawn arrived quickly. Olbrich decided he could wait no longer. The panzers started their engines and rolled forward out of the dip, making straight for a gap in the Pilastrino Escarpment. As they advanced they found themselves subjected to stinging attacks from the anti-tank guns of 3AA-T and also from five *portées* of 3RHA. These darted in, got off a shot, then darted back out, a new breed of gadfly in this land of pestiferous insects. Ignoring them, the panzers pressed on and reached the edge of the escarpment between Pilastrino and Sidi Mahmoud. They entered the gully and were emerging from this when they ran straight on to the guns of two RHA batteries. Lieutenant Chilver Stainer, the FOO for Chestnut Troop, had climbed into that troop's observation post, a wooden structure reaching 20 feet above ground level. He saw the panzers approaching, got off a warning to his guns, then scrambled down and took shelter in a well as they passed by. The gunners had scarcely needed his warning; they had been listening to the growing growl of panzer engines and so they had the advantage in that fraction of a second when the tanks emerged and the two sets of combatants came face to face. Their shells were already on the way while the men peering through the slits in the side of the panzers were still gaping. Some idea of the fury of that moment is given in the official Royal Artillery account: 'The first shot from No 1 gun set the leading tank on fire. No 2's first shot lifted the turret clean off another tank. ... soon there were 15 or more tanks firing at us with 75mm and machine guns ... during this period the only two officers with the guns were both hit along with four other ranks.'[26]

The panzers reacted quickly. Those able to, pressed forward in an attempt to reach and silence the guns. They got to within 500 yards, but the tremendous fire being brought to bear on them was too much. They faltered, then turned away from it. They began to withdraw, but as they did so they ran into their regiment's other battalion of panzers which had been following them and a confused mêlée ensued. Eventually the combined force veered to the east in order to outflank the guns, but they ran into the anti-tank guns of 3AA-T. Heavy firing was now coming in at them from all directions, and the resumed attack wilted under it. The panzers halted, turned, took to their heels and fled back to the gap. This took them across the path of Leakey's tanks which had arrived on the scene. He had just watched a Hurricane go straight into the ground within yards of his tank when a gunnery officer drove up to him and asked him to come to the aid of his guns. What happened then is best told in his own words.

'We swung right into battle line. I handed Milligan his cigarette and told him to start shooting. There was no need for me to indicate his target. "Load!" I yelled to Adams and away went another solid shot, tearing at the thick enemy armour. Soon the turret was so thick with smoke that I could only just make out the figure of Adams as he loaded shell after shell into the breech. We were firing faster than ever before and so were the other four cruiser tanks. It must have been a minute before the Germans spotted us and by then their tanks had received several hits from our shells. They appeared to panic because they started to turn in all directions, many back the way they had come. Then they were on to us and we could clearly see the flash of their guns. The tank on my left was hit several times and brewed up. I noticed one man of this crew dragging himself along the ground, badly wounded and machine-gun bullets were hitting the ground around him. I felt I had to give him cover. It was a stupid move because I presented the German tank gunners with a larger target and they took full advantage of it.

'"She's on fire, Sir!" shouted Adams. At the same moment Milligan's head fell back against my knees and looking down I saw that a shell had removed most of his chest. "Bale out!" I yelled and as I pulled myself out of the turret, what shells we had left began to explode. I saw Adams get out safely and we dashed around to the front of the tank to check up on the others. The driver flopped out of his hatch and Adams grabbed him.

One sub-turret gunner was dead and already his clothes were on fire. The other sub-gunner was lying by the side of the tank and he looked up at me and smiled; his right leg was shot off just below the knee, and the useless limb was attached by one small piece of skin. We were being machine-gunned. Somehow I got him over my shoulder and back to where I found a shallow trench. He straightened up, looked at his leg and said, "Cut it off, Sir. It's no use to me." I did so.'[27]

The panic which Leakey had witnessed is best described by one of his opposite numbers, Leutnant Joachim Schorm of 5PZR: 'Now we come slap into 1 Battalion which is following us. Some of our tanks are already on fire. The crews call for doctors who dismount to help in this witches' cauldron. Enemy anti-tank units fall on us with their machine-guns firing into our midst, but we have no time. My driver says, "The engines are no longer running properly, brakes not acting, transmission only with difficulty" ... the lane is in sight. Everyone hurries towards it. Enemy anti-tank guns shoot into the mass. Our own anti-tank guns and 88s are almost deserted, the crews lying silent beside them ... now comes the gap and the ditch ... the vehicle almost gets stuck but manages to extricate itself with great difficulty. With their last reserves of energy the crew gets out of range and returns to camp.'

There go the panzers!

It was not all cakes-and-ale with the gunners; it seldom is for the men who stand behind the flimsy shelter of the gun's shield. During the twenty minutes of the engagement the guns of Chestnut and E Troops had each fired more than 100 rounds, had had two guns knocked out and had suffered eight men killed and five wounded, two of whom subsequently died. The E Troop report describes how this happened: 'Just as our No 1 gun swung round to engage them [enemy tanks trying to outflank the guns] a 75mm shell landed on the trail killing all the detachment and setting fire to a box of cartridges. At the same time a gun of E Troop received a direct hit on the shield. The BSM, although wounded, manned the gun himself and continued to fire it.'[28]

Elsewhere amongst the gunners, a troop of 3RHA found itself surrounded and suffering casualties. Bombardier Williamson and Gunner

Aitchinson were both killed and Gunner Atkins wounded in the arm and leg. Atkins continued to fire his gun until a shell hit its piled-up ammunition. He then crawled away. Bombardier Rudd was in the company dug-out. He saw Atkins' plight, ran to help, and dragged the wounded man to safety, where Atkins, ignoring his wounds, loudly claimed to have knocked out eight enemy tanks. As for the *portées*, which had fought in the open, two of their five guns were knocked out and among the casualties was Lieutenant Robinson who had been killed. But the gunners had the immense satisfaction of knowing that they had faced the dreaded panzers and it had not been they who had backed off.

By 0703 hrs Rommel's all-out assault on the fortress had been held, then thrown back, leaving behind it the wreckage of seventeen panzers. This scattered trail of burning wrecks was a symbol of the other wreckage that had been wrought during that twenty minutes or so – the destruction of Rommel's dream of a triumphal entry into Cairo.

Where were Rommel's guns ... where were Rommel's infantry?
Questions need to be asked and answered. What had been happening at the gap in the wire which had resulted in the panzers rolling forward without the support of the other components of a *Blitzkrieg*? Where were their guns? Where were the machine-gunners who should have been wiping out the crews of the British guns?

The simple answer is, that they had been stopped in their tracks. The Australians in the posts that had been by-passed by the panzers had then come up on to their fire-steps, but not to surrender. Supported by their reserve battalion, 2/15th, they had opened a withering fire against anyone and anything that tried to follow the panzers. German guns had become jammed against the ditch where they came under the close attention of Rocket Troop and other RHA guns. By 0630 hrs Rocket Troop's three guns were claiming to have knocked out three enemy guns and two gun-tractors, and reporting that many German dead were lying around these guns. The final battering suffered here when the retreating panzers tried to fight their way through the shambles turned defeat into rout.

As for Ponath's panzergrenadiers, B Coy of 2/17th had put in a counter-attack against their position at 0600 hrs which had been supported by the infantry in the neighbouring posts. Far from being able to come forward and support the panzer advance, Ponath's force was now in scattered groups and the men in these were fighting for their lives. His situation was not enviable. He had seen many of his men killed and wounded, he had watched the panzers flee, he knew that the attack had failed and that he was now cut off. Crawford's men of 2/17th approached the stone house and one sergeant went forward calling out in case the building had been re-occupied by Australian infantry. He was immediately shot dead. That was enough for the rest of the patrol. Sergeant McElroy led a bayonet charge which resulted in the death of fourteen Germans and the surrender of the remainder. Ponath was not among them; he was out in the open with a larger group that included many who had been wounded. He decided to leave these last in the relative safety of a ditch and led the rest in an effort to fight free of the trap they were in.

Hynes of 1RTR now came into the act. He had been ordered to take his tanks from their position at R40 towards R33 to intercept the retreating panzers, but a ditch had prevented his doing so. Two of his cruisers had become stranded and so he sent his light tanks forward while the two remaining cruisers tried to free the stranded ones. The light tanks arrived on the scene just in time to help round up the remaining panzergrenadiers, and their arrival saw one of the few actions to disgrace this savage battlefield. Lance-Sergeant Hulme climbed down from his tank to accept the surrender of a group of infantrymen, one of whom dropped his hands, picked up a gun and shot him. Australian infantrymen who had seen this happen immediately shot the perpetrator.

Ponath, although wounded, refused to surrender and was killed. His had been a heroic effort. His regiment had been decimated, 150 being counted dead on the battlefield and 250 taken prisoner, many of whom were wounded. But these figures give only a partial picture: prior to the battle the ration strength of MG8 had been 1,400 all ranks. After the battle it was about 300.

There are versions which have Ponath and his men fighting on until the 20th without water and only succumbing when all their ammunition had been fired. This is not borne out by 9th Div's report of the battle which says that by noon that day the entire area had been cleared of the enemy. Nor is it borne out by Rommel, who wrote: 'We were unable to establish contact with Ponath's battalion on the night 14/15th April. A large part of the battalion had been wiped out. Lt Col Ponath himself, who had received the Knight's Cross for his exploits during the advance through Cyrenaica, had been killed.'[29]

A report written by 2/15th's Intelligence Section on the action describes how an A Coy patrol with two carriers commanded by Sergeant Keyes captured five officers and 89 men, and killed a German lieutenant-colonel and two men. It is possible that the dead officer referred to was Ponath. There are versions of the story that have him leading a suicide charge and being shot through the heart. Ponath has no need of such romanticism. He was a very brave man who served his country well beyond the call of duty. Like von Prittwitz, he had been driven to his death by Rommel's implacable will. He would not be the last to add his bones to that particular list.

The Easter battle in the air

So much for the battle on the ground, but the third arm of the *Blitzkrieg* had also been in action. Geisler's Fliegerkorps X arrived with the dawn, a total of 70 planes, some Ju 87s, some Me 110s, and with Italian G50s acting as escorts to these strafers and bombers. They ranged across the fortress, attacking the AA guns near the harbour and dive-bombing the gun positions and tanks, this first onslaught being followed by further attacks throughout the day. The sixteen big guns of the Heavy AA Brigade covering the harbour fought back; they were to fire a total of 1,200 rounds and claim three enemy planes shot down before the day was over, but they were also to lose one of their commanders, Lieutenant-Colonel McIntyre of 152HAA having been wounded by a bomb splinter and having to be evacuated from the port. The day ended with a final attack on the harbour during which the hospital ship *Vita* was hit and damaged in what 13LAA diary described as a 'dastardly attack'.

The RAF, too, joined in the defence of the fortress. The eight surviving Hurricanes went up to meet the first wave of attackers and a series of dog-fights took place, often immediately above the heads of the men battling on the ground. Thirty-eight sorties were made during the day and the squadron claimed to have shot down six Ju 87s, one Heinkel and two G50s, for the loss of three of their own planes. Flight Lieutenant Smith was killed while making a single-handed attack on five G50s, but before he was brought down he had shot down two and damaged a third. Pilot Officer Lamb failed to return from a flight. Pilot Officers Goodman and Millist, and Flight Sergeant Webster were all killed. The saddest case of all, if such an evaluation can be made of the totally tragic situation which every battle must become, was the death of Sergeant Webster. He was on the tail of an Me 109 when he was shot out of the sky by our own Bofors guns. Lamb's machine was discovered next morning, but he had not survived. Padre Cox of 258 Wing had the sad duty of travelling to all three plane wrecks so that he could bury their pilots in temporary graves on the spot.

Rommel probes the El Medauur sector

This was not quite the end of the Easter battles. On the 15th, several hundred Italian infantrymen supported by the Ariete Armoured Division's tanks attacked the posts held by 2/24th Battalion of Tovell's 26th Brigade on the Derna Road side of the perimeter. They penetrated between S13 and S17 but suffered many casualties and withdrew – though they did not get very far. They were pursued by a patrol from 2/48th Bn and 75 of them were taken prisoner. On the 16th, Rommel took personal command of an attack on Ras El Medauur. He sent in an Italian infantry unit supported by Ariete, but as soon as the latter came under fire its CO withdrew his tanks and not all Rommel's persuasion could tempt him forward again. Meanwhile the stranded infantry came under attack from a carrier platoon led by Lieutenant Isaksson of 2/48th. He had taken 97 prisoners when a German armoured car arrived on the scene and opened fire. The remaining Italians thereupon fled for the safety of the perimeter. Rommel tried to intervene with three anti-tank guns but was too late; the entire battalion of 62 Trento Regiment, a total of 26 officers and 777 other ranks, vanished through the wire and was on its way to Australia. Leading the German element in this attack was Rommel's adjutant, Major Schraepler.[30]

The final attack was a little more serious than these fiascos. It was again aimed at Ras El Medauur and in particular, at its hill. The approach march was made during the night and the attack proper followed an artillery barrage on the morning of 17 April. Thirty-two of Ariete's tanks accompanied by troop carriers appeared from the direction of Carrier Hill and made for Pt 209. A few of the tanks managed to get on to the hill but their supporting infantry were pinned against the perimeter wire. The tanks then came under heavy fire from 51FRG guns, directed from OPs in S19, S13, S11 and S2, and this forced them to retire. Lieutenant-Colonel Douglas, CO of 51FRG, who was acting as FOO in one of the posts, was wounded and had to be evacuated.

These concentrations of enemy effort against the Ras El Medauur sector did not go unnoticed by Morshead. He had already set a strengthening of defences under way, and he now ordered that priority be given to the laying of Minefield B. This was a belt of mines stretching across two miles in the hinterland of that zone's perimeter posts. This was to prove the wisest decision he would make during the whole of the siege.

So ended Rommel's first real assault on the fortress. It was frustrated by a combination of all arms. The Australian infantry-men, after having been 'softened up' by Rommel's barrage and blitz from the air, should have given up the ghost at the sight of his advancing panzers in the manner of all previous opponents. They broke that pattern. They allowed the panzers to drive by and then stood up in their posts and fired on the advancing enemy infantry until none were left to fire at. The British gunners stood to their guns until the panzers were almost upon them and then drove them back in panic. The British tanks came in at a critical moment and showed themselves to be full of fight. Not least, the RAF pilots took off from an airfield under constant attack, tore into an enemy far more numerous than themselves, and made dive-bombing as dangerous for the Stuka crews as it was for the men on the ground.

It would be pleasant to be able to say that a sense of elation seized the garrison on the night of 14 April, but it would not be true. We knew they had got in. We knew we had chased them back out. But we also knew that it had been a close thing, that they would be coming back, and that there were corpses by the dozen waiting to be buried. There was no elation, just reaction – part relief, part wondering what the next day would bring. We quite missed the historical significance of what that day had already brought – it had seen the first defeat of German arms anywhere during the war.

Rommel's conduct of the Easter battles

It is interesting to read the report of the battle written by Colonel Olbrich, CO of PZ5 Regiment: 'The intelligence gave out before the attack that the enemy was exhausted, that his artillery was extremely weak, and that his morale was very low. Before the beginning of the third attack the regiment had not the slightest idea of the well-designed and executed defences of the enemy, nor of a single battalion position, or of the terrific number of anti-tank guns. Also, it was not known that he had heavy tanks. The regiment went into action with unbendable will determined at all costs to break the enemy and take Tobruk. Only the vastly superior enemy, the frightful losses and lack of any supporting weapons caused the regiment to fail in its tasks. Thirty-nine tanks went into action, seventeen were shot to pieces by the enemy.'

There are implications here for Rommel's conduct of the battle. What improvements over the von Prittwitz affair had there been in his preparation of this much larger attack?

Neither panzer crews nor infantry could have been at the peak of efficiency. The infantry chosen to make the breach had been in constant action since first setting out across the desert from Fort Agheila more than two weeks before. The panzer crews had not had to fight anything in the way of a major battle, but they had been on the move in stressful conditions for a similar length of time. Their tanks had not received the servicing they required. Some had only just arrived from Mechili, a hard ride across the desert. On the other hand, the attacking force had the support of six batteries of guns, and the dive-bombers of Fliegerkorps X to soften up resistance to their advance. It also had several 88mm guns, without doubt the finest mobile gun in action in the desert at that time.

It was absolutely essential that the base of any gap that the pioneers were able to make in the perimeter defences be widened as quickly as possible in order to get these guns forward. Rommel had ordered the two Italian motorised divisions, Brescia and Ariete, to roll up the sides of the breach as soon as this had been made. This was not done; Brescia didn't arrive at all, and when Ariete did so, their CO asked for more time to prepare. Rommel would not wait. The attack went in without them and the breach remained a confined one, easily targeted by the British guns.

If Rommel had postponed his attack for two days he would have been using fresher infantry and better prepared tanks. He would have had Ariete to widen the base of his penetration. But there was another glaring deficiency which Olbrich highlights in his report. The men making the attack were in complete ignorance as to what they were up against. They did not have any maps of the defences until two arrived on the day of the attack, and those leading the attack never saw them. They had aerial recce reports but no aerial photographs, and the posts they were about to attack were so well camouflaged that from the air they could not be easily distinguished from the surrounding wasteland. The panzer crews did not even know that there was an anti-tank ditch until they blundered into it. From this distance in time it seems incredible that Rommel had not made a priority of getting as much information as he could from his allies about the defences which *they* had built. If ever there were need for thorough reconnaissance before an attack this was the occasion, yet the only reconnaissance made was by Rommel himself, using binoculars. To sum up: a less than fully efficient force was sent into attack blindfolded. Contempt for his opponents is implicit in these unaddressed deficiencies and in the opening statement of the Olbrich report, and contempt should never sit inside a future field marshal's knapsack.

It is interesting to note Rommel's reaction to this set-back. Ponath had wasted time trying to fill in the ditch. Olbrich and Streich were told, 'Your panzers did not give of their best', and both men were got rid of. Most telling was his comment in a letter to Frau Rommel, written the day after the defeat: 'Nothing of any importance from Africa.'[31]

What would Ponath have thought of that?

EIGHT

While, from the undergut of the sky
black birds nagged.
Strangers, meeting at night's noon
exchanged their hrrrmms!
We counted their comings and their goings
while our fleas slept.

Inside the fortress

What was it like during those early days of the siege for the men on the sea side of the perimeter? For the men in the Red Line it was a question of bending their backs and earning their sobriquet 'Diggers'. Morshead set them to converting their gun-pits to something more aggressive than funk holes. Surveyors working in the tunnels drafted sketches to show how the posts could be improved by adding more firing points and siting these for all-round defence. Engineers working in the town produced more than 500 periscopes and 200 Very flare alarms for use in the posts, a throw-back to the trench warfare of 1914–18. A thin belt of wire was woven around each of these posts and frontal wire was erected to link most of them. The mines which the Italians had sown in front of the Red Line were lifted, re-sown just inside the wire and boxed out to meet the anti-tank ditch. Spoke minefields were sown, with the post serving as the hub. Three aerial bombs, which could be operated either by electrical charge or by trip, were sunk in front of each Red Line post. When triggered, these leapt several feet into the air before exploding. Nor was the laying of mines confined to protection of the front-line posts. Two tactical minefields were laid between the Red and Blue Lines, the one in the Ras El Medauur zone receiving priority. As for those infantrymen being held in reserve in the Blue Line, theirs were not idle hands. They set to with their picks and shovels to convert this from a notional feature into a defensive reality.

One group of men were not happy in their forward positions. This was the dismounted KDG contingent who had been put under command of 2/23rd on the western side of the perimeter. When ordered to move in readiness for a counter-attack they asked: 'How do we counter-attack?' 'In the ordinary way of course,' they were told, 'how else do you think? Rifles and bayonets.' 'But we haven't got any bayonets, and if we had the men wouldn't know how to use them. We're armed with Brens, Boys Rifles and Vickers Guns. We aren't mobile enough for a vigorous counter-attack. Give us a job we're capable of doing.' 'Very well, the whole force will move up into the Red Line. All split up. One troop in S12, one in S13 and one in S19.'

The KDG CO, Major Lindsay, took a dim view of what he saw as mis-use of his trained wireless operators and mechanics and wrote to the CO of 2/23rd asking that they be taken out of line. This was done, but was accompanied by the slur 'windy'. The men of this famous cavalry regi-ment resented the charge. They claimed to be itching to have a go at something other than planes, although when an Me 109 came too close to their lines three of the KDG Breda crews almost came to blows over which one had shot it down. In the short term they were able to have their go, in the long term they were to prove the equal in bravery of any of Tobruk's troops, but by then the offending Australian officer had long left the fortress.

Life for the garrison at the beginning of the siege

I suppose that our own experience was pretty similar to that of all those not in either the Red or Blue Lines, specialisations excepted, and it must serve as a general description. We four had been in our new location and roles for less than a week, but had been too busy to do anything other than swipe at flies and scratch. Now that there was a lull in the action we could begin to make something out of our situation and environment. The sum total of my possessions was the tin of Gibbs toothpaste and the toothbrush, which I always carried in my shirt pocket and which had escaped with me from Mersa Brega. I had the clothes on my back, the boots on my feet and a water-bottle, and that was it. Jim and Charlie were little better off. Jock was reticent about what was in his haversack and we didn't press him. Our composite brigade had nothing in the way of stores. On the other hand our friends in 9th Div had fallen back in some order, did have essentials, and were amenable to pleas from their hard-up kin if that kin were prepared to take the odd insult along with the wherewithal. Then there was the town whose stucco and blancoed houses were empty of humans and open to itchy-fingered visitors.

We became gypsies, living on our wits, declining no offer in the way of dress or anything else. Within days I was wearing desert boots (Italian-officer-for-the-use-of); a dark blue pull-over, whose origin was probably still trotting around on its cloven hooves on South Island, and shorts (Australian issue, somewhat reduced by a sharp knife). I had collected an Italian water-bottle, fat and furry, and an Italian ground-sheet (also officer-issue, the ordinary Italian soldier being so disgracefully outfitted that nothing he wore was worthy of consideration). I had no headgear until I received a Balaclava in a comforts package; it arrived on 1 July, the hottest day in one of the hottest places on earth. I also had an Italian Beretta, with an ammunition clip, and one of those Italian rifles whose nasty four-flanged bayonet ended in a sharp point. Pre-war photographs sent around the world by Mussolini's propagandists had shown Italian soldiers leaping over the fixed bayonets of these rifles and I had imagined the Italian soldiers to be of Olympic stature and potential. When I saw the size of the rifles in question that notion went out of the window, but the rifles were pretty little toys and could puncture a target can of soil from a hundred feet.

We had no pup tents and slept wherever we chose to unroll our ground-sheets, first scooping a hole for our hips in desert fashion. It was a little primitive, but what more magnificent bedroom ceiling could a body ask for than the vast, star-strewn sky which was ours for the looking? During the day we rolled up our ground-sheets and left them on the chosen spot as a stake-out. That space was our home. When we were not manning the set we sat on it, ate on it, slept on it.

Our ACV was stationed as close to 9th Div HQ as possible. It was such an obvious target from the air that we hastened to festoon it with netting and scrub, and no vehicle was allowed to drive near it because of what a network of tyre tracks would signify to an enemy reconnaissance plane. The Div HQ was established in a series of caves which the Italians had burrowed and blasted under the escarpment and then solidified in concrete. Its corridors led into chambers which served as offices; ammunition was stored in some of the tunnels but most were already filling up with the bric-à-brac that is so essential to HQs, even Australian ones. One such room served as the Intelligence Office, and it was to here that we took the accumulated messages which arrived throughout the night from the KDG patrols. I became so associated with these messages that I was tolerated as part of the furniture, and not booted out as I would have been if it had been a British set-up. It was in this underground room during the night hours that I developed an appetite for military intelligence which has never left me.

We fed with the Australians. I had not previously mingled with them, and my only knowledge of their existence had come as a half-awake boy, dragged from my bed by my father to keep him company on his nocturnal wearing of earphones. Through their crackling we tried to make sense of a commentary coming from somewhere called Sydney on something called a Test Match. From these, and the authority of my father, I had learned that all Australians, especially those described as umpires, suffered from weak sight or even worse ailments. This had been poor training for existence with the real thing. I listened to them in the cookhouse line-up, in the tunnel, and around the two-up blanket. I learned that the central characteristic of that wonderfully psyched people was mutiny. I began to fear that I was surrounded by Fletcher Christians – there was always some NCO or Coy CO who was about to get a bayonet where it would do him no good at all. Then I realised that they felt the same way about their present environment, the sand was just as crook as the sergeant-major, and about the food and the men who cooked it. In time I came to realise that they were probably correct about all three.

The three 'F's
From the earliest moments we were plagued by three pests. all airborne, each beginning with the initial 'F'. First were the flies. The news that 30,000 hapless victims had been confined and compacted to await their attention must have winged its way across the top half of Africa, and on the wing, too, they answered it. From out of southern Chad and western Tunisia; from the sapless Sahara; from beyond the Sweetwater they must have come, for this black density which plagued us could never have been an indigenous population. They were always with us, always at us; at

the moisture in the corner of our eyes and our mouths and under our armpits, at every drop of sweat we managed to squeeze from our dehydrating bodies, at every morsel of food we tried to sneak into our mouths. They soared over and around our heads like aircraft in a landing stack. They alighted on us, died in their thousands under whatever weapons we could create, and in their dying seconds mocked us with their multiplicity. They were always with us, and if they now vanish from this account it is only to make room for humans.

Second in nuisance value were the fleas. We hadn't been in our location very long when we realised that we were constantly scratching at our ankles. Then red rashes appeared. Understanding came with horror and rage; the sand was alive – literally so – with fleas, and they were taking abode in our rolled-down socks, unsheathing their hollow needles and satisfying their hunger in the dark warmth they discovered there. The Italians took the blame. They had lived here for many years. They had bred and fed these tiny monsters until now they were as many as the grains of sand in which they passed their life cycles. We cursed the absent Italians and took off our socks. It did at least deprive them of their nests, but it did not keep them from their midnight feasting.

Third were the human fliers. We had first met those black-crossed villains on an early morning when they came from Sicily, frightened the life out of us, and departed leaving a trail of burning tents and vehicles behind them. All the length of the recent retreat they had pestered us, flying around unchallenged over our heads while picking out their targets: the 'A' vehicles first; wireless trucks, water-trucks, petrol trucks and anything wearing more than canvas. Then the softer stuff, beginning with the staff cars – all with an efficiency that had to be admired. They soon made it plain that, unlike the flies, they had no affection for us, but like the fleas they were after our blood. They were not as numerous, thank God, as their hairy-legged associates of the wing, but they were numerous enough and had six airfields within 25 miles of Tobruk from which to operate. In the days following his Easter defeat, Rommel ordered the change to siege tactics, and his bombers began the series of attacks upon the hub of our supply – the harbour and its ships, and on the supply dumps and water-points.

On 17 April, fifty Ju 87s dived from out of the sun on to one of the dumps. Dust was blanketing El Gubbi at the time and the Hurricanes were unable to take off. Next day it was relays of single bombers coming over from 0300 hrs until dawn, with El Gubbi as one of their targets. On the 19th it was back to the harbour and the day became one long scramble for those Hurricanes that were still able to take off. Every moment of their time they were in danger: at take-off, in the air, as they came in to land and most of all, while they sat waiting to be re-fuelled and armed. Nor was it simply the Luftwaffe they had to fear. A flight-path had been determined between the RAF and the AA defences, but by now everybody who had something which could fire was getting into the act and a plane was a plane – every plane was a target.

The Hurricanes took their chances and had their successes. Pilot Officer Spence shot down a Ju 87 over the town and then an Me 109, but in the town itself a command post was hit and the twelve unfortunates occupying it were all killed. On the following day the exhausted Squadron Leader Murray went for a rest in the Delta and Wykeham-Barnes flew in to take command of what was left of 73 Sqn. He was already a veteran of desert air battle, having shot down a CR42 in the early days of the Italian invasion of Egypt, and had been forced to bale out during the previous winter battles. He had won the first DFC to be awarded to a fighter pilot in the Middle East. He was now asked to do the impossible; to take on the might of Fliegerkorps X with no more than half-a-dozen patched-up fighters flown by tired and overstretched men. On the day he arrived the squadron's log read: 'It is not to be expected that pilots can, day after day, tackle 20 60 enemy aircraft with 5 Hurricanes at their disposal.'

Nor was it.

On the 22nd there were six scrambles to meet aircraft attacking the harbour and airfield. Thirty Ju 87s, twelve Me 109s and twelve G50s were counted in the raids. Flying Officer Goodman got a Ju 87 and shared a second with Free French pilot Sous Lieutenant Dennis. Sergeant Marshall was back on the score sheet with a G50, and then Dennis got his very own Ju 87 and crowned his day with an Me 109 which he shot down over Gazala.

Yet this magnificent effort was nearing its end. Enemy attacks on the 23rd were recorded at 1000 hrs, 1125 hrs, 1250 hrs, 1300 hrs, 1450 hrs, 1508 hrs, 1850 hrs and 1928 hrs. Wykeham-Barnes led four Hurricanes aloft at 1000 hrs and these were followed shortly afterwards by three more. A tremendous attack was developing over the harbour and airfield and the sky was reported 'full of aircraft', the seven British planes taking on sixty of the enemy. Wykeham-Barnes got a Ju 87 and an Me 109, Sergeant Marshall a Ju 87, Squadron Leader Litolff downed a Ju 87 and an Me 109, Pilot Officer Chatfield got a Ju 87. One of the AA Bofors guns shot an Me 109 from right off the tail of a Hurricane. But there was a price to be paid. Pilot Officer Haldenby was caught by an Me 109 as he was landing and crashed in flames. Flying Officer Martin was hit but survived the parachute drop. Wykeham-Barnes was set on by three Me 109s and had to bale out. He did so right over the town, giving the men below a good view of his descent, but not of his crash against the harbour wall, which put a dent in his leg. Sergeant Marshall's heroics came to an end while he was sitting in his plane, waiting for it to be re-fuelled. Strafed, he was hit in the shoulder and the back of the head and Leading Aircraftsman Webster of his ground crew was wounded in the lungs. Both men were got away from the plane and rushed to the hospital, where Webster died from his wounds. Pilot Officer Haldenby, who had climbed into his plane in mid-morning, was buried in Tobruk's cemetery that afternoon, a grim reminder of the transitory nature of the existence of a pilot in 73 Sqn on those fraught days.

Nor was the detached Flight B of 6 Squadron faring any better. Its Lysanders were a hazard and they were flown out, but several of the Flight's pilots remained and tried to carry out their reconnaissance work in Hurricanes. They had some success during experiments with the artillery, but their CO, Squadron Leader Weld, was lost in action. The demands on his Flight had been heavy and he had insisted on doing his share and more. He flew off one day and did not return. Flying Officer Fletcher took over until the arrival of Squadron Leader Legge. Finally, on the 19th, what was left of 6 Sqn was pulled out, leaving behind just two planes to continue reconnaissance flights. The engineers created a home for them in a nearby wadi where they could be hidden during enemy attacks and sally forth from it in the quieter moments.

Farewell to the boys in blue

On 25 April, 258 Wing was forced to call it quits. That evening the Hurricane squadron flew its surviving planes away from El Gubbi and their number was a measurement of the fight that had been put up there. Of the original three dozen which had flown up from the Delta only weeks before, eight patched-up planes took off. They left with honour, there was no rancour at their departure, only admiration for their bravery. Alas, their going was marred with tragedy. On the 28th it was the turn of the senior officers to leave: Wing Commander Johnson, Squadron Leaders Barclay and Cox (the padre), and Pilot Officer Beloe went to El Gubbi to take off in a Blenheim. Pilot Officer Allen and an unnamed air gunner made up the crew. As they were preparing to take off, news came in that six enemy planes had been plotted in the west. Johnson was told of this but decided they were too far away to be a danger. He was wrong. The Blenheim was scarcely airborne when word came that the enemy planes were now only seven miles away and approaching rapidly. It was too late for the horrified men on the ground to do anything. They watched the Blenheim pick up height and turn towards the sea, and it was there that the enemy fighters found it. They were on to it like a swarm of hornets and sent it down into the sea in flames. There were no survivors. Padre Cox, who only days before had buried the pilots of 73 Sqn, found his own unhallowed grave beneath the waters of the bay.

The departure of the flying element did not mean the end of the RAF's presence. Ten ground crew from 73 Sqn and six from 6 Sqn remained behind under command of Flying Officer Mathies. The remains of fifteen Hurricanes were scattered around the fortress and there was an acute shortage of parts for these fighters in the Middle East. Cannibalisation was the order of the day for these men. They travelled the length and breadth of the area, stripping the wrecks of anything that could be used again, especially the wings. These were shipped out on A Lighters which soon began the trip up Suicide Alley from Mersa Matruh. As these men roamed the fortress, spanners in hand, they must often have passed other men similarly equipped. This was the ROC recovery gang who were on the same recovery mission but for tank parts – sometimes they ventured beyond the wire in their search for anything that might be put to fighting use again.

There was a fourth 'F' which exercised the mind. During the first days we were getting two meals a day at the HQ cookhouse, a breakfast and an evening meal. Canned bacon or sausages and beans was the morning fare and the basics of the evening repast were corned beef and tinned vegetables. We had bully stew, and bully fritters, and sliced bully with mashed potatoes and mashed bully and beans. On rare occasions we had warmed-up M and V, our war's equivalent of the earlier war's notorious stew. There was in addition all the hard tack and corned beef you could carry away (until this dubious privilege was withdrawn), which allowed us to make porridge by soaking a couple of the biscuits in water or a touch of condensed milk on the better days, and adding any sugar you might have been able to scrounge. To heat this mess and the water for our brews we made our own stoves. These were the cubical aluminium cases designed to carry petrol. Their skins were too thin and easily fractured, so that they were nowhere near so serviceable as the German version, but they were ideal as stoves. You peeled away the top, filled them with sand, bashed holes in the side and then poured petrol into the sand and threw in a lighted match. Hey presto! A stove. On permanent 'high'.

Brewing up played its traditional army role. The British soldier's ability to hold up a battle until he has finished his brew is legendary and may it always remain so – it is in the tradition of Francis Drake, who did his share of soldiering as well as sailing. In Tobruk, where none of us was going anywhere and time became a nagging vacuum, the brew really came into its own. Any stray soul wandering past a rolled-up blanket was fair game to an invitation to have a cup of char and a share in the beating up of that ground-sheet's flies. In return would come an invite to drop in on the recipient next time you passed his way. Water was of course a fairly rare commodity. The ration varied, it was never strictly enforced but was done at the water point (which might be a water truck). If you ran short, you either borrowed, or hiked to the nearest water point. There was never any chance of a black market developing, the water we had tasted so awful that it was only in brew form you could get it down. We didn't do much in the way of washing, nor was it needed; the sand cleaned you off and your sweat evaporated the second it escaped the pores. But we continued to shave, ah yes. In circumstances which should have seen a flowering of beards to rival Old Testament lithographs we kept our chins hairless. Yet there wasn't a female within 500 miles. Amazing!

The A Lighters and the arrival of a chess player

There were two important happenings during the next few days. The first concerned our tank brigade, the second, ourselves. On 19 April 19 six strange shapes crept into the harbour. They were the very first of the landing crafts, although they weren't called that; for some reason they had been given the name 'A Lighters'. They were one of Churchill's better ideas and had been sent out from Britain in prefabricated form to be assembled in Alexandria. These six had brought in eight of those Queens of the early desert days, the Matilda (infantry support) tanks. The tank crews who came with them were men of D Sqn 7RTR, and they had had the pleasure of shooting up a mine while *en route* in HMS *Auckland*. This newly arrived squadron now took over the four Matildas already present and this allowed the 4RTR crews to leave the fortress and rejoin their regiment. Another six Matildas came in on A Lighters on the 30th, bringing the tank squadron up to full strength. The sight of the 'Tillies' was good for our morale, they looked so much more robust than the cruisers and they had an enviable reputation.

A word should be given to the Lighters and their crews. The vessels became the wallowing heroes (or heroines) of the coastal waters and harbour. They ploughed the route between Mersa Matruh and Tobruk bringing tanks and yet more tanks, and guns and yet more guns. They braved whatever the enemy might hurl at them, and this included submarines as well as bombers, while their own armament was minimal. They were sitting ducks, having neither speed nor manoeuvrability, and they suffered accordingly. The first to be lost to enemy action was sunk on 21 April. Not one of the six would survive the siege and precious few of their crews either, but the Royal Navy was never better served than by the men who sailed the A Lighters into and out of Tobruk harbour.

The second happening was more personal to us four – it was the arrival of Louis Angel. He wandered into our ken from God knows where, a desert gypsy like the rest of us, yet not quite so. He was a classicist, with expertise at chess and bridge as his second and third virtues, and thus was immediately odd to us. He was from Middlesex, that sunlit county in the deep south, where people drank pink gins and smoked Du Maurier cigarettes, which made him even odder. But he was a member of its Yeomanry, a Territorial regiment that had been absorbed by the Royal Signals, and this made him very important to us, it made him into another pair of hands and ears for our night watches.

The chess-playing propensity became something of a trial. He had a couple of pocket sets and he would hand one each to Jim and myself and would then play both of us at the same time, playing the two games simultaneously and blindly. He never failed to beat us because he had too much integrity ever to let us win as an encouragement. It reached a point where we vanished up the nearest wadi whenever we saw him approaching with that glint in his be-spectacled eye. Poor Louis, he tried so hard to civilise us; had the siege lasted eight years instead of eight months he might have succeeded.

Coincidental with his arrival was Jock's finding of a petrol-driven battery charger. He then went on a tour of the neighbourhood, taking batteries out of what he swore were abandoned trucks, until he had about a dozen. He next appointed himself Director of Battery-Charging Operations and Louis took his place on our rota. Jock's brows rose with happiness and his ulcers vanished.

NINE

We were all there,
*   Limey, Polack, Indian,*
Digger, Jew.
*   Guarding democracy from our holes.*

The fight for Carrier Hill

Rommel had no intention of sitting outside the fortress for long. He had placed road blocks across the Via Balbia to the east and on all tracks leading from the perimeter, but the disposition of his troops did not suggest permanence. He was waiting, and not too patiently, for the arrival of PZ15.

Neither did Morshead intend to sit on the laurels of his first victory. Barrie Pitt recalls his reaction to a newspaper headline which declared: 'Tobruk Can Take It': 'We're not here to take it, we're here to give it.'[32] The successful Easter defensive battle had shown how to take it: no surrender on the perimeter, defence in depth behind the perimeter until the enemy had been held, then ejection or destruction of any enemy trapped between the two lines. The strengthening of the Red Line and the building up of the Blue Line and the area between the two were only the defensive part of his strategy. The domination of the land between the two opposing forces was the way in which he intended to give it. Rommel must not be allowed to close up to the wire and establish himself in a position from which he could launch an attack without warning, nor could he be allowed to nibble away piecemeal at the defences. Morshead ordered his brigade commanders to make that outer space their own. Patrols were to be sent out into it every night on every battalion front. It must, and soon did, belong to 9th Division.

Given the interest which Rommel had shown in the Ras El Medauur sector, Morshead too concentrated his thoughts on it and, in particular, on a small hill about a mile outside the perimeter. This hill faced the much higher hill at Pt 209. Its reverse slope was hidden from sight, and was therefore an ideal place from which to launch an attack on Pt 209. By 20 April the enemy had dug-in a number of 75mm guns on the reverse side of the hill and the Fabris Battalion was protecting these. Morshead ordered that the Italians be taken out and the guns destroyed. It was to be an all-arms operation. The infantry would be C Coy of 2/24th, on foot and in carriers, led by Captain Forbes. Tank support would come from the Matildas of 7RTR. The flank of the attack would be protected from enemy armoured vehicles by the guns of M Battery 3RHA. A Lysander would fly above the area to hide the sound of the approach of the British tanks and, as a diversion, a feint attack against enemy positions on the Derna Road to the north would precede the actual attack.

The attack went in on the 22nd at 1640 hrs, when Captain Forbes led his men through the wire near R1. Unfortunately, the carriers got the bit between their teeth, raced ahead, and lost contact with the walking infantry. This was later regained on the hill, and two platoons of infantry together with the carrier force began to outflank the gun positions while the Matildas and the third platoon made a frontal attack on the guns. The Italians were taken by surprise but reacted quickly. They opened fire on the frontal attackers and momentarily halted these. Then Forbes led his carriers in a sweep to the rear of the position and opened fire from there. This allowed the frontal platoon to charge forward and break into the enemy position. After stiff resistance the entire hill was taken, together with sixteen officers and 350 other ranks. On the face of it this was a successful operation and it won Forbes a DSO, but in practical terms it was less so. Too much time had been lost in the initial stages and the destruction of the guns was only partially achieved; two were destroyed and the remainder had their sights removed. This little operation added another reference point to our maps, which had already seen escarpments named after a twisted little fig tree and a burned-out tank. From then on the little nub became known as 'Carrier Hill'.

Meanwhile the diversionary attack turned into something rather more deadly. A company of 2/23rd went through the wire in two groups. These attacked on each side of the Derna Road, and despite opposition from artillery and mortar fire managed to penetrate deep into enemy positions. The patrol led by Captain Rattray arrived back with 20 prisoners. The other, led by Lieutenant Hutchinson, turned its raid into a full-scale attack. It overran an AA battery, and fought its way to within a few hundred yards of two enemy gun positions. After a 5-hour battle during which 24 men were either killed or went missing and 22 including Hutchinson were wounded, the patrol withdrew, bringing in 87 prisoners and an assortment of captured weapons.

Two days later Italian infantry put in another attack on Ras El Medauur and were repulsed with heavy losses. While they were still in confusion, a strong fighting force from 2/48th went out after them and picked up two officers and 105 other ranks.

These skirmishes were a testing of the defences in the Ras El Medauur sector and a form of reconnaissance before the next onslaught. This took place at the beginning of the following month and became known to the garrison as the May Day Battles. By now, of course, Morshead was alert to

Rommel's interest in Pt 209 and the hill on which the trig point stood, and had adjusted his strategic thinking to meet the anticipated attack. This would be halted by protected minefields, supported by artillery, then counter-attacks would recapture any lost ground. The whole zone behind the hill was being transformed into a huge minefield and other weapons of defence-in-depth were being sited to protect that minefield. Resident gunners in the locality were 51FRG, whose guns were in the vicinity of Pilastrino and whose observers were on Pt 209 itself, and in the perimeter posts S19, S13, S11, S2, R1, thus covering all the bulge. Close by Pilastrino were the anti-tank guns and *portées* of 3RHA. On 29 April, the eve of the assault, Morshead's cruiser tanks were patrolling at 397430 (Ras El Medauur), 405425 and 406430 (Pilastrino), and the Matildas were in reserve.

As April drew to its close, enemy air attacks increased against the posts in this sector and the guns supporting them. At 1400 hrs on the 30th, E Troop, 1RHA was attacked. At 1730 hrs bombing was concentrated on this section of the perimeter, and this was followed by a 'tremendous' artillery barrage.[33] This crescendo heralded the end of the softening-up period, which should have seen the British guns silenced, the wire breached, the physical lines of communication between posts and HQs broken and the men in the posts intimidated. Next would come the attack itself. But where? All the signs pointed to Ras El Medauur and Pt 209, yet Rommel says in his papers that he launched feint attacks in both the Derna Road and El Adem sectors at this time. Morshead could never be certain that such attacks would not be developed into major strikes if they gained initial success. He was unable to commit his reserves, including the six Matilda tanks which had come ashore from an A Lighter that morning at 0830 hrs, until he was absolutely certain where the major thrust was taking place.

The May Day Battles: Rommel's plans
Rommel's plan of attack echoed that of his Easter assault but with an essential refinement; this time he intended to create a wider breach at the earliest stage and to broaden this before the second phase which would take his panzers and supporting troops through the wadis and into

the town. The initial stage would begin as soon as darkness fell, with the ubiquitous Major Schraepler leading the Pioneers of ENG33 in breaching the perimeter. The breach would then be exploited by infantry including RR115 and the panzergrenadiers of MG2 led by Major Voigtsberger. This was the sister battalion of Ponath's MG8, and could be expected to perform equally well, probably with thoughts of revenge in mind. The first target for the infantry was the hill at Pt 209, which was to be taken in a three-point attack – a central drive against the hill with simultaneous pincer movements around both sides. The panzers of PZR5, which had been brought back to full strength, would then enter the fortress, rally on the hill with its supporting anti-tank guns and artillery, and be ready to advance on the town via Pilastrino at first light. The panzers of PZ15 had still not arrived but that division's Infantry Regiment 104 had, and it had been rushed forward to take part in the attack.

The breach would be widened immediately it had been made, the Italian motorised division Brescia rolling up the left flank and armoured division Ariete doing the same on the right. Supporting the attack would be many guns including the batteries commanded by Gratti and Del Monti. General Kircheim had arrived back from hospital and Rommel put him in overall command of the ground operation.

All in all, the prospect looked good for Rommel. He had a much stronger force available than he had used in his Easter attack, and since he now held unopposed mastery of the air he would be able to order attacks on any points of resistance. However, there was a fly in the General's ointment and this one was of European and not African genus. Rommel's rapid rise under the patronage of Hitler; his subsequent successes in the subjection of France and the use made of this by Goebbels (which Rommel had done nothing to dampen); his no less irritating success as a military writer; his recent triumph in driving the British out of Cyrenaica, and last but by no means least, his combative personality had done nothing to endear him to the vons and barons and grafs, the traditional leaders of the *Wehrmacht*.

Halder, supremo at OKW, had been particularly affected and could find little to say in Rommel's favour. In his diary he described him as: 'The soldier gone stark mad'.[34]

Halder had decided that someone must go to Libya to bring Rommel back under the control of OKW and the man chosen for the task was General Leutnant Paulus, who was later to achieve lasting fame as the man who lost his army in a much colder clime. Paulus flew in on 27 April and toured the front-line units with Rommel. He appears to have had a right of veto over the proposed attack but he agreed to it with provisos. He was privy to secrets not available to Rommel: he knew that the great attack against Russia was about to begin and that it would demand all of Germany's resources. Until its outcome had been resolved there would be next to nothing available for the African Front.[35] The attack on Tobruk was to be allowed to go ahead because of the great value of the town's harbour, but it must be closely monitored and called off the moment it began to be too expensive. Rommel launched his attack with the shadow of Paulus across his battle map.

The sector which had been softened up was along a front of some 7,000 yards manned by Brigadier Tovell's 26th Brigade. He had 2/23rd defending posts S25 south to S12. On its left was 2/24th, holding posts S11 to R10 (covering Pt 209). The posts to the left of R10 were occupied by the men of 2/15th, a 20th Brigade battalion. Part of Tovell's reserve battalion, 2/48th, was in the important Wadi Giaida, which offered a way down the escarpment, and the remainder at nearby Maccia Bianca, a set of cross-tracks, one of which led to Pilastrino. The blow being prepared on the other side of the wire was about to fall on 2/24th, commanded by Lieutenant-Colonel Spowers. He had his A, C and D Coys in the posts and B Coy in reserve. Company OC Major Fell was in S2 on the hill itself, and Captains Rudge and Bird were in nearby posts. Rudge, however, took no part in the approaching battle; he had been wounded in one of the bomb attacks of the softening-up period. Supporting Tovell were the guns of 51FRG; the anti-tank guns of M and J Batteries of 3RHA, and of 24AA-T. Behind Forbes' Mount and covering the route to Wadi Giaida were the anti-tank guns of 26AA-T.

The May Day Battles: Day One, evening of 30 April 1941

At 1900 hrs enemy infantry and guns were observed to be gathering 3,000 yards to the west of Ras El Medauur and they were dispersed by gunfire. As the short desert twilight descended they gathered again and this time came forward under an intense barrage. The German engineers reached the damaged wire near to S3 and began to drag this away. Despite many casualties including their Coy OC, Leutnant Cirener, they managed to penetrate the defences in the vicinity of S3 and S5. The barrage moved forward from the wire to the posts and was closely followed by Voigtsberger leading his infantrymen. They infiltrated between the posts but left these to be taken by others, their task being to seize the hill. They divided into pincer parties according to plan and shortly before 2130 hrs moved on to the hill from the rear and occupied a stone house there. They then turned their attention to the nearby posts which had to be taken so that the whole hill would be in their hands and cleared for

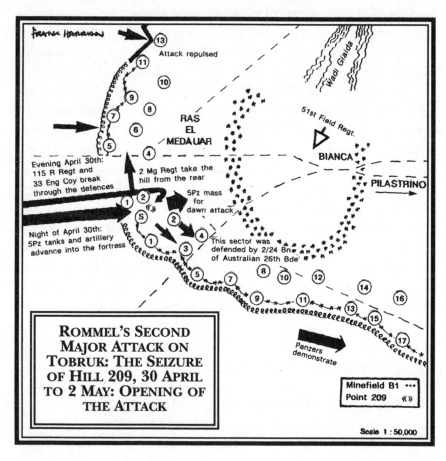

ROMMEL'S SECOND MAJOR ATTACK ON TOBRUK: THE SEIZURE OF HILL 209, 30 APRIL TO 2 MAY: OPENING OF THE ATTACK

the panzer rally to take place. One by one these were overcome and occupied.

By this time Morshead was well aware that the line had been penetrated, but did not yet know exactly where nor to what degree. All telephone lines had been destroyed by the barrage and the battalions under attack were cut off, so that no solid information was reaching him. The line from 51FRG to its OP on Pt 209 had been cut at 1915 hrs. It was restored at 2045 hrs but the operator on the hill was only able to say 'We are all right' before it was again cut. Captain Clapham went out with a party to restore the line, and had reached to within a thousand yards of the OP when he heard German voices. He tried to get nearer but was stopped by small-arms fire. He had bumped into Voigtsberger's advancing unit. He made his way to Spowers' HQ but unfortunately this was out of touch with everybody.

Another man who bumped into Voigtsberger's group was Sergeant Kierle, who was manning the left gun of C Troop, J Battery, which was protecting the minefield. Kierle found himself surrounded by enemy infantry who were trying to make a gap in the minefield by firing their machine-pistols at the mines. He took the sights from his gun and began to crawl back with the news of the penetration to his Battery HQ which was about a mile away, but he had to take such a circuitous route to avoid being captured that it took him from 0200 hrs to 0800 hrs to get there. So neither of the two earliest witnesses to the infiltration was able to get his news back to divisional HQ.

Spowers was just as helpless. He made desperate efforts to contact his men in the posts, but none of the patrols which he sent forward got through. Then at last Morshead received his first definite news. A patrol sent out by 2/24th's reserve company came back with five prisoners and they were all Germans. He now knew that an enemy force was in the Ras El Medauur region and that it was composed of Germans. He also knew what that signified. Maccia Bianca to Fort Pilastrino (the key point of the Tobruk defence according to a remark made by Rommel to his aide Schmidt)[36] was the route along which the enemy, now pouring through the breach, would be advancing.

How far along this route had the Germans reached by midnight? Quite a distance according to telephone messages reaching DAK from the units engaged in the advance. These reported Pt 209 captured, the Kircheim Group at Pt 182 to the east of Ras El Medauur and RR104 on its first objective. Supporting artillery regiments had moved inside the wire and were digging in on the position ordered for the following morning. The panzer force that was to attack Wadi Giaida had arrived, and its artillery was in a fluid situation as units relieved each other to the east of Ras El Medauur in readiness to support this attack. But not all had gone according to plan. Pioneer Bn 12 had had to be sent in to remove a troublesome bunker near S13 (this post never fell) and S7 and S8 were still in 'enemy hands'. Ariete had lost contact with its attacking force and its drive turned out to be 'useless'. The assault troops of Brescia, which had been ordered to break through on the left flank of PZ15 infantry, had preferred to 'run away' a kilometre to the right to get behind them. The enemy was replying to the advance with the heaviest artillery concentrations on all fronts but especially on the good roads from El Adem and Derna.

Nor was this the only resistance being met by the advancing German troops. The defenders in the posts under attack were fighting it out against a combination of small-arms fire, mortars, and even flame-throwers. By 0100 hrs of 1 May Pioneer Bn 12 was reporting the capture of S9 and S10 (erroneously) but had failed to take the most exposed Post S7, which held out until 0330 hrs. When it did finally fall, its handful of men had delayed Rommel's Juggernaut for six hours. The story was a similar one all along the line. At each post no more than a dozen men were hanging on, in many cases bereft of leadership and fighting on individual nerve and determination. To quote the greatest authority on this resistance, Rommel himself, who was right up with the action: 'The enemy fought with remarkable tenacity. Even the wounded went on defending themselves.'[40] At 0300 hrs DAK proposed a clearing-up of the enemy still holding out in the vicinity of Pt 209 and a rolling-up of R9 and R10, both of which should already have been done if Rommel's timetable of a dawn drive into the town from an established and secure base were to be adhered to. At 0400 hrs Rommel met CO Brescia and asked him to use his troops to roll up the posts on the north side of the breach. The General agreed, but informed Rommel that there would be a delay in assembling them for the task.

So, for Rommel on this May Day morning some positives and also a few negatives, but only a fool of a commander expects everything to go absolutely to plan. Every battle has its queue of variables waiting to intervene; sometimes these are human foibles, often they are logistic, occasionally elemental. Perhaps Rommel's greatest attribute as a field commander was his ability to bend intruding variables to his advantage. The one taking its place at the head of the queue on this particular morning was to prove beyond even his manipulation.

The May Day Battles: Day Two, 1 May 1941

Morshead meanwhile had been making what extra preparations he could to halt the coming attack. At 2350 hrs the RHA batteries had been warned that enemy infantry had probably penetrated the defences at S3, S5 and R5, and that a tank attack could be expected at first light. Among the observation officers who went forward in readiness to direct the fire from their guns were Captain Clapham of 51FRG, Captain Slinn of 107RHA, and Captains Hay and Goschen of 1RHA. The anti-tank guns of 24AA-T Coy had been ordered forward to Maccia Bianca and were already dug in there.

He had alerted Drew and the air in the ACV grew hot as that stationary vehicle filled with bodies and those bodies gave off the heat of tension. The first order was sent out soon after midnight; this was to 7RTR, to move two troops of Matildas to a position 3,000 yards of Pilastrino. At 0415 hrs these tanks were reported to be in position, and 7RTR was then ordered to move its remaining three troops of Matildas to Pilastrino where they would act as a reserve. The remainder of the tank brigade had been moved into designated areas: Rear HQ Sqn of 1RTR was at 40854302 (east of Pilastrino), B Sqn at 40594305 (west of Pilastrino) and C Sqn at 41274271 (covering the El Adem crossroads). The KDGs in their armoured cars and the 3rd Hussars in their light tanks were also patrolling these areas. It was at this point that Morshead gave an inkling as to what was in his mind, by asking 3rd Hussars to attach two of their light tanks as observers for 26th Infantry Brigade's reserve battalion (2/48th) in a counter-attack it was going to make at first light. He obviously did not intend to allow whatever had got inside the wire to remain there for very long. In the meantime he was holding back his main infantry reserve, the three battalions of 18th Brigade. Should the break-in be limited to a small penetration by the enemy in the posts, a counter-attack in battalion strength might restore the situation. If it were more serious, or if it should be paralleled by an attack elsewhere, he would have the reserve brigade in hand to meet the challenge.

His reasoning had been conditioned by other enemy activity during the night. Enemy tanks had been reported to be manoeuvring against the El Adem section of the perimeter in the region of the Easter attack. A patrol from 2/13th had routed a party of pioneers from out of the ditch in that area, and these had left behind equipment for breaching the defences. It was quite possible that the other claw of a pincer attack was intended there. As the attacker, Rommel held all the cards of bluff

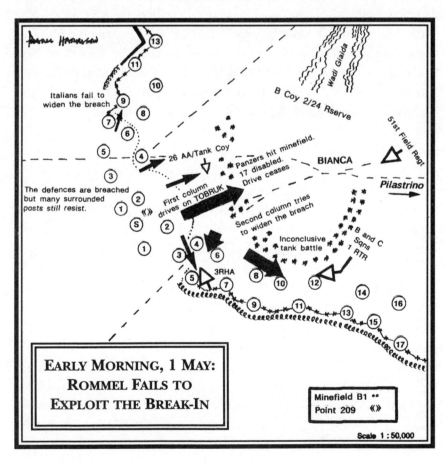

**EARLY MORNING, 1 MAY:
ROMMEL FAILS TO
EXPLOIT THE BREAK-IN**

Minefield B1 ••
Point 209 «»

Scale 1 : 50,000

and double-bluff, and all Morshead could do was to try to cover as many eventualities as possible.

Then the variable struck. At 0530 hrs Rommel was informed that the hill at Pt 209 was covered in thick fog and that the proposed attack could only proceed if the battle groups were re-arranged and the posts in their rear had been cleared. It had been his intention to use his panzers in a double thrust at first light, one against Maccia Bianca and the other to clear up and widen his base. Neither was possible in fog. He had no option but to postpone the timing of the thrusts and this he did, putting them off from first light until 0800 hrs.

There is no cold like the cold of a desert dawn. It is a long, slow strangulation of sinew, blood and bone. It seeps into your bedroll more silently than a secret lover, but its squeezing of your tissues is without love. Unconscious, deep in sleep you draw up your knees but they continue to ache, you curl into foetal form and the chill curls with you, so that you dream cold and come awake cold – into cold. You get up and hug whatever you have in the way of covering around and over you. You see monstrous shapes moving slowly in the strange, suffused light and hear muttered cursing, and you begin to see the flickering flames of sand burning inside a score of cans. On such mornings in those days more tea was brewed than in the whole of a Lancashire day. But on May Day morning in 1941 there were no flickering flames to hasten the dawn at Ras El Medauur. German and Italian, Australian and Briton peered into the grey mush and shivered, and not only from the cold. Generals do not choose to make their attacks at dawn simply because of its deceptive visibility. They do so because men of war discovered long ago that this is the time when man is most susceptible to the terrors of his imagination.

This day's dawn had a trick of its own to play on the peering antagonists. The heavy ground mist had fused with the dust raised by the night's barrages, so that when darkness withdrew beyond Gazala the mush remained, a curtain between the eyes and the enemy. Who would see whom first? The answer might well become a final knowledge. Not for a second did the peering eyes slacken.

At 0715 hrs the curtain was raised and all was revealed. Captain Hay reported from R14 that 20 to 30 panzers were on the ridge east of Ras El

Medauur. Within twenty minutes he had upgraded this to 60 tanks. By 0750 hrs 51FRG's guns were engaging enemy tanks whenever possible. From the skies above the battlefield came the first tactical reconnaissance of the day: 60 enemy tanks inside the perimeter and groups of 70, 100 and 70 approaching the perimeter along the Acroma Track. A second Tac R confirmed 60 panzers inside the wire. The wolf was on the prowl inside our house.

Here come the panzers! (2)

The way was now clear for the re-scheduled drives against Maccia Bianca and the posts on the flanks of the breach. Rommel launched both soon after 0800 hrs. The panzers and their supports on the hill at Pt 209 divided into two groups: one advanced towards Wadi Giaida, the other turned south-east and began to make its way behind the rear of the perimeter posts flanking the right side of the penetration. For the next few minutes the fate of the garrison hung in the balance. If the first group broke through, the town could fall before noon. If the second group opened up the breach, enemy re-inforcements would be able to enter at will. It was not only the fate of Tobruk that depended on the outcome of those thrusts. The entire British presence west of Suez dangled on the thread of the garrison's ability to resist.

The panzers making the drive against Bianca included Schorm, keeper of a diary. On the previous evening he had written: 'In the evening I drink a glass of Chianti with the Commander – our last drop. In Tobruk there is more of the stuff so we shall have to restock there.'

It was going to be as easy as that. Now Schorm was heading for Wadi Giaida where part of 2/24th's reserve company was entrenched. Standing directly in the way were the handful of anti-tank guns of 24AA-T under the command of Captain Norman. Perhaps Norman and his men had some of the blood of Frobisher in their veins. Undaunted by the size of the armada sailing towards them, they stood to their 2pdr pop-guns, waited until they could perhaps see the shining of eyes through the visors and then opened fire. One gun set a panzer on fire and hit two more. Others also registered hits, but these acts of resistance proved heroic suicides; the armada sailed onwards and over these gunners.

It was now the turn of the men of 2/24th. They watched grimly as the panzers rolled towards them, then, just when it seemed that nothing could save them from the fate suffered by the anti-tank gunners, the leading panzer slewed to one side and came to a crashing halt. Smoke bellied out from the ground beneath its tracks and began to curl upwards around it. Suddenly, the same thing was happening all along that onrushing line – not one after another, but almost simultaneously, fifteen ... sixteen ... seventeen panzers juddered to an explosive standstill, their tracks shredded, their sprockets splintered. Morshead's freshly sown minefield had reaped a plentiful harvest. It was not yet 0900 hrs but already Schorm's hope of Chianti was gone.[38] Although the battle would continue through two more days of often hand-to-hand combat, in those few moments Rommel's second great attack on the fortress had been lost. All the remainder of that day the panzers which should have taken the town would squat helplessly in the minefield, saved from utter destruction only because Spowers decided not to use the artillery against them in order to preserve the minefield.

The panzer survivors hung about on the edge of the minefield for a while but 51FRG opened up on them and then the anti-tank company of 26th Bde which had been on Forbes' Mount to the west of Bianca appeared on the scene and joined in. Several panzers were hit, but the shells from the 25pdrs created a local dust storm and the remainder were able to get away under its cover. How did our diarist feel during these traumatic moments? 'We attack ... tier upon tier of guns boom out from the triangular fortifications before us ... then things happened suddenly ... a frightful crash in front and to the right. Direct hit from artillery shell? No! It must be a mine. Five metres back a new detonation. Mine underneath to the left. Now it's all up.'

Poor Schorm! It was never like this in Poland. His luck held again, however, and he managed to get off the minefield and back through the breach. He was fast becoming the Houdini of the western desert.

The perimeter posts fight on

Meanwhile the attack against the posts was continuing. Hay, in R14, reported between twenty and thirty panzers on the ridge east of Ras El

Medauur and brought the guns of E Troop to bear on them, but the tanks continued their advance and began to attack the posts adjacent to the south side of the breach. The attacks followed a pattern, up to six tanks approaching and trying to keep a post's defenders occupied while machine-gunners and infantry got close enough to storm it. It was now that the conversion of the gun-pits into all-round defence bore fruit, because the panzers were attacking from the town side and not from the front. None of the posts was prepared to surrender; although the attacks would continue for much of the day, very few would be lost by its end. On the north side of the breach the enemy troops were making little and very slow progress. It took them all morning to occupy S5, S6 and S7, and the Italians who attacked S8, S9 and S10 were held off. During the afternoon Captain Malloch led a party of men from 2/23rd Bn into the last three of these posts and in the hand-to-hand fighting which followed, the Italians were driven out and this part of the front was stabilised.

And the tanks join in

The garrison's tanks were involved against both panzer thrusts. The first involvement came at 0800 hrs, when 25 panzers were reported to be threatening R9 and Hynes was ordered to intervene with B Squadron's cruisers. Leaving his light tanks behind, he advanced and opened fire on the panzers, but was soon driven off by a combination of panzer and anti-tank gunfire. Within ten minutes of his attack he himself was attacked by a flight of Stukas, an indication of the integration of German arms in this *Blitz*. All the cruisers survived the attack, a bomb which fell alongside Hynes' tank failing to explode. As soon as the raid was over Hynes moved off along the minefield to try to find a better firing position. He was joined at 1014 hrs by Walter Benzie's C Sqn (Benzie having taken over from Leakey because he was senior to him in age. Leakey was there as second in command). This combined tank force managed to get into hull-down position west of R10 from where they opened fire on the panzers trapped in the minefield. The shoot continued until 1135 hrs when Hynes led his tanks further along the edge of the minefield in search of a better firing position. It was not a wise move; the panzers retaliated furiously and scored an immediate success, penetrating the turret of his tank with an incendiary shell. The tank brewed and its crew baled out, two of the crew having become casualties. Lance-Corporal McConnachie then ran back to the burning tank and recovered its first-aid kit so that the wounded could be tended to. Meanwhile, the second tank in line had also been hit and its commander, Sergeant Cornish, had been wounded in both legs. He climbed out of the turret to warn his driver that he was heading for the minefield and was wounded a third time. Both McConnachie and Cornish were subsequently awarded the Military Medal for these actions.

The Matildas had done little other than make covering movements from left to right and back again throughout the morning, and there has been criticism of Morshead for splitting up his tanks and using them in penny packets in this way. It has been asked why he did not involve them all in a fight to the finish at the outset. This is to ignore the fact that he was still facing the possibility of a second attack from El Adem. It also ignores his plans for the counter-attack he was arranging, in which he intended the Matildas to play a leading role. Finally, it ignores what happened when he did bring in his Matildas later in the battle.

The guns in action once again

As in the Easter Battles, the artillery had played an important part in the resistance to this second offensive. Their work had been mainly, but not exclusively, on three fronts. They had driven away the panzers that had survived the minefield. They had attacked and dispersed enemy reinforcements when these debussed at the breach, and they had supported the infantry in the posts on the two flanks of the breach. As on 14 April, an outstanding feature had been the work of the artillery OPs. Hay was still directing his guns from R14, where he would remain all day. Goschen had gone in a light tank to Maccia Bianca at 0810 hrs to act as OP against the panzers which were menacing Pilastrino. Armoured OPs from A/E and 425 Batteries were on the ridge between R14 and Maccia Bianca. Clapham, who had been cut off at 2/24th HQ during the night, continued to observe from that area all day, using an 8cwt truck. He came under such heavy fire that he had to keep constantly on the move. Braddock of 51FGR kept his guns going even when under a strafing and bombing attack.

The firing programme of this regiment for the day gives an indication of the variety and amount of work performed around what was now developing as an enemy salient. At 0750 hrs its batteries were firing on the panzers advancing from Pt 209. At 0900 hrs they were engaging infantry debussing between S8 and S9. At 1200 hrs they were shelling dug-outs which the enemy to the north of Ras El Medauur were trying to capture. At 1250 hrs they were engaging panzers between S13 and S14.

In the afternoon the frustrated Rommel turned once again to his Stukas. At 1315 hrs they appeared over Rocket and B Troops. Down they screamed on to both gun positions. Troop B was unlucky, five of its gunners being killed and three wounded, two of whom died later. Rocket Troop escaped without suffering casualties. Both troops continued to engage the enemy. Indeed, the only time during the whole of that day when the guns fell silent was when they had become so hot they had to be rested to cool off. The commander of Tobruk's artillery, Brigadier L. F. Thompson, must have been proud of his gunners that night.

Thanks to this combined resistance, Rommel's time-table of attack fell far behind its schedule. It had lost momentum, and this is often the time when casualties begin to mount. Unless he could silence the guns and either delouse or get around the minefield his assault on the town would be in deep trouble. At 1400 hrs he issued orders that give an indication of his thinking at that time. The attackers were to establish a front line by that evening, running from R13/14 along the ridge to Pt 170, and from there to S7. This line was then to be held. These orders suggest three things:
  (i) a change of intent from assault to consolidation (even if only temporary)
  (ii) the acceptance of stalemate on the northern edge of the breach (at S7)
  (iii) the abandonment of an advance on the town via Maccia Bianca. And since his troops were still struggling to take R8 it placed the emphasis for the remainder of that day's action on a continuation of the thrust against the perimeter posts until all up to and including R14 had been taken.

Yet this second thrust of his attack was having little more success than had his attempted thrust towards Maccia Bianca in the early morning.

Once again British gunners were thwarting his efforts, this time, the men manning the 2pdr anti-tank guns of J Battery, 3RHA, which had been dug in behind the posts on the south side of the breach. When the panzers began their march behind the posts these gunners found themselves in a similar position to their ill-fated comrades in 24AA-T. They responded in the same way, standing to their guns, which had been dug in. Surrounded, attacked by tanks, machine-guns and infantry, they resisted. They had stood against the panzers of PZR5 on 14 April and had helped drive them away in panic. Now they stood against them again. Stubborn, brave, they fought their guns throughout the morning and into the afternoon, supported by the Australian infantrymen in the nearby posts. One by one they were silenced. The gallant Bombardier Rudd, who had run out under fire to rescue Atkins on 14 April, was in command of one of these guns. His crew hit tank after tank (alas, a hit did not necessarily disable) but then two shells exploded in the pit and Rudd was killed. By nightfall only three of the unit's eight guns were still in action, but they had held the enemy. He had not even got close to R14, his stated target for that night.

By early afternoon Morshead had a much clearer picture of the situation. Rommel had broken in and was believed to be holding all the posts from S7 to R7 inclusive, and also the hill and its environs. His advance on Maccia Bianca had petered out, but Kircheim was still in the minefield and attempting to delouse it. Rommel's attempt to widen the breach was continuing and could develop into a major threat. This put Morshead into something of a dilemma. On the one hand it was essential that he make a counter-attack before Rommel had time to strengthen the defences of the salient he had already won, and the Matildas would provide ideal support for the infantry making that counter-attack. On the other, he could not let the panzers roll up his perimeter posts without challenging them with his own armour.

His first decision was to use the Matildas in a counter-attack. The Commander of 7RTR was called to the ACV at 1300 hrs and given his orders. The squadron's role was to be two-fold:

(i) one troop of three Matilda tanks was to cruise around the tactical minefield which the enemy was trying to delouse (and stop them)

(ii) two troops were to co-operate with an infantry counter-attack from around the north of the minefield to pinch off the salient. It was Morshead's intention to trap those enemy units already in the salient, much as he had done on the previous occasion.

Neither of these actions took place. The cruise around the minefield was called off when two of the Matildas broke down on their way to it. Then Morshead's dilemma was resolved for him. At 1325 hrs panzers were reported to be advancing against R11 and R12. Fifteen minutes later they were reported to be attacking R8 and R9. This threat to the perimeter posts took preference over the counter-attack and the latter was called off. The cruisers and light tanks of 1RTR were ordered to the area but only to observe.

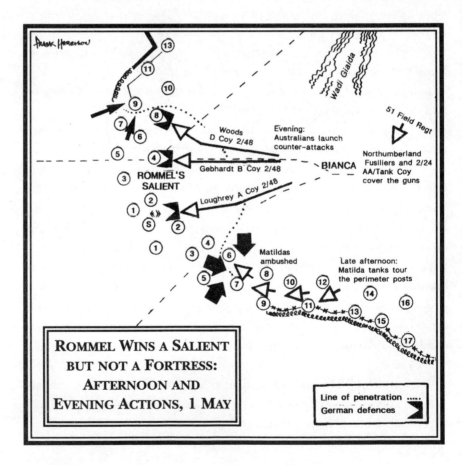

ROMMEL WINS A SALIENT
BUT NOT A FORTRESS:
AFTERNOON AND
EVENING ACTIONS, 1 MAY

Line of penetration .....
German defences

The Queen of the Desert is dethroned

There followed one of the critical tank battles of the western desert campaign, small though it was. As Hynes and Benzies were on their way to the scene they were told that R11 and R12 were under attack. Then they were told that the twelve men defending R9, eight of whom had been wounded, were being evacuated to R11 and R8. Two troops of Matildas were now ordered forward to the region but one became a casualty to dive-bombers *en route*, so that only five arrived at 1RTR's position. The Matildas then moved on to R12 with Hynes following in reserve, and they found that Australian infantry were still holding the post. Drew next ordered Hynes to make his way west along the line of posts up to and including R5, speak to the CO of each post in person, and restore any posts that had fallen. Hynes soon reported R11 as being in our hands ... then R10, then R9 and R8. Two Matildas were left at R8 while the other tanks moved along to R6. This too was still in our hands, but looking out from here Hynes saw a small group of stationary panzers. The infantry in the post told him that these were casualties, but while he was studying them he saw a German staff officer drive up to them and drop off several men. These climbed into the 'casualties' which then started up and drove away to the west, leaving a single panzer at R4. The adjutant of 1RTR had moved forward to investigate the situation and he now decided to take a closer look at this tank. He had gone only a short distance when he saw that behind this lone panzer were fourteen others. These began an immediate advance against him, and opened fire from about 1,000 yards. He retreated rather quickly to R6, and the troop of Matildas which had been waiting there was now sent forward to engage the enemy. This was the first time that Matilda tanks, which were designed as infantry support tanks, had met their German equivalents in the desert campaign.

By now, all the British tanks were under fire and Hynes' cruiser was soon hit. Its crew abandoned the tank and climbed on to the one commanded by the adjutant. The only two cruisers still mobile were ordered forward to help the Matildas, but one of these had already been hit and all its crew with the exception of the driver killed. The other three were withdrawing under heavy fire towards R8. As they fell back they were

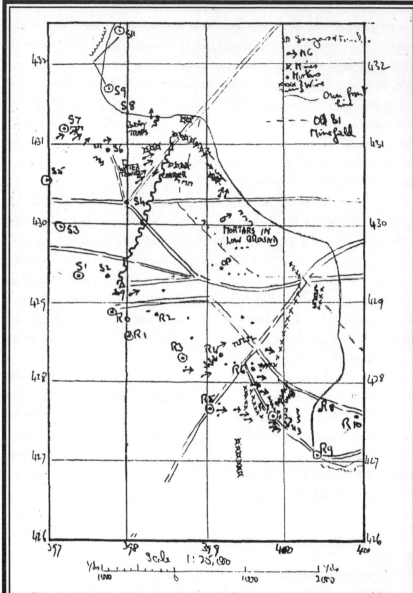

This sketch of the defences set up by the Germans after their capture of the salient during the May Day battles was drawn up by an Intelligence Officer for 1 RHA gunners. It shows the extent of the salient, running from R9 to S8, and inwards to take in the hill, Pt 209, which was being used as an observation post by the Germans. Noticeable are the strong defences on both flanks, against which the Australian attempts to reduce the salient failed.

attacked by eight more panzers which had come from the wire, and at the same time fourteen more panzers appeared from the north-east and threatened to cut them off. The British tanks were now under fire from three sides and in a desperate situation. The Intelligence Officer's cruiser tank was hit, and as its crew scrambled clear another three shells crashed into its turret and engine. It was then set on fire by enemy artillery. The adjutant's tank was the only cruiser still in action and he withdrew to R14 and asked Hay to order his guns to attack the enemy tanks at R8. Meanwhile, the Matildas had managed to halt the enemy advance from R4 but were under attack from the panzers in the north. One Matilda was hit and set on fire south of R8, a second became a casualty a little further to the south of this, and a third was disabled near R12 while it was trying to move around the southern flank of the panzers. The remaining two managed to reach R14, but their guns were both out of action. There was little now to stop the panzers from coming on and completing their work of destruction, but for some reason they turned away and made off through the fading light. The surviving British tanks were allowed to limp back to Pilastrino, taking with them the awful knowledge that the Queen of the Desert had just been dethroned.

The brigade's casualties had been severe. Three Matilda commanders, Lieutenants Rothwell and Fry, and Sergeant Chadwick, had been killed, together with Troopers Welling and Watts. Several more had been wounded, including Corporal Taylor, who later died of his wounds. Two Matildas had been totally destroyed (an impossible supposition only hours before) and two damaged, and two cruisers burned out. There was something of gain from the disaster, however; the intervention of this small and heavily out-numbered tank force and the resolution of its crews appears to have had a disproportionate effect on the enemy, causing the end of the attempt to widen the breach. DAK records show that the enemy over-estimated both the strength of the little tank force and its potential:

'1710 : Group held off counter-attack by 20 tanks. A few tanks shot up.

'1800 : Enemy renewed strong counter-attack with tanks and infantry along the whole front of the break-through with extensive increase in artillery activity ... the attacks completely pushed back.'

There is a feeling of tentativeness about the actions taken by this part of PZR5 during its attempt to broaden the base of the penetration. Perhaps the shock of the ambush suffered in the minefield by its other half was the cause. Perhaps the strong reaction of the anti-tank units; the incessant attention being given to them by the artillery; the stiff resistance of the infantry in the posts, and the readiness of the British tanks to have a go were all too much of a reminder of what had happened before. The failure to follow up what was undoubtedly a victory over the British tanks remains a mystery, although there are two possible reasons for it. Morshead's counter-attack was taking place at about that time and the second of the two reports quoted above suggests that this may have caused the withdrawal of the panzers in order to meet it. The RHA had another explanation; their response to Hay's call for counter-fire had come at once, they said, and in great strength, and had driven the panzers away.

Why then was this a 'critical' battle? Two reasons are offered:

(i) The destruction of the Matildas by enemy guns. For the first time the armour of the Matilda had been penetrated, not once but repeatedly. As usual for that time, it was assumed that the guns fired by the panzers had wrought the damage and in his report on the battle, Lascelles, who was the Tank Brigade Major during the action, wrote that the Germans had used their 'small tapered barrel gun for the first time'. He was probably referring to the 50mm gun which was phasing out the 37mm gun in their Mk IIIs at this time. I remember seeing this gun on German tanks but that was in the following year. Was it a panzer gun? The Mk III was at that time firing a 37mm gun which had a small bore, a long barrel, and a muzzle velocity of 2,445 feet per second. It was an anti-tank gun, but would have had to be within close range to penetrate the Matilda's 3in frontal and side armour. The Mk IV was firing a stubby 75mm gun which was most effective against static positions, but with its low muzzle velocity of 1,263fps would have to close the range considerably before it could hope to put out a Matilda. On the other hand, Rommel had several all-purpose 88mm guns, some of which he had tried to get inside the perimeter to act as anti-tank guns two weeks before. This gun had a muzzle velocity of 2,600fps, fired a 20lb shell, and had an effective range twice that of the British 2pdr gun. It was this ability to outshoot the

British tanks' 2pdr by a considerable margin that made it such a formidable opponent. It seems at least possible that this was the gun which created havoc among the Matildas on 1 May.

(ii) This leads on to the second notable feature of this particular action. Time after time during the next twelve months Rommel was to combine his panzers and 88mm guns in a tactical ploy which the commanders of the British armoured brigades fell for again and again; indeed the way in which they continued to charge into this sort of ambush denies them an intelligence faculty. His panzers enticed the British tanks into the chase which brought them on to the 88s which then destroyed them. The little tank battle of 1 May bears all the hallmarks of such an ambush, and there is the reference in the report of the action to enemy artillery setting one of the tanks on fire. If the guns he used in co-operation with his panzers on that day were 88s, this could have been the first execution of the tactic. On the other hand it could be that Rommel adopted the tactic as a result of its success on this occasion.

Whatever kind of gun used and whatever the tactic, the results were only too plain for the tankmen to see as they gathered around the stricken Matildas when these reached the rear areas. The great holes punched through the previously impervious armour spelled the death-knell of a myth. The Matilda was no longer invincible.

The Counter-Attack of 1 May

While the wounded Matildas were creeping away, Lieutenant-Colonel Windeyer was leading 2/48th forward to attack the salient. With the British tanks in trouble and unable to support him, the only help available would be from the guns which had been firing away all day and were ready to carry on doing so all night if asked. Windeyer was not happy about the counter-attack and no wonder. After using one company to re-occupy Forbes' Mount to the west of Bianca, which was necessary if his attack was to have a secure base, he would be left with only two companies from his own battalion and one on loan to him from 2/24th, with which to recover all the ground seized by the enemy that day. He felt that the whole thing was being rushed and asked that the attack be put off until dawn, but Morshead wanted the hill and its posts brought back inside his perimeter and was not prepared to allow their new occupants a whole night in which to consolidate.

The two companies set off from Bianca at 1930 hrs after a delay caused first by a bombing attack and then a mix-up in transport. As a consequence of these interruptions they left their starting-line twenty minutes late and this caused them to lose much of the benefit of the supporting artillery barrage. Captain Woods led D Coy on the right of the Acroma Track, his objectives being the posts from S7 to S3 on the northern side of the breach. Major Loughrey advanced on the left of the track, his objectives being Pt 209 and the posts on the southern side of the breach. They soon came into line with the waiting B Coy of 2/24th led by Captain Gebhardt which was to make a frontal assault, and this company got to its feet and joined them, using the track itself as its line of advance. The three companies marched with rifles at the port and bayonets fixed, their eyes peering through the thickening gloom, the stench of dust and cordite an acrid cocktail in their throats.

It soon became a bloody march. The companies on the left lost touch with each other. Woods headed for the Water Tower but came under heavy fire from the Germans defending S4, and was forced farther to the right. He persisted with his attack and got to within 250 yards of his first objective, losing men each yard of the way, but was then mortally wounded. Those few of his men still on their feet could go no further and that offensive ended. To the left of Woods, Gebhardt was suffering too; he had lost a third of his men on the approach march along the track and was now brought to a halt at a block across the track, defended by panzers and infantry. Roles had been reversed. It was now German infantry that stood to their guns in their freshly dug pits and defied the attackers. Despite desperate efforts the Australians could not break the block. Still further to the left, Loughrey reached to within 500 yards of Pt 209 where he too ran up against a formidable combination of machine-gun and panzer. Without tank support there was just no way forward.

At 2130 hrs Morshead called off the counter-attack, and those who were able to, carried their wounded away into the night. It had been a costly failure, its only merit being that it had thrown Rommel on to the defensive. On the night when he had expected to be inside Tobruk town, Morshead had wrested the initiative from him.

To sum up the situation at the end of this momentous May Day: Rommel had made a breach in the perimeter, three miles in length. He had taken fifteen posts, eleven in the outer ring and four in the inner. He had captured and held the hill. So far, so good. But on the south-east side it had taken him all day to occupy R6, and R7 was still holding out. On the northern side the Italians had failed to capture S8, S9 or S10. Kircheim had managed to get about a mile beyond the hill but had been driven off the minefield. Most telling though was the fact that both the panzer thrusts had failed, and that Rommel's revised objectives for that night had not been met. A worse consequence became apparent when the Afrika Korps casualties for the day began to be totted up. The DAK Diary reports that at 1200 hrs a 'defence front to the east of Pt 187 is being built up', and also that 'the remnants of Faltenbacher Battalion' were moving back to this line. The first part is hardly the stuff of an on-going attack, but it is the second part which holds greater significance. The report continues: 'The troops have suffered heavy losses especially of officers from infantry fire and flak from numerous bunkers which had not been spotted, and by very heavy destructive fire from artillery. Casualties average 50% and in some units more.'

This would not have made pleasant reading for the shadow looming over Rommel's shoulder. Nor would Paulus have enjoyed reading PZR5's casualty list for that day. Of the 81 panzers with which it began the attack, only 35 would be fit for action in the morning. After that moment of bitter accountancy Rommel's assault on the fortress was living on borrowed time.

In the ACV we were counting, too, and mourning, our own losses. All day I had watched the red and blue lines being brought up to date on the transparency over the brigadier's situation map by his IO, the red line marking the perimeter and the blue line showing the enemy positions. Time and again these had wobbled as posts were reported lost, and then new reports brought them back into the fold. Towards evening the two lines began to stabilise and assume the shape they were to keep for the remainder of the siege. It was quite the wrong shape so far as I was concerned. It were as if someone had taken a kick at a rather soft case-ball (as we called our soccer balls in those days) and had left a nasty dent in its side. From that night onwards the dent became known as 'the salient'. I never became amenable to that dent and it was not only from having its displeasing aesthetic annoyance in front of my eyes throughout the long watches. On that night it was not aesthetics which disturbed. I could not see how Rommel could be prevented from bursting the ball altogether when he resumed his kicking next morning. Nor was I the only one with this in mind. Lascelles wrote that we were down to a handful of tanks, that there seemed to be a large gap on the centre-line of the enemy's probable line of attack, that we had no more reserves, and that if the battle were to be resumed on the next day we could hardly hope to survive. He says there were many that evening who destroyed their papers and prepared to sell their lives dearly.[39]

The May Day Battles: Day Three, 2 May 1941
They did so prematurely. Once again the elements came to Morshead's aid. Patrols of KDG armoured cars and 3rd Hussar light tanks kept watch throughout the night but even panzers and their grenadiers have to sleep sometimes. And while they slept, dreaming perhaps of the shining sea they hoped to see on the morrow, the dust which had been pounded so hard twisted into the equally tormented air, the two fusing, as if to punish those who had caused such disturbance. Dawn on 2 May was dust; driven, harsh and hot dust; dust in the ears and in the hair and in the mouth; but most of all, dust in the eyes. Co-ordinated movement of armour was impossible, which was bad news for Rommel but good news for Morshead. It allowed him to ease troops into the yawning gap facing the apex of Kircheim's advance. Lascelles seems to have forgotten that Morshead still held 18th Brigade in reserve, He now sent 2/10th from that brigade into the gap and with them went 26AA-T. He ordered the NFS to take their machine-guns into the gap and to assist in this defence of Bianca. Throughout the morning these were the only troops who stood between Rommel and the guns of 51FRG, but they were enough, just. There was bitter fighting, Kircheim's infantry fought to get through to the minefield and at his most advanced point actually reached Bianca, but he was held there. The divisional diary speaks of 'the great gallantry of 2/10th Bn and its companions' in the fighting of that day.

In the afternoon an extraordinary sight was granted to the gunnery OPs when the storm suddenly subsided and the dust fell from the sky. Enemy infantry, guns and troop carriers were all huddled together on the hill, where they had gathered at the outset of the storm. It was a gunner's dream and the RHA went to work with gusto. The massed motley disappeared with the speed of rabbits disturbed at their midnight feeding.

The final action of the day came at 1820 hrs and it was from the air and against the British guns. Once again it was Rocket Troop which bore the brunt and once again the troop escaped scot-free; indeed the only casualty was one of the Messerschmitts taking part, Gunner Brunt bringing it down with a Bren gun. The RHA diary entry on that night read: 'During the day the enemy failed to improve on the positions he had gained.' They were too modest to add, 'Thanks to us.'

But the day ended on a note of alarm. At 1730 hrs a report came in to the ACV that 300 enemy armoured fighting vehicles were massing outside the perimeter. By dawn on 3 May the brigade's tanks had taken position for 'last-line' action. B Sqn was on the escarpment at 411428, and prepared to act as mobile anti-tank guns. HQ Sqn was at 410430 in a similar role. C Sqn was at 411431 acting as mobile reserve, and the remaining Matildas were between the RHA guns along the escarpment as far west as 406430. Dawn arrived, but not the expected panzers. At 0900 hrs the brigade was stood down. For the remainder of the day the tank crews were able to service their tanks and get some rest. Although we did not know it, Rommel's second great attack on the fortress was over.

The May Day Battles: Day Three, the second counter-attack

Rommel's assault had been delayed by the men in the perimeter posts, and held by a combination of minefield, artillery and tanks. Now came Morshead's third phase – the ejection of the invaders. He decided to use his reserve brigade for this, and to pinch out the salient. Two claws, each of battalion strength, would slice into the flanks of the salient and meet in the centre on the hill at Pt 209. At the same time a frontal attack against the hill would prevent Rommel from moving troops from there to help his flanks. The recapture of S7 and the posts to its south would be undertaken by 2/12th led by Lieutenant-Colonel Field from a start-line on the escarpment running east and west through S13. The attack on the centre would be made by 2/10th led by Lieutenant-Colonel Verrier. The attack on R6 and the posts north of it would be made by 2/9th with Lieutenant-Colonel Martin in command, from a start-line running north and south through R9 and R10. Artillery support for Martin's claw would come from the guns of 1RHA, and for Field's from 51FRG. It would be in the form of a creeping barrage timed to move on to the objectives at a rate of eleven yards in three minutes. Captain Armitage of 1RHA was to go in with the infantry to act as FOO for the guns.[40]

Tank support would be under command of the new leader of the Tobruk Tanks, Lieutenant-Colonel Brown, with three Matildas on the north flank and four on the southern flank. Twelve 3rd Hussar light tanks would be divided between the two. The Matildas would remain as reserve blocks in each case, but the light tanks would accompany the infantry and subdue enemy machine-gun posts wherever these were encountered. The attack was to take place in the dark with the (highly optimistic) aim of taking the enemy by surprise. Zero Hour was fixed at 2045 hrs.

The enemy was not surprised, in fact his position on the hill allowed him full view of the forward march of the attacking battalions towards their start-lines. He used his artillery against them to such effect that 2/9th were 35 minutes late in reaching theirs. When the attack proper began, the infantry soon ran into heavy machine-gun fire which drove them to ground, and caused the barrage to creep away from them. Then the light tanks which should have subdued these guns found that they could not operate in the dark, which was not surprising because they had never done so either in practice or for real, and they had to be withdrawn. Meanwhile, control of the infantry had been lost and the struggle for the posts had degenerated into the vicious individual clubbing and stabbing of a medieval battle. For several hours this military anarchy raged around and inside the posts, the attackers sometimes winning a foothold before being driven back. The northern claw was blunted and no posts on that flank were recaptured. The attack against the centre made some progress but was eventually brought to a halt. The southern claw also made some progress, but when its personnel got among posts R6 to R8 they were caught up in fierce fighting and their casualties began to mount. R8 was re-occupied and Captain Lovett fought his way into R7 with a handful of men, but an enemy counter-attack with flame-throwers drove them out again. At 0045 hrs the survivors of this battalion were withdrawn to R14, where they re-formed. They moved forward again at 0315 hrs, but by now it was getting too near to dawn, and that would have exposed them in dangerous positions. Morshead had no option but to call off the counter-attack and order a general withdrawal.

Next day I spoke to an infantryman who had got inside one of the posts. He described how he had crawled on his knees in the dark of a connecting trench, peering round corners, out of touch with anyone and not knowing what he was expected to do. He had his bayonet stretched in front ready to stick into anything that moved 'whatever bloody side the bloke might be on'. Tanks were blundering about in the dark, flame-throwers spurting flame into the posts with equal abandon and machine-guns spraying arcs of tracer in all directions. Yes, he had been scared, 'to bloody death, mate'. But his strongest memory was of not knowing 'what the 'ell was going on and who the 'ell was doing it'.

The frontal attack had been no more pleasant, both defenders and attackers suffering heavy casualties. Wilmot tells how stretcher bearers and ambulances were carrying away dead and wounded all the next day.[41] The brigade suffered 150 casualties, a high price to pay for the recovery of one post, but the psychological effect on the enemy was immense. One measure of the shock comes again from Schorm: 'Suddenly a wireless message. British [sic] attacking the gap with infantry. It is actually true ...' For after three days of *Blitz* and batter, the men who had suffered it and should, by rights and all previous German experience, have been queuing to surrender, had instead come out with their bayonets and thrown the *Blitz*-makers on to a desperate defence.

The May Day Battles: assessment of performances
The defeat of his counter-attack left Morshead with the problem of containing Rommel's salient. He did so by establishing and strengthening switch lines to cover each side of the penetration, these converging on Maccia Bianca. The Germans appeared content to remain within these, while they concentrated on strengthening their grip of the hill.

Meanwhile, Paulus signalled Berlin informing Halder that the Tobruk operation had cost the Germans 53 officers and 1,187 men in casualties. The signal said that it must be regarded as terminated and that it had only brought inconclusive, local gains. But Paulus did rather more than this; on his way back to Germany he added a rider which was to convert the military situation at Tobruk into a siege: 'Further to No 3 of Directive No 35457/4 Ref GeKados 2.5.41. The Directive is, that before a possible continuation of an attack on Tobruk in search of a decisive result the agreement of the Supreme Command of the Army (OKH) must be obtained, even after the arrival of the remaining elements of the 15th Panzer Division and of further reinforcements.'[42]

Rommel now issued an Order of the Day in which he said: 'This battle will go down in history as one of the hardest of the war in Africa.' But Orders of the Day are composed articles and may contain hidden excuses for set-backs. Better to turn to our Boswell of the panzers, who was still keeping up his diary entries, for a whole-hearted tribute written while the ice of that minefield and its defenders still chilled his veins: 'Our opponents are Englishmen [sic] and Australians. Not trained attacking troops but men with nerves and toughness, tireless, taking punishment with obstinacy, wonderful in defence.' To which, of course, should be added 'Scotsmen' and 'Welshmen'and 'Irishmen' and at least one 'Canadian'.

Morshead's performance

During the Easter Battles two commanders had been involved on the British side, Lavarack and Morshead, both of whom were Australians. Some of the credit for the success of those early battles should go to the former; he was at the time Morshead's nominal commander as well as being in command of 18th Brigade, and he had played a part in the arrangements of the defence force. He certainly deserved better than he subsequently received.[43]

During the May Day battles, Morshead was in sole and total command of the garrison and deserves full credit for limiting the German gains. His wisest move was made before the attack when he caused B Minefield to be laid as a priority, and by so doing denied the town to his opponent.

His positioning of his troops and weapons both before the attack began and during it provided a defensive barrier that could only be breached at a heavy cost in men and *matériel*. He did not panic during the hours when he was out of touch with what was happening in the critical sector and took up the reins as soon as this became possible. At no time did he completely surrender the initiative: his artillery, tanks and infantry were used to counter every move made by his enemy. At the critical point his reinforcements plugged the gap, and when he found the Germans too strongly entrenched in their salient to be ejected, he created switch lines which contained them within it. On a personal level, his calm and determination must have inspired all those who came into touch with him during the battles.

There remain two question marks about the direction of his side of the battle. The first concerns his use of the available armour. This has already been touched upon. In quantity, it was so limited in comparison with that of his foe that it had to be nursed. Using it *in toto* during the earliest phase of the battles might have stopped Rommel's attack before he was able to win his salient. Then again, it might not have, and Morshead would have been faced with the prospect of fighting the remainder of the battle without armour. There is also the question of morale; the loss of his armour in an early battle would have been a disastrous blow to the spirit of the garrison.

The second concern lies in his ordering of the counter-attacks. His resolution in resistance to enemy attack appears to have been matched by a similar fervour for counter-attack. His decision to send in Windeyer's battalion can be justified; it was made as soon as possible after the occupation of some of Morshead's 'territory' and that is standard practice – hit the enemy while he is still recovering from the exertions and casualties involved in the taking of that territory. Hit him while he is off-balance and before he has had chance to consolidate. But there are reservations concerning the method of counter-attack. Was Windeyer's force strong enough to achieve its objectives; could it have done so without tank support; should men have been sent in on an approach which was clearly visible to the enemy? Most importantly, should Morshead not have anticipated that men of the calibre of the Afrika Korps would make defence of the ground they had won a number one priority. Perhaps he had anticipated this and thought that the urgency for a counter-attack justified the risks involved.

His second counter-attack is open to more serious criticism. On paper it may have looked promising, a pincer movement of brigade strength supported by tanks and artillery, with the enemy being pinned down by a frontal attack. In practice it was a gamble; to make any attack without having made some sort of reconnaissance of the enemy and/or the position first is foolhardy, but in the circumstances no reconnaissance was possible. To make such an attack using combined arms demands exact inter-working and rehearsal. It is asking for trouble to throw units together into a situation where they are inter-dependent, without first getting them used to one another, their capabilities, and even more important, their limitations. To make such an attack at night is begging for trouble. The required exactitude is almost impossible to achieve, but confusion will come quite easily, as it did in this instance. The attackers lost their barrage, the tanks were unable to work in the dark, the commanders in the field lost control of their troops. None of these happenings should surprise. It ought to be a maxim for leaders that they set up the worst possible scenario and plan backwards from this, but that would probably be too negative for the military mind.

This criticism is of course being wise long after the event. It does not allow for the men in the tunnels who had been under strain throughout more than one night, who had fought the enemy to a standstill, who were convinced that the enemy must be got out of those perimeter posts as quickly as possible, and who were gifted with an attacking instinct. The second counter-attack was, like his first, a costly failure and was paid for in blood, and it might well be said that Rommel was not the only man to clamber over other men's bones. But if the counter-attack had succeeded, and if it had caused Rommel to lose the men he had injected into the salient, Morshead would have been acclaimed. It is too much like the tossing of two coins and as an Australian, Morshead would know all about the dangers of that pastime.

Taking the May Day battles as a whole, one can say that he contained the enemy, inflicting such losses on them that Rommel had to call off his assault, and then created switch lines which held. Rommel set out to capture a fortress and because of Morshead he failed to do so. Almost full marks therefore to Morshead.

Rommel's performance

While Morshead made the winning move before the battle began, Rommel did the opposite. Why did he not wait for the panzer element of PZ15 to arrive? There can be no reason other than impatience. With it he could have launched a massive pincer with one claw gouging into the defences at Ras El Medauur and the other at the point where the El Adem Road entered the fortress. Two drives could then have been launched on the town and its harbour, one through Pilastrino and the other through King's Cross. An alternative would have been a single attack at either spot using up to 150 panzers, and it is difficult to imagine that this could have failed.

His launching of his panzers across the minefield is astonishing. Did he think that Morshead had been sitting in the tunnel doing nothing? Two weeks previously, Ariete tanks had penetrated to the hill without encountering mines; did Rommel accept this as sufficient proof that the rest of the way into town was clear of such deadly weaponry? His engineers were inside the perimeter, so why did he not send them forward to probe the terrain before launching his panzers? In all his dashes across continental Europe he had never run into a minefield, never lost a tank on a mine. Did he think he was impervious to such things? Who knows? History only shows that he attacked yet again without having made thorough reconnaissance and that as a consequence his panzers squatted trackless in a minefield all through the day on which they should have been riding triumphantly into Tobruk.

To his credit was his breaking through the perimeter defences, his seizing of the hill, the creation of a salient, and the successful consolidation and defence of this. He held off the counter-attacks, inflicting heavy casualties on the garrison, but his own losses were the more significant.

An interesting question must concern the effect that the shadow which stretched across his battle map exerted. What would he have done on Day Four if Paulus had not been present? Everything about Rommel suggests that he would have resumed the attack and turned the battle into one of attrition. The casualties he had already suffered, and the intact condition of the defending forces, apart from their armour, suggest that he would not have won this either. He had one great problem and he knew it. He could not get to Morshead's guns and silence them. Given the quality of resistance he had already met, it is difficult to see him doing this, with or without the presence of Paulus.

Rather less than full marks therefore to Rommel.

TEN

Hey up there!
  If one of your bombers is missing,
look for him on the Bardia Road.
  He crumbles slowly,
buried dry.
  The desert does not weep.

Siege, sea and sand

Before the battles of May Day we neither thought nor felt that we were 'besieged'. We were inside the wire and resisting an enemy who was outside it. After the battles and the interdiction of Paulus, Rommel was forced to change his strategy from reduction by force to containment and slow strangulation and starvation. The strangulation would be by a ring of besieging posts in the historic tradition; the starvation, by using his bombers to deny the arrival of ships carrying the essentials of life.

Rommel needed to set up fortified positions; not to prevent succour arriving at Tobruk via the desert – there was no prospect of this with his forces holding the frontier passes – but to keep the besieged locked in. A 20-mile stretch of the Via Balbia, the only worthwhile road crossing Cyrenaica, lay inside the perimeter, so transport carrying supplies to his troops on the Egyptian frontier was forced to detour along the rough Acroma Track to El Adem and then on a wide loop which took it back on to the Via Balbia (the coastal Bardia Road). This desert detour caused increased wear and tear on both vehicles and men, but more important from Rommel's point of view was the fact that it was vulnerable to sudden sallies by the besieged force. Long stretches of it were within reach of patrols from the defenders' Red Line. The only alternative to the Acroma Track was Trigh El Abd, which lay even deeper in the wasteland. Protection of the track was therefore a primary function of Rommel's ring of posts. They had a second and equally important function – to house the siege artillery he was now assembling, which he would use to harass the garrison and the harbour. It was this second factor which determined the location of his investing posts; they must be kept beyond the reach of the British field guns which had proved so deadly in the battles just waged, and beyond the range of foot or carrier patrols. This resulted in the involuntary creation of space between the opposing lines.

Construction of the ring of posts began on the Derna side and continued south to the salient. By the autumn it had curved all the way around the fortress to the road block on the Bardia side which von Wechmar had originally had set up. It was not a continuous line, but a series of posts differing in size and function, from small 'listening' pits and sangars to large battalion-size defended zones.

Special consideration was given to the protection of the salient. From May onwards the defences which had been hurriedly created during the May battles were strengthened until they formed an almost impregnable arc from S7 to R7. Unlike the besieging posts, this was a continuous line and it was manned exclusively by German troops – for a long period by Inf Regt 115, the lorried component of PZ15. While this was being done, the Australians were whittling down as much of the salient as they could, Wootten's brigade chipping away at it until the two lines faced each other in trenches and gun-pits much as their fathers had done in Flanders 25 years before.

If this investment were the containing arm of Rommel's changed strategy, its fist was Fliegerkorps X, and this was aimed at the bellies of the defenders. The essential needs of the garrison were water, food and ammunition. Only slightly less needed were petrol, and reinforcements of men and of weapons. As early as 6 May Rommel was telling his wife: 'Water is very short in Tobruk, the British troops are getting only half a litre. With our dive-bombers I'm hoping to cut their ration still further.'[44] But water was available inside the fortress, if not of a sparkling variety. There was a pumping station capable of bringing up 600 gallons a day from sub-artesian wells in Wadi Auda, one of the dents in the coast to the north-west of the town. Two distilleries which had been built by the Italians on the south side of the harbour were able to produce 100 gallons of drinking water daily by distilling sea water. To these sources were added supplies brought in by tanker and stored in a large reservoir which had a capacity for 13,000 tons, but this water needed to be sterilised before drinking.

Since the fortress contained little apart from scrub and rock, all other essentials would have to be brought in by sea. Which meant ships and danger for them and their crews. With Fliegerkorps X now acting as Rommel's primary strike force, water supplies and ships became the primary but not the sole targets. The field guns which had caused him so much trouble were not to be left in peace either, but before them on the Stukas' priority list came the big guns protecting the harbour. Thus, keeping to the boxing metaphor, another contest was set into being, that between Air General Geisler, CO of Fliegerkorps X, clencher of the fist, and Brigadier J. N. Slater, MC, CO of Tobruk's anti-aircraft defences, the counter-puncher.

The Inshore Squadron

A report written by Colonel B. W. Pulver, Tobruk's Quartermaster-General, points to Rommel's changed strategy and its effects on shipping: 'For several weeks enemy action did not seriously interfere with the working of Tobruk harbour and depots, nor with the shipping *en route* to the port. From early in May however, enemy air action rendered daylight working of the harbour almost impossible and several stores ships were sunk or seriously damaged in the harbour and *en route*. It became necessary to restrict the shipping programme and to introduce closer protection by R.N. of ships during passage.'[45]

This brought in the old sea-horses, but the ones which came to our aid were not the great shires stabled at Alexandria, but the little trotters of the Inshore Squadron, commanded by Captain A. Poland: the British D and Ls *Defender* and *Decoy*, *Ladybird* and *Latona;* the Australian 'Scrap Iron Flotilla' *Stuart*, *Vampire*, *Voyager*, *Vendetta* and *Waterhen* (so named by Lord Haw Haw); *Napier* and *Nizam* and *Auckland*, the *Kingston* and *Liverpool* (whose ship's bell hangs still on the wall of Tobruk's War Cemetery). They were the steamships *Balmora*, *Liguria* and *Blue Peter*. They were the A Lighters (nameless except to their crews). They were the hospital ships, *Vita* and *Devonshire*. For all of these the days of test and trial were about to begin.

The men in the air

Geisler had moved his HQ into the Hotel Domenico in Taormina, Sicily, so as to be adjacent to the African coast. It was there that Rommel had found him in the first days of his African Command. It was perhaps at this initial meeting that the coolness which grew between the two men originated. Relationships between commanders of different services carry the strain of a struggle to maintain autonomy within co-operation, and since very few who reach High Command are shrinking violets, personalities often intrude. The relationship between the *Wehrmacht*, jealous of its historic role of supreme command, and the (upstart) Luftwaffe, with its favoured position under Goering which allowed it to maintain its own independent military arm, could not have been easy at any time. Rommel was no shrinking violet. His compulsion to dominate must have annoyed Geisler as much as it did most of those who had to live with him at the Command level.

At their first meeting, Rommel had countermanded one of Geisler's orders. Important Italians who had invested money in property in Benghazi had prevailed on the Air General not to bomb that town. Geisler had deferred to them in order to maintain harmony between the two nations at local level. Rommel had ordered Geisler to forget that consideration and to begin bombing the town immediately. Now he was demanding that Tobruk, its harbour, its installations, and the ships which travelled to, and sheltered there, should be brought under heavy and sustained attack. Tobruk was to be given equal status with Malta on Geisler's visiting list.

The men shooting them down

Defending the fortress from air attack were the guns of 4th AA Bde and 8LAA. The Brigade had a heavy section and a light section. The heavy section was composed of 152, 153 and 235 Batteries of 51HAA, which were defending the harbour. The light section was composed of 37, 38, 39, 40 and 57 Batteries of 13 and 14LAA. The first of these light batteries, together with 8LAA, was using Breda guns in its defence of the field guns, and they had 21 of these in the King's Cross area. The second two

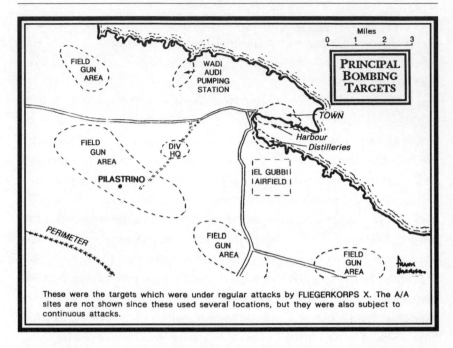

These were the targets which were under regular attacks by FLIEGERKORPS X. The A/A sites are not shown since these used several locations, but they were also subject to continuous attacks.

light batteries were defending the big guns of the heavy batteries. The searchlights around the harbour were manned by B Sqn, Royal Wiltshire Yeomanry. In overall command of the brigade was Brigadier J. N. Slater. The commanders were: 51HAA Lieutenant-Colonel McIntyre; 13LAA Lieutenant-Colonel Fisher; 14LAA Lieutenant-Colonel G. Eastwood. The actual gun situation at the end of April was :

152 Bty: eight 3.7in

153 Bty: eight 3.7in

235 Bty: four 102mm; four 3.7in

40 Bty: twelve static 40mm Bofors; one static twin-barrelled 37/54mm

39 Bty: six Italian field guns.

These totals were being constantly updated and changed as more guns arrived in the Lighters.

Slater was a regular gunner and a man blessed with energy and common sense. He was now having to learn on the job, dive-bombing being a totally new experience for the British Army. It was to prove an ever-changing job, as Geisler changed his tactics and Slater had to counter each change. One of Slater's virtues was that he was not prepared to accept a passive role for his guns or himself. He tried new tactics of his own, and eventually wrested the initiative from Geisler. His first major decision was that enemy bombers must always be met over the harbour by a barrage, appropriately named 'The Harbour Barrage'. Next, he ordered variations in the ceiling of the barrage so that the bomber pilot could never be certain at what height he might run into it. He set up alternative gun positions and had his guns moved about between these. He set up dummy guns, giving them a pseudo veracity by placing a real gun among a set of dummies. Finally, he devised various forms of protection for his guns. He insisted that the pits be dug deeper, and where rocky ground did not permit this, he provided alternatives. One position was surrounded by Italian ammunition boxes filled with stones. Others had diesel drums packed with earth and set as ramparts around a pit 2 feet 6 inches in depth, thus giving a height protection of 5 feet. Most important was his insistence that his crews stay at their guns under the most severe attack. There is no ambiguity in his orders on this point:

STANDING ORDERS FOR AA DEFENCE TOBRUK HARBOUR
> PART II
> (b) if the guns are attacked when firing the HARBOUR Barrage;
> (I) HARBOUR Barrage MUST be continued at all costs....
> (II) GPO can detach one gun (previously warned) to traverse in the direction of the attack and fire alternate fuses 2 and 4 at QE 70°

To which he added the following appendix:
> (a) The GCO will always order a Harbour Barrage if there is any likelihood of an attack on the harbour. It is preferable that a barrage be fired when no attack takes place rather than that the barrage be late.

TABLE 1.

Some idea of the strength of his barrage is given in the totals of shells fired by his guns during April and May:

	April	May
152 Bty	3,771	1,599
153 Bty	5,279	1,600
235 Bty	698	1,612
40 Lt AA	4,039	6,883
Totals	13,787	11,694

The large increase in 235 Bty's consumption during May is attributable to a delivery of four 3.7in guns to this battery half-way through April.

Despite what the QMG said in the report quoted earlier, the harbour and its defences did receive a lot of attention from the Luftwaffe during the early days of April when Rommel was trying to prevent what he saw as an attempt at evacuation. On the 14th all gun-sites were attacked and the resulting casualties included Lieutenant-Colonel McIntyre, 152 Bty's CO. On the 17th a supply dump close to the harbour was bombed by up to 50 planes. Two merchant ships commandeered by the Royal Navy, *Fiona* and *Chakla*, had been sunk by the end of the month. Ironically, in view of Rommel's suspicion that the ships were coming to evacuate the garrison, *Chakla* was *bringing in* troops (2/32nd Battalion) when she arrived on the morning of the 29th. She was bombed and sunk that afternoon.

The QMG was correct, however, in saying that attacks increased from then on. On 7 May there was an attack on the south-west corner of the harbour where two warships were sheltering, and despite the intense barrage put up by the guns one, a corvette, was hit and sank within three minutes. On the 12th, thirty assorted Jus spread their attacks between the distilleries, 4AAB HQ and B and G gun-sites. One 3.7in gun was put out of action temporarily but the distilleries escaped damage. On the 21st it was the guns again, and although one gunner was killed on D site it was noted that if the gunners kept firing their crews were safe. On the 26th there was again 'heavy bombing'. These are instances singled out from daily reports of air attacks.

The great heat and vibrations in the gun-pits, the constant thunder of the gun, the stench of burning cordite and the intense concentration of getting shells into the breech of the gun and hot spent cases out of the way, demanded much of the human frame. Soon, the almost non-stop standing-to to meet attacks and the strain of the attacks themselves began to tell on the men, but their numbers were too small to allow relief. In his work on the part the Navy played in the siege, Heckstall-Smith, who commanded one of the A Lighters, sums up the travails of the AA gunners: 'A blackened figure stumbles towards us, its clothing hanging in rags. It's my buddy, Phil, shouting that his gun-pit is on fire and his ammo exploding. He has already dragged a couple of his wounded from the blaze.'[46]

During the few days listed above, 153 Bty had more than 70 bombs dropped in its immediate vicinity, and the other batteries were receiving similar treatment. Major Elliot commanding 152 Bty noticed that its firing had thinned, that the men were becoming 'shaky', and that there were a few cases of 'anxiety state'. It wasn't surprising, considering what they were going through, but he had to do something about it and quickly. He re-arranged his crews as best he could and was a little happier after that when he was able to write: 'One thing is certain, the Hun dislikes us even more than we dislike him.'

The AA gunners were subjected to another type of bomb. This was the Italian anti-personnel bomb which, because of its resemblance to the domestic object, was known as the 'Thermos Bomb'. We had come across it on our first morning on the Libyan side of the frontier wire, so long ago it seemed now. One of the lads kicked what he thought was a rusted old flask and lost his foot. Now the Italians came over one night and saturated the 153 site with the horrid objects. All movement was stopped, but the bombs couldn't be left to wait in ambush for an unwary foot. Search parties scoured the ground from dawn onwards. B Section found and marked 63 of the things and 153 HQ beat that total by 14. A removal exercise was begun – find, lift, remove and blow up. Advice was sought from the experts. 'Dig around each bomb carefully, taking care not to shake it,' the gunners were told. 'Then tie a piece of string around it, attach the string to a wire and pull – but only after everybody has taken cover.' The gunners tried this, and about half the bombs were disposed of in this way. The remainder were towed to a pit and blown up. By 9 May 101 of these bombs had been dealt with and 40 still remained. There is no account of the number of fingers still remaining.

The men in the ships
The ships visiting the harbour had two main tasks: to bring in supplies, and transfer men into and out of the fortress. Morshead called for the building up of a 60-day reserve of all commodities on a restricted scale, with daily maintenance thereafter. This was not accomplished until July,

so for the first months of siege the supply ships were always working against the clock. A number of small stores-ships and schooners were used to carry general cargo, and were scheduled according to their turn-around times. For specialised commodities there were monthly trips – a petrol tanker, *The Pass of Balhama*, carried approximately 200 tons of POL, and a small schooner brought in cased petrol. There was usually a monthly delivery of about 80 tons of chilled meat which went to the men in the Red Line. In the early months of siege, transfer of men was mostly from the port. Pitt says that when Morshead took command, the garrison numbered 40,000 men, of whom 15,000 had nothing to contribute.[47] The latter included 5,000 POWs who were being held in a cage (literally speaking) near King's Cross. He adds that by the end of April the total garrison had been reduced to 23,000 men, all armed and ready to fight if called upon. A transfer of 17,000 outwards in two weeks seems very high and casts doubt on the initial figure of 40,000. The QM's report suggests that 30,000 were present at the beginning of July; this would represent the evacuation of 10,000 men by that time, and since the QM had the ration statistics his would appear to be the more realistic figure. Among the evacuees were the officers and men of 5RTR and 6RTR who left to rejoin their regiments.

Another shipping priority was the evacuation of the more seriously wounded to hospitals in the Delta. Two hospital ships, *Devonshire* and *Vita*, were employed on this duty. *Vita* entered the harbour on 4 May. Within 15 minutes of her arrival four Me 109s made a reconnaissance over the port and two hours later forty-two Ju 87s, two Ju 88s and sixteen Me 109s launched an attack in which more than 100 bombs were dropped. Twelve of these planes concentrated on *Vita*, dropping some 60 bombs around her. One scored a hit and started a fire but it was soon put out. Later the ship was hit again and had to be beached. Eventually *Devonshire* was also destroyed. No vessel sailing into or out of the port, whatever her markings, could expect to do so with impunity.

The stretch of water plied by these vessels between Mersa Matruh and Tobruk was given several titles of which 'The Spud Run' was perhaps the most used. I also heard matelots call it 'The Suicide Run' and 'Bomb Alley'. Heckstall-Smith says that the jetty in Alexandria from which they sailed was known as 'The Condemned Cell', and this is his description of what it was like traversing that deadly stretch of water: 'I know nothing more terrifying or demoralising than being dive-bombed – especially at sea. On land it isn't nearly so personal. But at sea, you're left in no doubt as to who is the target. What's more, there's no question of taking cover.'[48]

Yet still they came, these little ships and their brave crews. They hid alongside the wreck of the *Serenitas*, which had been converted to a quay by the engineers, and also alongside the beached *Marco Polo*, and it was there that the men of the harbour command slaved away at unloading them.

And here again, Morshead had been fortunate. The man who ran his harbour was Chief Control Officer, Lieutenant-Colonel J. O'Shaughnessy, MM, a veteran of the First World War and probably the oldest member of the garrison. He took up residence in a white house on the waterfront and it was from here that he directed the arrivals, the turn-arounds and the in-betweens. Within jumping distance of his house was his private machine-gun pit from which, he modestly claimed, he had shot down more bombers than the harbour barrage. Keeping him good company was the resident Officer in Command, Royal Navy, Captain F. M. Smith, another fearless soul. Their double-act became famous throughout the garrison as incomers who experienced it spread the word. Heckstall-Smith describes the two in action: 'Out in the harbour one of the Lighters unloading petrol alongside a merchant ship blew sky high. It was a ghastly sight. We could see the water burning all around her, and hear the dreadful cries of her crew, some of whom were burning like torches. A second later we saw smoke pouring from the forepart of the merchantman.

'O'Shaughnessy raced down the steps to the quay, and old Smithy came rushing hell-for-leather from his office. Together they jumped into a launch and were off to the burning ship. I shall never forget how the pair of them worked that night. Two of the oldest men in Tobruk, they were the first aboard and the last to leave. Unconcerned for their own safety, or the fact that at any moment the ship might blow up under them they manned the hoses and directed ops from the red hot deck ... in the small hours of the morning they came ashore with their clothes scorched, eyebrows singed, and feet blistered. But they had accomplished their task and saved not only tons of petrol going up in smoke and flames, but a merchant ship worth her weight in gold.'[49]

With men like this how could Morshead lose? O'Shaughnessy survived his private battles with the Luftwaffe, won the Military Cross and was promoted to major. Sadly, Smithy was to die at Tobruk the following year – killed in action of course. He sleeps within smell of his sea, the lantern with which he guided in the ships sits on top of his grave.

And the men on the ground
Apart from one highly unpleasant occasion and the odd desperate dash for a hole, Jim Gauton and I also accepted the fact of siege and that we were not likely to be eating fruit salad in the Empire Services Club for some time. We decided we weren't going to live on our ground-sheets any longer, but neither were we going to do any digging if we could help it. We went on a safari of the stretch of flat land below Solaro and found just what we were looking for – an abandoned hole. There was nothing fancy about it; somebody months before had dug a cube with sides of about 6 feet and stretched tin over it. Either he or the winds had covered the roof with sand, and then gone on their way. To get into it we had to remove half a ton of sand which had silted up the entrance. To get out of it we had to stand on an empty wooden box which had once held cans of corned beef. We moved in. The decision was ours to make. I doubt that any of the Brigade HQ officers knew or cared where we lived as long as there was a trained body sitting at the wireless set. As soon as we could, the two of us were off into town and making a search through its whitened and similarly abandoned homes. We didn't find much; the Australians of 6th Division and then of 9th Division had had first pickings and they were the nearest living things to locusts – indeed they were probably more efficient in stripping techniques. We did find tiled walls in one house and an oil lamp in another. The tiles became our floor and the lamp our single piece of furniture though we didn't need its light. We helped ourselves to one of Leggat's batteries and begged a bulb from our neighbours in the tunnels, and this drew company like moths on a

dark night. We were to live in this hole in the ground for six months, but mostly at night, it being far too hot down there during the daytime.

We were by no means the only ones to go to ground; anyone who hadn't found a hole to colonise took to spade and soon the flat resembled a slab of Swiss cheese. The news of this subterranean scoot travelled quickly across the Big Lake and into Europe so that William Joyce was soon taunting us: 'When are you going to come out of your holes, you rats of Tobruk?' This, of course, became our sobriquet, and is the title of the Association for the survivors of the siege.

This move towards domesticity was not the only change in our living conditions. Alas, we lost our places in the line-up at the divisional cookhouse. A cook had been produced from among the rag-bag at Tank Bde HQ and he opened a kitchen in a dip about 100 yards from the ACV. It was little more than a barbecue grill, next to which was a steel plate, both being suspended over a fire-pit. Its greatest virtue lay not in the food that it produced but in the heat it gave to our chilled fingers in the early mornings. This new messing arrangement resulted in varieties of bully which did not pretend to match that of 9th Div in either degree or disguise. Perhaps the constant threat of a lynching which hung over the heads of the Australian cooks kept them on their toes, but ours was a Regular Army brigade, conditioned over the ages to accepting the worst and usually getting it. With hindsight, and free now, thank God, from the small mercies of army catering in the field, I am sure that this carelessness towards the well-being of its men which was customary in those times, involuntarily produced one of the British Army's outstanding qualities – the ability of its rank and file to endure. They were at their most splendid when conditions were at their worst, because they had been trained by experience to expect little better.

Apart from one highly unpleasant experience and the odd desperate dash for a hole – any hole – we were mere spectators of the aerial attacks taking place over the harbour and the guns. When the two big battles ended it was back to the daily – and nightly – grind. The KDGs resumed their normal patrols, taking a continuous census of all movement of enemy transport in either direction along the Acroma Track to the south of the perimeter. Totals were passed every hour to whichever of the four of us was on watch. During the day we passed these on to the IO or his equivalent, and he would collate them. Such messages might read:

'1208 2 MT going west'

'1235 15 MT and 3 AFVs going west'

'1258 9 MT and 1 Water truck going east'.

Perhaps there was some worth in keeping sleepy KDG troopers out of their chaste cocoons; perhaps back in Cairo some statistician was earning himself a 'Mentioned' by collating these numbers during his time off from the Sporting Club and using the results to forecast the next month's action. The night reports were usually of the 'all quiet on the salient front' type. For the operator on night duty the hourly report was the opportunity to exchange a few words. We were of course unwitting of Captain Seebohm's eager ears listening somewhere out beyond the perimeter, taking in every word that we exchanged, weighing each for some tactical import, making as much out of our chit-chat as he could. We had an awful lot to learn about wireless security.[50]

Sometimes our frequencies would clash with those being used by the Italians along the other side of the perimeter and we would hear their Latin chatter and their '*Basta!*' – '*Basta!*'; voices in the night, enemies keeping us company, sharing our long and lonely vigil, while the great and neutral stars twinkled at man's stupidity.

And the highly unpleasant occasion? That happened on the evening of 4 May, and probably arose from out of Rommel's frustrations of the day before. The Luftwaffe came seeking the creators of that frustration, the co-ordinators of resistance, the HQs of 9th Div and 3rd Armd Bde – us! The men of the division didn't have too much to worry about; they were safe under hundreds of tons of rock, but all we had was the paper-thin wall of the ACV, which would have had difficulty stopping a sneeze. Two waves of bombers came over and gave us the treatment, yet surprisingly enough, the only casualties were a few empty ambulance trucks. We were beginning to learn that although Stukas made a lot of noise and left big holes in their wake, they were not all that dangerous, except to vehicles. Having said this, a rider must be added. It is unwise ever to treat with contempt anything which makes a big noise. During one attack Jim and I were standing watching the performance taking place over the harbour when a sneak stray dropped his cargo no more than fifty yards from us. Its explosion sucked the breath from our chests, caused our teeth to clash and left us deaf for the day, but otherwise whole. Yet its shrapnel slashed through the throat of a man who was about the same distance on the far side of us from where the bomb had landed. There is no way in which the idiosyncratic behaviour of shrapnel can be anticipated.

ELEVEN

Beyond the wire,
*   patrols periwinkled the sangars*
and all the Ities except one
*   were 'bastards' who'd tried to escape.*

On patrol

On 27 June of that year, Churchill wrote to his CIC General Staff claiming that the besieged forces were four or five times as strong as the besiegers, had a hundred guns and ample supplies. There was no objection to their making themselves comfortable, but they were expected to hold this highly fortified zone against four and a half thousand men, even if the latter were Germans.[51] His arithmetic had obviously not improved since he was a backward schoolboy. Forgetting for the moment his over-estimation of our gun strength and his ballooning of our supplies, he also appears to have misplaced two Italian divisions which were perhaps trying to make themselves comfortable on the other side of the perimeter wire, not to mention double the number of Germans he gives, who were protecting their salient. If he had added a nought to his total of besiegers he might have been nearer the mark, but still well below the 70,000 enemy troops who eventually sat out there in the posts they were then constructing. He would have had no need to worry, however. Ming the Merciless was the last man to let anyone become comfortable. As already mentioned, Morshead had ordered his brigadiers to make that strip between wire and enemy line their own.

Every night Australian infantry patrols went out into that space. It is not difficult to glamorise night patrolling; there is something of both fox and wolf in its stealthy creeping and stalking, its final pounce and ruthless killing. British Army lore told from the days of Kipling how Pathans took command of the night hours on the mountains of northern India, how men woke without their ears or did not awaken at all. Some of this glamour has attached itself to the men of 9th Division who became both foxes and wolves in Libya's cold and dark nights. No enemy trying to sleep in that space was allowed to close his eyes on the day and be sure of opening them on the morrow.

The patrols varied in size and purpose. They might be a small group going out to check on a sangar which had suddenly appeared out there, they might be going in search of a prisoner for intelligence purposes. They might be a few men going out to listen for enemy chatter or movement. Sometimes, as on 13 May, they would be part of a mixed patrol which included armour.

One night when I took a SITREP into Div HQ, I came across an Australian infantryman guarding an Italian prisoner who had been picked up earlier that night, and who was waiting to be interrogated. The man's face was almost as green as his uniform. I stopped for chat. 'There was sixteen of the bastards,' the Aussie told me. 'The other fifteen all tried to scarper, so we had to do for 'em, didn't we?' I returned to the set musing on the ability of the Australians to tell a tall one with the straightest of faces. As if any patrol would bring back only one prisoner from sixteen enemy encountered. Not long ago I was reading through some papers dating back to the siege when I came upon a report of how a patrol attacked sixteen Italians of whom only one survived. I was in the very civilised surroundings of the Imperial War Museum's Reading Room at the time. I looked around me at the heads bent to their quiet, peaceful work and I remembered that night and the man's words and I shivered. It was as if the building's central heating had suddenly been turned off.

There were the celebrated 'love and kisses' patrols. These were made daily between Red Line posts to ensure that there had been no infiltration during the previous night. A section from one post would go halfway towards the adjoining post, where it would find two sticks lying parallel. The patrol would change these to the X position. When the corresponding section from the other post arrived it changed the sticks back to the parallel position, ready for the next day. If the sticks had not been changed, the patrol would go the whole way to discover why not. When patrols went out at night they were geared for the job – soft-soled desert boots, or socks pulled over the outside of the boot. They carried bayonets and grenades, except for the officer who would have his pistol. They might take a tommy gun or two. But the essence of the patrol was silence until absolutely necessary, and then the quick burst of action or firing, followed by an even deeper silence.

Dismounted patrols

Patrolling was not restricted to the Australians although they were the recognised masters – patrolling had become synonymous with the name of Australia's 9th Division. The dismounted section of KDGs had been having their moments in the Red Line. During the action of 2 May Lieutenant Taylor counted 30 shells arriving in his wadi in a very short period. On the 4th the grounded troopers were attached to 2/23rd at Fig Tree Ridge and the officers of the section together with Sergeant Waterson set off in a 15cwt truck to make a recce of their locality. Their truck broke down after going 50 yards. They tried again, and this time the truck caught fire. Their third attempt was made in a 3-tonner which they managed to get to the top of the pass where they were met by a barrage of 75mm shells which fell like hail around them. They abandoned the truck and took to the rocks. That night the section was told by the CO of 2/23rd: 'We are putting in an attack. Tomorrow this place will be as safe as a public park.' In pouring rain they watched the attack go in. It was shelled all the way in and all the way back. So much for the safety of public parks in Tobruk.

On 8 May 2/12th replaced 2/23rd in the Red Line. The KDG section was given the task of holding the line from S27 to S14. They moved into the best and deepest holes. When they were settled in, the usual carrying party was sent back to meet the food truck. It consisted of four men, Troopers Birch, Hamberton, Kinchin and Smith. They made their way to the pick-up spot, met the truck, and collected the rations. When it got dark they set off on the return journey. All went well apart from the stumbling and cursing until they were only 50 yards from the forward position. At that moment the skies above exploded and all hell was let loose around and over them. Their approach had been spotted and every step of it monitored, until they arrived within mortar range. Caught in the open, the four men had no chance. Birch and Hamberton were killed immediately. Smith was severely wounded. Only Kinchin was left untouched. Instead of taking to his heels he stayed with Smith, somehow got him on to his back and managed to half carry, half drag him to safety.

The cavalry family is very close, and the KDGs were not about to leave two of their own lying out there for long. Captain Arkwright and Lieutenant Christal went forward to recover the bodies but were driven back by heavy gunfire. Later that night, Christal and Sergeant Waterson made another try, and this time they reached the bodies and brought them out. In the meantime, Kinchin still had a job to do. He set off alone, returned to the bloody spot, found what food remained and carried it to Lieutenant Richardson who was in the gun-pit. It was eaten at last, but not with any relish.

The 'windy' remark still rankled, and eventually the dismounted KDGs were able to remove the slur. On 29 May Captain Palmer led a patrol of two officers and eight men through the wire for the first time. Palmer had a tommy gun and the others were armed with bayonets and grenades. When they were through the wire the party divided, a sergeant and three of the men making a demonstration opposite S25 while Palmer led the others up the Derna Road to within a few yards of an enemy post. They charged it in true Australian fashion. Palmer killed four of its occupants with his tommy gun and the Dragoons with him despatched several more. The platoon's only casualty was Sergeant Waterson who was hit in the throat. He was evacuated to hospital but was back with his unit and in action again by September. Among Dragoons cited for their work on this patrol and for other actions were: Captain Palmer, Lieutenant Franks, Sergeants Foster, Battersby and Berryman and Trooper Kinchin. Shortly after this, Lieutenant Franks suffered severe burns and had to be evacuated.

And armoured patrols

On 6 May, Lieutenant Massey of 7RTR took a troop of Matildas to the salient to deal with a reported infiltration from that position. A severe dust storm was blowing and since visibility was down to almost nil he decided to go forward by truck, find the Australians in the locality and determine the situation. Instead, he found Germans. He was being escorted to their Regimental HQ when his escort got lost in the storm and blundered into R8 which was still in Australian hands. Roles were reversed, and Massey made his way back up the line of posts to his patrol. 'Where the hell have you been?' his men wanted to know.

On the 8th a troop of C Sqn cruiser tanks went through the wire at R33, taking with them a sapper officer to destroy three enemy guns which had been abandoned about half a mile outside the wire after the Easter battles. The action was successful, the guns were destroyed and the tanks returned unopposed through the wire. Not all patrols had such a happy return. On 13 May a foray was made against Italians manning the road block on the Bardia Road and against Wadi Belgassem. The attacking force consisted of a troop of Matildas led by Captain Johnstone, two troops of cruiser tanks from C Sqn 1RTR and two KDG armoured cars. The supporting infantry from 2/43rd were led by Captain Jeanes and were in carriers. This little party went out from R75 at 0600 hrs, the plan being for the Matildas to advance north-east towards the Via Balbia and make the attack on the block, while the cruisers and armoured cars took up observation positions on their eastern flank. Unfortunately, visibility was not more than 100 to 200 yards and the leading carrier driver lost his way. The Matildas, who were following him, hit the road before they should have. They set off along it in search of their objective and the cruisers watched them vanish into the mist. Visibility got worse and one of the Matildas became detached from the other two and strayed away to the north where it blundered into an enemy position and came under heavy machine-gun and anti-tank gun fire. Its commander, Sergeant Cooper, engaged the anti-tank guns and knocked out two. He then turned south in search of his comrades. Fortunately for him, he did not find them, and eventually was able to make his way back to the waiting cruisers. Meanwhile a mistaken signal caused several of the carriers to withdraw into the perimeter before they should have done, leaving a much reduced infantry support. The remaining carriers charged some enemy positions but several were knocked out in the process. The infantry baled out and fell back on foot towards the perimeter. Manning the posts in this area were men of the Royal Australian Service Corps who were serving as infantry, and they came out and covered the withdrawal.

At 0700 hrs the observation party was told that the infantry were back inside the wire, and its commander decided to send a troop of cruisers in search of the two Matildas and order the withdrawal of the remainder of his group. The investigating party moved north to the road and at last came in sight of the missing Matildas. They were not moving and were surrounded by enemy troops. Before the cruisers could interfere they were seen and immediately came under heavy anti-tank fire. They had no alternative but to withdraw, and were ordered through the wire at 0830 hrs. Johnstone, another officer and six crewmen were lost in this costly little affair, and Italians captured some days later reported that some had been taken prisoner. Officers from the Matilda squadron then went out to try to discover what had happened to their comrades. With field glasses they were able to see that the cupola had been knocked clean off one of the tanks. It was the second time this had happened to a Matilda during their short time in the fortress, and one wonders if this had been another instance of the power of Rommel's 88mm gun. The shocked officers recommended modifications to the structure of this tank to give it a flatter turret. Alas, the modifications were never made – at that time no one in the UK was thinking beyond quantity production, even of useless weaponry.

Operation 'Brevity': a very brief feint

On 15 May the Brigade was asked by Morshead to make a feint against the salient. Although we were unaware of it for some time, this feint was part of Wavell's first attempt to come to our rescue. It was associated with an attack on the frontier posts held by the Afrika Korps and their Italian allies, the idea being that our feint would draw Rommel's armour to the Tobruk area, leaving the frontier posts ripe for the plucking. Code-named 'Brevity', a more apt name for the operation could not have been chosen. There were two parts to the feint. The first part involved an attack on enemy infantry who had been reported to be on high ground 800 yards west of S15. The three cruisers serving as 1RTR HQ were to make the attack, accompanied by Australian infantry. Moving off from the foot of the escarpment, the troop advanced under fire towards the post. One cruiser broke down but the other two, commanded by Benzie and Leakey, advanced to Fig Tree, where they came under artillery fire. They took to a wadi along which Leakey advanced until he reached S15. He reported this post clear of enemy and Benzie joined him there, the Australian occupants being 'delighted' to see them. At 0935 hrs the tanks recommenced their advance, following the infantry who were about 1,000 yards ahead. When the enemy saw them coming they abandoned their positions and the infantry moved in. At 1030 hrs Benzie was able to report his mission completed and the tanks returned.

The second part of the feint was pure demonstration. Three troops of cruiser tanks under command of Lieutenant Geddes crossed the Pilastrino Road and went to Pt 152. They then went west for 800 yards before returning to Pt 152. Next, they went north over the escarpment, moved east in a wide sweep in full view of enemy positions in the salient, before again returning to Pt 152. From here, they drove north-west to Wadi Giaida where they were again in full view of the enemy. They then returned to their original positions. The Brigade was told later that there had been some reaction to these activities by Rommel, but obviously not enough to affect the happenings taking place at the frontier.

The last Tank Brigade action of the month was on 30 May. Panzers were known to be lying up about 6,000 yards south of the perimeter, and an unnamed but enthusiastic FOO from A/E Bty 1RHA was sent forward to see if he could find them and bring his guns to bear on them. He went out in an armoured car escorted by two light tanks and Leakey's three cruisers.[52] The FOO and the light tanks advanced to the high ground west of the El Adem Road and the cruisers moved to the east of them where they settled in a hull-down position.

At first, no panzers were seen, and the FOO brought his guns into action against some enemy posts he had spotted near by. This soon brought a reaction; ten panzers came north astride the road and the FOO informed Leakey. The tank officer ordered his troop into battle line and moved forward to cover the withdrawal of the FOO. As he did so he sighted the enemy and recognition must have been mutual. The panzers stopped and opened fire with their 75mms. Leakey replied and a small battle got under way. The FOO now brought his guns into action and one of the panzers was knocked out. Three more enemy tanks were then seen to be coming down the escarpment from the direction of El Adem, and Leakey withdrew a little. The FOO had not yet been spotted and he remained where he was, still directing fire on to the enemy. But it was becoming obvious that the panzers were manoeuvring to cut Leakey off from the perimeter, and he advised the FOO to withdraw. The advice was accepted and the party returned unscathed through the descending dusk to the port of entry. The conclusion drawn from this little venture was that the enemy patrol being maintained near the El Adem Road could be rapidly reinforced from El Adem. It was scarcely an earth-shattering discovery.

For the four of us working the HQ set which was directing these actions, these were interesting parentheses in the monotony of days of nothing but patrol reports. Not only were we in on the ordering and reporting ends of the actions, we were also in on the debriefing summaries, when the tank men concerned would come to the ACV to report verbally to the Brigadier. I listened to Hynes and Benzie and Leakey of the black beret fraternity tell of their good 'shoots' beyond the wire, and then went off into the tunnels to pick up what I could of the doings of the desert-booted, down-under brethren who had gone along on these shoots either in carriers or on their feet.

TWELVE

But ...
> *there was tenderness too.*
> *Graves could smell the sea.*

The other wire, and the thrice-cursed attempts to relieve the garrison

When we talked about the patrols, and they were often a topic of conversation when word got around about a particularly deep penetration by one, we spoke of 'going through the wire'. There was another wire, of course, the one which Mussolini built to keep the Egyptian Arab on his proper side of the frontier. It began on the coast below Bardia and ran south past Sidi Omar and Maddalena to the northern tip of the sand sea at Jarabub. It was a hedgerow of wire some eight feet in height and a couple of yards thick. It was a rusting monument to egotism and stupidity – what camel in a desert, any more than a buffalo on a prairie could be expected to order his life to lines on a map? But it had some uses, as a geographical reference, for example, or as an aid to a lost soul who could go west or east, depending, until he hit it (as Rommel once did) and then turn north. It might have caused a half-day hindrance for any Bedouin with a pair of pliers in his camel roll and a Senussi girl friend on its opposite side.

It was movement across this wire that we were anxious to hear about. Wavell had asked Morshead to hold out for eight weeks, by which time he had hoped to assemble forces strong enough to return to Cyrenaica and relieve us. We discounted the man's problems in the Aegean, we knew little of the revolts in Syria and Iraq which were also plaguing him. We looked to him to carry out his promise and we watched with interest any happenings along that distant wire. 'Brevity' had been Wavell's first attempt to keep his promise. Two others were to follow, Operations 'Battleaxe' and 'Crusader'. All three operations had something in common. Each was thrice cursed.

The first curse

The first curse was political interference. We had already suffered (personally) the consequences of such interference at El Agheila at the beginning of the year, when a victorious army which had Tripoli at its mercy was ordered by London to halt at that desolate spot. Its experienced infantry divisions and tanks were taken from it and sent to Greece, in the hope that this would lead to the formation of an Allied front against Germany in the Balkans. This was political lunacy. There was no military force in existence in continental Europe at that time that could possibly have stood up to the Wehrmacht and the Luftwaffe for longer than a few days. Within the month, panzers were storming through Greece, Allied armies were perishing in its mountains, British ships were going down in its straits, and the British aircraft that we needed so desperately in the desert were being shot out of its skies.

The ordering of that expedition showed a total lack of appreciation of the true military situation and possibilities (which was repeated in the following year at Dieppe on the opposite edge of that mainland). It showed a refusal to accept the lessons of the defeats of Poland, of Belgium, of France. It was claimed as an honourable keeping of our word to the Greeks. It was nothing of the kind; they had not wanted us in the first place, they knew they were quite capable of defeating the Italians, and did not want the presence of British troops which could only result in the arrival of the Wehrmacht, which it did.

Meanwhile, the anorexic 2nd Armoured Division was left to hold the front at El Agheila, and after its single and ill-fated brigade was scattered across the wadis south of Jebel Akhdar, its dead commander was blamed for the disaster by the same politician who had demanded the transfer of the troops. Now, while the corpses were still floating ashore along the Greek coastline, he was urging Wavell to give him an immediate victory in the desert. It was necessary in order to show his friend across the Atlantic that the US Ambassador in London was wrong in what he was telling America, and that Britain *was* still worth backing. The launching of 'Brevity' was a consequence of political interference.

The second curse

The second curse was inferior weaponry. Smithers tells how before the war and during its first five years, British designers and engineers were incapable of producing a tank worthy of the crews brave enough to get inside them and take them against the panzers and Rommel's 88mm guns.[53] In the thirties, the designers and planners appear to have been divided between those of the trench mentality, who eventually produced the early Matilda, a heavy slow tank carrying a machine-gun and intended for use in combination with infantry (hence the prefix 'I' for Infantry), and those of the cavalry mentality, who produced a faster, less heavily armoured cruiser tank with which to contend withenemy tanks. Thus, from the very beginning, two diametrically opposed types of battle were being anticipated, each with its adherents. To these psychological differences was added the practical complication of a discrepancy in speed between the two types. Given this discrepancy, a cohesive tank strategy was almost impossible to achieve even had the will existed. Nor was either tank fitted properly to carry out its designated role. The Matilda was eventually given a 2pdr gun but this could not fire high-explosive shells, a fact which astonished Rommel, while the skin of the cruiser was nowhere near thick enough to survive in a close-up, tank v. tank battle.

Nor was it only strategic philosophy that was awry. The great industrial scandal of the Second World War was the pouring of vast investment in money and energy into the production of thousands of tanks that were so unfit for action that they never saw any. Centaurs and Covenantors, not one of which fired a shot in anger, Crusaders, driven by an engine designed in 1917, which did well even to reach the battlefield. Matildas and Valentines which were still being produced two years after they had been shown to be obsolete, and shown so in battle, the true testing ground. All still carrying the 2pdr gun whose uncapped shells bounced off the sides of Rommel's Mk III and M IVs as though they were peas. Most still trundling to the front on their tracks because there were no tank transporters to carry them.

Major Tapley, a man who knew better than most what was going on at the desert frontier, wrote: 'Inevitably crews were sent into battle with unfit and inadequately equipped tanks, with unfortunate effects on morale at the "sharp end" and on planning calculations further back.'[54]

The astonishing thing is that men were ever persuaded into British tanks, but this is said with hindsight. Despite what had happened on May Day we inside the fortress still had confidence in the ability of our Matildas to take flak, and if there were doubts these centred on the cruisers (which were all well beyond their selling date). It was accepted that both had to go in under fire for half a mile or so before there was any point in firing their own guns, and it was hoped that the Matilda would have the strength of body, and the cruisers the speed, to carry them through this dangerous phase. Even then it was the panzer's gun which was feared, the part played by Rommel's 88mms not yet having been realised and understood.

The third curse
This lay in our military leadership. Despite, or perhaps because of, whatever training it received at the Staff Colleges, its strategic and tactical con-

ceptions in actual combat proved naïve in the extreme. Yet so ingrained were these, that those holding them were quite unable to adapt to the fluidity of a desert campaign. They were equally unable to adapt to the instinctive and intuitive decisions made by Rommel when on the move, faulty though these sometimes were. For those who would root the problem in the fact that most of these high-ranking commanders were infantrymen whose First World War trench experience inhibited their decisions concerning mobile battle, it should be remembered that panzer-expert Rommel was also a veteran of that war and of those trenches. Indeed, his best-selling book was an Infantry Manual. The difference was that his mind had been able to transcend that supposed handicap.

To take strategy first. The aims of each of the three operations listed above were the destruction of Rommel's armour while in a concurrent separate action the enemy occupying the frontier posts was to be eliminated. In each operation the achievement of the first aim was seen in terms of a cruiser-tank v. panzer mobile battle. The achievement of the second aim was seen as an infantry-supported-by-Matilda static action. The battle between tanks would take place wherever Rommel could be forced to bring his panzers into action. The infantry battle would take place at the fixed locations of his frontier defensive posts. Thus, from the planning stage onwards, tactical dispersal was ensured by strategic compartmentalisation. Cruiser tanks were remote from Matilda tanks, cruiser tanks were remote from infantry, artillery was divided between the two or chasing between the two. Armour was to seek Rommel in the wide open spaces while Matildas and infantry were battering their heads against a static line – never the twain to meet. As Bayerlein, Chief of Staff to the Afrika Korps, was to write later: '... their main mistake was that against all tactical principles they scattered their forces instead of concentrating them on the decisive spot, there to fight with a superior force.'[55]

Indeed they did, in every major encounter until the topography of the El Alamein bottle-neck put a limit on dispersal. The great criticism of the senior British commanders as they came, and almost certainly went, was that they seemed incapable of learning the simplest of lessons. Was this rigidity of mind, commented on by Rommel, the result of Staff College courses or because the promotion system was bringing the less adventurous ones to the top? Or was it, as Jim Gauton put it, that the colour of one's corduroy trousers was a more acceptable measurement of military merit than any other? Whatever the cause, only O'Connor, Campbell, Auchinleck, when in the field, Morshead and Freyberg were anything like a match for their German counterparts in desert warfare.

There was no compartmentalisation in the Afrika Korps. Rommel seemed able to conjure battle groups containing engineers, panzer-grenadiers, pioneers, anti-tank guns, field guns, armoured cars, and panzers out of thin air, and also to produce the men to command such combinations successfully. With the exception of the 'Jock columns' which were never more than harassing units, the British had nothing to compare with them. Armoured units which were supporting infantry might come under command of that division's commander but only for the duration of the battle, after which they would resume autonomy within their laager. Tanks were tanks and guns were guns and infantry were a nuisance to be tolerated only for so long as was necessary.

Leadership at the lower level of the armoured units was certainly brave, and this was often its own undoing. All Rommel needed to do was show an Allied tank battalion CO a few of his panzers and the charge was on – on after the retreating panzers. – on to his waiting 88mms – on to destruction. If ever a general had his work made easy for him it was Rommel. Having said this, it must be added that I write from the serenity of my desk, with little hanging upon my words, and far from the turmoil and tension of battle.

So much then for the three curses. They may not have been exclusive to the Desert Army, but it was in the desert campaigns that they found full and malevolent expression. Well intentioned the politicians may have been; hard working the civilian engineers must have been; brave the generals undoubtedly were, but history does not forgive easily. The men at the sharp end could not appeal to Mr Speaker; they were not able to have a tank withdrawn because its specifications did not meet with desert requirements; they had no say in the choice of their leaders. Their fate was to burn in their tanks before they could get near enough to the enemy to fire its gun, or to bleed into the sand while waiting for support to appear which had broken down miles away.

'Brevity': the first failed attempt to relieve Tobruk

Halfaya Pass had to feature strongly in any fighting on the frontier. It is one of only two gaps through the escarpment which towers above the coastal strip at Sollum, the other being the coastal road. Possession of either allows access to the inland plateau above the escarpment and thus, to Fort Capuzzo. 'Brevity' was an attempt to seize these passes and the frontier posts, and then to knock out the German armour as it came to their rescue. Under pressure from Churchill, Wavell began the operation in the early morning of 15 May, with General Gott in command. He sent the cruisers of 2RTR on a flanking attack aimed at a desert crossroads near Sidi Azeiz, where they were to cut the enemy line of communication and prevent Rommel from interfering while 4RTR Matildas and a motorised Guards Brigade captured the frontier posts. At first all went well, Halfaya was stormed and Capuzzo and Sollum were captured. Unfortunately 2RTR did not reach its objective and a quick riposte by Rommel put the cruisers in danger of being cut off. They withdrew, and with this flank protection gone the other arm of the operation was forced

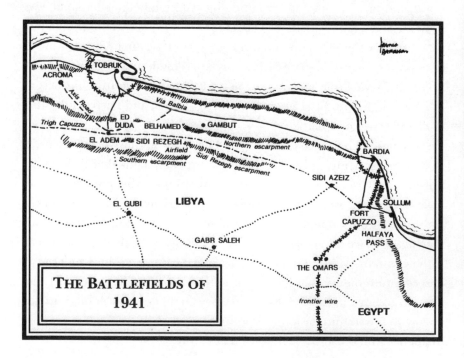

to follow suit. Within 48 hours of the commencement of the attack Gott had given up all its gains apart from Halfaya, where he left a garrison. On 27 May Rommel retook it by storm.

'Brevity' was important for its consequences rather than as a battle. Rommel took note that Halfaya Pass, Fort Capuzzo and Sidi Azeiz were on Wavell's target list, guessed that there would be a repeat performance and prepared for this. He resorted to the tactics which Morshead had used to stop him at Ras El Medauur – mines and artillery. His chief gunner at Halfaya was Hauptmann Bach, one of the great characters of the desert war. This ordained minister was 50 years old, had been called up at the beginning of the war, was commissioned, became CO of a rifle regiment, and then of the anti-tank unit which had the 88mm guns. Ordered by Rommel to fortify the pass, he personally sited the five 88mms and the new 50mm anti-tank guns he had received. He also had the turrets removed from the knocked-out Matildas that were strewn about the pass and had these dug in. He sowed the area of the lower approach with mines and anti-personnel mines. By the time he had finished, Halfaya was no longer simply a pass, it was a death trap. The approach to Capuzzo from the south is covered by the Hafid Ridge, on which is Pt 206. The approach to the Azeiz crossroads is covered by the Sidi Azeiz Ridge (in fact a series of small ridges). Rommel turned both these sites into tank traps, armed with guns and mines, and at Hafid he included four of his tank-killing 88mm guns among the anti-tank artillery.

'Battleaxe': the second failed attempt to reach Tobruk

Apart from the two feints we had nothing to do with 'Brevity'. Indeed Morshead, who would have had to provide the troops if a break-out had been planned to coincide with the operation, only learned about it two days before it began, an astonishing situation in which to be placed.

'Battleaxe' was different. This was to be a three-phase attack. First would come the destruction of Rommel's armour and the capture of the frontier posts (a repeat of 'Brevity'); then the link-up with TOBFORCE (the garrison), and finally, the expulsion of Rommel's army from Cyrenaica. Churchill set the aims: there was to be a decisive victory and Rommel was to be destroyed. To ensure success he bullied all the tanks he could from the War Cabinet and insisted that the convoy carrying them must risk the dangers of the Mediterranean. He told Wavell that 307 of Britain's best tanks were on their way through the Mediterranean.[56] In the event, 238 arrived, the remainder going down in the one ship sunk by the enemy. The convoy was named 'Tiger', the tanks it brought were its 'Pups'. Alas, their bite, if measured by firepower, was still by milk teeth. The political pressure now began. Churchill demanded that these tigers be put into action at 'the very earliest moment' and suggested that no German should remain in Cyrenaica by the end of June.

Poor Wavell! In one hand he held this signal, in the other a report on these 'best in Britain' tanks. There were fifteen old cruisers, 21 light tanks, 135 Matildas and 67 of the new and untried Crusaders. Each of the Matildas had to spend up to 48 hours in the workshops before it was fit for action. All the tanks needed sand filters and none had been given desert camouflage. Some of the Crusaders were without wireless sets and none was available. None of the Crusader crews had been trained in the use of this new tank. Wavell was ordered to encompass the defeat of two panzer divisions using this mish-mash. Never less than honest, he signalled Churchill that success was doubtful. Neither the armoured cars nor the tanks were a match for those opposing them and the tanks were unreliable mechanically.[57] Then, like every good soldier in the merciless grip of a political leader, he launched an attack in which he could have had little confidence.

On 14 June Middle East Command informed Rommel that it was about to make a sudden surprise attack on him. It did so involuntarily – Seebohm's team had picked up the single code-word 'Peter' being repeated all the way down the British lines of communication. The alert Seebohm went at once to Rommel and forecast that this was the order for an attack to begin next morning. Rommel put the Afrika Korps on full alert at 2100 hrs. PZ15 was moved into position south of Bardia; 5LT was brought forward from the Tobruk area, and Bardia was placed on full alert. When Beresford-Peirse sent the attackers through the frontier wire next morning everything had been done to ensure that they got a warm welcome.

'Battleaxe': the battle

The attack was made by three columns. The 11th Indian Brigade supported by Matildas made a frontal attack on Halfaya and Sollum. The centre column consisting of the Guards Brigade and Matildas got up on to the plateau and advanced on Capuzzo. On the left flank, 7th Armoured Brigade's Crusaders drove forward to Hafid Ridge.

The attack on Halfaya was a disaster. The two troops of tanks attacking the pass from below ran on to its minefield, were battered by its guns, and four were lost. The twelve attacking from above made the long drive on to the escarpment from the south and ran on to Bach's waiting guns. A despairing cry was heard from their leader, Major Miles: 'They are tearing my tanks to pieces.'[58] Only one tank returned from this encounter.

The Matildas approaching Fort Capuzzo ran on to Pt 206, where they suffered losses, but 80 tanks went on to take the fort. When PZ15 counter-attacked they were repulsed. These were the only British successes of the day.

On the far left, a sad and shocking story was unfolding as Crusader after Crusader broke down on the march.[59] Those which managed to keep going advanced on Hafid Ridge. That evening they were tempted into a charge. They took the first ridge, charged the second, and ran into the mouths of the waiting 88mms. They paid the usual price.

'Battleaxe' lasted three days and at one time its outcome teetered in the balance. Then, in a move which proved decisive, Rommel switched his armour and concentrated it against the British rear. There followed a fighting retreat by 4RTR's Matildas which allowed the major part of the British force to slip back over the frontier. Much of its armour did not. There are conflicting accounts of the number of tanks lost by the British. Behrendt, Rommel's Intelligence Officer, says that 64 'I' tanks and 23 cruisers were knocked out.[60] Schmidt says that he and Rommel counted 180 British tanks left on the battlefield, but it is hard to imagine Rommel wasting his time in such a way.[61] German losses amounted to twelve panzers, an indication that the battle was largely between British tanks and German guns.

One major lesson which should have been learned from the battle was that Rommel was just as adept at fighting a defensive action as he was an offensive one. A second lesson was that the combination of mines and guns was quite as deadly when used by the Germans as it had proved when used by Morshead. Guns and mines; after 'Battleaxe' those should have been the last two words on which every desert general closed his eyes at night.

TOBFORCE's role in 'Battleaxe'

On 2 June, Tobruk Tanks got a new Brigadier. He was Colonel Davey, and he had come to lead a proposed break-out. He and Lascelles immediately got down to making plans for this operation. On 14 June, Davey issued Brigade Order No 101. Under its instruction the Brigade, less D Sqn 7RTR, was to break out of the fortress in conjunction with Australian 18th Brigade. With the main force would be:

M Bty of 3RHA using six Bofors portées

one company of infantry from 2/10th Battalion

one troop of anti-aircraft armoured cars from 4 AA Brigade

two FOO parties from 1RHA.

With 18th Brigade would be :

1RHA

three Australian anti-tank batteries

two companies of the NFS

D Squadron 7RTR

one troop of KDG in armoured cars.

The objective of the break-out was to be El Duda, a ridge about seven miles out from the south of the perimeter. This ridge dominated the Trigh Capuzzo. Slightly to the north-east of Duda was another ridge, Bir Belhamed. To the south of Duda and Belhamed were the two escarpments of Sidi Rezegh. Between the two sets of ridges and escarpments lay the Trigh Capuzzo; they thus formed a potential bottle-neck to traffic travelling either east or west along this track. When TOBFORCE linked up with the advancing 7th Armoured Brigade they were to join together in the destruction of what was left of the Afrika Korps, which would, the planners hoped, be attempting to escape through that bottle-neck.

We were eager to get out into the open. The very thought of shaking the claustrophobic shackles from our ankles acted as an aphrodisiac, and we waited impatiently for the code-word which would send us out to the open arms of the desert ... and waited ... and waited ... and then one morning we read the brief notice pinned up by Lascelles:

(1) In yesterday's fighting in the Frontier area severe losses were inflicted on the enemy and 800 prisoners were taken. In the air our fighters shot down 12 Stukas and 6 fighters during a dive-bombing attack on our forward troops.

(2) Considerable reinforcements have reached the enemy and following our capture of Capuzzo, numerically stronger forces operating against the left flank of our attack have succeeded in stopping it.

(3) The operations contemplated in 3rd Armoured Brigade Operation Order No 101 of 14 June 1941 and their exploitation in accordance with Operation Order No 104 are accordingly postponed for the present.

It was a nice piece of writing and worthy of any advertising agency. It was also Lascelles' final service for the brigade. He left shortly afterwards in the last destroyer to leave during moonlight. For three hours he sat in a barge, ducking to the occasional shell sent over by the 'Bardia Bill' group, and then at last got aboard. He was given 'an excellent supper and plenty to drink'.[62]

The failure of these operations caused changes in Cairo and Tobruk. They meant the departure of Wavell in the typical Army 'someone must carry the can' and the equally typical political 'it won't be one of us' syndromes. As for the garrison, since there was now no possibility of relief in the foreseeable future we were ordered to take on the complexion of a defensive force. The question of supplying the garrison for months instead of weeks had to be faced. Measures were taken to ensure the best economy of shipping:

(1) Reduction in the personnel of the garrison by evacuating all 'useless mouths'; line-of-communication and base units, and other arrangements. This brought the ration strength down from 30,000 in June to 24,000 in July.

(2) Concentration of MT repairs. These were to be carried out only on Class A vehicles, i.e., AFVs; ambulances; water-carriers; wire-

139

less vans; RAOC technical vehicles. This brought about a considerable saving in shipping space and allowed the evacuation of 2/1 Australian Field Workshop and several RASC workshops.

(3) Curtailment of the daily maintenance tonnages to 180 tons at first, but subsequently to 145 tons.

We must have been useful mouths. We stayed, and by now wouldn't have wanted it any other way. Were we not Founder Rats of Tobruk?

THIRTEEN

'Hold fast' the old man growled,
and so we clung,
rats, on the great cheese of Africa.
Knowing that if we were not crisped
sand would be in our shoes
for ever.

Summer of siege: down to the sea in little ships

The desert may not weep, but it shows indecent haste in its timing and its seasons. Its sun, for example, does not linger. One moment it is the high and mighty Ra, sailing its Memphitic sky; the next, it is plummeting, a huge red bomb, beyond the western escarpment without so much as a bang to signal its descent into the underworld.

The desert does not have a dusk. Nor did it have a spring that year. We were into shimmering horizons almost before we had time to take off our shirts. 'Mad dogs and Englishmen,' Coward wrote, went out in it. He should have been with us that summer; he would have added a few other nationalities to his refrain. The fortress became a huge browning pot, we bleached into Vikings, we sweated salt until we could scrape it from the armpits of our shirts. We lived in the worst possible conditions that could be devised for products of an industrialised civilisation (if the oxymoron can be accepted): intense heat; rigid rationing of water whose foulness made a mixed blessing of the rationing; dust between the teeth and the eyes; rashes between the toes; monotonous and constipation-inducing food; constant threat from the skies and from the siege guns operating behind the salient and down the Bardia Road, and flies, flies, flies! We lived like that not for days, or weeks, but for months, and we throve on it. Back in Cairo the lads who went out in the *Balmora* would be carrying out those essentials of professional soldiery which vanish at the sound of the first shell: spitting polish into their boots; whitening their webbing; throwing salutes to puff up the already pompous. We had neither time nor desire for such Napoleonic nonsenses. We weren't soldiers, we were gypsies fighting a war.

Jim learned through the code which he and his family were using to get around the censors that a cousin of his who was something in the Royal Navy was in town, and we decided to go in and say hello. We found the man and he was so pleased to see Jim that he insisted on taking us on a tour of the harbour in a motor launch. It was such a treat after having been sand-bound for so long, to feel a whole ocean just waiting to be dragged along by the ends of your finger tips. The harbour was littered with wrecks and we zig-zagged around and among them, pausing for a running commentary on how they had come to be there. What a shame to spoil such an afternoon, but suddenly our host was whipping the craft around and sending it through the water like a *Bluebird* on Lake Coniston. He must either have had paranormal sense where big black Maltese Crosses are involved or hearing which stretched all the way out to El Adem airfield. He got us into the shadow of one of the wrecks and switched off the engine in the very second that the sky became a howling horror.

I don't like being bombed. I have never met anyone who does. I have been bombed by the Luftwaffe, the Italian Air Force (from a great height), the RAF and the US Army Air Corps, and I didn't appreciate any of it, but Heckstall-Smith was right, being bombed at sea is the worst. Our sailor told us not to worry, the pilots wouldn't waste their bombs on a ship that was already a wreck – he seemed to have great faith in their marksmanship. I didn't. I covered my ears and prayed. The great guns on the cliffs roared and the planes screamed in their dives and their bombs blasted the air and concussed all senses. We were in the eye of a hurricane but it was not the oasis of calm that writers describe, it was a noisy hell and it was terrifying and through every one of those seconds that dragged like slugs I was expecting to vanish from the earth and was praying as fast as I could that it wouldn't hurt.

141

And then it was over. And there was the most profound silence. Did I really hear the sailor speak of a waste of bombs, and then of a cup of tea? All I wanted to do was get as far from this beautiful bay as my legs would take me and never ever to come back. 'No, thank you very much,' my wise Mancunian comrade told him, 'we have to get back to the set.' We were going along a jetty as fast as decency and honour would allow when a late and lonely bomber dropped his stick across our bows. If you are ever in an air raid keep your mouth open, it will save your eardrums from bursting under the unequal pressure. My memory of that afternoon sail is of dust in the mouth at the foot of the harbour wall. Dust in the mouth? Well, that's the memory.

Summer of siege: friends and neighbours beneath Solaro escarpment

'When you've got friends and neighbours
The world's a happier place.'

Those wartime troubadours, Flanagan and Allen, used to sing these words in their heyday. Tobruk was full of neighbours; some were friends, many were characters. Jim Gauton, for example, who did not have too great an opinion of the intelligence of anyone who carried the mark of authority on his arm or his shoulder. He had been on too many Territorial Army camps, had watched too many men of authority trying to order up a marquee. He had a special curl of his lip reserved for such people, and a phrase which I would hear at least once in every day– 'Bloody loonies!' He came into my life just when I was beginning to lose my fundamentalist faith in the infallibility of the Army I had joined, and he nudged me a little further along that path. It was a necessary development, a healthy scepticism does no harm when one is putting one's life into the hands of higher authority, but the loss of any kind of faith is a painful business.

Then there was Charlie Jones, our resident Canadian and a quiet man. I learned more about him in a single hour one night than I had in weeks. We were sleeping on the northern side of Solaro beneath the escarpment and under the stars. Enemy gunners had ranged on its crust and were working through a programme. It was a much-interrupted conversation, we would hear the 'tump!' of the distant gun, pause for the sw-i-i-i-sh of its incoming shell, accept the bang at the back of our heads, then resume the conversation. Charlie told me of his life on the western prairies; how, during the summer vacation his mother would pack food for him and he would jump a freight train in Edmonton station and ride east, looking for work on farms, earning his board across hundreds of miles before returning for the fall semester. This ability, psychological and physical, to uproot oneself and take off into the unknown without consideration of security astonished me, a town boy, who had (previous to my Government-sponsored tour) considered a bus journey across that town to be something of an undertaking.

In return I inducted him into the culture of a cotton town, told him how, as a child I lay awake in the early morning listening to the split edges of a bamboo cane rattling against the windows of neighbouring houses as the knocker-up called them to their slavery in the mills of the town. Told him how you knew an army was abroad in the dark of those mornings by the tramping clatter of clogs against cobbles. Told him how I had learned to leg-spin against the base of a lamppost. Told him the rules of street-corner courting. We were not only making our different and distant worlds known to each other, we were also bringing them back to ourselves. At some stage in that night the shelling stopped but we had both been too many miles away to notice that.

There was Bowton William, a portly cockney who had the important job of eradicating all signs of vehicular activity from around the ACV and, later, from around our underground HQ. He sat, brush at the ready, and after we had had a visitor on wheels he would get to his feet and amble about, whisking sand over any tracks that might have been made. 'Could 'ave been doing this at Brighton,' he once told me, 'except I'd have been getting paid proper there.' Not that Bill needed money. He was the richest man in the garrison and as important to many men in that garrison as the Brigadier his brush was protecting. When night fell, he put away the brush and strolled over to the caves where the two-up school was located. Australians, as I knew them, would bet on anything that moved, crawled, flew, or fled, but especially on two flying pennies. They would put their shirts and their wives' blouses if they'd been able to, on the way those two pennies would fall to earth. In Tobruk they would stake their rum ration (saved nightly until they had a full bottle), their appropriated Lugers, and any pair of boots they might have fallen over on their way to the two-up school. The men of Melbourne, plus a few foolish Englishmen, Scots, Irish or Welshmen, crouched over the blanket above which the coins soared. A generator that had been intended to feed the authorised activities of the tunnels had been hijacked to allow light from a single bulb. Its central illumination made monsters of the excited men as they crouched, cheered or cursed the coins and the tosser of coins. It was a scene made for Daumier.

Bill was anything but foolish. Starting a run of luck in the early days of the school he had become its uncrowned king. By day he swept the sand – masses of it. By night he swept the money – masses of that too, into his back pocket against the day when it would buy him a house in Lambeth. And did it with the same dignity, despite the fevered atmosphere. He was 'Bill' to every Australian who visited that blanket, surely the most famous Englishman in the garrison.

There was George Maers, the owner of the painted feet. I was suffering from an ingrowing toe-nail, not a very glamorous affliction but a painful one which would eventually cost me half the toe. Somebody told me that an Anglo-Indian medical orderly had set up his tent not too far away on the same flat as our hole and I hobbled in search of him. I saw the white patch of cloth with its manufactured red cross and I approached the tent from the rear. As I walked round to the front the first thing I saw was a pair of bare human soles and they were purple! I couldn't stop myself from laughing. The owner of the feet was at first aggrieved, but then a smile spread across his face. I had met George Maers, Corporal, King's Dancing Girls, and wireless operator to Major Lindsay, who commanded that armoured car company. I must have spoken to him dozens of times during the night watches, now here he was in the (purple) flesh. He was stretched out on a camp bed, suffering from sand-itch between his toes, and the orderly had just finished painting his feet with gentian violet. 'It could have been worse though, couldn't it?' George protested, and the three of us went into hysterics at the thought. As we laughed away on that sun-scorched day we were not to know that I would be the only one of the three to survive the siege.[63]

There was Jim Pearce from Bristol, tall, dark, laconic of phrase, quick with a smile and ever hospitable. We had joined up together at Belle Vue Zoo in Manchester in the dim and distant past; had chipped away at the ice with pick-axes when that city's canal railway points had succumbed to the terrible winter of 1940; had become separated when Jim went to the RHA and I went to 3 Armd Bde; had last met when those two outfits were sharing the rear-guard on the first retreat, and had snatched a quick chat while shells were flying over our heads somewhere south of Mechili. Jim was now only an escarpment or so away, and we visited whenever we could.

There was Stormy Gale who almost killed me, but that is for a later part of this account. There was Sidney Eisbruck, tank man, who had been seconded from 1RTR to Brigade HQ as tank gunner on the Brigadier's tank, which often saw me on its set when he went riding in it. Sidney (and I never called him Sid, it would not have seemed appropriate, though I can't even now think why) was a Jew, and proud of that. His London family had not wanted him to join the Army but he needed to show by his presence that Jews were not afraid to fight for their country. I had never thought otherwise; I only knew one Jewish boy back home and he had volunteered for the RAF. Sidney was as brave as they come and ours was a warm friendship.

There was the priest, Australian, and plump of belly which protruded like a melon above his shorts. These reached down almost to his ankles, so that one way and another he was something of a landmark when he went walk-about. His chapel was in one of the caves and it was there that he said Mass on Sundays for those who had been able to distinguish one day from the next dozen. He had tied a string across the ceiling above his altar and a chameleon, gift from one of his desert parishioners, balanced on this and slid through its repertoire of greens and greys while it learned Latin and waited upon an aerial visitor. We heard the priest's Latin, transformed into Aussie idiom and we watched the circling fly.

'*Darminoos vorbiscoom*'

Would it? Wouldn't it? Would it?'

A pause at the altar.

Silence in the cave.

All eyes on the fly, calculating the parabola of its flight.

WHANG!

With the speed of lightning – no fly. And so fast we hadn't even seen the uncurling of the tongue.

'Et coorm spiritoo tuo.'

We emerged one Sunday from the benediction of Mass into the tail-end of an air raid. An enemy plane tore through the sky towards us, it was very low and smoke was pouring from it. It was being chased all the way by every gun along the escarpment and its pilot was fighting for a life already lost. When his final twist bounced the plane against the rocks and it burst into flaming bits, scattering its mortal, we gave a great cheer. Our Christianity, alas, was as thin as the sliding skin of the chameleon.

And there was Tommy, the lad I didn't meet. I learned through the code I was operating with my family that one of my father's apprentices was with the RHA guns and not too far away. I set out to find him. I found the wadi where his battery was and as I approached a group of men sitting there I was searching faces and hoping to spot him before he spotted me. I didn't. He had been killed just two days before. He lies in the cemetery beneath the slope of a hill two miles out from Tobruk town. It was a place I never visited.

A Canadian then, a Mancunian, two Cockneys, a man of the southwest, a gunner, a Dragoon, a Tankie ... in other words, my little ambit was a fair cross-section of the men of the garrison and they are offered in this vein. But there was also the socialising in the wider world, which meant jawing with the Aussies. On one of my walk-abouts I came upon a small opening which led into a great cavern. I entered, and found myself at the rear echelon of one of the battalions in the Red Line. Their non-essential kit was stored here and preserving it from passers-by were two men of that battalion. One was Les, second name never learned, the other was surly, first name never offered. Together they expressed the schizophrenia of that great ex-Dominion. Les was friendly, a good soul and always ready to share a brew. He was from a town called Preston, which made us kin I suppose. His companion was the opposite of all these things and came from a wooden cave in Sydney. I could have been a German so far as he was concerned, indeed, he might have been more friendly then.

They were a strange lot on the whole, these distant cousins of ours; bloody-minded, elementally tough, roughly humoured, full of contempt for the Poms in their midst at one moment, telling you how much they wanted to see Piccadilly before returning to their upside-down position, in the next. Typical behaviour in fact of any teenager who is divesting himself of the reins of parenthood.

Summer of siege: in the seas and skies of Tobruk

And while we did our little socialising, the attempt to starve us out grew apace. Geisler and Slater continued their battle throughout the summer apart from a slight pause at the beginning of June and in the latter part of July; Geisler sent his twin-engined fighters over the town and down the coastline and Slater greeted them with his barrage whenever they appeared over the fortress. It was cut and thrust between the two. Slater introduced a new element, two anti-aircraft rocket guns that fired parachutes into the sky, a small explosive charge dangling from the parachute on the end of a wire. These guns were regarded with suspicion by the more orthodox gunners, but on 1 July Lieutenant McIlwraith of 152 Bty opened their account by using one which brought down one of the enemy planes. Geisler replied in kind on the 29th of that month by dropping mines by parachute. These were to plague the Royal Navy until the very end of the siege, one sinking HMS *Chantala* in the harbour on 7 December.

During the first six months of the siege, the garrison suffered more than 750 air raids in which up to 150 enemy aircraft were destroyed, a drain on the pilots of the Luftwaffe that seems to have escaped the historians of both sides, who appear to have been mesmerised by the air battle over Malta. In May there were 43 attacks; in June there were 52, with four Jus being shot down over the harbour on the first day of that month. July saw the highest total of all with 82 aircraft downed over the fortress. A pattern developed. The appearance of a single Me 109 usually signalled that dive-bombers would soon be on the way. Their targets were fairly consistent – any ships either in or near the harbour, AA guns, Wadi Auda's pumping-station, the distilleries, the field gun positions. The station was hit but its pumps continued to work. Its buildings were left in their semi-destroyed state to suggest that they had been abandoned. Somehow, the distilleries survived many attacks.

By July it had become far too dangerous and costly to work the port during daylight hours and any ships in the harbour were laid up under camouflage until nightfall when the place became a hive of activity. Most of the supplies were now being brought in by the A Lighters. The programme called for two to arrive and unload their cargo of 200 tons every 48 hours, but this schedule fell to five a week on average. Destroyers put their pride to one side and became supplementary cargo boats. In this way, and with the help of a store ship and two schooners, the shortfall was made up.

All along the coast the one-sided battle was fought, ships trying to make it from Mersa Matruh to the harbour during the hours of darkness, and fighters catching them *en route* and circling above their masts like swarms of desert hornets. The lumbering Lighters tried to swat them away with their pom-poms. The destroyers fired everything they could lay hands on. The sloop *Grimsby* was lost off Tobruk and *Flamingo* and *Cricket* were both damaged. The *Stuart*, skippered by Captain Waller, made 22 trips before leaving the run on 27 August with one of her engines out of commission. The *Vendetta* beat that with no fewer than 28 trips before she was withdrawn to return to Australia. And for those which made it to the harbour there was no guarantee of safety; HMS *Sidonis* and two Lighters were sunk there on 29 May.

Towards the end of June the shortage of petrol had become so acute that all swanning around inside the fortress had been halted by order. It was decided to risk the *Pass of Balmaha* in a dash to the port with 750 gallons aboard. She came up the coast escorted by the sloops HMS *Auckland* and HMAS *Parramatta*. They were spotted. The first wave of Stukas caught the little convoy as it approached Tobruk. Forty planes attacked and made their mark. *Auckland* was hit several times and her crew took to the water, clinging to whatever bits and pieces their ship had discarded when she turned turtle and sank. The other two ships were too busy fighting off their attackers to be able to help their comrades in the water. When darkness fell and the last of the planes departed, the battered *Pass of Balmaha* and *Parramatta* were still afloat. They were joined by *Vendetta* and *Waterhen*, and the rescue operation began. More than 160 men were lifted from the sea and taken aboard *Parramatta*, which took them back to Alexandria. The petrol ship was taken to tow by *Waterhen* and brought safely into the harbour.

It was not the first time that *Waterhen* had come to the rescue. When the hospital ship *Vita* was hit and damaged on 14 April, she took her in tow and when that failed, took off the wounded patients, doctors and nurses and carried them to Alexandria.

She was soon to die in our service. On 29 June she and HMS *Defender* were caught approaching the harbour and were attacked by bombers. *Waterhen*'s engine room was holed beyond the possibility of emergency repair and *Defender* came alongside to take off her crew. She was doing this when a surprising addition to the attacking force arrived on the scene, but from beneath the sea, not above it. It was one of the U-boats recently ordered to the Mediterranean by Admiral Dönitz. *Defender* drove her back under and then resumed her efforts to take *Waterhen* in tow, but she was beyond rescue. George Hynes, that magnet for the Stukas, was returning to the garrison and had a ringside view as this heroine of the seas and siege sank from sight. Such was the work of *Waterhen* and her sisters and their crews that summer, arduous, frightening, often bloody, always dangerous and absolutely essential.

Summer of siege: along the salient

There was no lack of action along that other fringe where the strand was of twisted and spiked wire, the surf a spattering of Spandau or Bren-gun fire. Rommel was so concerned to keep the hill he had won that he stationed eight or nine battalions in and around the salient; at one point in the summer these included between two and three battalions of Artillery Regt 33; two battalions of RR115; one battalion of Inf Regt 107; two battalions of Inf Regt 104 and personnel of either MG2 or our old enemies the rebuilt MG8. It will be noted that these were all crack German units. They were subjected to a third and last attempt at reduction of the salient, and after that failed, to constant sniper fire that won the awe even of those suffering it.

This final attempt to wipe out the salient was made by infantry only and it began in the early hours of 3 August. The two battalions making it came from 24th Brigade, and they were supported by some fifty guns belonging to several RHA batteries and Australian 2/12th Field Regiment, all under command of 51FRG. The attack was again in the form of a pincer, with each claw aimed at one of the two flanks of the salient. Captain Conway led 2/28th against S7 on the northern side of the salient and Captain McCarter led 2/43rd against R7 on the southern flank. The artillery concentrated on enemy artillery located behind Pt 209 and the NFS used their Vickers against the posts under attack.

The barrage began at 0325 hrs and the infantry went in five minutes later. The story was the same in both attacks. Preliminary rushes carried the attackers across the minefields to the anti-tank ditches and wire, but they then came under intense mortar and machine-gun fire. This pinned the attackers against the wire surrounding the posts. Casualties strewed the minefields and began to mount as the men triggered the anti-personnel mines that had been planted in the ditches. Despite these horrific hazards the two groups pressed on in what were fast becoming suicide missions. Both assaults were whittled down to single-figure attacks, and then to individual efforts. McCarter was forced to call off his attack when he, all his officers and most of his NCOs had either been killed or wounded and he had only 23 men still fit for action. A desperate, do-or-die effort – and it was more often die than do, resulted in the seizure of S7. Conway, Lieutenant McHenry and a score of men clung on to it all through the next day before being overwhelmed.

Australia bled badly that night in what was perhaps the most bloody battle of the siege to date, and questions could be asked about the sense of launching an operation when the enemy had had three months in which to make sure that any attack on the salient would be costly in the extreme. However, this little battle saw an example of humanitarianism that was rare in the insane inhumanity of war. Sergeant William Tuit, a 2/43rd stretcher-bearer, took a truck flying the Red Cross flag on to the killing ground in the south in order to gather the wounded and recover the bodies of the men of his battalion. With him went their padre, Father Gard, and stretcher-bearer Keith Pope. They were allowed to approach the enemy lines and Wilmot used Truit's words to describe what followed: 'A German stood up with another flag like mine. He shouted something like "*Halten. Minen!*". We could tell we were on the edge of a minefield because we could see the bodies of thirteen of our chaps lying there. A couple of Jerries came out with a mine-detector and guided a lieutenant and a doctor out to us. I told the officer we wanted to pick up our dead and wounded. He replied in English. "Very well, but only one truck and only two men at a time. You must not come any closer than this. We will send your wounded out."

'They brought out four wounded and let the truck come up to take them away. Then they carried out the bodies of fifteen dead and helped us with those still on the minefield. I told the doctor we were four short and he replied that three of our wounded had been taken away in ambulances that morning, another, badly wounded had chosen to stay because his brother had been taken prisoner. When the last of our dead had been brought to us, the lieutenant told us we were not to move until they were all back in the post and had taken in their flag. He went back; his men went below. He lowered his flag and I lowered mine. I saluted him, and he saluted back, but he gave me the salute of the *Reichswehr*, not of the Nazis. Our armistice was over.'[64] As the War Diary of 7RTR says, 'Great credit due to the German C.O.' So it was, and also to Sergeant Tuit and Padre Gard.

As for our sniping – Major Ballerstedt, Commander of RR115, wrote: 'Enemy snipers achieve astounding results. They shoot at anything they recognise. Several NCOs of the battalion have been shot through the head with the first bullet while making observations in the front line. Protruding sights in gun directors have been shot off, observation slits and loopholes have been fired on and hit, as soon as they were seen to be in use. For this reason, loopholes must be kept plugged with a wooden plug to be taken out when used so that they always show dark.'[65]

Summer of siege: inside and outside the wire

Four happenings of note punctuated that summer for the men at Tobruk Tank HQ under Solaro. The first was when that HQ went underground. One morning, a squad of pioneers (British version) appeared and began to dig a large hole on the flat and to the west of our little home. Jim and I took turns at guessing its purpose – 'The Brig's doss-down' was his first effort, but our Brigadier was thinner than a jerboa and the hole being dug would have housed several million of those long-tailed little friends. 'The Officers' Mess,' I thought. 'Yes,' Jim agreed, 'where they can eat all those cakes sent from Australia that we never see.'

But when the hole had been roofed and camouflaged and we had been invited in – on a permanent basis – the mystery was solved. The cavity was to replace the ACV as our HQ. It had three rooms, one for the Brigadier, one for use as the Orderly Office and the last was the Signals Office, complete with sets. Henceforth we were to work down-under, and Bill was to sweep an even wider berth.

The second happening arose through the idiocy of some bureaucrat in Cairo. He conjured up one of those schemes which appear ideal on paper but prove nonsensical in the real world. In the rush to get 1RTR into the fortress in April, its A Sqn had had to be left behind, and was at the time somewhere on the frontier. On the other hand, 7RTR had all its men and tanks on the frontier except for its D Sqn, which was manning its Matildas inside the fortress. *Ergo* – transfer the men of 7RTR's D Sqn into 1RTR and call it A Sqn, bringing that regiment to full strength in the fortress. Transfer the men of 1RTR's A Sqn to 7RTR, bringing that regiment to full strength on the frontier. A neat solution, and one worthy of mention in some future Honours List. Also, one worthy of the mutiny which followed when news of the proposed switch of personnel reached the garrison. The men of D Sqn were outraged. Many had been with 7RTR since it was formed in 1937 and had fought under its colours in France and in Libya. When they were informed of the switch 126 men asked for interviews. The men of the cruiser regiment were equally enraged at the thought of losing one of their squadrons which had shared in their dash across the desert to destroy the Italian Army at Beda Fomm. Whoever thought up the scheme had no conception of the *esprit-de-corps* on which the British Army had been built. For a few days there was great upset, then Lieutenant-Colonel Brown of 1RTR wrote 'a good letter' to Brigadier Keller, commander of the Tobruk Tanks at the time, complaining about the cross-posting and the idea died the death.

The third happening was the delivery of mail, weeks of it which had been piling up on some wharf at Alexandria. Among Charlie's sheaf of letters was the vital one informing him that he was a father. Those two nights in the hotel at Thursley had resulted in the creation of a daughter. He took out and read that letter so often that he must surely have known its words by heart, but I suppose the physical feel of the thing was needed to convince him of the fact that another tiny being was now part of his world. This news caused an involuntary adjustment where Jim and I were concerned. From now on Charlie was no longer 'one of us', the carefree. He had moved apart in the most mysterious manner, and paradoxically, we began to father him in many small ways.

The fourth happening was the appearance of speckled bread on our menu instead of hard tack. Apparently this was being baked in town from a stack of flour which had been in store there for some time. It wasn't exactly white, nor was it exactly brown, but its cross-grain was speckled with darker flakes. We had been eating it for several days when the cook let out that the darker flecks were dead and cooked weevils. Since the alternative was the tooth-cracking biscuit, there was only one thing to be done – toast the stuff on his hot-plate until it was the same dark brown all over.

For one member of the Brigade, we were leading too quiet a life and he set about livening it up for himself. This was Captain Leakey of 1RTR, whose little raids through the wire had had to stop with the introduction of petrol rationing. The Australians had established listening outposts as much as two or three miles outside the wire and to the south-east. Leakey volunteered to join the Australian Army as a Private so that he could get out there. He was made an 'Honorary Corporal' and allowed to take stance in the most distant of these posts with two Australians, Bennet and Heyes, but with orders to get out fast if the enemy appeared. At 0530 hrs one morning the enemy did appear, but the three men sat tight. In the close-order battle that followed, Leakey fired his tommy gun while the other two used a Bren and grenades. When the enemy reached the post, Leakey killed two with his revolver. The remainder of the attackers fell back, leaving eighteen of their number dead and several wounded. The three men then evacuated the post, running the last few hundred yards to safety.[66]

Several of these posts, originally begun as Australian listening posts to the south and south-east of the perimeter, were subsequently developed into something rather more than this. They took on names: 'Bondi', 'Plonk', 'Jack' and 'Jill'. The last two were soon to feature largely in our lives and would stay in our memories for ever

And so the summer drifted on and away – greater heat, fatter flies, bully by the bucketful accompanied by vegetables in the form of white pills to be taken every day when you could remember. On some days a truck took those men free of duty across to a wadi on the coast, and here we peeled off and either swam or played in the cooling waters of Mussolini's lake under the protective watch of a couple of machine-gunners on the rocks. Blue skies above, a darker blue below, becoming almost black where the two made a horizon, a fringe of surf bubbling quietly between the Persil-white boulders. What more could a body ask? Fish, apparently. Not taken in the traditional and sporting way but in the hungry way of the soldier. A hand-grenade, Italian or British, the fish didn't know the difference. 'Out of the way, you blokes!' A soaring grenade, a muffled explosion and a spout of water. Then the search and the gathering in, the barbecue fire and sizzling fish flesh. We sang all the way to the ocean on those days, and all the way back, and our favourite was 'She'll be coming round the mountain when she comes' and we weren't thinking of the train that inspired the song, and we never sang 'Lili Marlene' because at that time we'd never heard of the lady.

Summer drifted on and away, a summer of nicknames that became 'household' names: 'Bardia Bill', the big gun that chased the little boats scudding around the harbour but never hit one; 'Salient Sue', his sister, who banged her offerings against our escarpment; 'Eskimo Nell', the busiest of those little boats; the 'Dinkum Oil', our home-produced newspaper; 'Pedlar Palmer', Royal Australian Navy, but late of the Chinese Lancers, dauntless skipper of the *Maria Giovanna*, who won fame through his cussedness on the Spud Run until the Germans kidded him into captivity lower down the coast; somebody called *Auk* who sent messages from Cairo. Names and names. We became stupefied in the sun, using names as roots of an existence whose daily processes became so familiar that they could be done with half a mind while the other half day-dreamed. Then suddenly the sandy foundations of that existence shifted.

PART TWO: BREAK-OUT
The Story of British 70th Division

Remote from pilgrimage, a dusty hollow
*   Lies in the Libyan plain:*
And there my comrades sleep, who will not follow
*   the pipes and drums again:*
Who followed closely in that desperate sally
*   The pipes that went before,*
Who heedless now of Muster or Reveille,
*   Sleep sound for ever more.*

In days of peace, when days of war were nearing,
*   My comrades who are dead,*
Once in a while looked up the dark track, peering,
*   Where fate and glory led:*
For these, the chosen of their generation,
*   This was the path it took,*
That ended in the sand and desolation
*   Ten miles beyond Tobruk. **

ONE

Strangers in the night

In a very loose way the break-out can be said to have begun during the night of 18/19 August, because although it was not until November that the bridges over the ditch were crossed, it was on that August night that the changes in personnel began which would see an entirely new division undertake the challenging task. The morning of 19 November seemed no different from any of the preceding hundred mornings when Jim came to relieve me from the set. 'Odd bods,' he said. 'What?' 'Odd bods.

* Extract from 'Towards The East' by Bernard Fergusson, Black Watch Regiment .

155

In the caves. Bloody loonies.' 'Odd? What do you mean, odd?' 'Can't speak English.' 'Free French?' 'Can't speak French either. Told you, they're bloody loonies.'

As soon as I'd had the obligatory brew I went up to the cave to see what 'odd' was. I found that Les and his companion had departed, that the cave was filled with strangers, and that Jim was right, they could speak neither English nor French. This wasn't surprising because they were Poles, come to Tobruk with the specific intention of killing Germans. Or so they told me in graphic terms, with paralingual thrusts and stabs of the arsenal of knives and bayonets which they were sharpening and polishing. They laughed when I first tried them with my French, in fact they laughed all the time, and they were behaving as if they had a date that very afternoon – with Rommel I think, which made them the oddest of bods. Every last one was doing something warlike, stripping a Bren, cleaning the barrel of a .303, taking a grenade to pieces and re-assembling it. The oddest thing of all was that this warlike preparation was taking place beneath a gallery of Holy pictures, The Madonna of Czestochowa mostly, but other religious icons – which had replaced the Aussies' Lana Turners and Betty Grables overnight.

What was it all about? Who were these followers of the Black Madonna who seemed so eager to push their noses into our war? They were members of the Carpathian Brigade who had come to take over from Australian 18th Brigade, the members of which were at that very moment feet-up on a ship's rail somewhere approaching Mersa Matruh.

Politics had reared their ugly head again, this time Australian politics, and in both military and civilian circles. General Blamey wanted all Australians in one corps under Lavarack (and himself of course), and preferably well to the east of Suez. The new Australian Prime Minister wanted all the Australian troops out of the garrison before their mothers, fathers, wives and sisters voted in the forthcoming election.[1] Put those two lustings together and not even Churchill could resist them. The Aussies were going, every man Bluey of them, and these were the first replacements. Men of the eagle for men supposedly of the spade, but just as handy with the bayonet. Mid-Europeans in place of Antipodeans. Heel-clickers instead of midnight creepers. It seemed an odd swop at first, but less so as the idea sank in. In the place of rugged independent men had come men fierce for independence. In place of volunteers who had crossed an ocean to stand shoulder to shoulder with their northern kin had come men who had crossed frontiers to take revenge on those who were oppressing their kin. In all the world who had more cause to hate the Germans than these, their nearest neighbours? As for the incongruity of grenade beneath Holy Virgin, this too was proper; for them the grenade was also an icon, they had come to wage a holy war. The Italians, they laughed at. The Germans, they licked their lips over. They were a fearsome, mad crew to be in possession of the weaponry scattered around them, on that morning in that cave.

A miracle of organisation
The exchange of 70th Div for 9th Div was nothing less than that – at each of its ends. It was carried out in three waves, or operations:

'Treacle' (19–29 August)

in: Polish 1st Carpathian Brigade and a Polish Cavalry Regiment

out: 18th Brigade, 18th Indian Cavalry and 152nd LAA

'Supercharge' (19–27 September)

in: British 16th Inf Bde, Advanced HQs of 70th Div

32nd Army Tank Brigade (32ATB) and 4RTR

out: 24th Bde and Australian 24th Field Park Company

'Cultivate' (12–25 October)

in: HQ 70th Div, British 14th and 23th Inf Bdes

One Czech Inf Bn and 62nd General Hospital.

out: 9th Div HQ and Divisional Troops

26th and 20th Bdes and Australian 4th Hospital.

The convoys sailed from Alexandria. The men travelling in them weren't told their destination, but they would have had to be very slow not to have guessed within minutes of leaving that port and turning into the setting sun. Indeed, the 2nd Leicesters expressed relief that it was Tobruk; they had feared going to Cyprus and finding themselves in another Crete situation.

Most of this huge lift was carried out by destroyers working in pairs: *Encounter, Havoc, Jarvis, Jaguar, Kimberley, Kipling, Nizam* and *Latima*, all made the run with one or other of the fast minelaying cruisers *Latona* and *Abdiel* accompanying each pair. A third destroyer in each convoy carried stores. In addition to the men and stores aboard these ships, 48 Matilda tanks of 4RTR and six light tanks were brought in A Lighters, these last sailing from Mersa Matruh. One man to leave the fortress was Brigadier Slater, defender of the port. One to come in was Major (Jock) Holden, who was to take over D Squadron 7RTR.

Moonless nights were the chosen times for arrival and departure, the destroyers being allowed 30 minutes to off-load. Two descriptions of the disembarking tell of its rapid but effective organisation. Brigadier Willison, of 32nd Army Tank Brigade, wrote: 'As ships had to be far away from Tobruk by dawn they could only stay in the harbour for a specified time, whether or not their cargo had been unloaded; and the method for everyone leaving the ships was by sliding down a sloping board, sometimes on to the quayside and sometimes on to partly submerged ships in the harbour. Everyone had the fun of being grasped by the seat of the pants and made to land in this unusual manner.'[2]

Even brigadiers!

For 2nd Leicesters it was rather more dignified: '27 September ... at Tobruk. Disembarked in 10 to 15 minutes. Our slippers helped ... from Kimberley on to a wreck and from there by pontoon bridge to the shore. Greeted by Aussie ASC who took us in remaining 10 tonners left in Tobruk. Received into Div Reserve by (oddly enough) our affiliated regiment Aus 2/32nd Bat and we renew our acquaintance with holes in the ground full of the usual desert dust and fleas, but this time mice are added.'

Wilmot watched this group come ashore; he describes the scene: 'As one destroyer tied up alongside the wreck at the end of Tobruk's main wharf, British Tommies began streaming down the narrow gangway, across the wreck and on to the jetty. There was no clank of iron heels on the steel plates because they all wore rubber-soled desert boots. They needed them. The gangway was narrow and they were more heavily laden than an Arab mule. Nevertheless, 300 padded off in ten minutes.'[3]

He adds that the Diggers were on the ship in five.

There were casualties. During 'Treacle', *Phoebe* (cruiser) and *Nizam* were damaged by aircraft. On the last night and last leg of 'Cultivate' the

158

convoy was attacked by bombers and a U-boat. Between 1900 hrs and 2300 hrs there were fifteen low-level attacks on the ships. *Latona* was hit by bombers and sank. *Hero* was damaged. To continue the voyage would have been to risk every ship and every man sailing in her, and the convoy was forced to return to Alexandria. This was bad news for 2/13th and the men of 20th Bde HQ who were waiting at Tobruk to be disembarked. They returned to the Blue Line. The 20th Bde personnel were taken off on 12 November, but 2/13th remained, not only to continue the Australian presence to the end of the siege, which was right and proper, but also to carry the Australian bayonet into action at the most critical part of the break out battle.

The passage of C Sqn 4RTR during that period is worthy of mention. They came in on the Lighter A7, accompanied by A2 and A8. They were sleeping on the tarp coverings when they were brought out of their slumbers by the sound and flashes of shells. Shells at sea? They dismantled the Besas (BSA machine-guns) from their tanks, brought these top-side, steadied them against stanchions and searched for targets. They soon found one, a U-boat surfaced and firing at them from about 150 yards' distance. The Lighters scattered and engaged the U-boat with their 2pdr guns. It disappeared, only to arrive again at a distance of 50 yards on the port side of A7. The skipper of the Lighter, Sub-Lieutenant Dennis Peters, using a tommy gun, and Trooper Weech, using his Besa, both claimed hits. The skipper, bursting to have a U-boat to the credit of his lumbering vessel, was all for ramming her, but the 4RTR CO, mindful of his precious tanks, had to say no. The U-boat vanished, the passage was resumed, and Peters called the Tank CO to the bridge to share in a victory bottle of whisky.

One of these three Lighters, A8, returned to Mersa Matruh, but A2 and A7 carried on to Tobruk. At 1700 hrs twelve enemy planes appeared but they were driven off by the Lighters' escort. At 2200 hrs they were bombed by two aircraft and at 2400 hrs they were shelled by guns on the coast. They arrived off Tobruk at 0130 hrs, to find themselves in the middle of a severe air raid. All this before they had even reached the port.

There is a sad tail-end to this account. Both A2 and A7 returned to Matruh carrying repairable engines. On this return passage they again encountered a U-boat but this time only managed to get off a despairing signal before both were sent down with all hands. Perhaps Peters should have been allowed to ram after all.

The Royal Navy had come up trumps yet again. During the three-part exercise it took 15,000 men away from the fortress and brought in a similar number. At the same time it brought stores vital for the break-out. The figures for 'Supercharge' alone give an indication of their feat: troops in 6,308; troops out 5,444; wounded out 500+; stores in 2,100 tons. All achieved with speed and efficiency under tremendous pressure.

The RAF returns

Nor was it only the Royal Navy. Morshead had a major fear about this exchange of troops. What if Rommel should attack the fortress in the middle of one of the operations? He had arranged for the exchanges to be made through the medium of the Blue Line so that the perimeter posts would be manned throughout, but any attack might catch incoming troops on the move or before they were settled in to their weapons. His ground patrols could not penetrate far enough to determine Rommel's intentions and he decided that he had to have aerial reconnaissance. By this time, however, El Gubbi was so vulnerable to air attack that it was not available for take-off. He ordered a new strip to be built closer to the harbour and had his engineers erect two new hangars in wadis at the north-east corner of El Gubbi. These were camouflaged so that they were practically invisible from the air, and each was capable of harbouring a Hurricane. An underground hangar was also created, with a wooden platform which could hold a Hurricane. It was worked by a system of rope pulleys using barrels filled with rocks as counter-weights, and it had a sliding roof.[4]

Despite its ingenuity the underground hangar was never put into use. The other two were. Two pilots of 451 Sqn RAAF, 'Wizard' Williams (Christian name unknown), an Australian, and Geoffrey Morley, an Englishman, flew up from their base at Sidi Barrani. The guns were taken out of their planes to make them lighter and cameras were fitted in their place. Morshead greeted Morley and told him that he wanted a check on enemy activity during the evacuation. The pilot flew his first mission on

ON PATROL

Above: Australian infantry make a fine silhouette as they move up to the Red Line. (Imperial War Museum, E4855)

Below: 'We're not here to take it – we're here to give it,' said Morshead, and this patrol on their way through the perimeter wire were the ones who did the giving. The officer carries a Tommy Gun; his men have fixed their bayonets. (Imperial War Museum, 5498)

Above: The patrol returns, bringing back its wounded. This photograph shows the rough terrain that covered much of the fortress. (Imperial War Museum, E5503)

Left: Lance-Corporal John Hurst Edmondson, VC, the first Australian soldier to win the Victoria Cross in the Second World War. During Rommel's first attack on Tobruk he showed 'resolution, leadership and conspicuous bravery'. (Australian War Memonal, 100642)

LIFE GOES ON

Above: 'For you the war is over.' Surviving panzer-grenadiers of Ponath's 8 Machine Gun Regiment captured during the Easter battle await transport to the PoW cage and the beginning of their long journey into captivity. (Australian War Memorial, 007475)

Below: A group photograph taken in Tobruk in the week before the break-out. The proud boast and the water bottle suggest that at least some of the men were operating the distillery in the damaged building behind them. In the background is the church of St Anthony. Its nave had lost its roof to bombs so that when you looked up you saw the clear blue of a Libyan sky, but its tower remained undamaged, despite all the dive-bombing. (ROTA)

Australian troops manning a Bren gun in one of Tobruk's many damaged houses. During an enemy air attack everybody who had anything that could fire used it, making every moment hazardous for the unwelcome visitors. More than 75 enemy planes were shot down over the fortress.
(Imperial War Museum, 5136)

Above: 'Smudge's' dug-out – a typical Rat of Tobruk's hole out on a flat. Untypical is the Blenheim In the background, suggesting that this hole was close by the airfield at El Gubbi. The rough, rock-strewn terrain is general in this part of the Libyan docert. (ROTA)

Below: A harbour barrage gun crew takes a few moments off in order to attend a religious service, but they stay close enough to their gun to bring it into action at a moment's notice. Ammunition for the gun is stored in a bunker. Army chaplains were important members of most units throughout the siege. (Imperial War Museum, E4832)

Top left: Men of D Company, 2nd Leicester Regiment, manning a firing-step in a post on the Bardia side of the Red Line. Behind the Bren gun is Private Thompson, and with him is Private Len Greaves. Behind them is Wadi Zeitun, and beyond that lies the Mediterranean. (ROTA)

GUNS AND GUNNERS

Lower left: RSM Clarke in front of one of the Italian guns captured at Tobruk in 1940. The Italians removed their sights but Clarke made new ones, thus bringing the guns back into action. They became known as 'Mr Clarke's guns'. RSM Clarke was killed during the break-out. Left to right: RSM Clarke, Sergeant Cauldwell, Gunner Rolfe and Gunner Patten. (Jack Warner, ROTA)

Above: Mr Clarke's guns in action at Tobruk. (Jack Warner, ROTA)

Below: Every kind of desert headgear is being worn by this group of 1 RHA gunners, including the one worn by the Aussie who has found his way in to the picture. (Jack Warner, ROTA)

Above: The men and one of the guns that stopped the panzers. RHA gun crews pose on the trailer of one of the battery's 25-pounder guns. These were the men who brought Rommel's panzers to a sudden halt during his first attack against the fortress. (Imperial War Museum, E6576)

Left: Lieutenant-Colonel Williams (holding cap), CO of 1 RHA, with his second-in-command, Major ('The Bull') Turner, outside the cave which served as their HQ in Tobruk. 'What are you doing here?' Willison asked Williams on El Duda ridge, 'you should be with your guns.' 'I am... they're right behind me,' Williams answered. (Jack Wamer, ROTA)

THE TOBRUK TANKS

Right: HQ of 1st Royal Tank Regiment in a tunnel-cave under one of the escarpments. The former Italian garrison's engineers had converted these caves into underground rooms linked with tunnels, the most notable being those occupied by 9th Australian Division HQ under the Solaro escarpment. (The Tank Museum)

Below: Captain Phillip Gardner, VC, (left) with other officers of 4 RTR in front of one of their Matilda tanks. Tank names began with the initial letter of the alphabet corresponding with the number of the battalion. This tank was perhaps named DEFIANCE. The photograph was taken In Tobruk shortly before Captain Gardner won his VC by going to the aid of two KDG armoured-car crews who were trapped in a minefield and under heavy enemy fire. (The Tank Museum)

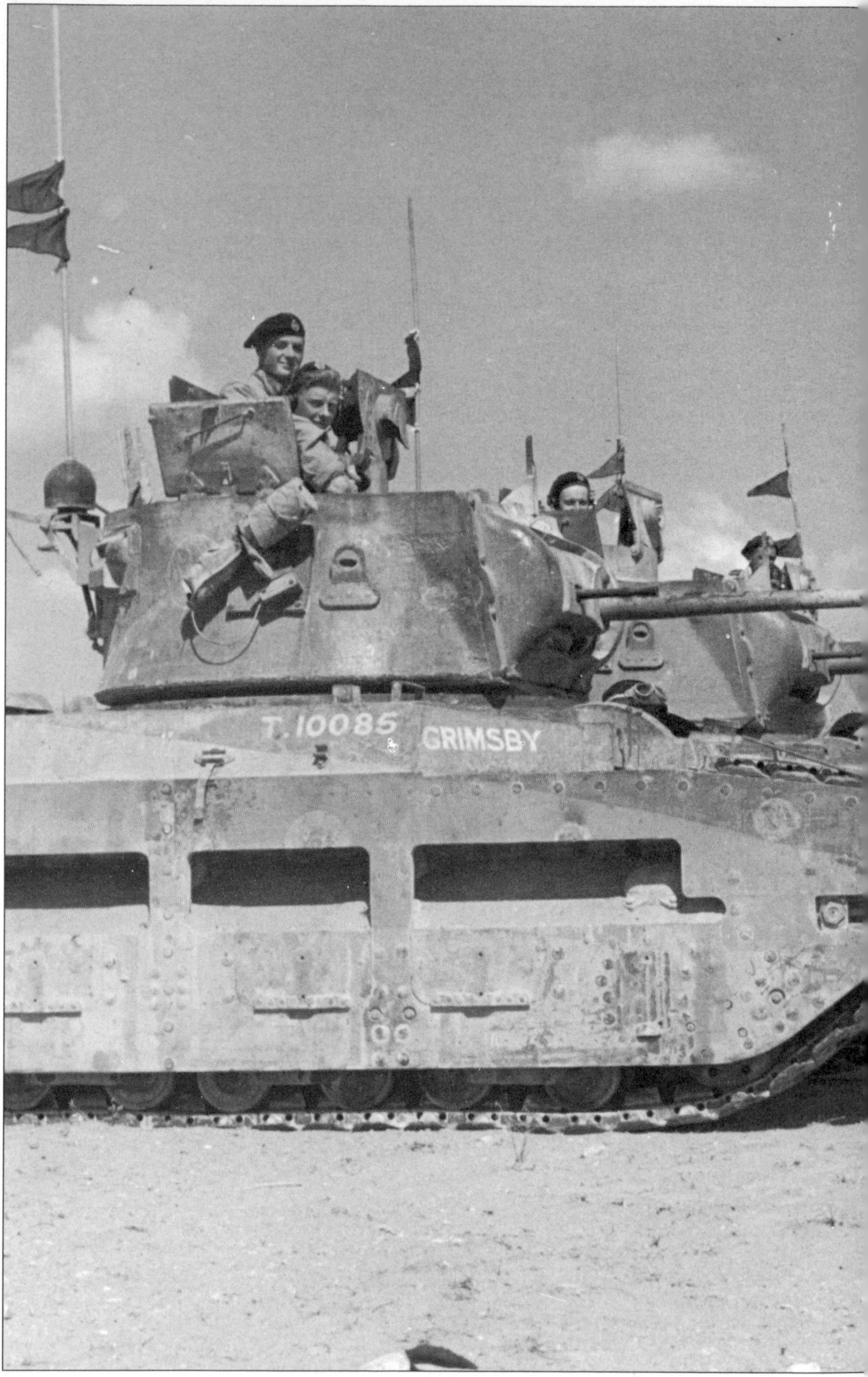
T. 10085
GRIMSBY

Above: Two King's Dragoon Guardsmen standing by their Marmon Harrington armoured car. The three-man crew consisted of a commander, driver and wireless operator. On the left is the car's belt-fed Vickers Mk 1, with a spotlight fixed beneath it. The spotlight was operated from inside the car. On the far side is a Boys .55 anti-tank gun. There was also a Bren gun which was mounted alongside the No.2 driver. The wireless set can be seen through the open rear doors, and sand tracks are fixed to the car's side. (ROTA)

Left: D Squadron of 7 RTR line up just before the break-out. It was these men who took the first enemy post, 'Butch'. Their Matilda tanks were designed for work with infantry and yet their 2-pounder guns could not fire high explosive-shells. Strong and well armoured, they had been the 'Queens of the Desert', before the arrival of Rommel's 88mm and 50mm guns put an end to their reign. (Imperial War Museum, E5550)

THE PROVIDERS

Above: A lighter being unloaded at the makeshift quay by pioneers. These cumbersome, undefended craft brought tanks, guns and supplies to the garrison. The boxes being unloaded here each contain two aluminium petrol containers. Not one of the lighters was to survive the dangerous run up from Mersa Matruh. Unglamorous vessels they may have been, but the Royal Navy was never better served than by the men who brought them into Tobruk harbour. (Imperial War Museum, E8433)

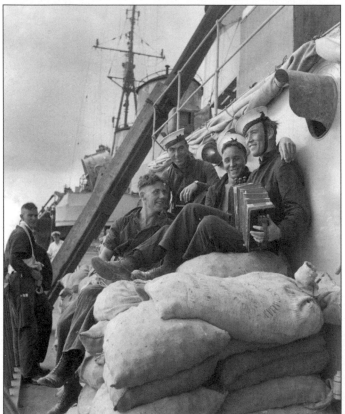

Left: Although the deck of their destroyer has taken on the appearance of a vegetable market stall in the desperate need to get food to the garrison, the matelots can still enjoy a song. (Imperial War Museum, E6195)

THE BREAKOUT

Above: General Morshead (9ADV), known to his men as as 'Ming the Merciless', the defender of Tobruk (left), and General Scobie (70 Div) who relieved him, in conversation before the hand-over of the fortress in October. (Imperial War Museum, 6215)

Right: Generalfeldmarschall Erwin Rommel, fearless, inspirational, chivalrous; but also stubborn, reckless and demanding – was a Desert *Wolf*, not Fox. He deserved better of his nation. (Imperial War Museum, GER1281)

Above: Brigader Willison using his model of the break-out operation. Behind him are the junior commanders of the Infantry and tank battalions which were to make the break-out. The small squares show the line of perimeter posts from which the break-out was to be made. The zig-zag line is the anti-tank ditch, and the irregular shapes are the posts to be attacked. Through the window can be seen the entrance to the HQ caves under Solaro escarpment. (Imperial War Museum, E6852)

Below: On 'Tiger' after the battle. Sergeant McNichol of the Black Watch, plays Pipe-Major Roy's pipes while German first aid men tend the wounded of both sides. Only an hour before, the tin-hatted Scots have crossed that ground under intense fire from this post; now they enjoy a cigarette, while in the background, men of the German 90th Light Division begin their long march into captivity. (Imperial War Museum, E6797)

Above: The first men to get through to Tobruk by land meet its defenders on Duda Ridge. Under the Union Jack can be seen the 4 RTR standard. Within hours the link would be broken and these men would be fighting for their lives. Left to right: Captain Humphries (4 RTR), Lieutenant-Colonel Brown (1 RTR), Lieutenant-Colonel O'Carroll (4 RTR), Brigadier Willison (32 ATB), Lieutenant-Colonel Hartnell (19 NZ Btn), Major Holden 7 RTR, Captain Blundell (19 NZ). (Imperial War Museum, E6899)

Right: Camouflage painted, this ACV had served as HQ for the Tobruk Tank Brigade during the siege. It reverted to its more normal mobile role in the break-out, and is here seen on 'Tiger', shortly after the capture of that enemy position. The canopy is rolled up because of the constant need to be on the move to evade incoming artillery fire. Left to right: Captain George Hope, Brigade Major Windsor, Brigadier A. Willison. The author is standing at the rear, and an operator sits at the No. 9 set. (Imperial War Museum, E6867)

Left: A rare photograph of Captain Jackman, VC, of the Northumberland Fusiliers. One of the few in his battalion who were not Geordies, he was a leading figure in the break-out, forever asking Willison to give him targets for his Vickers teams and twice appearing on the scene at critical moments to turn the tide of battle He was killed on Duda Ridge on the evening of the day he won his Victoria Cross. (Stonyhurst College)

Left: The entrance to the War Cemetery in Tobruk where the men of the Commonwealth who died there are buried. Carved on the obelisk are the words:

'THIS IS HALLOWED GROUND FOR HERE LIE THOSE WHO DIED FOR THEIR COUNTRY'

They were chosen by General Morshead, who wished to honour the men of all nations who lost their lives in the battles for Tobruk. The ship's bell is from HMS *Liverpool*, a Royal Navy cruiser which operated along the 'Suicide Run' during the siege. (ROTA)

27 September, across Acroma, and was able to report 'nothing of moment'. He flew three such Tac R missions and one gun-spotting flight during the three weeks he was with us. Nothing is known of Williams's work apart from photographs showing him beside his Hurricane inside the fortress, but it can be assumed that it was similar to what Morley did. The two planes were serviced by the same small group of RAF grounds-men who had remained behind as plane scavengers.

Goodbye to Ming the Merciless

The withdrawal of the Australians meant that their commander had to go also. Before he departed the fortress, Morshead visited as many as possible of the units which had served under him. He also wrote to those British units that were to stay behind. He told them that it had been his wish that they all go out with the Australians but he had been over-ruled. One unit he visited was 107RHA. They thought the Australians were looking forward to getting back to civilisation but all of them appeared genuinely sorry not to be in at the kill. To the men of the big guns around the harbour he said: 'The fine discipline and steadiness in action of the AA Batteries have been an inspiration to us all, and we are sad to sever an association which has meant so much to us in the execution of our task here.' To the men of the Tobruk Tanks he wrote: 'Would you please convey to all ranks of 32 ATB farewell greetings from the Australian 9th Division. We are confident that future events will bring them additional fame and confirm the proud motto they bear ('Fear Nought'). We are grateful for all they have done for us in the defence of this fortress and trust that the course of the war will enable us to serve together again.'

And we in turn were more than grateful for what he had done for us. He, and his GSO1, Lloyd and GSO2, White. His Brigadiers: Wootten (18th Bde), Murray (20th Bde), Godfrey (24th Bde) and Tovell (26th Bde). Most of all though, we were grateful to the ordinary Australian soldier who had spent his days in those gun-pits along the Red Line and facing the salient; his nights in the no man's land beyond the posts. He was leaving us now, and fate would decree that we would never again fight alongside him. He was also, alas, leaving behind many of his comrades on that slope within scent of the sea, lads who would never know Lindwall and Miller, or Lillie and Thomo.

For Morshead, Tobruk had been a triumph. His steadfastness under attack had been infectious. He had met everything that Rommel could throw at him, and had inflicted two defeats on the man. They were to meet in the field twice more and on each occasion Morshead would repeat the treatment. If Rommel had a nemesis (other than Hitler) it was Morshead.

New faces in the Red and Blue Lines

By autumn the battalions in the front lines had names instead of numbers, and some were quite famous names.

TABLE 2

The composition of the three British infantry brigades was:

14th Brigade	16th Brigade	23th Brigade
2nd Black Watch	2nd King's Own	1st Durham Lt Inf
1st Beds and Herts	2nd Leicesters	4th Border Regt
2nd York and Lancs	2nd Queen's Own	1st Essex Regt

The artillery remained the same as before with the exception of 152HAA which had left the fortress.

It will not have escaped notice that the garrison now had a new tank force, 32nd Army Tank Brigade. This is not quite as it appears. On 18 September HMS *Jaguar* slipped into the port and disembarked the three 'W's; Willison, Windsor and de Winton, the Brigadier, Brigade-Major and Signals Officer of this new brigade. They made their way from the harbour to our underground HQ where they took over from the current residents. Next morning Willison reported to Morshead that 3rd Armd Bde had been relieved by 32nd ATB. This word 'relieved' is a misnomer to say the least; the new brigade consisted of 1RTR, D Sqn 7RTR and C Sqn KDG, which names readers will recognise without too much difficulty. We had not been relieved at all, we had been taken over. That night, Brigadier Keller and Brigade-Major Silvertop embarked for Alexandria and we were left to our new masters.[5]

The new brigade's growth was very rapid. Next day Lieutenant-Colonel O'Carroll, DSO, commander of 4RTR, arrived and established an HQ for his regiment. On the day after that, the first of his Matildas came in on three A Lighters. They moved off to Spanish Farm, where they lay up among derelict vehicles until dark. From there they went to tank standings which had been dug for them by men of 1RTR. On 26 September four more shipments of Matildas came in, and yet more on 1, 11 and 19 October. This brought all 4RTR tanks and personnel into the fortress.

TABLE 3
The brigade's armour now stood at a total of 166 fighting vehicles:

'I' Tanks	*A9*	*A10*	*A13*	*Lt Tanks*	*Armd/cars*	*Scout cars*
69	6	9	13	34	29	6

Of considerable interest to us four was the new Officer in Command of 32nd Army Tank Brigade's Signals. He was Major de Winton of the Middlesex Yeomanry (now part of the Royal Signals) who had come ahead of his squadron. I don't know if he had been advised that there was already a Signals presence at the HQ, and that it had been operating to everyone's satisfaction for six months, or if he simply 'found' us. It must have been strange for him, straight out from England, to find himself with unexpected underlings who were so much more experienced than he or his men of what went on at the sharp end of military communications. It was no less strange for us to be meeting a new 'boss' who had arrived up the blue from out of the blue, so to speak, after our many months of very well-functioning autonomy. My first meeting with him was when I bumped into him outside the HQ dug-out. He was wearing an Army greatcoat which reached quite low, rather like those worn by German officers when on parade, and also a peaked cap. The result was to make him appear even taller than he was, and that was well over the six-foot mark. I wondered what I looked like to him, in my NZ sweater, scuffed, Italian officer boots, really short Aussie shorts, and a few weeks' collection of sand in my ears. Pretty appalling I should think.

We summed each other up but kept our verdicts to ourselves. Shortly after this introductory meeting I was standing outside with him when a shell landed on our side of the escarpment and about a hundred yards away. 'That was pretty close, Sir,' I said with the sang-froid of someone who had been putting up with that sort of thing by the day. I had hardly got the words out of my mouth when over came a second, this time about fifty yards away. 'That was closer, Harrison,' he replied, more than matching my sang-froid. Then we both remembered that the third time pays for all, especially where shelling is concerned, and we abandoned sang-froid altogether and departed in haste. He was reputed to be a Marches Baron, whatever that may be, but he was a fair man and determined to give his brigadier the best possible service, which was our aim too.

By the time his own outfit arrived to take over he had seen us at work and he put efficiency before familiarity. We four continued to play leading roles in the Brigade's communication arrangements, formal authority or none.

Our other new master was Brigadier Willison, DSO, MC, and known to the Tank Fraternity as 'Ant', probably because of his appetite for work. He had been an infantry man in the First World War, twice wounded and twice mentioned in dispatches. He had also won the DSO and the MC and Bar. But that was then, and now was now. How would this intense, thin man who must have been every day of forty-five (an immense age!) shape up against the demands of desert life? It was hard enough on young men; what would the chill of its dawns do to his ageing bones? Would he need all the fire in his veins just to keep himself warm?

We soon found out. Ten days after he had taken over he issued his first instructions:

32 ATB Op Inst No 1.

1. List of units

2. In the event of an attack being made upon the fortress the Brigade will assemble as follows (detailed)

3. a. 4 RTR will be the principal unit used to engage and destroy any enemy AFVs which have penetrated the perimeter

   b. 1 RTR will move to outer flank of 4 RTR and cut off the retreat of enemy AFVs endeavouring to withdraw

   c. KDG will delay and head off the enemy formation until the tanks arrive

   d. 7 RTR will remain in reserve

4. In the case of more than one enemy formation of AFVs penetrating the perimeter they will be defeated in detail and be destroyed successively

6. When a formation has been defeated 4 RTR will be prepared to follow up any AFVs which manage to escape. They will be pursued into the enemy FDL which will be shot up and their fire subdued so that our own infantry can advance to better positions if ordered.

8. OC KDG will be prepared to detach 2 further troops of armd cars to assist in destroying parachutists if this form of attack is used. It is unlikely that such attacks will be continued after the first flights of paras have been disposed of.

These were the answer to our unasked questions: 'engage and destroy'... 'cut off the retreat'... 'defeated in detail' ... 'pursued' ... 'disposed of'. These weren't the words of a thin-blooded old soldier, but of a man who was itching to get on with the said destruction and disposal as soon as he was given the opportunity.

What kind of a man was he in addition to being fierce? I was coming out from the dug-out one afternoon and he must have been close on my heels. An Australian DR came tearing up to its entrance, pulled up his Norton with a skid that shot half-a-ton of sand down into the underground suite, and without dismounting, threw that day's official mail through the entrance. Willison exploded. He told the Australian exactly what he thought of him and it was not complimentary. The DR gave him a long stare, grinned, said, 'Get ——— !', kicked his starter and vanished in another cloud of dust. 'No discipline at all, these Australians, Harrison,' Willison snarled. 'No, Sir.' Then his face creased in a grin. 'But I wouldn't be without the buggers, they know how to fight, by God!'

And I grinned too. He was going to be all right.

TWO

The best laid plans o' mice and men

The summer shimmered away through August and into September and we passed its days in going about our daily doings, little aware of all the planning that was going on out there in the greater world beyond our string of wire – the plotting, the organising, the games of bluff and counter-bluff. To get an idea of the degree of this plotting it is necessary to leave the fortress and take a look at that greater world.

Rommel was still determined to capture Tobruk, then, with his western flank finally secured, drive to Suez. Auchinleck was determined to destroy the Afrika Korps, relieve Tobruk, seize Tripoli, then, with his western flank secured, meet any new threat which might develop in that melting-pot to the east of Suez. Both men were devising strategies which they hoped would bring about these happy, if opposing, results, and re-organising and re-equipping their armies so that they would be able to satisfy the demands of the strategies.

Rommel had to ensure that the British forces on the frontier would not be able to intervene during the critical hours of any attack he might launch against the fortress. Auchinleck had to get his attacking units up on to the plateau and into battle positions of his choosing before they were discovered. Both men had to consider the logistics involved in transporting, arming, feeding and watering huge numbers of men in an environment which provided nothing helpful but whose harsh terrain and elemental extremes increased logistic demand while making its satisfaction even more difficult.

Autumnal plotters: Rommel

Throughout the summer Rommel worked as feverishly as only he could, bringing his dispositions and troops to that pitch of perfection which would translate strategy into victory. His frontier defences were transformed from a few defended posts into a 25-mile line stretching from Sollum in the north to Sidi Omar in the south. This defensive corset was manned by the Italian Savona Division, stiffened with whalebones of German units. At its critical points were groups of 88mm and 50mm guns, and its whole length was protected by minefields. He now had the experience of the success of Hafid Ridge to add to that of his failure at Maccia Bianca and this was a man who did learn from his experiences. He insisted on supervising the transformation personally, which meant that nothing was left to chance. He demanded that the defences along the frontier wire be capable of holding out for three weeks should the situation require it, and did everything he could to ensure this. They were to protect his eastern flank while he finally disposed of the stubborn defenders of the fortress.

On the Tobruk front, the track around the outside of the perimeter which the Axis troops had been using for more than six months had now become almost impassable and Rommel demanded that a new by-pass be built. Three thousand Italians from 21st Corps set to work on the kind of task at which they were so proficient, and within three months they had completed the road. It was given the name 'Achsenstrasse' (Axis Road) by its builders. It ran slightly to the north of the old Trigh Capuzzo, and passed close to the south-east of El Duda before descending the Belhamed Ridge and turning north to join the Via Balbia on the coast. Given TOBFORCE's projected role in the failed 'Battleaxe' operation, this road's proximity was of great interest to those who would spearhead any break-out.

Meanwhile major changes were taking place in the organisation and content of the Axis armies. The Italian Commander-in-Chief, Gariboldi, was replaced by Bastico, who thus became Rommel's immediate superior if only nominally in so far as Rommel was concerned. Bastico's command was divided into two parts, Panzergruppe Afrika and Corpo di Manovra.

TABLE 4
The composition of these two organisations was:

Panzergruppe Afrika: Commander Gen Rommel

Afrika Korps (DAK)	Corpo d'Armata XXI
(under Gen Crüwell)	*(under Gen Navarini)*
PZ15: Gen Neumann-Silkow	Bologna Regt: Gen Gloria
PZ21: Gen von Ravenstein	Trento: Gen Stampioni
90 LT: Gen Sümmermann	Pavia: Gen Franceschini
Recce Bns 3 and 33	Brescia: Gen Gambon
	Savona: Gen di Giorgis
	Artillery: Gen Böttcher

Corpo di Manovra: Commander Gen Gambara
Ariete: Gen Balotta
Trieste: Gen Piazzoni
Corps Artillery

It will be seen that Rommel's command had increased greatly; in fact he had taken over the entire Italian Army apart from its armoured and motorised regiments and its artillery. Two new formations had appeared in the ranks of Afrika Korps, PZ21 and 90LT Divisions. The former was the old 5LT, which had been re-named and strengthened around the two tank battalions of PZR5 (whose commander was now Oberst Stephan). Its infantry element was RR104 (commanded by Oberst Knabe) and it had under command Arty Regt 104 and Eng Bn 20. Its reconnaissance was Recce3 (commanded by Oberleutnant von Wechmar). Thus it was a typical panzer striking force containing all the elements for either attack or defence.

The other division, 90LT, was entirely new to the campaign. For some time after its arrival in Africa it went under the tongue-twisting name Div zbV Afrika (the Afrika Division as it is often referred to). It was an infantry division with strong artillery and other support, and was to become a major force in the battles ahead. Its two infantry units were Inf Regt 155 (commanded by Oberst Marks) and Afrika Regt 361 (commanded by Oberst von Barmby). It had three artillery battalions, one of which fired 88mms, and also a reconnaissance unit – Recce Battalion 580 (commanded by Oberst Homeyer). Afrika Regt 361 is of special interest. It was composed of Germans who had left Germany during the rise of Hitler to supreme power, and had volunteered to serve in the French Foreign Legion. When France fell, these men were in an unenviable situation since they were considered to have deserted the Fatherland; indeed, there is a reference in DAK communiqués to their being 'made up of Africans released from prison'. They had been given the opportunity of redeeming themselves in the German Army and had been sent to Africa because of their desert experience.

PZ15, one of Rommel's original two divisions, was centred around the two tank battalions of PZR8 Regt, now commanded by Oberst Cramer. Its infantry component was RR115 and its artillery Arty Bat 33. Also under command were Eng Bn 33, and Recce33 (commanded by Oberleutnant Heraucourt).

Finally, Rommel had been given an 'artillery train'. This was a group of artillery regiments entitled Artillery Command 104. Under Major-General Böttcher, its armoury was a powerful mix of 21cm, 150mm and

105mm guns that had been shipped over to assist Rommel in the reduction of the Tobruk Fortress. We were destined to become only too familiar with this noisy train.

Rommel had received more reinforcements than is generally recognised; indeed, the ration strength of DAK rose by 44 per cent between May and November. He also received additions to his own staff: Oberstleutnant Fritz Bayerlein as his COS and Oberstleutnant Siegfried Westphal as Operations Officer. Westphal was to make a significant intervention at a critical moment in the coming battle. Less welcome were Leutnant General Gause and his staff who appeared on the scene at this time. Rommel thought (correctly) that Halder was attempting to impose his authority through the medium of Gause, but the latter was content to serve as liaison with General Bastico, and friction was avoided.[6]

The disposition of Rommel's troops during this period took care of the differing strands of both his short- and long-term strategies. The most important part of the salient was held by units of 90LT replacing RR115. The remainder of the perimeter was held by the three Italian divisions Brescia, Trento and Bologna, reading from west to east, one each of these astride the three main roads leading from the fortress. As noted earlier, the frontier defence line was manned by the Savona Division, stiffened at intervals by other elements of 90LT. The desert flank was covered by the Corpo di Manovra, the motorised Trieste being at Bir Hacheim to the south-west of the fortress and the tank division Ariete at Bir el Gobi, an important desert crossroads to the south-east. Both had supporting artillery. The two panzer divisions were located between Tobruk and the frontier. The Italian Division Pavia was being held in reserve.

Rommel was actively planning his next attack upon the fortress. PZ15 and RR155 were to make the break-in, supported by Böttcher's artillery, while PZ21 held itself ready to repel any interference from the British forces along the frontier. In preparation for this attack the two panzer divisions and RR155 were undergoing intensive and meticulous training in which Rommel again took a central role. The instructions given to 90LT units illustrate the degree of this training:

Divisional Command No 1.

For the preparation of the attack on Tobruk.

The troops after arrival in training camp must be immediately trained for their approaching task: Attack on Tobruk. All preparations for this must be made immediately so that precious time is not lost later. Three weeks are to be allowed for training.

Training Material

(1) Attack :

(a) Approach under our own very heavy fire. Fire protection from a position on flat ground covered only with camel thorn, about 1,000 metres outside the enemy post and after placing our own artillery. A storm of fire from a distance of 200–300 metres over flat ground against a fortified front, consisting of concrete emplacements armed with 1–2 PaK and 2–4 MG, arranged as on the sketch enclosure 1. For plans of the separate installations see the enclosed blueprint 2-4.

(b) Proceed over about 6km open flat country and attack while on the move through a rocky position existing behind continuous barbed wire fence, from a zone about 1 km deep in which nests of MG provided with surrounding fences arranged at an interval of 200–600 metres in dug-outs. In the MG sector there are also a few battery posts. ½ to 1½ km behind that lies an unconnected, apparently unoccupied system of trenches.

And so on. They show that the training was meant to simulate the actual battle ahead, with the use of live ammunition and photographs and replicas of the Tobruk defences. Furthermore, although concentrated it would be thorough, lasting over a period of three weeks. When the attack proper was launched, every man taking part would know his role, there would be no faltering, and no leaving of panzers high and dry without infantry and artillery support. It was a far cry from the over-confident, almost insouciant approach of his other two attacks, but Rommel had learned. He was concentrating his mind on taking the town, with all the intensity of which he was capable.

Not unnaturally, towards the end of his summer Rommel began to consider what the British might be up to. They had been quiescent for the better part of three months, the longest period of silence from them since he had been in Cyrenaica. Why was this? Were they also quietly preparing to attack. That would be very inconvenient in view of his own intentions. There was only one sure way to find out and that was to probe their side of the frontier wire, and there was only one man who could do so to his satisfaction. In September, he decided to go on safari.

Autumnal plotters: Auchinleck

Auchinleck also spent the late summer working on his plans, dispositions and logistics. A new army was created. It was named Eighth Army and it consisted of two corps. These were XIII Corps and XXX Corps. The former had an infantry bias with armoured support, the latter an armoured bias with infantry support. When it came into being at midnight of 26/27 September 1941, the composition of Eighth Army was:

TABLE 5

Eighth Army: *Commander Gen Sir A. Cunningham*

XIII Corps: *Maj-Gen A. Godwin-Austen*	XXX Corps: *Lt-Gen C. Norrie*
4th Indian Div: Maj-Gen F. Messervy	*7th Armd Div: Maj-Gen W. Gott*
5th Inf Bde: Brig D. Russell	4th Armd Bde: Brig A. Gatehouse
Indian 7th Bde: Brig A. Anderson	7th Armd Bde: Brig G. Davey
Indian 11th Bde: Brig R. Briggs	Support Group: Brig J. Campbell
NZ 2nd Division: Maj-Gen Freyberg, VC	*S. African 1st Div Maj-Gen G. Brink*
4th Bde: Brig M. Englis	S. African 1st Bde: Brig D. Pienaar
5th Bde: Brig J. Hargest	S. African 5th Bde: Brig B. Armstrong
6th Bde: Brig H. Barrowclough	22nd Guards Bde: Brig J. Marriott
	Recce Units: 4th/6th S. African Armd
1st Army Tank Bde: Brig H. Watkins	Cars and 11th Hussars and KDGs
Reconnaissance: Central India Horse	
	Oasis Force: Brig D. Reid
	Indian 29th Inf Bde
	S. African 6th Armd Cars.
	NB. 22nd Armd Bde (Scott- Cockburn) would later join XXX Corps.

Eighth Army's Commander was the General who had so recently defeated the Italians in Abyssinia, and he had been chosen presumably on the back of that fine victory. But he was now going to have to wage war over very different terrain, and would be directing his army into vast spaces instead of over the tops of mountains. He would also be commanding a much larger force, whose major striking power would be armoured, an element of whose many idiosyncrasies he knew little, if anything.

On his arrival to take command he discovered that two options had already been prepared for him by the planners. One was an echo of O'Connor's successful cross-country dash to cut off and destroy the Italian Army at Beda Fomm, but this later version saw Eighth Army curving deep into the desert and looping round in Rommel's rear to capture Benghazi. Cut off from his source of supply, Rommel would either be brought to battle or forced to pull back into Bardia, and do his own 'Tobruk' or 'Dunkirk from there. This plan carried two flaws. The first was logistic. The thought of the quantities and detail of supplies needed (and needing to be carried) by the advancing army must have petrified Cunningham's QMG. The second flaw was in the reading of Rommel's character. He was not a man to sit and starve behind fortifications, and Dunkirks were not in his vocabulary. He was certainly a man to take his panzers through the wide open door to the Delta which this plan would have allowed him.

The second plan called for an advance into Cyrenaica to mask the enemy's frontier forces while the British armour was destroying Rommel's armour. Tobruk would then be relieved and the enemy frontier posts would fall like figs into Cunningham's hands. In other words, an enlarged version of 'Battleaxe', but with the emphasis put on the destruction of the Panzergruppe and capture of the enemy's frontier posts a secondary priority. Discussions churned on for weeks, but eventually this was the option chosen, with a few modifications, one of which was the use of Tobruk garrison troops to cut off the panzer divisions by blocking the Duda bottle-neck. This plan too had flaws, some major, some minor, and they began to show almost as soon as Eighth Army crossed the frontier. But for now it is sufficient to give the text of a note written by Auchinleck for transmission to his commanders: '... it is essential to concentrate the strongest possible armoured force ... any subsidiary movement which might require detachment of tanks, other than I tanks, for their local protection against possible attack by enemy armoured units must be foregone in the interests of ensuring the strongest possible concentration of fast armoured units for the decisive battle.' These were words which should have been painted in large letters on the side of every British commander's battle wagon. Unfortunately they weren't.[7]

There was action as well as talk. The larger the force, the more complex its logistic arrangements, and Cunningham's force was three times the size of the one taken into Cyrenaica by O'Connor. The British tried to relieve their problems of supply by extending the railway an extra 80 miles beyond Mersa Matruh to Misheifa. At the same time they put in a water pipe-line which reached a further ten miles west of Misheifa. They also set up a series of supply dumps (soon to become known as Field Maintenance Centres) at Sidi Barrani, Thalata and Jarabub. These were huge depots covering several square miles. As Cunningham's army advanced, the FMCs would be moved forward under the protection of 22nd Guards Brigade.

Autumnal plotters: Willison

The overall Commander of Tobruk was General Ronald Scobie, and he had delegated command of the break-out to Brigadier Willison. Willison and Windsor spent a great deal of time in the underground bunker preparing detailed plans. These were typed on an old Oliver typewriter by the Orderly Sergeant, and since no one expected a German or Italian spy to come creeping in at night the typewritten sheets were there for the night-time wireless operator to read during his quiet hours. Thus one signalman at least was kept aware of what lay ahead for himself and the brigade.

Willison faced difficulties which Rommel was spared. His space for manoeuvre was limited. He could not withdraw men from the Red Line in order to give them large-scale training without putting the line at risk. Most important of all, German aircraft were apt to fly over the fortress at any moment of the day or night so anything that he did was likely to be immediately observed. As a result of these inhibitions, most of the training had to be theoretical. A sand model was made of the sector to be attacked and officers and tank crews who would be making the attacks were required to come to Brigade HQ to study it.

There were two practical essays. One night a full-scale battlefield was taped out as soon as it got dark. At dawn next morning, when it was hoped that the Luftwaffe pilots would still be abed, a practice attack took place. This was the only actual practice made by two of the three units which had been chosen to spearhead the break-out. It could not of course involve that third and most important unit, the artillery. The main lesson to come from the practice was that, given the distance of 5 kilo-metres which had to be crossed to reach the enemy posts, the infantry would have to run to keep up with the tanks. One wonders what Rommel would have made of that discovery.

The other practice effort was concerned with delousing the mine-fields which would certainly be encountered beyond the wire. The KDGs undertook this dangerous task, and six sappers came to live with the squadron for a month. They taught the Dragoons how to lift anti-per-sonnel and anti-tank mines, and how to render them harmless.

This was the extent of Willison's preparation. The contrast with that being made by Rommel is stark, and to say that the training inside the fortress was 'intensive', as Willison did in his account, is to distort the meaning of the word.[8]

The lull before the storm

While all this planning and plotting and swanning around was taking place, the men of Tobruk went about their daily work: watching out from the Red Line; banging away with any gun they had from all corners of the fortress at enemy planes which came visiting; unloading the midnight ships; servicing their tanks; cleaning out their gun-barrels and rifle breeches; patrolling the wire and taking reports from those making the patrols, and of course, burying the dead, because always there were the bombers and they rarely departed without leaving their mark.

We cursed the moon on those late summer nights, we watched it grow from thin apricot slice into full fruit, knowing that the week of its ripening would bring unwanted and unceasing company. Fourth Air Fleet had taken over the night-time bombing and made a psychological weapon of it. A single bomber would cruise around for hours until his fuel was almost gone before dropping his bombs. In the meantime another bomber would have arrived and he would carry on this war of nerves. You lay in your hole and you listened to that unmistakable sound 'vroom'... pause ... 'vroom'. You lay, and were sure that when your tormentor decided to release his bombs they would pick out your tiny hole in all of that vast desert on which to drop them and after the blinding flash there would be no need for any-body to come looking for you. We grew to hate the moon. As we watched the apricot grow into a melon, we hated the moon.

Men got edgy on those nights. We were ordered not to fire at aircraft that came over after dark, and then we were ordered to cease firing on any idiot who was showing a light from his cave. The order wasn't put in quite those terms; it said that we had to 'make a request that the light be put out', then make a report if it wasn't. Offenders who took the law into their own hands by trying to shoot out the light were threatened with court-martial.

There was a night when word of mouth carried the news that 'Win-nie' was going to make a speech, and that the big wireless van, which stood near the ACV and was our link with Cairo, was going to pick it up and amplify it. We gathered in the dark, squatted around the van, a cir-cle of cigarette sparks in the night, the strangest audience the man ever had, and one that was not going to miss a word that was coming from the distant homeland. Then we heard the voice. What cunning use of slurp and gravel and pause and stress. What value he could twist from the most ordinary of words. I remember that he spoke about the massive bombing of German cities which was then taking place. The Germans didn't need to stay under it, they could go out in the fields and watch the home fires burning. There was a roar of laughter at this First World War sally. We cheered. We were witless then of screaming babies and of men not much older than babies who were also screaming in their fast-falling funeral pyres.

Rommel on safari

The operation was given the name '*Sommernachtstraum*' (Midsummer Night's Dream), an apt title in view of its touches of Saturnalia. Two Groups went along, both from PZ21. One led by Schutte took a northern route along the escarpment towards Egypt, the other led by Stephan took a route to the south of Schutte's. Rommel and von Ravenstein accompanied Schutte, Rommel apparently behaving like a schoolboy playing hooky. At about mid-day both columns converged at the spot where Rommel had expected to find the British dump. He had with him a convoy of empty trucks which he had anticipated taking back crammed to their canvas tops. Alas, the cupboard was extremely bare. All they found were some discarded tins of bully beef and a few empty beer bottles.

One of the units with the column captured a truck which turned out to be the Orderly Room of S. African 4th Recce, and which contained two men and a lot of written material. Von Ravenstein worked up a little excitement about this, but it was nothing like enough to satisfy Rommel. He hurried both columns farther into Egypt, but the fun of the day's outing began to drain away with the falling sun. Jock Campbell's Support Group, which was attached to 7th Armd Bde, appeared on the flank of one column and began to pepper it with their 25pdrs. Then lack of fuel halted the panzers and while they were waiting for their fuel trucks to come forward a South African patrol which had arrived on the scene called for an air strike. British planes appeared overhead and the Germans were subjected to a series of bombing and strafing attacks. Casualties began to mount; they included Rommel's driver, and the General himself had a narrow escape when a shard of shrapnel tore the heel from his boot. Seventy casualties had been suffered and 30 vehicles had been destroyed by the time the column got moving again, making this a very expensive safari. To make matters worse, one of the tyres of Rommel's Mammoth went flat, leaving the Commander of the Afrika Korps and his senior officers at the mercy of whoever might pass that way. The foolishness of this escapade and Rommel's insistence on prolonging it placed the entire German investment in Africa in the balance. Poor Schmidt had to struggle alone with the huge tyre while the other officers watched. He managed to get the spare on but it was dawn before they recrossed the wire into Libya and could breathe easily again. Rommel's luck had held once more. Or had it? He had lost so many men and vehicles belonging to PZ21 that he had to postpone the date of his intended attack on Tobruk. Hardly a fair exchange for a few tins of bully-beef.

And what did he gain from the trip?

(i) The knowledge that the frontier zone showed no signs of preparation for an impending attack by the British. The papers which had been found in the captured truck appeared to support this assessment. In fact, they were nothing more than unit replacement orders, but Rommel's Intelligence Unit saw them as clear evidence that the British, far from planning an attack, were preparing to withdraw beyond Mersa Matruh.

(ii) The conviction that he could continue his own planning for the reduction of the Tobruk garrison without having to cover his frontier flank (which is more or less what he had been hoping to find).

Or so we are given to believe. Yet there are accounts which are in conflict with one another concerning how much Rommel knew about Cunningham's preparations. Pitt says that the raid seriously misled Rommel, that he even believed that the Australians in Tobruk were his main enemy, rather than the British in Egypt.[9] Lewin thought that Rommel called off the raid even more convinced that he was right, and that his reluctance to consider a pre-emptive strike by the British was the consequence of myopia.[10] As supporting evidence of this myopia we are told how he threw a set of aerial maps to the ground without even studying them because they showed British preparations to be at a very advanced stage.

Yet there is the strong possibility that Rommel knew every move that Auchinleck and Cunningham were planning. Colonel Fellows, the US Military Attaché in Cairo, was privy to all British intentions and planning, and was regularly transmitting a distillation of these secrets to Washington. He was using a code which had been broken by the Germans, and Rommel was receiving daily copies of this distillation. In other words, it was Ultra in reverse. Hoyt says: 'It was as if Rommel were being briefed every day or two by a British Staff Officer'.[11] He is of the opinion that by the autumn of 1941 Rommel was well aware of whatever the British were planning.

Which opinion is correct? Was Rommel ignorant of the true situation building up on the Egyptian side of the frontier, or was he fully aware of it, and if so, why did he order 'Sommernachtstraum'? Perhaps the answer lies with Major General von Mellenthin, Rommel's Intelligence Officer. Here he is, speaking on 11 November to the Italian Liaison Officer:

'Major Revetria (Italian Head of Intelligence) is much too nervous. Tell him not to worry, because the British won't attack.'[12]

And at a later date he writes: 'Actually, we were very perturbed at the possibility of a British offensive, and Rommel took competent measures to meet it.' He adds that it was because Intelligence reported that a British offensive was likely that Rommel decided not to commit PZ21 to the attack on Tobruk, and ordered PZ15 to be ready to withdraw (from such an attack) at 24 hours' notice to support PZ21 if the need arose. There is nothing myopic about these arrangements.

Von Mellenthin has another important thought to add; it is his estimate of how long it would take a British offensive from the frontier seriously to interfere with a German attack that was taking place against Tobruk. He put this at three days and says, 'In the meantime we hoped to capture the fortress'. In other words, Rommel was well aware of the probability of a British attack and was balancing the future operations of his two panzer divisions accordingly.[13]

These comments, coming from a man so close to Rommel's thinking, suggest that Hoyt is correct, that Rommel was aware of what Auchinleck and Cunningham were up to, but was intent upon capturing Tobruk and was prepared to take any risk in order to do so. If that were the case his safari was a bluff, perhaps to satisfy his critics at OKH. This, together with his deception of his Italian allies, is in keeping with his paranoia about interference with his plans from any source, but especially from those who might hinder them.

The choosing of the day

Rommel was considering the ideal moment to launch his attack, and calculating when the state of the moon would best accord with the completion of his preparation and training. Cunningham was making similar calculations but with an added impetus – a hectoring voice (far from the field of action, of course) was bombarding him with gratuitous advice and exaggerated expectations, telling him that 'For the first time British and Empire troops will meet the Germans with an ample equipment in modern weapons of all kinds. Now is the time to strike the hardest blow yet struck for final victory, home and freedom. The Desert Army may add a page to history which will rank with Blenheim and with Waterloo.'[14] Cunningham perhaps lingered over that word. Any student of military history in his desert army would have remembered with some misgivings that the air over Blenheim and Waterloo became rank with the stench of blood.

And so, like two brides preparing for the most important day of their lives, the two Commanders dithered, chopped, and changed, and then settled. Rommel decided to open his attack on his birthday, 15 November, then changed this to 20 November. Having made his decision, he and von Ravenstein flew to Rome, where they joined their wives for a short holiday. Cunningham chose almost the identical date for his big day, and this was the major difference between metaphor and fact. Neither of these two brides intended being late to church. On the contrary, a race was under way to get there first.

THREE

Things that went 'bump!' in the night

Now that the two opposing forces facing each other across the perimeter wire were making plans to launch major attacks – one outwards, the other inwards, the space between them took on even greater importance. For Rommel it was a question of getting close enough to cut down the approach march for his attack, and of preventing his preparations for this from being monitored by Australian or British patrolling of that space. For the Australians in the first place, and the British when the Australians had departed, it was a matter of keeping the space clear of anything in the way of posts which might be used as launch-pads against the fortress, and of observing enemy activity.

During his last few weeks at Tobruk, Morshead had been concerned to keep Rommel away from the perimeter. Panzers had taken to approaching the wire in the south-eastern section of the perimeter and on three occasions in the nights of early October they had advanced to within 1,000 metres of it. It will be remembered that the Australians had established two or three posts outside the wire in this sector, and that 'Bondi' and 'Plonk' were two of these. It was these posts that the enemy were probing, and Morshead decided that this must be stopped. He ordered Willison into action, and this Brigadier of the Tobruk Tanks needed little urging.

At 1940 hrs on 9 October, Major Gough took A Sqn of 4RTR through the wire. He was under orders to investigate enemy tank movement around the two posts and to drive away any panzers in the locality. The tanks were guided through the minefield and out of the wire by men of 2/17th who were holding that part of the perimeter, and they then set off for 'Plonk'. They had been ordered to switch off their engines when they got there, to listen for the sound of panzer engines, and to attack any panzers they heard. On their way to the post they were met by a few infantrymen who told Gough that they were the only survivors of an enemy attack on 'Bondi'. Gough ordered his tanks to continue their advance on 'Plonk' and then head for 'Bondi' at full speed.

The Matildas, travelling in trident formation as a precaution against mines, had gone about a mile beyond 'Plonk' when Gough reported what he thought were black blobs on his left front. He warned his men to be ready to open fire but not to do so until ordered. The tanks advanced another 40 yards and at that point Gough gave the order to open fire. The whole squadron did so, and the blobs immediately responded in kind. Gough had got off four rounds when his own tank was penetrated by a shell. His gunner was seriously wounded, Gough was blinded, and his driver suffered shell-shock. Fortunately, at this critical point in the little battle, the enemy ceased firing and began to withdraw. Gough recovered sufficiently to be able to take his tanks back to 'Plonk, and they came back through the wire at 0145 hrs.

Two days later, the same squadron was ordered to recapture 'Plonk'. This time they would be accompanied by infantry from 2/17th and would have artillery support (which included smoke) from 1RHA. The infantry arrived late, and the effect of the smoke was lost because of a high wind, but despite these set-backs the squadron got on to 'Plonk' and poured Besa fire into it for about ten minutes. This brought return fire from artillery and from panzers which had appeared on the squadron's front and left flanks. Two panzers were hit and one of these blazed, and the firing from the enemy occupying 'Plonk' ceased. However, the patrol's CO decided that the density of machine-gun and artillery fire being brought to bear was too much for him to risk trying to get the Australians into the posts.

On 12 October Willison issued Order No 4: 'The enemy are in PLONK and also in new sangars at 41454185. Enemy anti-tank gun is at 41134186. 2/17 are manning newly-dug post 500 yds west of PLONK (GOOMA). 4 RTR is to provide protection until further orders. B Sqn will do so during the night of 12/13.' Before this order could come into effect the Australians were driven out of 'Gooma' and B Sqn's orders were modified so that it became a standing patrol in the vicinity of this new post. The squadron moved through the wire at 0015 hrs on 13 October and took stance as ordered. At 0300 hrs Lieutenant Andrews reported the presence nearby of an Italian working party which was making quite a lot of noise. He called out to the party in German, hoping to fool them, but instead, his squadron became the reception centre for a barrage of anti-tank fire. The Italians had been the bait of a trap, and now the Matildas found themselves under fire in a three-sided ambush. Five Matildas were hit, none seriously, and the squadron was able to withdraw from the trap. A cruiser squadron with its thinner armour would have fared much worse.

It was now obvious that Rommel's troops were in strength in this locality and intended to stay there. On 13 October it was reported that 'Tugun' had been captured by the enemy, and that 'Tugun', 'Bondi' and 'Plonk 'were being linked with sangars and wired extensively.

And men that crept quiet in the night

As the Australians withdrew from the Red Line and their places were taken by the British, it fell to the latter to probe this closing-in by the enemy upon the perimeter. They took up the patrolling of their predecessors but with two differences. First, they were not able to penetrate to anything like the distance because of this closing-up, and secondly, their patrols were investigative rather than aggressive. Some idea of the nature of these patrols and of the lessons learned from them is gained from reading extracts from reports. On 6 October Lieutenant Scott had led out a patrol from R13, taking a bearing of 207° for 2,750 yards, then on a bearing of 90° for a further 1,100 yards, before returning to re-enter the wire at R15. He reported: '... no enemy m/g fire until the last 30 yards of the first leg. After 2,700 yards a path was crossed and a tripwire was found immediately after this.

'I went forward with the RE for about 10 yards. I encountered a suspicious scrub branch lying on the ground. After investigating, a three-pronged AP mine was found underneath, about ½in of the prongs being exposed. M/g fire on a bearing of 140° approx yards away at this position. RE saw lines of Teller mines behind the AP mines. It would appear that the field was guarding a strong point and I would assume it to be Pt 166. Enemy movement could be heard from the escarpment and a noise which we thought to be a compressor working ... the minefield appears to be laid about 300 yards from their position.'[15]

On the next night 2nd Leicesters sent out two patrols. Sergeant Munns took eight men through the wire at R61, and Lieutenant Newman took seven out from R67. Munns went forward on a bearing of 157° for 2,400 yards, then on a bearing of 90° for another 600 yards. At the end of his first leg he found himself between two enemy posts that were not connected up with wire, and his patrol went to ground some 30 yards from the posts. Enemy parties were working both inside and outside these. Those working outside were thickening up the wire fence around a post. The patrol saw some vehicles come up and begin to unload wire and wooden pickets. It heard a pneumatic drill and what seemed to be a cement-mixer at work. The party withdrew for 100 yards before setting out on its second leg. Lieutenant Newman's patrol saw three large parties strengthening enemy posts.

After one month in the line the battalion reported that the enemy had systematically encroached all around their sector of the perimeter, and added, 'Why they stayed back so far and let us have OPs so far out before is a mystery.' The departed Australians could be forgiven their chuckles if ever they read that. But change there had been, and it was not by chance. On 8 November the same battalion reported great change in enemy dispositions since they were previously in the sector. 'The enemy has occupied BUTCH and are erecting strong points there, while they are also fortifying the wrecked plane area at 42404208. At BUTCH itself they are within 1,000 yards of our anti-tank ditch while the night before we arrived a patrol of Beds and Herts caught in enemy fixed lines at approx 42344210 lost 8 men. This was ground over which we had wandered freely just over a month ago.'

Men from this battalion made a total of seventeen patrols between posts R71 and R81 during the 13 days from 29 October to 11 November. Unfortunately in early November it was reported that there were no mines in front of enemy post 'Jill'. There may not have been at the time the report was made, but there certainly were when Willison took his brigade against that post some days later.

And a tank that went 'crash!' in the night

I never knew Gale's first name. He was 'Stormy' from the moment he arrived at Bde HQ from 1RTR as a tank driver in answer to a request from Willison, and I suppose I should have remembered that such requests usually allow a unit to off-load. That is not to say that he was not a good driver, rather that he was one of those persons to whom things 'happen' too often for the unit's comfort, and such a person is a dangerous element in the confines of a tank. Stormy came to take part in the second of the tank excursions to 'Plonk'. He was to take a light tank beyond the wire, where it would act as wireless relay between the Matildas and the HQ dug-out. De Winton detailed me to act as operator, and since we would be the only crew, I would also serve as tank commander. The brief was simple. I would take reports from the patrol and transmit them to Willison in the dug-out. This could have been done directly without any difficulty, but this part of the night exercise was in fact a testing for the communications set-up which we would use when we broke out through the wire.

My part in the action was fairly peaceful although time dragged because it was quite lonely out there; we were in the dark and Gale was not allowed to leave his seat and join me in the turret. There was some shelling at the end of the patrol as the Matildas came back and the enemy artillery tried to catch us bunching up to re-enter. We made it without any problems, then the leader of the patrol reached a wadi where he decided to laager for what was left of the night. He gave me the

183

option of staying with his tanks or returning to Solaro. I chose the latter. Off we went on a half-moon night along the El Adem Road until we reached King's Cross, then along the eastern side of the escarpment towards the town. We were driving its bends, the sea encroaching through the dark crevices to our right, a wall of rock to our left. I was head and shoulders out of the turret, dozing, but the wind chill keeping me from dropping off altogether. The bends came and went in a soporific way until the horrific instant when I realised that this next was one bend we weren't going to make. The tank was heading straight for the rim of the road and nothing could stop it from going over. I managed to drop down inside the turret and then everything became a question of grab and cling to, and over and over, and crash and smash. One of the crashes was against the back of my head; it was the battery coming loose and being tossed about as though weightless.

When I came to a few seconds later I found myself upside down inside a tank which was also upside down, and so far as I knew, scant inches from the sea. I groped around, trying to orientate myself. I was quite stupid after the thwack on the head. Then I heard a shout: 'Harrison, where the bloody hell are you?' 'Here,' I answered.

I was fumbling around. I found that one half of the turret lid had snapped to and would have beheaded me if I hadn't managed to drop inside. There was enough space to get my head and shoulders through but there I stuck. All this time Gale was shouting advice at me. Now he asked, 'Have you got your coat on?' Of course I had, wasn't it night and hadn't I been half out of the turret? Of course I had. Now I wriggled free of it and tried again. This time I managed to get out. We stood together and stared at the tank. We were both thinking about the retribution which would fall on our heads next morning. 'What happened?' I asked, then answered myself, 'You went to sleep, didn't you?' 'Me ... go to sleep ... did I heck as like.' Then, in a flash of inspiration, he said: 'I got reverse steering.'

Reverse steering. One track idling on a bend while the other whirled, the discrepancy throwing the steering into reverse. Was that it? Who was I to argue? The tank I had been in command of lay upside down at the foot of a cliff and I was faced with an unpleasant trudge back to camp where I would be faced with an even more unpleasant Tank Corps

Sergeant-Major. 'Reverse steering,' I would tell him, with all the authority of someone who knew what that meant. I practised the words as we set off on the long trudge to our holes. We had covered a couple of miles and were approaching the town when the bombers came over. Stormy would go no further. We were crossing a small culvert at the time and he elected to crawl into this and resume his disturbed sleep. I thought of spiders on my face and decided to carry on. I walked through the raid and it was a big one. Was that evidence of my courage, or of the superior strength of a tank battery over the human skull, or was my mind too full of the impending interview? Who knows?

I reached the fork in the road where one branch turns towards the town and the other towards distant Pilastrino. I took the latter. That walk was an eerie experience, parachute flares falling like a monster display of the northern lights; transforming the land beneath into a pink moonscape; all to an orchestra whose instruments vied in dissonance – the crashing cymbals of the 3.7in guns, the quicker beat of the Bofors, the ratt-a-tatting of the Bredas. I was walking through the world's greatest ever disco.

I went directly to the Sergeant-Major's hole. 'Sir!' I called out. 'What do you want?' asked a deep-down voice. 'It's me, Sir. Harrison. I've lost my tank.' 'What do you mean, lost your tank? You can't lose a tank.' 'Over a cliff, Sir.' 'Where's Gale? Is he dead?' 'No, Sir. He's under a bridge.' 'What's he doing under a bridge?' 'Kipping.' There was some muttering to himself which sounded like cursing and I said, 'We got reverse steering.' I heard him growl 'Reverse steering my arse. Don't you know there's a raid on?' 'Yes, Sir, I've just walked through it.' 'Then you're a bloody idiot. Get away from my hole!'

And parachutists who didn't arrive in the night

On 13 November the first ship to arrive in the harbour for almost three weeks came alongside bringing Lieutenant Alcock and the rest of de Winton's Yeomanry squadron. The poor lads scarcely had time to get a mouthful of Tobruk's dust before they found themselves standing to all night with the prospect of having to repel paratroops. On the 15th Scobie was warned that an attack on the fortress by land, sea and air was imminent. It will be remembered that this was the date originally chosen by Rommel for his attack before the change to the 20th of the month. Given the hindsight of Ultra, it would appear that this was the source of the stand-to warning. The first date had been picked up by interception, hence the word 'imminent'. As for the paratroop element, 90LT had not yet taken on that name and part of it was travelling under the title '*Sonderverband*' which means 'Special Detachment'. Someone at Bletchley Park must have put two and two together and made five.

The entire garrison was put on Red Alert. The RAF ground crew at El Gubbi stood to at their Lewis guns from dusk to dawn ready to protect that airfield. All units of 32ATB received verbal warning in the early afternoon, and at 1850 hrs Brigade-Major Windsor issued the following written orders under an 'immediate' designation: 'Information has been received that there is an impending attack on Tobruch [*sic*] by paratroopers and from the sea in rubber boats. Especial vigilance will be maintained. All units of 32 Army Tk Bd 'STAND TO'. One Bty 1 RHA is in action about 412429 and is protected by infantry from Bn SIDI MAHMOUD. The Bty will engage seaborne landings EAST of harbour. One Bty 1 RHA is in action area NORTH of ARIENTE rd junc. and is protected by inf from Bn ARIENTE. This Bty will engage seaborne landings WEST of harbour. O.P.s and coast watching parties patrol the sea coast. 7 R Tanks and Tps KDG will engage any enemy landing in the area of the DERNA Road Landing Ground [the former Lysander airfield] and Plain in particular protecting the H.Q.s of Bns holding the Western perimeter and Western Brigade HQ WADI EL GHESSIMA. They will make every endeavour to engage the enemy before landing from the sea. Tps KDG on GUBBI AERODROMES will remain in those areas engaging enemy where found. 1 R Tanks will detail Sqns to protect HQs and tps in area EAST of road TOBRUK–EL ADEM and the area FT ARIENTE–Tobruch. Sqn Cruiser tanks will remain present locality and form Bde Reserve in case of attack on perimeter. All enemy will be DESTROYED when and where found and tanks will engage enemy by troops or singly. Control may be decentralised by Commanders when necessary. ACK.'

The presentation of the order suggests the hurry in which it was produced, but its instructions are fairly comprehensive. Within thirty minutes 1RTR was dispersing to its ordered positions:

A Sqn to the area east of the Tobruk–El Adem–Bardia Road fork

B Sqn to the area west of this to the line from Fort Ariente and
Pilastrino

C Sqn remaining in its normal laager position with a probable task
inside the town.

No enemy arrived that night either by sea or from the air. Next morning
O'Carroll, CO 4RTR, issued more detailed orders to his regiment which
suggested much burning of midnight oil. They are worthy of consideration because in addition to demonstrating the determination to root out
any enemy who might be so foolish as to drop into the regiment's zone,
they also show O'Carroll's tactical awareness of how to meet all aspects
of such an attack.

(2) INTENTION

It is the intention to defend Tobruk at all costs

(3) METHOD

(a) 4 R Tanks will remain in their present localities

They will be in Brigade Reserve

They will stand to until further notice

A Sqn will be prepared to operate in the area between the Road inc
FT PILASTRINO RAS EL MEDUUAR and the road excl TOBRUK
–EL ADEM

C Sqn will be prepared to operate in the area incl the Rd TOBRUK–
EL ADEM East to the coast

B Sqn will remain in Bn Reserve

(b) SPECIAL ARRANGEMENTS AGAINST PARACHUTE
TROOPS.

Each Sqn will organise their lorry drivers and fitters and clerks into
fighting patrols armed with Thompson submachine-guns and
rifles and pistols where allotted. Each light tank of the Sqns will
be prepared to hunt down and destroy parachute troops. The
fighting patrols will move on foot and operate from behind the
cover of old lorries, etc., seeking out and destroying the enemy
as he lands, and before, if possible.

B & C Sqns will be responsible for the hunting down and destruction of all parachute troops landing, or attempting to land in the

area of their present locations. They will co-ordinate their
arrangements, mutually.

A Sqn will send their fighting patrols on to the top of the escarpment South of their present location, and will occupy the walls in
the vicinity of the O.P. at Pt 144 (Sq 409429) and engage parachute troops attempting to land in that area. The Sqn light tank
will operate in that area also.

BHQ Sqn. All lorry drivers and the L.A.D. will be organised into a
fighting patrol under the command of Capt Stuart. They will be
prepared to operate on the plain to the Westward of their present location, co-ordinating their plans with B Sqn.

All BHQ Fitters and Sigs will form a fighting patrol under the command of the RSM. This patrol will be in B Reserve.

Three HQ light tanks will be dispensed as under 2 under command
to Captain Stuart for operating on the plain on which he is
located. 1 under command to O.C. A Sqn for operating on the
plain above his present location.

In addition two Dingos will be under Command to Captain Stuart to
operate with his light tanks.

ACTION DURING AERIAL BOMBARDMENT

During any heavy air bombardment, Troops will remain under
cover, but emerge at once on the bombardment lightening or
easing. It is then that the airborne troops will attempt to land.
They will be sought out, engaged and destroyed, no time being
given for them to take cover or organise themselves.

They will be engaged in the air before they descend.

The enemy may be wearing British uniform or a uniform similar to
it. Anyone not wearing the British Distinguishing mark, will be
arrested once the airborne invasion of TOBRUK has commenced.

ADMINISTRATION

Meals – At normal times, look-outs will be provided during meal
times.

Medical – RAP in present location. The MO will arrange for one
ambulance to be ready to move forward to collect wounded.

NB. The reference to a 'distinguishing mark' is a mystery.

FOUR

Break-in: Rommel's plan

The coincidence of the two Field Commanders both choosing almost the same day for launching their opposing attacks has already been mentioned. What is even stranger is, that while the defenders intended to make the break-out on the south-east corner of the perimeter, they had chosen almost the identical location selected by Rommel for his break-in attack. A map exists which shows the attack on the fortress, proposed for November. It was drawn by Rommel using differently coloured pencils,

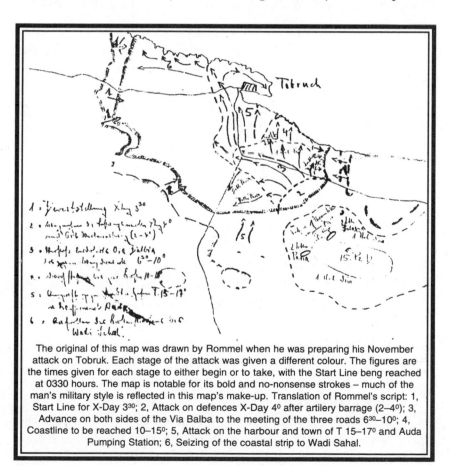

The original of this map was drawn by Rommel when he was preparing his November attack on Tobruk. Each stage of the attack was given a different colour. The figures are the times given for each stage to either begin or to take, with the Start Line beng reached at 0330 hours. The map is notable for its bold and no-nonsense strokes – much of the man's military style is reflected in this map's make-up. Translation of Rommel's script: 1, Start Line for X-Day 3³⁰; 2, Attack on defences X-Day 4⁰ after artilery barrage (2–4⁰); 3, Advance on both sides of the Via Balba to the meeting of the three roads 6³⁰–10⁰; 4, Coastline to be reached 10–15⁰; 5, Attack on the harbour and town of T 15–17⁰ and Auda Pumping Station; 6, Seizing of the coastal strip to Wadi Sahal.

and is simple and direct. The attack was to be against the south-eastern side of the perimeter. PZ15 supported by infantry and guns would smash through the perimeter defences at 0200 hrs under cover of an artillery barrage, and would advance along both sides of the Bardia Road as far as King's Cross. The strike force would divide there, one arm heading for the town, the other for Solaro, and the British HQ. When these had been taken, the coastal strip beyond the town would be seized.

Rommel had moved crack troops into the posts on that side of the perimeter, and it would be they who would make the attack. He had taken great care to keep the movement of these troops secret as his orders issued on 7 November show:

PREPARATION FOR THE ATTACK ON TOBRUK.

The following arrangements have been made for the attack on Tobruk.

(1a) Com zbV Afrika must in the night of 10/11 November with the co-operation of Bologna Div replace the garrisons of support bases 2, 18, 19, and 20 in the section of Bologna Div with parts of the assault troops, to the strength of one battalion.

(b) In the course of the exchange the heights of Magen Suesi must be occupied and prepared for defence.

(c) Parts of P1900 dug-in in the region of Ht 19 and to the south must be replaced by zbV Afrika.

(d) To camouflage the replacement, Italian forces to the strength of a company to be left by Bologna in the support posts. It is important that during daylight, German soldiers show themselves as little as possible.

(e) The take-over of the whole section by Com zbV Afrika must follow in the night of 20/21 November up to 0300 and must be reported to DAK.

(11d) Absolutely no impression of preparation for attack must be given to the enemy by the garrisons of the B posts and the positioning of the artillery. Movement on, from, and to the B posts and gun emplacements by day is absolutely forbidden. The soldiers must wear Italian helmets which will be lent by Bologna Div.

These orders move 90LT (then still zbV Afrika) into the posts from which the attack was to be made. Elements of Bologna Div were to remain as camouflage, but the bulk of that division was to be withdrawn. Thus, instead of launching themselves at Italian infantry as forecast in the break-out orders, the Tobruk force (TOBFORCE) would be charging out against Sümmermann's 90LT, these last in heavily defended posts, which was a vastly different proposition.

Break-Out: Scobie and Willison's plan

Major-General Scobie had designed a five-point plan which would carry the break-out forces through the enemy encirclement and on to Ed Duda, where they would meet with S. African 1st Div, who were coming up from the frontier.

> Phase I was to see the capture of 'Butch'
> Phase II was to see the capture of 'Tiger'

Phase III was to be a sweep by 1RTR around the enemy's rear

Phase IV was to be the capture of 'Jack'

Phase V was to be the capture of the El Duda ridge and link-up with the South Africans.

And Rommel was not the only one who was preparing a surprise. For the first time in the desert campaigns the British 3.7in guns were going

BREAK-OUT: THE AXIS OF ATTACK BY TOBFORCE

The intended axis of attack to be taken by TOB-FORCE during its breakout from the Tobruk perimeter. Confusion arose because of the mislaying of a start line and the obscuring of reference points by the smoke and dust of battle. This caused elements of 4 RTR and B Coy Black Watch to veer to their left and attack JACK during Phase II instead of Phase IV as scheduled.

to be used as field guns in support of these actions. Three were moved from their sites protecting the harbour and dug- in in the Pilastrino area. They were given four tasks:

(1) To afford AA protection to the field and medium artillery positions in the east and centre sections of the corridor (once this had been made).

(2) To provide harassing fire on El Adem airfield, thus denying the enemy unlimited freedom to land troops or supplies there.

(3) To carry out c/battery and harassing tasks as requested by the CRA.

(4) To engage such Fleeting Opportunity targets as seemed worthwhile and provident.

At all times anti-aircraft targets were to have priority.

By this time there was a counter-battery team functioning in the fortress. It was directed by Lieutenant Scrimgeour, who had drawn up a system which allowed daily detailing of the location of enemy guns. It, too, would play its part in the break-out by doing just that.

They waited, the men of zbV Afrika, wearing their borrowed hats in 'Butch' and 'Jack' and 'Jill', for the word which would send them through the perimeter wire into the fortress; and the men on the opposite side of the perimeter wire waited too, listening for the word which would send them out of the fortress and against 'Butch' and 'Jack' and 'Jill'. A word that would not be uttered until the South Africans were approaching El Duda on the escarpment to the south-east of the fortress.

FIVE

Break-Out D-3: on the Eighth Army front

Cunningham won the race. In the watery dawn of 18 November, Eighth Army began to pass through Mussolini's wire. It had been moving forward for two days, streams of vehicles of every shape, size and degree of aggressiveness. These came together to form rivers and eventually a flood which surged against the gaps in the dam and burst through them into the flat and inviting emptiness beyond. The metaphor is apt, the advance taking place during the most torrential storm in Libya's memory. Rommel's forward air bases became bogs and closed the eyes which should have been reporting this advance. This rain, together with the icy cold it carried, was to become the hall-mark of the battle ahead, replacing dust as its elemental accompaniment.

Fourteen brigades of fighting men passed through the wire, led by 11th Hussars, the symbolic heroes of British history, who took 22nd Armd Bde through, and followed by a S. African Recce Bat, who took 7th Armd Bde through. Then came the KDGs (less our Squadron) who took 4th Armd Bde through. Behind these armoured regiments were the New Zealander and South African and Indian divisions, military representatives of the greatest empire the world has known. The largest army that Cyrenaica had seen or would ever see rolled and bounced and clanged forward, and when Rommel was told about it, he refused to accept the advance as anything other than a reconnaissance in force. At least, that is the lore.

There is something awesome about being carried along on a human tide, The heart is stirred, the spirit is uplifted, both swell with an optimism which is contagious, so that it too becomes a tide and as unstoppable as the humans who carry it. Eighth Army was high on optimism. It shrugged off the cold of dawn and its cursing of the terrain was cheerful. It was an invading army, on the hunt in enemy territory, the taste of victory on its tongue before the quarry had even been sighted. And yet ...

The flaws in Cunningham's plan

Kippenberger, who was to become a major-general, subsequently wrote: The whole Eighth Army, Seventh Armoured Division, First South African Division, The Second New Zealand and Fourth Indian Divisions moved westward in an enormous column, the armour leading. The Army moved south of Sidi Barrani, past the desolate Italian camps of the previous year, along the plateau south of the great escarpment, through the frontier wire into Libya, south of the enemy garrisons in the Sidi Omars and wheeled north. Then, just as we were rejoicing in the conception of a massive move on Tobruk, disregarding the immobile frontier garrisons and crushing everything in our path, the whole Army broke up and departed different ways.'[16]

For that was Cunningham's plan. Thirty Corps rolled on massively to its appointed stance in the area of Gabr Saleh, where it would await Rommel's armour, which would be forced to react, and be destroyed when it did so. Thirteen Corps wheeled to face north-east and put itself into position to reduce the frontier posts. Fourth Armd Bde took stance between the two where it could protect XIII Corps' desert flank while still remaining part of XXX Corps. Here was the first, and major flaw in the strategic plan; the two corps had been separated both geographically and in function. The risk of compartmentalised and widely dispersed actions which had cursed 'Battleaxe' had been built yet again into 'Crusader'.

The second flaw was in the selection of Gabr Saleh as the site where the British armour would await Rommel's reaction, which must certainly be to bring his own armour into battle there. Criticism has been voiced that if the huge force had carried out this 'wait and see' part of Cunningham's plan it would have thrown away any advantage gained by its surprise advance. This need not have been so, had a better choice of site been made. There was no reason why Rommel should rush to Gabr Saleh. His frontier posts were prepared to hold out for three weeks. The one site whose occupation would have compelled him to intervene quickly would have been the bottle-neck of the Sidi Rezegh–Belhamed–El Duda triangle, and especially the escarpments which came together there to dominate the Trigh Capuzzo and the new Axis bypass. There were three of these: the first was the northern escarpment, and at the western end of this were two features which would become crucial in the battles ahead. They were Belhamed, on the northern edge of which was the hill Bir Belhamed, and El Duda, a ridge about seventeen miles from Tobruk town. The second, sometimes referred to as the Sidi Rezegh escarpment, overlooked a desert airfield and also the Trigh Capuzzo which ran through the plain below. On this ridge and to the east was Pt 175. The third was the southern escarpment, and Pt 178 was on this escarpment, in a north–south line with Belhamed. If these escarpments had been seized on the first day and held in strength in concert with TOBFORCE, all Rommel's troops to the east of that bottle-neck would have been in jeopardy. However, this is all by the way. Although Gabr Saleh had been pre-selected as the site where the armour would concentrate, this plan was almost immediately dropped.

The third flaw was in the role given to 4th Armd Bde. This role had resulted from pressure exerted by the infantry divisions at the planning stage. Apparently they were nervous about going into the desert against Rommel without having tanks under direct command. True they had the Matildas of 1st ATB, but apparently these were not sufficient. Cunningham gave way. The cruiser brigade which should have been acting in concert with its two sister brigades against Rommel's armour was detached from them and anchored in space. As a consequence it was of no real use to either corps but was itself dangerously exposed.

The fourth flaw was in the composition of Cunningham's armoured force. This consisted of 210 Crusaders (the unreliable tank), 90 older cruisers and 173 Stuarts. Superior in number to the Panzergruppe and faster, it was on the other hand inferior in both fire-power and armour, the panzers having recently had front and side protection added. It was therefore essential that this tank force have a strong anti-tank artillery component as an integral part, as did the panzers.

A comparison of the opposing artillery strengths shows that the British armoured corps was superior in the number of guns and it could be expected that this superiority would be used in concentration alongside the tanks.[17]

DAK (only): 40 field guns (105mm) and 20 medium guns (150mm)

    63 anti-tank guns (50mm)

    21 anti-tank guns (37mm)

    12 x 88mm guns

XXX Corps (only) 132 field guns (all 25pdrs)

    16 medium guns (calibre not known)

    168 anti-tank guns (2pdrs)

    28 anti-tank guns (18pdrs)

However, the German 50mm gun was to prove almost as deadly against British tanks as the 88mm. Moreover, Rommel had twelve of the latter which could be towed into action by tractors alongside the panzers. To counter the effect of these powerful anti-tank guns it was essential that the British artillery (and machine- guns) be in close support of the tanks. This did not happen. The artillery continued in its semi-autonomous state, the tank brigades in theirs. The armoured battle was expected to be won by superior numbers of inferior tanks, but the anchoring of 4th Armd Bde in space would take away even that spurious advantage.

And the destruction of that plan by Cunningham and his commanders
Already though, on this first evening of arrival in the battle zone, Cunningham's plan, flaws and all, was being tossed into the dustbin of history. If Cunningham and his corps commanders had intended keeping to it, there should at the very least have been some preparation for receiving the enemy attack at Gabr Saleh. There was none. Instead, the question which seems to have remained unasked by any of these men during all their planning, 'What if Rommel's armour doesn't come to Gabr Saleh?' suddenly began to nag them. When it didn't immediately arrive on the scene they appear to have become obsessed with a need to retain the initiative. Gott began the rot. His recce units had reported Ariete on his desert flank at El Gobi. He ordered 22nd Armd Bde to clear them out in the morning, and to occupy that locality themselves. The remainder of his armour would meet (and presumably defeat) the German armour somewhere to the north-west of Gabr Saleh. Gott was guilty on two counts here. He was ignoring Auchinleck's diktat of 30 October concerning dispersal of tank commands, and he was sending an untested brigade against an armoured division holding a fortified position. His optimism for the brigade was vying with his contempt for that enemy division. The stricture on contempt for one's enemy applies no less to British generals than to their German equivalent.

Finally, the General himself killed off his own plan. The man who should have been insisting upon concentration, that evening confirmed the order to 22nd Armd Bde to occupy El Gobi on the following morning, supported by S. African 1st Div. He then ordered 7th Armd Bde and the Support Group to occupy the Sidi Rezegh escarpment. Thus, the three tank brigades which had come in concert to destroy Rommel's armour at one spot were now to be the corner points of a triangle whose legs were getting on for thirty miles in length. The corps could not have been better dispersed had that been Cunningham's original intention.

It would appear that both strategy and tactics had changed during that day. Cunningham's new orders placed emphasis on 'the relief', which can only have meant relief of Tobruk. This had suddenly become priority number one, while destruction of Rommel's armour seems to have taken a back seat. The ease with which a closely argued and finally agreed geographical stance, together with a policy of priority in the destruction of Rommel's armour, were both abandoned, did not augur well for confidence in future decisions, tactical or strategic. Indeed, it argued that the momentum of the advance (and perhaps the mesmerising effects of that great space in which they now found themselves) had affected the Commanders to such an extent that henceforth decisions would be 'off the cuff', would more often than not be reactions to enemy initiatives, and would arise from localised situations, conditions and personalities. In the battles to come there was to be no sense of centralised control, nor could there have been given such chopping and changing of plan by a Commander who was for most of the time at Fort Maddalena, 80 miles from the nearest action.

SIX

Break-Out D-2: on the Eighth Army front

By the afternoon of 19 November all three of the dispersed brigades were in some sort of action.

Scott-Cockburn's 22nd Armd Bde consisted of Yeomanry regiments and, as Lewin says, when thinking of their military behaviour, it is the line of a Keith Douglas poem that comes to mind: 'It is not gunfire I hear but a hunting horn.' The Yeomanry heard the horn at El Gobi, attacked, and knocked out more than thirty Italian M13 tanks, then chased the fleeing foxes – straight on to the waiting minefield and enemy guns. They had no supporting infantry or guns and by the time they managed to get out of the trap, had lost half their tanks. The battles of 'Brevity' and 'Battleaxe' might never have been fought. Davey's 7th Armd Bde took the airfield at Sidi Rezegh but not the escarpment which dominated it, the lack of infantry support again being a contributory factor in this lack of total success. As for 4th Armd Bde, in a touch of irony it would have taken a military Socrates to devise, half of Afrika Korps was on its way to where the whole of XXX Corps should have been entrenched and waiting to destroy it, but where it would find 8th Hussar's single regiment of tanks. The armoured cars of Recce3 had shown themselves on Gatehouse's northern front and, unable to resist the temptation, he had sent his other two tank battalions in a chase after them. Thus the British armour which was to have been concentrated at Gabr Saleh was now scattered all over the desert.

'We must not lose our nerve'

So spoke Rommel to Crüwell on the first night of 'Crusader'. Next morning he released a Battle Group to the DAK Commander. It consisted of 200 panzers, the large majority of which were Mk IIIs and Mk IVs, and its artillery component included four 88mm guns. Led by Oberst Stephan, this powerful group came upon 8th Hussars in the afternoon, and the outnumbered Hussars charged into the enemy ranks without hesitation. A confused battle was fought in clouds of dust, and only ceased when darkness fell on dust and tanks. The Germans remained on the battlefield while the Hussars withdrew into a night laager, convinced that they had given as good as they had taken. If victory there was, it is usually credited to Stephan, though the question why, with such an vast superiority of armour he did not annihilate the Hussars, is never asked.

All in all, then, this second day of 'Crusader' was a poor one for the reputations of the commanders on either side. The only ones to emerge from it with any sort of credit were Davey, who had at least occupied the Sidi Rezegh airfield and destroyed some planes there (a limited success), and Gambara, whose corps had repulsed 22nd Armd Bde. But if the British commanders had been less than intelligent in the arrangements they made, their men had been more than brave in the way they had carried them out. They had fought well, if foolishly, at El Gobi. They had shown great dash at Sidi Rezegh. They had fought head-to-head with Stephan's panzers. They had chased off the huge armoured cars of Rommel's reconnaissance battalions. Herein lay the seeds of future nettles. Not unnaturally, given the confusion of desert battles, they thought they had inflicted much more damage on the enemy than was the case. They so reported to their commanders, and these so reported upwards. A day in which the western desert was pock-marked with actions was followed by a night that was peppered with optimistic analysis, out of which Sidi Rezegh emerged as the new logical location on which to concentrate. Cunningham ordered the Support Group to get on to the escarpment next morning, accompanied by 22nd Armd Bde and S. African 5th Bde.

It had been a long, full and hard day, and the troopers, the gunners and the infantrymen of these units rolled themselves into their blankets and tried to create enough warmth on another bitter night to get to sleep. But while they beavered down in search of that warmth, Sümmermann's men were also beavering away – getting on to that escarpment, setting up machine-gun posts there, dragging heavy guns to where they would do most damage to anyone or anything on the airfield below. And Rommel was ordering Crüwell to take the whole of DAK in search of the British armour on the morrow and to destroy it. For many of the men in those blankets their next sleep would be even colder.

Break-Out D-2: on the Tobruk front

Inside the fortress 19 November had been a long day for the men who were under orders to make the break-out, but it was the emptiness of their day which made it seem so interminable. Men waited all over the fortress for the single word which would set them on the march to the start-line. At 32nd ATB HQ the seaweed was taken down from the ACV and she was dieseled up and ready to roll for the first time in almost nine months. We were a little fearful – not of going out there, but at the thought that we might not. The last time we had seen a British Army it had been streaming backwards in disorder, or clambering on to the *Balmora* to get away even quicker. Twice since then one had been on its way to relieve us but had failed to arrive. Why should this time be any different? That was the 'down' position of the rationalisation see-saw; the 'up' position had us sitting waiting while Eighth Army did it all by themselves. Would we be the bridesmaid at this desert wedding? That was a thought almost too awful to bear.

I was at one of the sets in the ACV. The other set was tuned into 70th Div HQ, from whom the all-important word would come. A wireless silence was in force throughout the garrison and I was able to indulge myself with a little searching of the waves. Suddenly I heard an English voice, it was so clear, and yet it could only be coming from somewhere out there. I listened.

'How many can you see?' the voice asked.

'About fifteen, I think.'

'That's two each. Good!'

I knew at once that the voices belonged to tank men, and that they were not a million miles away. I looked at Willison; all I needed to say was 'Sir!' and he would immediately reach for his headphones. I knew that he would have loved to listen to the next few minutes of that conversation. But de Winton was only feet away, he would know that I had left the net and that was not permissible. Reluctantly I let the knob click back on the net. Later, when the news of the actions of that day trickled back to us, I took it for granted that I had been listening to 7th Armd Bde's tank crews as they arrived on Sidi Rezegh airfield. Now I am not so sure. 'That's two each. Good!' sounds much more like a Yeomanry reaction than one from regular tank men. Had I been listening to the men of 22nd Armd Bde about to begin their charge at El Gobi? I have often wondered if either of those optimistic gentlemen survived the next hour.

Yes, 19 November was the longest day of the siege for us, but the sun did eventually fall from grace and we too sought warmth but not in our hole. There was no singing that night, no flipping of cards. We kipped down alongside the ACV ready to react to a midnight word. I was not to know that I had seen my tiled floor for the very last time.

Break-Out D-1: on the Eighth Army front

On the morning of 20 November Crüwell set out in search of XXX Corps. He had word from Recce3 that they had been attacked by tanks near Sidi Azeiz the previous afternoon and must have remembered that on both the previous advances the British armour had made a hook movement which took them into this area. He decided to use his two panzer divisions as hammer and anvil on which to destroy his opponents. PZ15 was sent along the Trigh Capuzzo to attack from the north, and the three elements of PZ21 (Stephan Group, Knabe's infantry and the remainder under von Ravenstein) were ordered to concentrate at Gabr Lachem. They were to cut the British armour's escape route and attack from the south. Stephan now had to cross in front of 4th Armd Bde and while his panzers were doing this they had a brush with the British tanks. Stephan stuck to his orders, refused to become entangled in combat and continued his march. This gave 4th Armd Bde the quite false impression that they had inflicted such a trouncing on this formation during the previous evening's battle that the Germans were now running away.

When the various parts of PZ21 met up and reported no trace of British armour at Sidi Azeiz, Crüwell faced a dilemma. He realised that the British force holding Sidi Rezegh airfield represented Cunningham's main thrust, and that there was nothing hostile in the Gabr Saleh region apart from the armour with which Stephan had clashed on the previous evening. He decided that he should get back to Sidi Rezegh as quickly as he could, but first dispose of this element of Cunningham's dispersed armour. But Stephan's panzers had run out of fuel and there was no prospect of a supply before that evening. Crüwell ordered them to get back to Sidi Rezegh as soon as they were able, then sent PZ15 to deal with the British armour at Gabr Saleh. These orders were intercepted, and Cunningham ordered 22nd Armd Bde to leave the El Gobi area and go to the aid of its seriously threatened sister brigade. The result of these moves by both sides was that the German Command had also dispersed its armour and that yet again the British were unable to take advantage of this because of its own dispersed state.

If the two German panzer divisions had been able to combine against 4th Armd Bde the latter would have been in a parlous position; so too might have been 22nd Armd Bde, had it arrived at the tail-end of 4th Armd Brigade's demise. As it was, Neumann-Silkow found the British tanks in hull-down position; a battle developed in which they fought well, and they were only slowly driven from the field. Just before dark 22nd Armd Bde arrived on the scene. The battle petered out and the British followed their usual custom of going into laager, thus ceding the battle-field and its knocked-out tanks, British and German, to the enemy, who promptly set about recovering both.

Meanwhile, on the Sidi Rezegh front, Sümmermann's Afrika Regt 361 had made a dawn counter-attack against the airfield. This had been repulsed, as had a follow-up attack at 0800 hrs. The remainder of the day had seen the airfield being subjected to heavy artillery fire from Böttcher's guns on Belhamed.

'Pop!'

At midday, the British Command was making decisions based on wildly misplaced optimism. The Commanders of the two corps had been told that German panzers had run away from battle at Gabr Saleh that morning. Those armoured units which had engaged the enemy reported that they had given as good, or better, than they had taken. The troops engaged on the airfield had driven off two attacks and concentration was now taking place there. Royal Air Force reports were telling of a stream of enemy vehicles heading westwards as though a general retreat were under way. Everything seemed to point to a victory in the making, so that now seemed the time to bring out TOBFORCE and to block that bottleneck.

That afternoon we heard the word 'Pop!'

SEVEN

Break-Out Day on the TOBFORCE front

If the approach march of the Eighth Army had been something of an organisational triumph, the movement of TOBFORCE to its start-lines was no less so, if on a much reduced scale. It began immediately after dark on the night of 20 November, and during the next few hours 159 armoured fighting vehicles, an infantry brigade, the guns of one and a half artillery regiments and hundreds of trucks moved into the sector behind a line running from R60 to R80, many of them arriving via the Bardia Road and climbing through the gully on to the escarpment. The soft vehicles came first; Captain George Hope's B Echelon, carrying fuel, ammunition and food, had been assembled and marshalled and brought up early so that they would not gum up the approach of the fighting vehicles. Then came the hard vehicles of A Echelon, the tanks and armoured cars, steel segments of a long, twisting and venomous snake: O'Carroll and Holden's Matildas; Brown's cruisers; Lindsay's armoured cars with George Maers of the purple feet riding with Lindsay. The infantry came up that road too, but soon left it and made their own way across country.

As the columns advanced towards the forward defence line they came to their first hazard, our own minefields. Eight routes had been cleared through these by Royal Engineers working under directions from Lieutenant-Colonel Duchesyne, RE. The gaps were 36 yards wide and were marked by candle-light in the fashion of an aircraft runway, but with the candles sheltered inside tin cans so that they could not be seen from the air. The vehicles crept along these channels and out to designated areas, each unit reporting its arrival to Brigade Major Windsor, each getting its name ticked off the list, like little boys getting on to the coach at the beginning of a school trip.

Gradually the attacking force built up. The three infantry battalions which had drawn the short straws came into the forward line led by Brigadier H. Chappel. By 2300 hrs all companies of 2nd Black Watch were in place, with their commander, Lieutenant-Colonel Rusk at R66A. At 2345 hrs 2nd King's Own arrived in the rear of R66 where all compa-

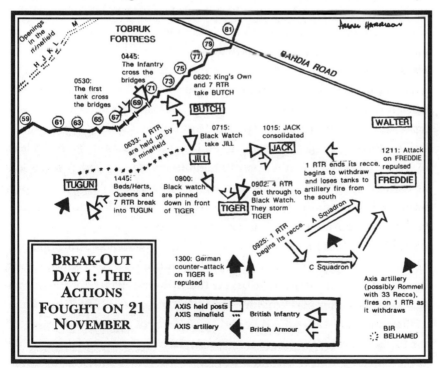

nies were visited by Major H. Creedon, Acting CO. This wise man sent his men to their ground-sheets with a rum ration inside them. Lieutenant-Colonel Gilroy brought in 2nd York and Lancs and the brigade was then complete and under overall command of Brigadier Willison. Groups of silent and unseen congregations, whose members had left their homes and travelled thousands of miles, and had undergone scores of hours of training for this moment, faced it as best they could. Perhaps some said prayers they hadn't spoken since childhood or since they last earned free cake and tea at a Salvation Army hut. Perhaps the scholars among them thought on the imagined words of another man from the distant islands from which they had come, spoken on a foreign field before such a dawn as the next might be:

He that outlives this day and comes safe home,

Will stand a tip-toe when this day is nam'd'.

There would be many who would not have that opportunity.

All the time while they had been arriving, other men were working in the ditch. Another section of Duchesyne's Engineers had gone out to this as soon as darkness fell, their task being to erect the four bridges across which the tanks and vehicles would cross. One pair of bridges was set in front of R67, the other pair in front of R69. At 1900 hrs Captain Godberg had led out a platoon from A Coy, 2nd Leicesters, his brief being to investigate the zone covering the start-line from which the King's Own would attack 'Butch'. He had returned at midnight to report the zone all clear of enemy patrols. Two other patrols had then gone out. The first was led by Lieutenant Kinnersley and its role was to mark the lines of advance from the bridges to the tank start-lines; the second, led by Captain Chambers, was to provide the taping party with cover.

They must had found it eerily quiet out there – at least until 0300 hrs. Then from the west side of the perimeter came a burst of gunfire. It was the signal that the Poles had begun their diversionary feint, taking all that weaponry they had brought with them to use against the oppressors of their nation. There would be little in the way of mercy on that side of the fortress during the hours to come. An hour later the noise increased as the Queen's Own began their diversion, this time a little nearer to the actual break-out site. This was the signal to the main attacking force that their moment was fast approaching. It was also an element of deception, being used to hide the noise of the tanks as they began their slow crawl towards the bridges. The men in the taping party heard the engines in spite of the gunfire. They looked for a reaction from that dark void ahead, but none came. There was no movement, no sudden shouts of alarm. The enemy slept on, his sentries too, apparently.

At 0515 hrs the men of the King's Own moved out through the Leicesters, crossed their appointed bridge, and assembled on their start-line. On their way out they were passed by Chambers leading back the taping party. There was no one ahead now save the enemy. They squat-ted on their heels in the rubble of the desert, watching their comman-ders, and waiting. Suddenly the perimeter behind them erupted. The sky flashed apart scores of times in a handful of minutes. The Beds and Herts in the nearest Red Line posts, virgins to this kind of blooding, watched with awe as shell after shell crashed on to 'Butch'; their diary later told of a miracle when night was turned into day.

It must have been as frightening to the attackers as to those about to be attacked. They were upright now, on their feet, watching officers whose heads were bent to wrist-watches, finding the minute finger and following it on its climb to the summit. 0620 hrs. Down came the raised arms and the King's Own began their march on 'Butch'. The break-out had begun.

The taking of 'Butch'

Four carriers led the way, the men following in line abreast, grenades in pouches, bayoneted rifles at the port, their hearts and stomachs God knows where. But at that moment of heart-in-mouth came some reassur-ance – the big and burly shapes of ten of Jock Holden's Matildas rolled up alongside.

The enemy was no longer sleeping. The enemy was up and reacting furiously with his own guns, but they were firing on the wrong range. The advancing men heard the shells whistle overhead and fall behind them. Perhaps this helped them quicken pace in the last yards but the tanks were first into the gun-pits. They crushed and tore away the barbed screens and the infantry rushed through the gaps they made. D Coy was the first to get inside. With a communal yell of encouragement they dashed to the heart of their objective where they fought 'magnificently'. Scarcely ten minutes after the commencement of the attack the success signal was being fired and Holden was reporting the first victory of the break-out. But there had been a price to pay for the victory – 30 men of the King's had been killed including Lieutenants Faulkner, Pritchard and Thompson. Sixty-nine others had been wounded including Captain Bellamy. Six men were missing. More than one hundred casualties to take a few holes in the ground. It was the beginning of a pattern which would develop over that day and those still to come. Death would never be far from the men who fought over the holes in this scrap of wretched desert.

The survivors were not allowed to dwell on their bloody trophy. Into 'Butch' came a detachment of the NFs and soon the music of their guns could be heard as they took on the enemy in 'Tiger'. The surviving King's Own got to their feet and moved off to their next target, 'Jill'. Alas, if 'Butch' had been bloody, 'Jill' was to prove even worse.

Meanwhile, the men in the Red Line were learning about Rommel's little surprise. Eighty prisoners were taken at 'Butch' in a post where the attackers had expected to meet the Italian Bologna Division, but they were all Germans. Confirmation that he was attacking Germans and not Italians came flooding in to Willison, now in a cruiser tank and across the ditch. Fired with their victory, the men of D Coy had stormed the crest beyond 'Butch', taking one small post after another, and in each case their captives were German. A Coy reported identical news. Prisoners began to be brought back through the wire, 40 into R64, eleven into R71, followed by eighteen more, and then another 109 – and all were Germans. The shock of this discovery was not a pleasant one, and that is not to decry the Italian infantry. Despite Rommel's set-backs against the garrison, the German soldier still carried an aura of invincibility. Those given the task of smashing through fortified positions and racing for El Duda might have approached it with a little more caution had they known that it would be German not Italian troops in those positions.

The presence of Germans where they had no right to be was not the only shock of those early moments in the break-out. Enemy shelling was far heavier than had been anticipated. For some days Rommel had been bringing his artillery forward to 'Tiger' and its vicinity in readiness for his own attack. This included guns ranging through 105mm, 155mm and 21cm. They came into action at the onset of the battle and were to make existence anywhere in the corridor now being created, a very hazardous business indeed. The enemy had 210 guns in the Tobruk area as against the sixteen 25pdrs which were in the corridor with Willison. Many of these guns were searching for the bridges and soon that whole locality was wreathed in dust and smoke. Visibility became reduced to yards and this caused some confusion at the bridges, and no little difficulty in finding start-lines. Heckman wrote that a sort of British congenital effect became evident; 'There was no overall commander in the foremost line of the fighting; the various branches of the service worked side-by-side independently.' [18] This is true only in the limited sense of immediacy. Willison was as close to the action as he could get and was in as much control of all units as was possible, given the confused nature of the battle then unfolding. He was in direct control of the tank units by radio, he had Armitage of 1RHA alongside in a light tank and acting as OP for the artillery, and he was in communication with the infantry commanders through the tanks supporting their units. Once the action was under way, of course, it was directed by the commanders of those units but there could be no doubting among them as to who was in ultimate control.

The taking of 'Jill'

The 2nd Battalion Black Watch had reveilled at 0445 hrs and had been given a rum ration to go with their tea, a strange libation on which to send Scotsmen into battle but no doubt very welcome on this 'bitterly cold night'. They moved through the forward lines, crossed the bridges and followed the white ribbons which took them to their start-line. Within the hour they were on it and awaiting both Zero Hour and their tank support. With them were D Coy Beds and Herts, who were to follow up the Scottish attack and help to consolidate 'Jill' as a corollary to the capture of 'Tiger'. But where were the tanks? That was the question the Scots were asking as they listened to the attack going in on 'Butch'. The answers to that question were trying to push their way through the congestion at the bridges and not finding it easy. At Z Hour (0630 hrs) they had still not arrived. The Scots gave them two more minutes but then had to start their march or lose their barrage. Major Blair gave the signal and led B Coy forward to attack 'Jill'. Close behind came the rest of the battalion: D Coy led by Captain Benson; C Coy led by Captain Boyle; HQ Coy led by Captain Barry, and A Coy led by Captain Evans. They marched to the skirl of their pipes in the dawn of a day which was to prove as bloody and brave as any in that proud regiment's long and distinguished history.

At Z+4 minutes the tanks arrived but some were too far to the left of their line of advance. Two reasons have been offered for this. The accepted version is that their start-line tapes had been laid askew. Lindsay gave another cause. He said that he saw an armoured car go up on a mine immediately ahead of him. He turned to the left to avoid becoming a casualty himself and was followed by the tanks in question. Whatever the cause, C Squadron's Matildas which had been detailed to lead B Coy Black Watch into 'Jill' now found themselves leading D and A Coys of the King's Own against that post instead. But not for long. On the previous evening the Germans had completed an extensive minefield stretching across from 'Tugun' on the west to circle the front of 'Jill'. The British tank commanders had been told the way was clear and they ran straight on to these mines. Within seconds Willison was faced with the problem that had destroyed Kircheim's attack on Pilastrino. There were two differences this time. He had made some provision by having KDG trained for just such an emergency, and his infantry was already on the march.

When the Scots came through the dust and smoke to the front of 'Jill' they saw that more than half their armoured support and all their Carrier Platoon less one carrier were out of action in the minefield, some of the vehicles already on fire. The King's Own, who had gone in with them, were pinned to the ground about two hundred yards in front of well-sited, well-wired posts. It was a critical moment and the Scots answered the crisis in typical fashion. The men of B Coy made a series of dashes which took them across the open space and into 'Jill', which they took at the point of their bayonets. 'With unflinching courage and a dash that could only be described as magnificent, every man pressed home his attack until the last German had been killed or captured,' says their diary of that action. But at what a price: three of the company's officers had been killed and two were seriously wounded. The company had been reduced to 20 per cent of its fighting strength and the 2,000 yards over which it had advanced was studded with rifles whose bayonets had been driven into the ground to indicate where the wounded lay.

The taking of 'Tiger'

By 0715 hrs the Beds and Herts had followed the Scots into 'Jill', and the Black Watch were able to press on to their main target – 'Tiger'. They would have to go it alone, their tank support either lying motionless behind them or cruising to right and left in desperate efforts to get through the barrier of mines. The Scotsmen could not wait – they had a time-table to keep to. They went on alone.

By now, the cruiser tanks of 1RTR had arrived on the scene after having been held up at the bridges. Benzie's C Sqn was in the lead when it too hit the minefield. Four tanks were immediately disabled and came under sustained fire. The tank commanded by Sergeant Ashwell was hit and its crew had to bale out. As they were doing so, Trooper Clark was hit and killed by a sniper and fell back inside the tank. Sergeant Frost's tank was next in line. His crew dismounted under fire and Trooper Spencer was killed in front of the tank. The surviving men from both tanks were captured. Lieutenant Ellison and Sergeant Rendell, commanders of the other two tanks, managed to get away with the rest of their crews. A Sqn had been following Benzie when Lieutenant Young saw some British infantry lying in the open. He ordered his troop to open Besa fire on enemy infantry in sangars who had been harassing these men. Sergeant Shields killed several machine-gunners, then A Sqn withdrew and rallied to the north-west of 'Jill'. They thus missed the minefield.

Meanwhile, Lieutenant-Colonel Brown of 1RTR and Rusk of the Black Watch had been conferring with O'Carroll of 4RTR. It was essential that the cruisers get out and resume their sally behind the enemy posts, and at 0905 hrs Brown was ordered to send his A Sqn north of 'Tiger' and then around to the west, to bring them back on to their intended course. As the squadron moved off on this detour they came under heavy fire from the west. The tank in which the Squadron CO,

Major Sir F. Coates, was riding was hit, he and Corporal Watts were wounded and Trooper Beukes was killed. Sergeant-Major Alexander managed to get Coates on to his tank and out of the firing line. He thought that Watts was dead but in fact he had managed to bale out and was lying unconscious close by. Captain Plaistow then took command of the squadron. All the British tanks were now either beached in the minefield or frustrated on the wrong side of it, and the euphoria of the quick victories at 'Butch' and 'Jill' was fading fast. Into this moment of crisis came the KDG armoured cars with their Royal Engineer hitch-hikers. Lindsay led them to the verge of the minefield, halted there, and in full view of the enemy posts, their crews and the sappers dismounted and began to grub up the mines. It was a pity that the Australian who had made his adverse comment about the Dragoons was not there to watch them during these moments. He would have had a different word for Maers and his mates had he watched them crawling on their hands and knees under fire, groping for the horrible lice of that battlefield. They stuck at it until they had cleared a gap wide enough for the cruisers to nose through and soon through it, and out, and on their safari.

During these travails being suffered by his brigade, Willison had been in his Command Tank at the edge of the minefield, with Charlie on his set. Now he called for an extra effort from his tanks: 'To Fourth Royal Tanks ... employ your reserve squadron. You will capture "Tiger" ', and: 'To First Royal Tanks ... swing wider ... you must break through.'

And somehow they did. First went the seven surviving tanks of C Sqn, Benzie leading the way with his head out of the turret and throwing a salute at Willison as he passed by. They were followed by A Sqn, RHQ Sqn and B Sqn in that order. Once free of the mines they turned south-east and set course for 'Tiger', which they were to skirt in their drive into the rear of the enemy. The Matildas followed them and resumed their interrupted march on 'Tiger'. Willison too tried to follow but his eagerness to be up with his men took him on to a mine. Almost immediately his tank was hit by a shell but the crew managed to bale out unscathed.

'Tiger' was obscured by clouds of dust and smoke and it was difficult for O'Carroll to identify his target among the many other posts and gun-pits in the locality. The Matildas of his C Sqn went too far left and became involved with some Black Watch infantry in a battle for 'Jack'. B Squadron ran into a strong-point 2,000 yards north-west of it in the 'Tugun' area. They attacked this, captured it, and garrisoned it with infantry before moving on. Only A Sqn found the right line and these few tanks headed straight for the post. Meanwhile, ahead of the tanks, the Black Watch had been making their way through the same choking dust and smoke in search of 'Tiger'. Their march had its musical accompaniment; rising above the incessant rattle of small-arms and machine-gun fire, through the scream and crash of shellfire, they heard the pipes every step of the way. Pipe-Major Rab Roy had played them on to 'Jill', now he led them through the smoke, his 'Highland Laddie' a musical beacon in their blindness. He was wounded and got up again. He was wounded a second time, this time in the legs, but again he got up and resumed playing.[19]

By now B Coy, which was in the lead, was suffering terribly and had lost all its officers, but it was exacting payment in kind. One platoon came upon a post hidden in scrub and 'neutralised' it. A second enemy post was attacked through a gap in its double-apron wire and its defenders were cleared away by bayonet and grenade. But the attrition was telling on the company. By the time they reached to within 200 yards of what later became known as 'Spandau Ridge' most of the company had become casualties and the few survivors were driven to ground.

The remainder of the battalion had advanced to the left of its scheduled axis of attack because of an error in the laying of the battalion start-line. The officer leading this section had spotted an observation post which was standing on a commanding piece of ground. The bulk of the small-arms fire they were being subjected to seemed to be coming from this direction, and he decided (correctly) that this was 'Tiger'. He pointed his men in that direction and they marched towards it. Although they had been advancing under very heavy fire, these men were still maintaining the formation in which they had set out from their start-line, an indication of both the leadership they were being given and the discipline with which it was being followed. History was repeating itself. The sons of the generation of the Somme marched behind their Commander just as their fathers had for his father, and he led them into the same withering

211

machine-gun fire that their fathers had suffered. One would have thought that the memory of the heaped corpses of that war would have ended this pattern of behaviour for ever. It hadn't. What obedience is this which makes one man march behind another to the death of both? Whatever it is was present on that day in front of 'Tiger'. Major Pitcairn, second in command of the battalion, and Captain Wilder, second in command of C Company, had both been killed and eight other officers wounded on the march, but this hadn't stopped the advance. When Pipe-Major Roy had been hit a third time and could not go on, Sergeant McNicol had picked up his pipes and 'Highland Laddie' continued. Then the point was reached when the 200 men still on their feet could get no farther and were forced to go to ground. Even then the heroism of these men endured. Lieutenant Hill and CSM Scott set up an OP for stragglers and dispersed these as they came up with the rest. Both men were obvious targets but they stuck it out until Scott was killed and Hill wounded.

And then at last, when it was almost too late for the Scotsmen, help arrived. Matildas appeared through the dust and came grinding past, their guns belching at the post. The Adjutant of the Black Watch Battalion got to his feet and urged his men to follow the tanks. He was killed almost immediately, but the Scots were up and advancing again. Major Roberts found the tracks made by the vehicles which had been bringing supplies to the post and he led his Matildas along these, through the mines and into the rear of 'Tiger' on its south-west side. B Squadron crashed through the gun-pits on the front edge of the site. The two squadrons met in the centre of a far more extensive system of defences than had been anticipated – a mile and a half deep and a mile wide. A classic attack then took place in which the tanks subdued the machine-guns while the infantry knocked out the crews of the anti-tank guns. The bayonets of the few Scots who had made it all the way helped to end all resistance. Together the Matildas and the Black Watch had pulled the teeth of 'Tiger'.

By 1015 hrs the position (for it was much more than a post) was in British hands and the Black Watch could take stock of their situation. Of the men who had taken that strange early-morning libation, barely one-quarter had made it into 'Tiger' – only five officers and 160 men.

Together with the Matildas they had captured twelve field guns, 30 Spandaus, a flame-thrower and 500 prisoners. Theirs had been a victory equal in sacrifice and achievement to any in their proud regiment's history, but the sacrifice was heart-rending. Six officers and 58 men dead, and 196 wounded of whom fifteen would not survive. Shocked medical orderlies from both sides of the combat began to work on the wounded of both sides, while long lines of prisoners began their weary walk into captivity. The remnant of the infantry battalion began the essential task of consolidation, knowing that the seizure of a position is only the beginning of an action – it then has to be held. Captain Berry and personnel of the battalion's HQ took up positions on the front face of the position. A Coy under Captain Ewan covered the right face, the remainder the left.

Behind them on the battlefield the tank and armoured car crews were doing what they could for their dead and wounded. Sergeant Corbett took a light tank into the minefield, dismounted, and rescued the unconscious Watts. Lieutenant Manby's crew came out carrying a wounded officer from 4RTR. Lance-Corporal McKeand of 7RTR had been a gunner in one of the knocked-out Matildas. He had remained in the minefield and had cleared about 30 yards of mines. Now he turned his attention to the wounded infantry lying about him. The KDGs had had one man killed and ten wounded during their mine-lifting; they had also lost eight armoured cars, one Dingo and a 15cwt truck. QMS Swineburn, who went out to try to rescue some of those vehicles, was hit in the pelvis and died out there. When one reads of the Desert War and its reconnaissance units it is usually the 11th Hussars who draw the attention and rightly so; they were in from beginning to end and did many great things. But no armoured car regiment's work in the two years of those desert battles surpassed what was done by the KDGs on the morning of the break-out.

The sweep by the cruisers
The cruisers of 1RTR had by-passed 'Tiger' and moved south on their sweep into the rear of the enemy. A Sqn was held up but C Sqn knocked out a machine-gun post on the fringe of the position as they passed by and then went for six enemy guns that Benzie spotted, firing as they advanced. They got to within 100 yards of the guns before swinging left

in line and then halting about 600 yards away. No further movement was observed around the guns and the squadron continued south as far as 'Wolf'. This post had a lot of tents and the tanks used their machine-guns on them. Benzie informed Willison, who was now in the ACV, that the post was strongly manned and then continued east and south-east passing through unwired positions. The squadron then turned north and their right flank passed through a site which contained four field guns and twelve anti-tank guns, all of which were unmanned.

The cruisers were now heading towards 'Freddie' and at 1300 hrs A Sqn was ordered to attack this post. Captain Plaistow took the squadron forward in battle line, his own tank in the centre. As they closed in, they saw C Sqn about 2,000 yards to their south and coming from the direction of 'Wolf'. They also saw men moving about on 'Freddie'. For some reason, Plaistow thought that the men they could see might be friendly and he ordered his tanks not to fire. It may be difficult for the historian to understand how he could make this mistake, but the historian is not privy to the fever of anticipation held by those breaking out, who thought that at any moment they might bump into the advancing Eighth Army. Indeed all eyes had been watching from first light for the red flares in the south-east which would announce its arrival.

Plaistow was not a foolish man; he risked his own neck but not his squadron. He had his tanks get into hull-down position before going forward to investigate. He discovered that the occupants of 'Freddie' were far from being friends. His tank was hit by two shells, he was seriously wounded, his driver, Trooper Nichols was killed and the remainder of his crew, Troopers Billings, Clark and Williams were all wounded. For the second time in little more than two hours the squadron had lost its commanding officer.

The squadron's other tanks opened fire and were joined in the attack by Benzie's group to the south of them. Lieutenant Richards now took command of A Sqn. Leaving his light tanks he advanced on 'Freddie' with two cruisers on each side, and under their covering fire he brought out all Plaistow's wounded. Meanwhile, C Sqn was taking most of the flak from the post. Benzie was hit and wounded.[20] Sergeant Turner's tank brewed up and its crew baled out. Lieutenant Hayter's tank was hit four times. The tanks withdrew, but Lieutenant Dawson returned under fire to rescue the crew of the burning tank.

The sweep now completed had shown that both 'Wolf' and 'Freddie' were strongly defended, and the regiment began its planned withdrawal with this information. It was not allowed to do so in peace. As it moved away it came under heavy fire from guns about 2,000 yards to the south. A Sqn was following C Sqn and took the brunt of this fire. Two tanks received direct hits. Sergeant Corbett, Troopers Crighton and Ratcliffe were killed and Troopers Bracey and Lynch wounded in one of them, Sergeant Burgess was killed and Troopers Roberts and Mottram wounded in the other. The guns which wrought this damage hold a special interest for the historian, as will be seen later.

The taking of 'Tugun'

For months Rommel's bombers had been the thumb on our throat as they squeezed our life-line. Now we had a thumb on his throat. It was a tiny thumb; 'Butch', 'Jill', 'Jack' and 'Tiger' were in our hands and being consolidated. This took us half-way to El Duda, where the throttling would really begin. It was also a sore thumb. Resistance had been much stiffer than expected and casualties reflected this. As early as 0945 hrs Willison was warning 70th Div HQ that he did not have enough infantry to hold the captured posts against the expected counter-attacks. As a result of that warning Scobie sent men from the Beds and Herts forward to 'Jack' and 'Tiger'. And it was a narrow thumb – too narrow, and as a result, the captured posts were now under fire from all sides. Most troublesome was that coming from the gathering of gun-pits which had been designated 'Tugun'. Already one attempt to take this locality had failed when B Coy 2nd Queen's had been driven back. Willison was pondering his next moves when at 1300 hrs the expected counter-attack came in against 'Tiger'. A troop of 88mm guns accompanied by lorried infantry was reported to be advancing against the post from the south-east. They began firing on the Matildas from about 2,500 yards and continued to advance until they were about half a mile away. The British tanks then opened up with their machine-guns and the counter-attack faded away.

Willison was now facing something of a dilemma. His programme for the day called for him to continue, post by post until he had his tanks on El Duda. He could hardly do so with a hostile 'Tugun' dominating his western flank, but he did not now have sufficient tank or infantry strength to subdue 'Tugun' and, at the same time, go for El Duda. Which was the greater risk, committing tanks against 'Tugun', which might leave him with insufficient strength to go for Duda, or making the attack on El Duda with a hostile 'Tugun' menacing his extending flank? And where were the South Africans, who were supposed to be advancing to meet him on Duda? He asked 70th Div about this and was told: 'No information at the moment.' At 1439 hrs he told Scobie: 'Tank state is 26 'I's, twelve armoured cars, six cruisers and six lights. At present these are concerned with defeating counter-attacks. 'I' tanks are only strong enough for the attack on El Duda if synchronised with attack by 1st S. Africans from the south.'

At 1445 hrs he took the decision and the risk. He sent Holden's Matildas accompanied by A Coy, Beds and Herts and B Coy Queen's Own against 'Tugun'. It was a successful move. By 1537 hrs they reported that they had taken all their objectives, the Queen's finishing off the battle at the point of the bayonet. In this action the Beds and Herts took 185 prisoners and these were all Italian. Here was an indication of the demarcation lines between the German and the Italian forces. Hardly had Willison been given the news that 'Tugun' was in our hands when he was told that 'Plum' was off. This was the code-word for the attack on El Duda. The news was both a relief and a disappointment to him – disappointment because he had looked forward all day to the moment when the siege would end as he shook hands with a South African on Duda Ridge; relief, because it would allow him time to rebuild his battered armoured vehicles. Fortunately, he held the battlefield on which the disabled tanks lay, and he had a first-class recovery unit waiting eagerly to work on them. Tank recovery and repair was to become a notable feature of the action in the corridor.

With Duda now definitely off that day's menu, Willison went back to the wire to meet Scobie, and they settled the disposition of troops for the night. The Black Watch survivors would hold 'Tiger' and 'Jack'. Beds and

Herts would hold 'Tugun' and 'Jill', with their Commanding Officer, Lieutenant-Colonel Hassell, taking charge of the 'Tugun' flank. King's Own were to hold 'Butch'. O'Carroll now had only 25 serviceable tanks; he was to leave one squadron on 'Tiger' and withdraw the remainder inside the perimeter for servicing.

And so the first day of the break-out came to an end for TOBFORCE. All its objectives had been achieved apart from the ultimate, Duda Ridge, which had been put on hold because of the failure of the South African brigade to appear there as planned. The Force had advanced four miles on a two-mile front, and the sweep into the hinterland by 1RTR had provided information as to what lay beyond the advance positions. The day's bag included 40 field guns and more than 1,000 prisoners, most of whom were German. But these objectives had been taken at a heavy cost to the attacking forces. At the close of the day's fighting the number of armoured fighting vehicles available to Willison was down from the original 158 to only 40. Each of the infantry battalions had taken many casualties, the Black Watch in particular being reduced now to a holding role.

At some time during that very long day I found myself standing outside the ACV near 'Tiger'. The area was strewn with paper – copies of '*die Oase*' and '*Signal*'; highly coloured regimental song books of the Italian unit which had so recently had its home here; photographs by the dozen, most showing the extravaganzas of Latin studios; letters, scattered and trampled into the earth. It was an astonishing phenomenon which repeated itself at every captured post. Strange is the detritus of battle.

A lone Scot was standing guard over a group of German prisoners, who were squatting in the dust. They were the first Germans I had seen and I gave them a good hard look. They looked hard themselves, lean, wrapped in the long coats they had been wearing to keep warm when their sleep was so rudely interrupted. Their faces were caked with the dust of the day. Most would have looked down on their guard had they been standing. Now he looked down on them, and they were not enjoying the experience, they were silent, sullen. The first hours of prisoner status are not pleasant.

'We'd never have got in there if you tankies hadn't got up to us,' the Scot told me.

Then, as we stood chatting, a long, long line of 15cwt vans pulled out from the rear of the post and began to make its way past us in the direction of the perimeter. Each bore the white circle and red cross emblem of the Field Ambulance Service. They came so slowly, creeping hub deep in the pounded dust. We fell silent as they passed. People have a habit of saying: 'I'll never forget the time when ...' when what they mean is 'I've just remembered something and you are going to have to listen to it.' But I never could forget that long line of vehicles carrying the wounded from their battlefield, and also carrying many young Scots who would never know Delaney or Docherty, Dennis Law or Kenny Dalglish.

Break-Out Day: on the Eighth Army front

Where were the South Africans? To answer this question it is necessary to return to the previous evening, when Eighth Army had taken to its blankets firmly convinced that it had given Rommel's armour a drubbing and already had it on the run. This was why 'Pop' had been called, and TOBFORCE brought out from the fortress. This false impression was reinforced on the morning of the break-out when Neumann-Silkow, acting on Crüwell's orders, took PZ15 back to Sidi Rezegh. The two British armoured brigades, 4th and 22nd, came out of their overnight laager to find PZ15 withdrawing across their front. Scott-Cockburn sent his Yeomanry squadrons in chase and they had a couple of tiffs with Neumann-Silkow's rearguard, but the panzers were under strict orders not to linger and so they did not turn and engage. The British armoured brigades took this as confirmation of their superiority over the panzer divisions.

Meanwhile, the Rifle Brigade of the Support Group had seized the escarpment overlooking the Sidi Rezegh airfield in a very bloody battle and were licking their wounds up there. In so doing, they had cleared the way for an advance on Tobruk by Davey's 7th Armd Bde, which would coincide with the TOBFORCE break-out. Davey now ordered 6RTR forward to meet the Tobruk sortie and they drove across the airfield and down the escarpment towards El Duda. They were perhaps watching eagerly for sight of Willison's men but what they saw as they crested a ridge were four 88mm guns awaiting their arrival. Rommel was waiting for them in person; he had picked out that spot as being crucial the moment he heard that the men of Tobruk had begun their break-out, and had hurried there, picking up part of Wechmar's Recce3 and the four guns *en route*. The cruisers of 6RTR charged forward, the 88mms opened fire, and within a very short time Eighth Army's first attempt to reach TOBFORCE was over, the British tanks decimated and on fire. None survived.

That was only the beginning of 7th Armd Bde's troubles. At about the moment when 6RTR were coming under the cosh, Davey was told that enemy tanks were approaching from the south-east. Perhaps he had heard the wildly optimistic reports of panzers fleeing with British armour hard on their heels. Perhaps he thought that all he needed to do was to put a block on the progress of these panzers until the pursuing British tanks caught up with them, or perhaps he simply reacted to the appearance of an enemy force by challenging it. Whatever his reasons, he left his reserve tank regiment, 2RTR, to mask the airfield and led his last regiment, the 7th Hussars, against the might of two panzer divisions. This was dispersal to the ultimate, and sheer lunacy. Neumann-Silkow's 50mm guns destroyed the Hussars before they could even get within firing range. Among the first to be killed was their Commander, Lieutenant-Colonel Byass. While they were staggering under this blow, PZ21 arrived in the north and joined in the slaughter. When they had finished off the Hussars they turned their attentions towards 2RTR on the airfield. By midday, when the men of TOBFORCE were so anxiously looking to the skyline for the dust clouds which would signal the arrival of their friends from Egypt, those friends were fighting for their lives and mostly losing them.

Nor was it only the tanks who suffered. The Support Group on the airfield and on the southern escarpment was also overwhelmed. The day was distinguished, if such a word may be used for such a day, by the determined bravery of the unfortunate British troops on the ground. It was exemplified by the actions of Rifleman Beeley who died storming an enemy post on the Rezegh escarpment; by Lieutenant Ward Gun, who fought his anti-tank gun to his death; by Brigadier 'Jock' Campbell, who drove up and down the airfield all the time the battle was being fought, rallying his guns, at times leading the tanks into attack in his staff car. All three were awarded the Victoria Cross, two of them posthumously, but Victoria Crosses seldom win battles.

It is almost impossible to believe that on that evening a cable was sent from Cairo which reported: 'It is authoritatively stated that the Libyan battle, which was at its height this afternoon, is going extremely well. The proportion of Axis tank casualties to British is authoritatively put at three to one.' [21]

Davey presumably, was not one of the authorities quoted.

To answer the question then. The South African brigade which should have been approaching El Duda to link with TOBFORCE was still somewhere to the south of the southern escarpment; there had not been the remotest possibility of their arriving on that day, nor was there in the immediate, or even the foreseeable future.

Two questions arising from the actions of Break-Out Day

Two wrong impressions which have been given currency about the work of TOBFORCE on Break-Out Day need to be refuted. In his work on the Desert Generals, Barnett says: 'In fact the major event of the day had been that Rommel had personally stopped the sortie of the Tobruk garrison with a scratch force.'[22] This was not so. Rommel had stopped 6RTR in the manner described above, and it is possible that he had then taken his 'scratch force' to intervene against the sortie. In this case his guns must have been those which knocked out the three cruiser tanks of A Sqn 1RTR as also described above, but it will be remembered that these tanks had *completed* their sweep into the rear of the enemy and were withdrawing according to plan when they came under fire from these guns. It is true that Rommel stopped the Eighth Army from arriving on El Duda (in the persona of 6RTR) but he did not stop the sortie. This remained short of its first-day target only because of the uncertainty of the location of the relieving forces and the need for Willison to bring his armoured force up to sufficient strength to continue the push. Other historians claim that the assault had faltered by mid-afternoon and that other assaults to take secondary objectives beyond 'Tiger' were thrown back. Rommel is said to have organised robust counter-attacks which were causing TOBFORCE to have to fight bitterly to retain the ground they had won. In fact, the counter-attacks on that day were anything but robust. With the exception of El Duda, TOBFORCE had taken all its objectives, and although it had suffered severely in doing so, was prepared to continue had that been called for. The only reason Willison did not go for El Duda was because he was ordered not to do so.

EIGHT

Break-Out D+1: on the TOBFORCE front

In contrast to the previous day, this one was fairly quiet, that is if one discounts the incessant shelling which searched and probed the little corridor through every hour of daylight. At 0930 hrs Scobie put Willison in the picture regarding Eighth Army. He told him that 7th Armd Bde and the Support Group had suffered considerable casualties east of Sidi Rezegh, and that S. African 1st Div was still at El Gobi. There was to be no advance on El Duda until the position of that army was known. This was as well; although Captain Price and his RAOC Recovery Team had worked through the night to bring tank strength up from forty to more than eighty, 1RTR had only eight cruisers and thirteen light tanks still running. Lieutenant-Colonel Brown had lost the commanders of two of his squadrons and had been forced to combine A and B Sqns under command of Major Bouverie Brine. Nor was this shortage of cruiser tanks the only problem facing Willison. Daylight had shown the Beds and Herts on 'Tugun' that they were merely on the edge of a much more extensive system of fortifications than they had realised. They were now staring at enemy guns, dug in no further than 800 yards away. The threat that these guns posed towards any attack which Willison might launch against El Duda remained very real and potent.

Willison was also of course, still being plagued by the question of when he was to go for El Duda, the main objective of the break-out. At 1050 hrs he was informed that the attack on this feature was back on again. At 1205 hrs this was rescinded. No one seemed to know what was happening 'out there' although for some reason optimism remained high. Then another problem arose for him. A second post was located to the south-west of 'Tiger' and adjacent to the line of advance against El

221

Duda, which would put the eastern flank of an attack on Duda at risk. This post was reported to be wired and was probably as heavily mined as had been 'Jill' and 'Tiger'. It would have to be taken before any attempt upon Duda could be made. Willison gave the order for this newly discovered post, designated 'Lion', to be attacked at noon, but the tracks forward from the bridges were so churned by the traffic and shelling that it was 1423 hrs before the York and Lancs battalion, which was to make it, reached their start-line. The infantry were accompanied by a squadron of O'Carroll's Matildas and went forward under cover of a barrage by the guns of 1RHA, which had crossed the bridges on Break-Out Day. When the infantry charged into 'Lion' they found that it had been already abandoned. They were the lucky ones; it was not often that such good fortune favoured the Tobruk infantry. Meanwhile, the Beds and Herts had been suffering harassment from the guns in their neighbourhood as they began to inch further into 'Tugun'. An evening attack made no progress and it became obvious that a major effort was going to have to be made if the area was to be cleared of those guns.

At nightfall, the AFV count was 34 'I' tanks, nine cruisers, 20 light tanks and thirteen armoured cars. Captain Palmer, the Dragoon who led the KDG fighting patrol on the Derna Road, took a 3-ton truck on to the battlefield to see if he could rescue any equipment from the wrecked armoured cars. He came back with a Luftwaffe pilot whose plane had been forced down in the corridor.

While the attack on 'Lion' was under way the sky to the south-east began to attract attention. Twists of smoke were weaving their way upwards above Sidi Rezegh, dark smoke which spoke of burning oil and rubber. They became more numerous, their peaks flattening and eventually joining together to form a long smudging of the sky. All eyes turned to study that smudging. 'Something is going on over there,' must have been said a hundred times or more by the watching men of TOBFORCE.

Something was.

The New Zealanders enter the scene
At 2040 hrs Willison was called to 'Tiger' where Black Watch had installed a field telephone, and he spoke to Scobie. He was told that

advanced elements of Eighth Army were heavily engaged at Sidi Rezegh, but that a New Zealand brigade had been ordered west along the Trigh Capuzzo and that it was accompanied by a squadron of infantry tanks. It had been ordered to help clear the situation at Sidi Rezegh and free XXX Corps to proceed to El Duda. The New Zealanders were too far away to be of immediate assistance, but TOBFORCE must help by engaging as many of the enemy as possible on its side of the Sidi Rezegh pocket. Willison immediately ordered that 'Dalby Square', a position south of 'Tugun' and slightly west of 'Lion', be attacked next morning, and he sent 7RTR back into the fortress so that Holden's Matildas could assist the Polish Carpathian Brigade in making a diversionary sortie on the western side of the perimeter.

The day closed on yet another problem for Willison. His guns had been firing almost non-stop for two days and were running out of ammunition. Scobie asked GHQ for an urgent delivery but was told that his request could not be met at present. Plans had to be made for the conservation of whatever ammunition remained in the corridor. It goes almost without saying that throughout all the fighting which had taken place, the FOOs had as usual been directing their guns from forward positions. Lieutenant Morrison of Chestnut Troop had had a narrow escape when a 21cm howitzer shell hit the tracks of the light tank from which he was observing. Fortunately for him and his crew, the shell failed to explode.

Break-Out D+1: on the Eighth Army front

As the morning passed, Cunningham was at last achieving some degree of concentration. The remains of 7th Armd Bde were to the west of the airfield and 22nd Armd Bde was approaching that area. Fourth Armd Bde was to the south-east of the airfield and KRRs were holding the Sidi Rezegh escarpment. When S. African 5th Bde completed its movement to Pt 178 on the southern escarpment, he would have his armour in possession of the airfield, with its northern and southern flanks covered by the infantry on the two escarpments. The anticipated arrival of the NZs with their 'I' tanks would then bring Belhamed under his control. He was hoping that all these movements would be completed by the next day;

the concentration would then be sufficiently strong for the short move to El Duda and the link-up with TOBFORCE.

Rommel was not prepared to wait until the next day. He had taken over the command of DAK and he launched three attacks against the forces in the Sidi Rezegh area. He sent Knabe's infantry against the KRRs. He sent Stephan's panzers against the armour on the airfield and he sent Oberst Marks' RR115 against whatever enemy might be on the southern escarpment. His three thrusts caught his opponents off balance. Stephan's panzers burst upon the remnants of 7th Armd Bde and elements of the Support Group, taking them by surprise. There was a brisk tank v. gun battle and then 22nd Armd Bde appeared on the scene, made yet another charge – across the airfield – straight on to the waiting 88mms. Their tanks went up in flames before they were near enough to the enemy to get off a single shot. These burning cruisers, whose commanders had failed to learn the lesson of El Gobi, were the source of the smudge in the sky which had so intrigued the men of TOBFORCE.

Once again Campbell was to the fore in this battle. Standing upright in his car he led the tanks into one charge after another, but only one outcome was possible. The arrival of 4th Armd Bde might have delayed it a little, but a battlefield conference between Gott, Campbell, Gatehouse and Scott-Cockburn recognised the inevitable. The British fell back on Pt 178, only to find that the South Africans had not arrived there. They were pursued by the panzers and were only saved from total annihilation by the combined gunnery of 60FRG and 3RHA which gave cover to the retreating tanks. Cunningham's armour eventually went into laager that night well to the south of this point.

While this battle was taking place one just as hard was being fought on the Rezegh escarpment. The Riflemen had been holding Knabe's attack when they were suddenly attacked by panzers which had wheeled north from the airfield and circled to attack them in the rear. They were overwhelmed and driven from their positions.

Thus nightfall found the British (and Commonwealth) presence at Sidi Rezegh limited to a toehold on the eastern end of the southern escarpment, and Cunningham's dream of a strong concentration there blown away with that day's desert wind. As if this were not enough disaster for one day, Cramer was bringing PZR8 into the area after nightfall when he ran straight into the HQ of 4th Armd Bde. His Major Fenski was quicker on the uptake than the British tank men and he bagged the entire HQ plus the tanks of the 8th Hussars who were supposed to be protecting it.[23] Gatehouse happened to be away at the time but he had now lost his communication links and his staff. It was tantamount to a hen having her head cut off but still needing to lay her eggs on the morrow.

It was probably as well that TOBFORCE were ignorant of all this as they sought to snatch what little sleep they could between the icy squalls and the flying shells – ignorant that one after another the tank regiments of XXX Corps had presented themselves for a battering and had been duly battered; ignorant that Rommel was planning an even bigger battering for the next day; ignorant that instead of arriving some time on the next day, the South African brigade for which they had been watching for two days was about to disappear for ever.

Break-Out D+2: on the TOBFORCE front

On this Sunday morning Willison was at work early, issuing orders for the attack on 'Dalby Square'. There were four parts to his plan :

> 1RTR were to demonstrate and to protect the right flank
> 4RTR were to go south around the extended tail of its minefield
>   and then turn north to take it in rear
> The York and Lancs were to make a frontal attack
> 1RHA were to fire a supporting barrage.

There were to be two objectives, 'Dalby Square' and 'Bondi', but the attack on 'Bondi' was only to go in if Eighth Army had arrived on the escarpment (this was an indication of how little either he or Scobie knew of what had happened to XXX Corps on the previous day). By 0720 hrs there was no sign of Eighth Army, and twenty minutes later Scobie told Willison to go ahead with the attack at 0930 hrs, but reiterated his injunction about the 'Bondi' attack. At 0830 hrs a report came through from Eighth Army that between 80 and 100 hostile tanks were moving towards Tobruk from the south, and that another 30 were assembling ten miles south of El Adem. This was shattering news, since it was from this direction that Willison and Scobie were expecting their 'friends' to arrive.

Although it was obvious that these friends would not be arriving on this day, Willison decided to go ahead with his attack on 'Dalby Square', if only to straighten out that side of his corridor.

Suddenly, into the middle of all this uncertainty and growing sense of unease there sprang a more immediate 'family' crisis. There had been so much rumour and so little real knowledge about the movements of the South Africans that Lindsay had sent out a patrol of two armoured cars to look for them. Lieutenant Beames was in one, Lieutenant Franks in the other. They were in the vicinity of 'Wolf' when they came under heavy fire. Beames in the leading car ran on to an enemy post and his car was hit. His driver, Trooper Crouch, was killed instantly, and Beames was hit in both legs. He managed to get out of the car but was wounded again, this time in the arm, and fell to the ground. The second car stood off and was giving covering fire when it too was hit and Franks and his crew, Troopers Peters, Cleland and Norbury were all wounded. Franks was ordered to withdraw. This message was acknowledged by someone, but nothing was seen or heard of Franks himself. An artillery FOO told O'Carroll that he had seen two armoured cars being knocked to pieces near 'Wolf'. O'Carroll contacted Major Pritchard of C Sqn, who immediately sent two of his tanks to help the armoured cars. One of these was commanded by Captain Philip Gardner.

Gardner went forward, located the cars, and ordered the second Matilda to give covering fire while he brought out either the cars or their wounded occupants. He reached one car, decided to tow it out, and climbed out of his tank. Then his problems began. He found that he couldn't budge the tow rope fixed along the side of his tank. He went to the rear of the tank and tried the one attached there. This came free, but in order for him to be able to use it, driver Trooper Robertson had to turn the tank round. Gardner signalled to him through the tank visor to do this, and he began the manoeuvre. The men inside the tank turret had no idea what was happening and Lance-Corporal McTier, who was firing the Besa, suddenly found himself being turned off his target. Trooper Richards, the wireless operator, who was now acting as loader, put his head out of the turret to find out what was happening and was killed immediately and fell back inside the tank. McTier's face was pressed against the rubber pad surrounding the gun sight and he failed to see what had happened. When his ammunition ran out he turned to ask for another belt and saw his friend on the floor. It was a bad moment for McTier, but a desperate moment, too. He climbed out of his seat, man-handled Richards'body so that he could traverse the turret and then risked putting his own head out of the turret. He saw what Gardner was doing, and remained in that highly hazardous position so that he could transmit Gardner's orders over the Tannoy to the driver. Gardner had secured the rope to the car when he saw Beames lying on the ground. He picked up the wounded officer, lifted him into the car, and then signalled McTier to order the driver to move off. At that moment Gardner was hit in the leg and knocked off his feet. Robertson advanced the tank but the pressure on the rope was too great and it snapped. McTier saw what had happened, and although his face was bleeding from a 'splash' he remained where he was and ordered Robertson to move the tank back.

Gardner now gave up the attempt to tow the car away and he lifted Beames out of it, carried him to the tank and got him up on its rear lou-vres. He made a last visit to the car to make sure there was no one left alive in it, and then climbed up next to Beames. As he did so he was hit again, this time in the arm. By now, the guns of E and O Troops 1RHA had been brought into action by Goschen and Armitage, one of whom had probably given the original report, and they were trying to keep down the heads of the enemy who had been firing from the post. McTier took command of the tank and ordered Robertson to retire at full speed. He then fed a new belt of ammunition into the Besa, returned to his gun seat and kept up harassing fire as the tank withdrew. The other Matilda moved forward in order to draw the enemy fire away from Gardner's tank, and then McTier climbed out to help Gardner hold on to the wounded Beames. This is how they came out from the action.

I was inside the ACV with Willison throughout this drama, which was reported in snatches through O'Carroll. Willison was on edge until the final report brought Gardner to safety, then he turned to those present inside the ACV and said: 'That man is going to get the Victoria Cross,' and so Gardner did. Trooper Richards was awarded a 'Mentioned', the only posthumous award that can be given other than the VC. Lance-Corporal

McTier won the DCM, but had to wait until 1947 before he could collect it, the original citation having been lost. When Gardner's tank came past the ACV on its way to the workshops, Willison marched out, came to a halt, and saluted the tank and what was left of its crew. It was a memorable moment. It was also Robertson's only reward; his citation was disallowed because he had received the Military Medal in a Gazette of the previous month.

The taking of 'Dalby Square'

While all this was going on, the attack against 'Dalby Square' had begun, and had uncovered another man who was to earn the ultimate laurel before the week was out. It began with the demonstration by 1RTR's cruiser tanks, which advanced on a line to 'Tiger' and then wheeled to the south of 'Tugun'. The composite B Sqn was in front and C Sqn followed in reserve. At 1005 hrs the leading squadron came under fire from four troops of guns at what became known as 'The Walled Village'.

The advance continued until at 1022 hrs the squadron was in position south of 'Tugun'.

Meanwhile B Sqn of 4RTR had left its start-line at 0930 hrs and had begun its march around the tail-end of the minefield protecting 'Dalby Square'. A and C Sqns followed, with the intention of developing the attack towards 'Bondi' after 'Dalby Square' was taken. The York and Lancs infantrymen who were making the frontal attack on the latter post had come under heavy machine-gun and mortar fire and were taking casualties. The tanks also came under attack from guns which were firing over open sights and three Matildas were hit and disabled. It was a tricky moment with both tanks and infantry stalled and suffering. Fortunately for both, Captain Jackman of the NFs was at hand. He came up from the south with Lieutenant Ward's 14 Platoon and saw what was happening. He approached in a wide circle which took him into the enemy's right flank, where they captured some positions. He then set up his machine-gun crews and proceeded to knock out the crews of the anti-tank guns that were causing the hold-up. Jackman then jumped into his truck and raced away, returning with 13 Platoon, which joined in the action.[24] Jackman's intervention was crucial, the attack was resumed and 'Dalby Square' fell at 1105 hrs.

By this time, York and Lancs had taken so many casualties that they were too weak to hold it without help. They called forward their reserve C Coy who found themselves in a hornets' nest. The whole area was an enemy redoubt and the British tanks were attracting such heavy fire that they had to withdraw.

Two hours after the seizure of the position came the first counter-attack. It was driven off by a combination of the York and Lancs, the disabled tanks and Jackman's machine-guns. Sergeant McKay of the NFs won a DCM for his part in the action. Jackman, who was one of the 10 per cent in the battalion who were not Geordies, had become a familiar figure at the ACV with his daily (and almost hourly) visits in search of targets for his guns.

'Dalby Square' was not the only gain by TOBFORCE on this day. While the York and Lancs were battling for it, the Beds and Herts were having a go at the guns they had seen on the previous day. A Coy made the attack. They advanced in 'great style' and had taken the guns by 1030 hrs. They then saw a second group of guns about 1,000 yards to their south-west. They went for those, too, making their bag for that day 180 prisoners and 32 guns. There was more to come. Their B Coy was told at 1230 hrs that the remainder of 'Tugun' had been evacuated by the enemy and they were ordered to occupy it. They moved out to do so and immediately came under mortar and small-arms fire from the supposedly empty trenches. In spite of this the attack went in in 'magnificent style', three gun-pits were captured and Lieutenant Ablitt and RSM Kemp especially distinguished themselves. By this time the area was being blanketed by enemy fire and the Beds and Herts were pinned down in the pits they had captured. It was evening before a carrier platoon could get through to them and take away their wounded. For the next few days the regiment hung on in these fraught positions, guarding the all-important western flank of the break-out bulge.

Willison was now grappling with two practical problems: his guns were running out of ammunition and his infantry had suffered far heavier casualties than had been anticipated. The original break-out plan had envisaged a short, sharp assault lasting no more than two days, by which time the link-up with the outside forces would have been achieved. This plan was now in shreds because of the non-appearance of the South Africans and the stiffer than expected resistance of Sümmermann's troops. Willison had already used five battalions of infantry as against the three called for by the plan and each had taken heavy casualties. A sixth was now brought forward – 2nd Leicestershire Regiment, commanded by Lieutenant-Colonel Phillip. It came into the corridor during the night; A Coy went into 'Jack'; B Coy covered the space between 'Jack' and 'Butch'; D Coy went into 'Butch', and HQ Coy went into 'Jill'. This allowed the King's Own to be withdrawn from the corridor.

When Windsor wrote the summary for the day he was able to say for a third time that all TOBFORCE's objectives had been met and that 250 prisoners had been taken. The corridor now extended for five miles and was four miles in depth. The tank state showed 34 'I' tanks, thirteen cruiser tanks, 22 light tanks and fifteen armoured cars fit for action.

So far as I was concerned there was a strange curtain to the day. That night there was more than the usual interference on the air waves and I had to revert to key to get messages through. As I strained my ears to pick out the thin and tiny dots and dash responses I found that they were in competition with the violins and brass of some intrusive orchestra. This civilian invasion of our world of battle was an eerie reminder that out there was something other than bombs and shells and trucks carrying away the dead and wounded. How distant that world was from us, though, and not only in space.

Break-Out D+2: on the Eighth Army front

The feast of All Souls' Day, when Roman Catholics of all nations pray for the souls of the dead, is celebrated in Germany on the third Sunday of November and is known as *Totensonntag*. This particular *Totensonntag* was to add many more to the remembrance lists on both sides of the warring divide. But it opened happily for Eighth Army. The New Zealanders had paused for the night in their advance towards Sidi Rezegh, and woke at dawn to discover that they had parked themselves alongside Crüwell's Headquarters. They promptly seized it and all within it. Like Gatehouse, Crüwell was not at home and so escaped capture, but he had lost his staff and communications, and this was at a higher level and therefore much more serious a handicap to DAK than it had been for Gatehouse. If it seemed that at last Lady Luck had moved over to Eighth Army, that was an illusion, she did not linger long.

Dawn had found the Germans in strength at Sidi Rezegh. Afrika Division 361 held the second escarpment; Knabe was on the airfield and RR115 was along the southern escarpment. To the east of Knabe was PZR5 and to the south of the Afrika Division was PZ21. As for their opponents, XXX Corps was grouped very loosely on the plain to the south of the southern escarpment and Armstrong's S. African 5th Bde was in a three-sided box south of Pt 178 and facing RR155. Transvaal Scottish held the north side of this box; Regiment Botha held the east side, and S. African Irish the west side. The brigade's B Echelon of soft vehicles was crowded into the open south side. To the west of the box was 22nd Armd Bde, and to its east were remnants of the Support Group. The other brigade of Pienaar's S. African 1st Division which had been ordered to join Armstrong had made only a little movement towards doing so, but its B Echelon had somehow found itself to the south-east of Armstrong's box. It was upon this wide-spread gathering that Rommel's next blow would fall.

Rommel had decided to destroy what was left of XXX Corps and concentrate his armour for the task. He intended to use the typical hammer and anvil tactic with Crüwell in overall command. A direct strike by the combined panzer divisions from the north would drive the British and South Africans on to the tanks of Ariete, which were approaching in the south from El Gobi. There was to be an emphasis on the left side of the panzer attack which would result in this developing into a containing arm so that none of the British armour would escape. These orders were contained in a long message which had been seized by the New Zealanders when Crüwell's HQ had been captured, and it is not known how much of them Crüwell had read before he set out on his destructive march. In the event he modified his orders, discarded the pincer tactic and set off for the south to pick up Ariete with which he intended to join the panzers and launch a massively concentrated drive from the south against the open side of Armstrong's box.

On his way to pick up Ariete, he drove straight through and over Pienaar's B Echelon and the Support Group, but he encountered a good deal of scattered resistance, particularly from the gunners and anti-tank gunners in the area. These clashes were a warning to Armstrong and he heeded it. The threatening presence of the enemy to his front did not allow him to make a complete about-face, even if he had had time for this. Nor could he withdraw without inviting attacks from front and rear while he was trying to do so. But he was able to get most of the gunners in the area to come into the box, and these included the guns of Support Group and the anti-tank gunners of 3RHA. He also had the surviving tanks of the combined armoured brigades close at hand.

The battle for Armstrong's box

Crüwell assembled his strike force with Ariete on the left, PZR8 in the centre and PZR5 on the right. Behind this line of tanks were his motorised infantry regiments, 155 and 200. The attack opened with a barrage from Böttcher's heavy guns firing from Belhamed. Then the line of panzers swept in on the box, with the motorised infantry in close support. It was a steamroller of a charge, but the defending guns met the attacking tanks head-on over open sights. This drove back Ariete, but PZR8 continued its march with PZR5 on its right. Together they broke into the box, but at a price – Zintel, CO of RR115, was killed as he stood erect in his armoured carrier. So too was Major von Grolman, his Battalion CO. Their regiments were decimated and the many panzer casualties included Major Fenski, Leutnants Wurth and Liestman, who were leading columns of panzers, and tank commanders Leutnants Koser, Adams and Pisat.[25]

Individual fighting broke out all over the box as the panzers fought their way northwards and their supporting infantry engaged the gun crews. The South Africans fought back. The British tanks tried to intervene but were too few, and those which survived had eventually to make a desperate charge to get away. The scene became one of smashed guns, smashed and burning tanks, smashed bodies. The accompaniment, a cacophony of screaming shells and human cries. Man did his worst to man at Sidi Rezegh on that Sunday of the dead.

Nightfall found the South African Brigade (which had been chosen to relieve Tobruk) no longer in existence. The palm of victory went to Crüwell on that day, but the evening's reckoning converted it to a crown of thorns. It had been a day of the dead for his victorious panzers and panzergrenadiers as well as for his opponents. Far too much of the Afrika Korps had been lost in the winning of it. Could Rommel afford such losses? Writing well after the event, von Mellenthin said: 'Our motorised infantry suffered heavy casualties, most of their officers and NCOs were killed and wounded – while the panzer regiments lost 70 tanks out of 150. This was our highest daily loss in the Crusader battle, and gravely weakened our armoured strength.'[26]

Rommel arrived at DAK HQ on El Adem airfield enthused by Crüwell's victory and convinced that he was on the point of finishing off all British resistance. He had no time for other considerations, certainly not for the negative vibes which Crüwell's casualties from that day's victory should have caused him. This was a failure to face facts for which he would eventually have to pay. Auchinleck had flown in to Eighth Army HQ in answer to a request from Cunningham, whose earlier optimism had ebbed fast once the true nature and results of those earlier armoured clashes had penetrated. He was met by a situation which was deteriorating by the hour and by his Field Commander who was doing so by the minute. Auchinleck, helped in his decision by information from Ultra which exposed the frailty of Rommel's supply position, changed the strategy from the original plan of quick destruction of the Afrika Korps to one of a gradual grinding down of this fine force until it could no longer sustain its presence in Cyrenaica. 'Crusader' was to become a battle of attrition and Rommel's losses in his Totensonntag victory saw the beginning of that grinding down process.

NINE

Break-Out D+3: on the TOBFORCE front

The most significant happening on this day was that TOBFORCE was placed under the command of XIII Corps; this was because the New Zealanders of that Corps were now the nearest friendly troops. General Godwin-Austen looked to the meeting of his men and TOBFORCE on El Duda, but before this could happen he needed to hold the whole of the Sidi Rezegh pocket. He therefore asked TOBFORCE to synchronise attacks against enemy posts on the eastern side of the corridor with attacks which the New Zealanders were going to make against Sidi Rezegh and Belhamed. This would put those enemy troops under attack from front and rear.

The Leicesters were to open proceedings by making an immediate attack in the area of the wrecked aircraft, which was to the north-west of the two enemy posts, 'Freddie' and 'Walter'. Willison's 32nd ATB (less 4RTR, which was to be saved for the attack on El Duda) was to attack and take these two posts from the south, then swing left astride the Bardia Road and take the block which had been set up on that road. As it turned out, none of these attacks took place on that day. At 0810 hrs Willison held a conference with his Commanders at his battle HQ – a table beneath the canvas flap hanging from the ACV. It was to plan three actions:

    (i) against Ed Duda

    (ii) against the Bardia Road block

    (iii) support for an attack to be made by the Poles.

That evening he issued a Battle Order for the first of these proposed attacks. During the day, meanwhile, various infantry movements had taken place in the corridor. The Leicesters settled into the positions they had taken over from King's Own during the night, and were now covering the eastern side. Beds and Herts were in 'Tugun' on the opposite side. York and Lancs were in 'Lion' and to its south. Black Watch were in 'Tiger'. Willison's requests for more men to replace the many casualties his supporting infantry had suffered was answered at 1600 hrs when a new battalion came under his command. This was 1st Essex, led by Colonel Nichols who had been informed that his battalion was to take part in the attack on El Duda and would help cut the Axis Road and link up with the New Zealanders. At 2100 hrs he took his men forward into the corridor.

The warning about the diminishing stocks of ammunition was also being addressed. Willison was informed that 600 tons were being rushed up by ship, and men were standing by to unload it. Careful rationing had improved the position somewhat, so that his gunners had 554 rounds per gun in hand.

Peace in the corridor on this day allowed the infantry to carry out the duty which every soldier owes to his comrades. The York and Lancs diary for the day reads: 'Consolidation and burial by all companies.'

But the peace was comparative. The corridor was seldom free from the noise of those 210 guns ranging on the corridor from all sides. This caused a particular problem for the men in the ACV who were planning and running the battles in that narrow strip of desert. Their vehicle was turning out to be schizophrenic, highly unpopular with those who should have loved it but didn't want it anywhere near their positions because of its tell-tale appearance, but altogether too popular with the men manning those external guns who would have loved nothing better than to see it go up in smoke. The only way to live with this last problem was to accept that eventually Böttcher's gunners were bound to find it, and hope that you were elsewhere when they did so.

One man who was very fortunate in this respect was Jim Gauton. His head appeared at the open door of the ACV and gave that 'Come and look at this' jerk. It was a quiet moment, wireless-traffic wise, and I was able to slip out of the vehicle. I followed him to the rear of the 8cwt wireless truck he was manning. He pointed to its floor without saying a word. He didn't need to, a huge chunk of shrapnel was wedged in the centre of it. The truck had been on the move down one of the tracks when the shell exploded behind it. This fragment of the shell had bounced and skidded along the track and used its last bit of unnatural energy in an effort to cut him in half. He had watched helplessly throughout the whole performance. I gaped. He said in outrage, 'Bloody loonies!'

Break-Out D+3: on the Eighth Army front

Now, at the moment when he had the armoured component of Eighth Army lying on the ropes and awaiting his final uppercut, Rommel astonished his commanders and all military historians. He had several options available:

    (i) With TOBFORCE committed in the corridor, leaving the perimeter so thinly lined, he could have attacked the fortress and won his heart's desire, probably with ease. Tobruk was more at his mercy on the night of 23 November than at any time in the preceding eight months.

    (ii) He could have cut off TOBFORCE and annihilated it.

(iii) His panzers could have toured Sidi Rezegh and the locality, destroying all the left-over bits and pieces of XXX Corps.

(iv) He could have gone in search of Eighth Army's supply dumps.

(v) He could have carried out a combination of these.

He did none of these things. He decided to launch a typical thrust deep into the heart of his enemy. He sent the whole of Panzergruppe on a dash to the frontier where it was to destroy what enemy formations it found there; cut Eighth Army off from its supply (and escape) routes; seize their railhead and the dumps there; relieve the Axis forces locked in their frontier posts, and then drive on to Suez. He told Westphal: 'This will be the end of the campaign. I shall finish it with a single stroke.'[27]

It was a grand conception which would feed historians with endless fodder on which to chew. Unfortunately for Rommel, the grandeur of conception was lost in a script which, in its unfolding action, could well have been written by Buster Keaton – had it not been for its accompanying tragedies.

Rommel joined von Ravenstein's PZ21 in the van of the chase; next came PZ15, and finally, Ariete. They went south through Gabr Saleh to Trigh El Abd, and used this as their axis of advance to the frontier. This took them through the north-eastern section of the S. African 1st Bde where several British HQs had gathered. The reactions of these when a phalanx of panzers appeared on the near horizon can be imagined. Grouse on the Twelfth of July never took to wing so quickly as these gentlemen warriors sought their own horizons – north, south or east, but certainly not west. Rommel ignored them. The panzers drove relentlessly onwards, pausing for nothing, passing almost within sight of FMCs 65 and 62 but missing these in their haste, although von Mellenthin later claimed that Rommel knew of their location through captured documents but was more concerned to destroy the armour. This may have been so, but it was a missed opportunity; without the supplies in those dumps Eighth Army would have withered on its desert vine.[28]

By 1600 hrs Rommel was on the frontier but at some cost. In his wake was a trail of broken-down panzers and scattered units whose exhausted men were fast losing the euphoria of the previous day's victory. He now gave orders for the next morning. The two panzer divisions acting as pincers on each side of the wire and supported by Ariete on their western flank would drive the New Zealanders against his double line of minefields and the Axis troops holding the frontier posts. Recce33 would advance to Habata, close the escape route south of the Omars, and seize whatever it could find in the way of supplies. Another group would capture Eighth Army HQ which was at Maddalena.

These orders indicate his lack of knowledge of the true situation. His troops no longer held the Omar posts against which the New Zealanders were to be driven; they had been marched away as prisoners of war when those posts were captured on the previous day. Nor does he appear to have known that two of the New Zealand brigades were miles away to the west, where one of them was actually pressing in on Sidi Rezegh.[29] Finally, he did not know the state of his own troops; Recce33, for example, was by now a spent force and quite incapable of carrying out the task he had set it.

Having given the orders, he set off on a typical Rommel adventure across the wire with his Chief of Staff, General Gause, and promptly got lost. Crüwell bumped into them, but the three could not then find a way back through the wire. Three German Generals, one the Commander of an Army, the other of a Corps, and the third, a senior staff officer, spent the night on the wrong side of the wire in a captured ACV, with British troops streaming past but taking care not to disturb what they took to be sleeping British VIPs. For a second time Rommel had put the entire German involvement in Africa at risk. For a second time he got away with it. But while he was out of touch with his troops the advantage was once again swinging towards his battered opponents.

While this dash to the frontier was under way, Auchinleck was writing a directive that considered the two options which he saw as being open to his Field Commander.[30] He told Cunningham that he could either withdraw to a line based on Gambut–Gabr Saleh or even farther back to the frontier, or he could continue the offensive. He wrote: 'The second course is to continue to press our offensive with every means in our power.' He went on to say that this was the right and only course to take, and added: 'You will therefore

(i) Continue to attack the enemy relentlessly using all your resources even to the last tank.

(ii) Your main immediate objective will be as always to destroy the enemy tank forces.

(iii) Your ultimate object remains the conquest of Cyrenaica and then an advance on Tripoli.'

This directive was unequivocal. It determined that the struggle would be continued in Cyrenaica and that it would be decided in favour of the side which could best survive attrition. The questions of resources in human as well as *matériel* terms – psychologically as well as physically – together with the organisation of supply, became paramount. Auchinleck was counting on his being superior to those of his opponent.

Break-Out D+4: on the TOBFORCE front – The taking of 'Wolf'

On the morning of 25 November, TOBFORCE's fifth day in the corridor, Scobie asked Willison to consider making a second break-out at another point of the perimeter, presumably to draw German troops away from Sidi Rezegh and relieve pressure there. The Poles were pleading for

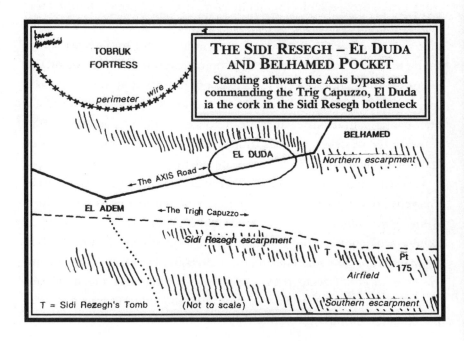

THE SIDI RESEGH – EL DUDA AND BELHAMED POCKET

Standing athwart the Axis bypass and commanding the Trig Capuzzo, El Duda ia the cork in the Sidi Resegh bottleneck

TOBRUK FORTRESS

perimeter wire

BELHAMED

EL DUDA

Northern escarpment

← The AXIS Road →

EL ADEM ← The Trigh Capuzzo →

Sidi Rezegh escarpment

Pt 175

Airfield

T = Sidi Rezegh's Tomb (Not to scale) Southern escarpment

some action and would be the supporting infantry. O'Carroll and Holden went to view the suggested area, but following their inspection of the terrain for the proposed second Tobruk front the idea was dropped. Next came a minor flap when it was reported that Eighth Army intended attacking towards El Duda at 2100 hrs. This report was subsequently cancelled and orders were then given for two night actions. In the first of these, A Sqn 4RTR and the York and Lancs battalion were to attack 'Wolf'', a strongly defended and mined post about a mile and a half wide and half a mile deep. In the second, the Leicesters were to attack to the east of 'Butch' in the locality of the wrecked plane, with D Sqn of 7RTR as their support. This locality was also strongly defended and had successfully held off an earlier attack. The capture of 'Wolf' was a necessary preliminary to the attack on El Duda, the one against the wrecked aircraft area was intended as a widening of the base of the perimeter.

Both attacks went in under moonlight at 2100 hrs. A Sqn attacked 'Wolf' from the front while B Sqn went around the right flank. The infantry advanced in leaps and bounds as and when the opportunity offered. Unfortunately A Sqn ran on to mines and soon had four tanks rendered immobile. Deprived of this support, York and Lancs began to suffer casualties, but the Matildas of B Sqn managed to penetrate the post's defences and by 2230 hrs the infantry were inside 'Wolf' and claiming it as theirs. While it was being consolidated it was discovered that other enemy positions in the vicinity were so close that the infantry would be hard-pressed to hold it, so when the other tanks withdrew in order to rally, a squadron of cruiser tanks moved in as support.

The attack in the wrecked aircraft area was carried out by B and C Coys of 2nd Leicesters. The leader of B Coy, Captain Bryan, had two platoons forward, one under Lieutenant Parish and the other under Sergeant Forrester. His third platoon, commanded by Lieutenant Gilroy, was following as the reserve. When they were within 200 yards of an enemy position, Forrester's platoon bumped into a German patrol. The tanks opened up and five Germans were killed, but the tanks had begun to bunch and suddenly one went up on a mine. The others stopped immediately, and the infantry out in front of them came under heavy fire. Bryan was with one of the forward platoons where the battalion's

239

Signals Officer had managed to run a field telephone line to him. He reported the position over this and was told to contact the officer in charge of the Matildas. He did so but was informed that because of the mines they dared not move in the dark. Nor could they open fire because they could not distinguish between enemy and friend. Bryan was ordered to keep his company where it was until dawn, when D Coy would attack behind the reserve tanks. He and his men settled down to a most unpleasant night during which any movement brought a hail of fire down on their heads.

At this point a runner arrived from Lieutenant Vanderspar's platoon bringing Bryan news that Vanderspar had seized part of the position but was being hard-pressed to hold on. Bryan immediately sent Lieutenant Gilroy with the reserve platoon to help, but as soon as Gilroy and his men began to move they became the centre of enemy activity and Gilroy was seriously wounded and his platoon was forced back.

Vanderspar's had been a noble effort. He had led 13 Platoon into the attack accompanied on his left by 15 Platoon commanded by Lieutenant Collett. Both platoons came up against the same enemy strong-point together. Vanderspar cut an opening in the wire protecting the post and his men ran through this, attacking and killing most of the defenders. The trenches on the other side of the post were still strongly held by the enemy, who were firing at least three machine-guns from there. Collett then went for these trenches while Vanderspar's platoon gave them covering fire. It was not enough; Collett's men had suffered the fate all infantrymen fear, they had become trapped on the wire and were being shot to pieces. Collett, Sergeant Truluck, the three section commanders and many of the platoon were either dead or wounded. Vanderspar and his platoon were now in an unenviable position. He was clinging to a small section of the post, he had several men wounded and he was fast running out of ammunition. Sergeant Hearson volunteered to go for help and crawled out through the wire. He was later followed on the same dangerous mission by Private Withington. As described above, one of these two men made it to Bryan but the first attempt to get help through to Vanderspar failed. A second attempt was then made by Lieutenant Hallam's platoon, but Hallam was shot down on the way forward

240

and the platoon was taken over by Lance-Corporal Smith who managed to get through to the beleaguered men.

It was clear to Vanderspar that even with these reinforcements he was not strong enough to evict the enemy from the rest of the post and he decided to withdraw as soon as the moon went down. It was a desperate wait; their wounded were in pain, the dead and dying on the wire, and themselves still drawing enemy fire. It was a desperate prospect ,too, the wire to be negotiated and the machine-gun and small-arms fire to be braved. At last the moonlight faded and Private Griffiths, who had been wounded on the approach to the post, crawled out and cut an exit breach in the wire. Lance-Corporal Smith then led the way and the remainder followed, with Vanderspar in the rear. They suffered more casualties as they went.

In the early hours of the following morning Captain Walker brought up D Company and they stormed into the post which had cost the battalion so dearly. They found it empty. An unsung county regiment led by youngsters, not all of them commissioned, had fought a desperate battle in a desolate spot far from Leicestershire, while the good folk of that county slept in their warm beds. It was a story being repeated often as the holes in that wretched patch of earth were fought over, died over, won – and then abandoned.

Break-Out D+4: on the Eighth Army front

This second day of his dash should have given Rommel his decisive battles along the frontier posts, their wire and their minefields. But this supposed master of concentration was dispersing his armoured force with an abandon that would have done credit to any of Eighth Army's commanders. He sent Neumann-Silkow north against Sidi Omar. He divided PZ21, sending von Ravenstein (without its panzers) through Halfaya to sweep up the eastern side of the wire. Stephan was ordered to take its panzers up the western side.

The Commander of Recce33 was told to drive to Habata and cut the rail link there, and Recce3 was sent to capture Eighth Army's HQ at Fort Maddalena. Since Ariete was being delayed back down the track by S. African 1st Brigade, these arrangements meant that Rommel now had his

Panzergruppe in five different locations. The inference must be that he considered any opposing force which might be encountered by his dispersed units would be incapable of anything more than resistance at battalion level. He appears to have forgotten that regardless of the strength of the British and Commonwealth ground forces, they still had an air force and that it had treated his midsummer ramble harshly. They now began to repeat that treatment. Stephan was about to attack British troops near Sidi Omar when his column was strafed and he was killed. There are stories of Rommel's personally taking him to a field hospital and standing by while the surgeons worked on him. If true, this did nothing for Stephan.

Major Mildbrath took command, and launched two attacks against Indian 7th Brigade. In the first of these he was driven off by the guns of 1st Field Regiment. In the second, he was punished roundly by an assortment of guns attached to the brigade. As for the remainder of PZ21, according to von Mellenthin, it wandered about without meeting any enemy. Neumann-Silkow wasn't faring much better. He did come upon a tank repair depot set up in a wadi by 1st ATB, where about eighteen damaged Matildas were being repaired under the supervision of Major Rawlins. Some were almost ready for action, others were almost wrecks. Warned by radio that panzers were approaching the wadi, Rawlins set about arming and re-fuelling the tanks, and selecting crews for them. When the panzers arrived he took his scratch group out of the wadi to face them. It was outnumbered two to one and some of his tanks had jammed turrets and could not traverse their guns. They fought their corner and a handful managed to battle their way out into the open, but the outcome was certain. One by one they were hit and set on fire. Rawlins was killed while firing a tommy gun outside his wrecked tank. Not a single man survived. They were a handicapped but legitimate target, a few more bones to be scrambled over. Their sacrifice was to be measured only in terms of the delay they might have caused to Neumann-Silkow's panzers.[31]

As for Recce33, it was battered from the air, lost many of its vehicles, ran out of petrol and never even began the advance on Habata. Meanwhile, the other reconnaissance group which had been sent to capture Fort Maddalena was called back before it reached that location.

Such were the actions fought by Rommel's armour along the wire. None came anywhere near to ending the campaign at a single stroke. Ariete and the South Africans were still standing each other off along the Trigh el Abd at great expense of ammunition for little result.

On the opposing side, the day was marked by the advance of the New Zealand troops and the resuscitation of parts of XXX Corps. The NZs received orders from Godwin-Austen to seize the escarpments in the Sidi Rezegh–Belhamed pocket. General Freyberg sent them in on a night attack, 4th Brigade going for Belhamed on the northern escarpment and 6th Brigade for the Sidi Rezegh ridge. The former captured their objective, but the Italian Bersaglieri Regiment fought well, and retained their hold on the ridge escarpment, confining 6th Bde to the airfield.

The day had seen a small tactical change in Eighth Army, with the breaking down of what remained of the Support Group into columns. These were sent into the blue with orders to harass the enemy wherever they could find them. They were of mixed arms and never of a size large enough to make any significant intervention, but their presence across Rommel's lines of communication must have had its effect, especially on the mental state of a fast-tiring army. These columns were christened 'Jock Columns' in honour of Campbell who, as might have been expected, led one of them.

It was perhaps on this night when I had my last chat with George Maers. It is hardly possible to distinguish one of those days from another, or one night from the preceding night. There was no real rest; we might snatch an hour or two, trying to keep warm inside a ground-sheet by the side of the ACV, often with freezing rain on the face, mud for company and the enemy's succession of flares to remind us that we were almost surrounded. Days, too, became a part of that pattern ... at the set ... on the move, but never more than a mile or so, and always being followed by Böttcher's reminders that he did not have our survival in mind. The hours became confused, day followed night, followed day, but on this night Lindsay had come in to see Willison and I went out to find Maers. I didn't like what I found. He was depressed and jumpy, and that was not my man of the purple feet. He had been asked to do too much and it was beginning to tell. 'He's mad,' he said, of Livesey. 'That's why they call him the Mad Major,'

I answered, trying to lighten him a little. 'No. He is mad. He's going to get me killed.' 'Never! You'll be okay.' 'I'm telling you. He will.'

TEN

Break-Out D+5: on the TOBFORCE front

At first light of 26 November, O'Carroll sent his C Sqn against 'Wolf' and this time it was taken, together with the CO of Bologna and 200–300 of his men. York and Lancs, who went in with them, also captured 26 Bredas, twelve Fiat light machine-guns, twelve 3.7mm anti-tank guns, four mortars and two 88mms. These last had been dug in so that their barrels were no more than 12 to 18 inches above ground level and they had fired many rounds. After the attack only 42 men were available to defend the post and there were several messages from them reporting enemy tanks gathering to their south. O'Carroll eventually sent some Matildas to deal with these and they promptly departed. TOBFORCE also made an attack against the Bardia Road block, but this was driven

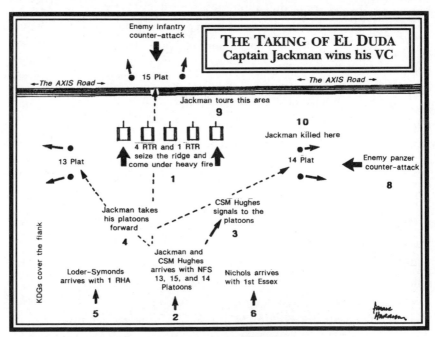

Based on a map in the official history of the Northumberland Fusiliers.

back by heavy machine-gun fire when 400 yards short of its objective. Major Waring was among the casualties of this action.

Then, at 1048 hrs, came the message for which we had been waiting so long. It was from 70th Div and it read: 'Our troops now in possession of all ground on top of the escarpment towards El Adem. Get your "I" tanks up towards El Duda and establish contact at all costs.'

If Willison had been flagging (and there hadn't been any signs of this) this order galvanised him. Within three minutes the code-word 'Plum' had gone out to all the tank regiments and to Lindsay of the KDGs. Willison himself was already on the way to the start-line to organise the attack. O'Carroll had been on his way to the perimeter when he bumped into Willison. He was told that 'Plum' had been ordered, and that his tanks were to lead the attack followed by 1RTR and then the KDGs. Infantry support would be provided by 1st Essex and NFs. In close support would be 1RHA with Captains Goschen and Escher going along as FOOs for B/O Batteries of this regiment and Captains Morrison and Armitage for A and E Batteries, while 149 RA were to be the anti-tank support.

In view of the urgency expressed by 70th Div, Willison discarded his previous timing of attack and simply ordered the attacking units to get across the start-line as quickly as they could. At 1125 hrs he ordered 'Don't wait for anybody. Everybody up on to the ridge!' By now this gathering of TOBFORCE's armour had been spotted by the enemy and the tanks were coming under very heavy fire. Willison ignored it. At 1146 hrs he ordered 'Advance!' and the charge to Duda Ridge began.

The taking of El Duda

Thirty-four Matildas, fourteen cruisers and sixteen light tanks, and whatever armoured cars Lindsay had managed to get to the scene, took part in the attack. It should have been a stately charge, since it was geared to the 12mph of the Matildas, but too much fire was falling on the five miles of open ground being crossed to allow for stateliness. O'Carroll's tank was knocked out and his gunner killed but his men went in without him, C Sqn on the right, B Sqn on the left, A Sqn in reserve. Perhaps they were a little too stately for Willison, because at 1223 hrs he was ordering: 'More speed! Much more speed!'

The leaders reached the foot of the escarpment and began to climb. As they crested the ridge they came under intense fire from the front and the left, but behind them was Willison and he was no less aggressive. 'Attack with greater vigour!' he ordered. By 1320 hrs the great prize was his. The Matildas were on the escarpment, 4RTR on the right and facing right, 7RTR on the left and facing left. The armoured cars stayed at the foot of the ridge but the composite cruiser squadron went beyond, as far as the Trigh Capuzzo. Willison, too, went forward. As soon as he could after the ridge had been occupied he was standing on the Axis Road and looking for the friends he had been told were on Belhamed. All he could see coming from that direction were enemy shells and he told 70th Div so: 'Belhamed is not held by friends but on the contrary is heavily defended.' There had been confusion perhaps, between the locality Belhamed and Bir Belhamed, the hill on its northern side. There was no confusion about the shells raining in on the ridge which were uniformly hostile. The square mile or so of the crest was under heavy fire from several sides: guns from the southern escarpment firing from the front of the position, guns on Belhamed firing from the left front, and a troop of long-barrelled high-velocity guns, probably 88mms, firing from the foot of Belhamed in the left rear. What Willison later described as a 'torrent of shells' was crashing on to the ridge and creating so much dust that the tank men couldn't see whether they were being opposed by panzers or artillery. He asked O'Carroll, who had made it up the hill, if the hold on the escarpment was strong enough to justify his calling up the infantry, and O'Carroll told him: 'If the men are half as frightened as I am we shan't be here much longer.' At that moment Major Loder-Symonds, DSO, of 1RHA, appeared at Willison's elbow. Willison asked him what he was doing in the middle of a tank battle when he should be with his guns. 'I am with my guns,' he was told. 'They're coming up the hill right behind me.'

And so they were. So too was Captain Jackman, and this was one time when he didn't need to ask for a target. Under a plan worked out prior to the attack, CSM Hughes jumped from his truck and, standing in the open, used a flag to direct the three machine-gun platoons to their positions. Lieutenant Sanderson took 13 Platoon across the Axis Road on to the south-west slope of the ridge. Langley set up 15 Platoon's guns in the centre of the position. Jackman led Lieutenant Ward's platoon across the front of the feature between the Matildas and the enemy guns, braving the intensive fire this movement caused, and set these guns where he wanted them. Their heavy chattering soon joined in the cacophony, and as they located the enemy gunners and began to wipe out their crews the enemy firing grew less. Once again Jackman had arrived in the nick of time and once again his appearance had turned the tide of battle. On this afternoon on Duda Ridge his tiny detachment was to win twelve decorations including the Victoria Cross, three DCMs and several MCs and MMs, an astonishing haul.[32] But where were the infantry who should have been doing the consolidating? Where were the Essex? Therein lies one of the sadder stories of the break-out.

At 1155 hrs they had joined the NFs on their start-line. At 1230 hrs they watched the tanks advance on their objective. At 1330 hrs they were ordered via the radio on a KDG armoured car to advance at once. Their advance went well during its early moments, the flat ground allowing their vehicles to maintain a fair rate of progress, and the battalion was out in the open ground and following its carrier platoon when a flight of fifteen Maryland bombers and its escorting fighters passed overhead. They had seen these planes on their outward flight and had exchanged recognition signals, but before they could repeat the signals the bombs were dropping;and on to them. Several fell among the Carrier Platoon, its commander, Lieutenant Lawrence, MC, was killed and the platoon suffered 50 per cent casualties. Major Robinson, the officer commanding D Coy, and several of his men were also killed. This was a horrific and shattering blow, and it was some time before the remainder of the battalion could be got back into its advance. Then Lieutenant-Colonel Nichols steadied his men, and leaving his dead and wounded behind, set off for the ridge again. They came up the hill soon after the arrival of the NFs and Nichols set up his Advanced HQ at the foot of the escarpment. He established communication via back-pack sets with his companies, and when the Senior FOO of 1RHA reported to him, he asked that FOOs should be sent to each company. By 1450 hrs he had his battalion established along the highest part of El Duda.

They were just in time. Shortly after this the first counter-attack came in. It reached to within 250 yards of B Coy's position before it was driven back, leaving 30 dead and 50 prisoners. At 1700 hrs the second counter-attack was launched, this time against the depleted D Coy. It was a pincer attack, infantry and tanks coming in from the west and tanks from the east. It too was driven off but at the cost of Lieutenant Parry and several other ranks killed. By now, this company had suffered 25 per cent losses. In its exposed position, HQ Coy was also losing men from enemy shelling. Once again the familiar story was being repeated, an infantry battalion taking heavy casualties in the corridor. By evening 1st Essex had lost three officers and 60 men either killed or wounded, but hard as it must have been for Nichols to watch his family dying around him, he had the heights to hold. He had the living to preserve. He set off around his companies and helped organise their defences; he got the men to dig in and create firing points and by midnight all his companies were wired in. His work, on what must have been a personally harrowing day, was outstanding.

While the charge on Duda was taking place, Willison received word that the New Zealanders were going to make a night march across Belhamed to join TOBFORCE on that escarpment. At 1620 hrs Lieutenant-Colonel Hartnell, CO of 19th New Zealand Battalion and Lieutenant-Colonel Yeo, CO of 44RTR were given the following orders :

(1) TOBRUK GARRISON IS ON EL DUDA.

2) You will join them there.

3) You will fire green VERY flares on approaching and they will do likewise.

The 'I' tanks were to go at top speed on a narrow front, followed by the NZ infantry advancing on a 300-yard front. They had to cross 10,000 yards of uneven and unfamiliar desert occupied by the enemy and they had to do it in the dark. It was a tall order, but the men on Duda neither knew, nor worried about the whys and wherefores; enough that at last these often-promised friends were on their way.

It was 1830 hrs when they arrived, with Major Gibbon at their head, leading a squadron of Matildas. These were the first outsiders to make contact with Tobruk by land since 10 April, and although this shaking of a few hands on a disputed height could scarcely be described as a 'relief', at least there was a photographer to record it. A Captain Keating, I believe, popped up as if by magic, camera in hand, and took the obligatory snap of Willison and Hartnell greeting each other.[33]

The next visitors were awaited with mixed feelings. At 2130 hrs Lieutenant-Colonel Yeo led in six more Matildas and more NZ infantry, who had taken 200 prisoners *en route*. Yeo was the father of Captain Bill Yeo, the Adjutant of 1RTR. Earlier in the day, Bill Yeo had been chatting with George Hynes about the approach of his father, whose voice he had been listening to on his tank radio, when a shell from a 21cm gun exploded next to his tank. He was killed instantly and Hynes received a minor wound. When the colonel came in he was taken to one side and told of his son's death. Shortly after that he left with his tanks to make his way to Belhamed. That ride must have been filled with despair for the man. But his was not the only tragedy to hit TOBFORCE that day. At 1500 hrs Jackman set off on a tour of his guns on Duda. Fusilier Dishman told of what happened next: 'Captain Jackman came and lay down on the gun line and began to observe through his binoculars. He then gave us the order to fire on a truck and motor-cycle. "Give them a burst," he said, and just as those words were said a mortar bomb dropped just in front of our left-hand gun wounding three and killing Captain Jackman and Corporal Glare instantly.'[34]

In fact five men were killed and eight wounded. The brave Jackman, who had walked among flying bullets all this day and on many others, was felled by a chance mortar-bomb towards its close. He died unaware that his determined courage had won for him the Victoria Cross, the third to be awarded to men of the garrison.

At the time of the meeting of Hartnell with Willison, the face of the corridor was a mile wide and it stretched between eight and nine miles from the perimeter. At its widest point about half-way down it was five miles broad. Beyond this line only 'Wolf' and El Duda were held, and this part of the corridor was only being kept open by the mobility of Brown's cruiser tanks, which were continually driving off the many attempts to cut it.

Break-Out D+5: on the Eighth Army front
Westphal, in charge at El Adem now that Rommel had gone to the frontier, watched TOBFORCE take El Duda and the advance of the New

Zealanders with foreboding. He had been unable to get in touch with either Rommel or Crüwell for two days and had no idea where they were. He decided that the whole Axis position around Tobruk was in danger of crumbling and, taking the bull by the horns, spoke to von Ravenstein by radio. He described the threat now growing against the immobile besieging force and suggested that von Ravenstein return and attack the New Zealanders from the rear. Von Ravenstein was only too happy to oblige. He re-crossed the wire, had a brush with the New Zealanders on the frontier which cost him 40 men, then headed for Bardia to refuel. He met PZ15 who were coming out from that town and they told him that Rommel was there. He went in to report the arrival of his troops to Rommel and was the recipient of an outburst of rage. Rommel had thought that von Ravenstein was deep inside Egypt and about to attack the railhead. When von Ravenstein informed him of Westphal's order Rommel shouted that it must be a fake, but he did not countermand it, and this was significant. Instead he told von Ravenstein to get his division along the Via Balbia to the Sidi Rezegh area. He then ordered Neumann-Silkow to clear up the frontier area and then to also get back to Sidi Rezegh. The dash to Cairo now became a dash back to the Libyan cockpit.

The removal of Cunningham

On the British side this day saw a dramatic development, when Auchinleck removed Cunningham from command and replaced him with one of his own staff, Major-General Neil Ritchie. It was a strange appointment. Ritchie had previously served as a divisional commander of a division, and was now being asked to take over an army containing two corps, each of which was commanded by a soldier senior to himself. This in the middle of a battle which was not going too well. Ritchie, however, accepted the role and flew out to Maddalena that afternoon to relieve the despondent Cunningham. Meanwhile, the New Zealand 6th Bde completed the capture of the Sidi Rezegh escarpment. The situation at the Sidi Rezegh–Tobruk end of the conflict was now much happier for Eighth Army, but for how long would that be the case with the panzers streaming westwards again?

This day is one which I can place firmly among the kaleidoscope of days and nights I spent in the corridor. Some of 1RHA's guns had been set in 'Tiger' to support the attack on Duda. They soon came under heavy counter-fire from a battery of extremely big guns. We were also in 'Tiger', if a little way from the guns. I came off the set during this time and walked out into the shelling. I didn't take to it. I found a hole as quickly as I could and got into it. It was already occupied by four of the Black Watch who were playing cards. The shells whistled and crashed all around us, each seeming closer than the last but the players ignored them. They called out their hands and threw down their cards and cursed whoever won in language which needed an interpreter. I waited for the shell which I was sure would at any moment claim the kitty. The tension down-under was too great for me and I just had to get back out on top, where at least I would be able to see what was happening. I did see. One of our guns on the site took a direct hit. I saw the gun go over and the men around it scatter. A few minutes later it was firing again.

ELEVEN

Break-Out D+6: on the TOBFORCE front

TOBFORCE was on Duda. Tobruk had been relieved. Or had it?

For this was the day on which Godwin-Austen signalled Scobie, 'Impossible for New Zealanders to go further than the ground already held; they are expecting trouble from the south-east, and now it is Tobruk's responsibility to hold open the corridor to El Duda and to hold El Duda at ALL COSTS.' When he spoke of 'corridor' he was not necessarily referring to the one so dearly bought by TOBFORCE; there was now the other corridor linking TOBFORCE with the New Zealanders on Belhamed.

It was also a day of downpour which reduced visibility to next to nothing. It was wretched weather in which to fight and perhaps this was why the enemy confined his activities to shelling. At 1120 hrs Willison was informed that KDGs were now down to 50 per cent of their original strength; they had not suffered their casualties in any major encounter, theirs had been a slow bleeding, car by car, day by day. Yet they were still carrying out their patrols; one troop, penetrating beyond Duda, discovered a complete enemy workshop, and tanks were sent out to destroy it.

A situation report arrived from 70th Div which said that as soon as possible after Sidi Rezegh, Belhamed and El Duda were firmly established, the NZ Division would continue west along the escarpment to a general line of Tobruk to the El Adem–Bir El Gobi track, and that TOBFORCE would conform on the north. This meant that TOBFORCE would have to take 'Plonk' and 'Bondi'. The positive note was pleasing but the message was puzzling. The NZ Division had suffered many casualties in its attacks at Sidi Rezegh and Belhamed, and there was no way in which it could alone consolidate that pocket and at the same time advance along the proposed line. Presumably the consolidation was to be carried out by others, 22nd Guards Bde perhaps, or S. African 1st Bde, whose commander had so far shown a remarkable ability to keep his brigade in the field but out of trouble. True it had held up Ariete, but much of that action could have been written by Gilbert and put to music by Sullivan, especially its ending, when the brigade withdrew for its sleep and allowed Ariete the freedom of the road it had been blocking all day.

New orders from the fortress put an end to all such speculation. At 1420 hrs came news that the NZs were expecting trouble from the southwest. It was followed at dusk by a warning from XXX Corps that 70th Div could expect a heavy attack from the east. Suddenly, alarm bells were ringing all over the corridor. All Beds and Herts companies were warned of the importance of holding on to 'Tugun' until the end, no matter what the cost, and 1RTR was ordered to leave El Duda and get into a position from which it could maintain the sides of the corridor.

At 1645 hrs, Captain Bennet, Willison's liaison officer at 70th Div, came into the ACV with a copy of Godwin-Austen's message. In it he suggested that O'Carroll take command of the El Duda position while Willison remain in 'Tiger' in command of a portion of the forces plus the squadron of 44RTR's Matildas and the NZ Battalion. The suggestion made sense; what was to come might well develop into two battles, one for Duda ridge and the other against the walls of the corridor. But it was to lead to misunderstandings concerning the routing of orders and to cause friction between Willison and 70th Division's staff officers.

On El Duda O'Carroll now had under command 4RTR, D Sqn 7RTR, one squadron of 44RTR and one troop of 1RTR. For artillery support he had 1RHA and a platoon of anti-tank gunners. His infantry was 19th NZ Bn, 1st Essex and a company of NFs. He called a meeting of the officers commanding this conglomerate. Nichols of the Essex was there, so too were Lieutenant-Colonel Hartnell, Loder-Symonds, whose guns were on the escarpment, and Jock Holden, wearing his woolly hat and scarf against the cold that plagued this corner of the wasteland. The position was explained to them. The action was agreed by them. If attacked, there would be no withdrawal.

The return of the Aussies

The attacks began before dusk. The first, against 'Wolf' by 30 Italian tanks, was not effective. Then came an attack on El Duda from the south-east, and this too was beaten back. The last attack of the day was against 'Tiger' and was made by six AFVs; two of these were destroyed and the others retired. When news was received that PZ21 was moving west along the Trigh Capuzzo and was being followed by PZ15, TOBFORCE knew that these had been probing attacks only, and that the real fireworks were about to be ignited. The night closed with everyone preparing for a hard morrow. Essex spent most of it sowing their position on Duda with mines which had been lifted from the perimeter.

Scobie now faced a serious problem. His infantry had drained away to the extent that those he had left were having difficulties holding on to their gains. Fresh attacks by them would be problematic, resistance to major counter-attacks would be limited. He had no divisional reserves left. But there remained one first-class fighting force within the garrison. This was the Aussies' 2/13th, which had missed the boat when the remainder of 9th Division was evacuated. Scobie turned to its commander, Lieutenant-Colonel Burrows, for help and it was offered at once. The battalion was placed on orders to move up to the perimeter. With this offer came other support – two troops of Polish artillery.

Break-Out D+6: on the Eighth Army front

The information 70th Div had passed to TOBFORCE was incorrect; it was PZ15 that was advancing along the Trigh Capuzzo, and PZ21 was following along the Via Balbia to the north. Rommel was in a hurry again – his orders to von Ravenstein and Knabe to return to Sidi Rezegh had gone out at 0200 hrs, By first light Neumann-Silkow was already at his task of cleaning up the frontier, and this early bird caught NZ 5th Bde in its laager. There was a short sharp battle in which the infantry and guns put up a good fight but had little chance against the panzers, Neumann-Silkow captured Brigadier Hargest and 800 of his men. Then Rommel arrived and told him to get back to Sidi Rezegh as fast as he could. He also recalled the group which he had sent to attack HQ Eighth Army at Fort Maddalena, one of whom was his former aide, Schmidt.

The third arm of the tank force which only two days before had been ordered into its great crusade of destruction was Ariete. It had sneaked past S. African 1st Bde and arrived at Bir Ghirba, where it was busy shelling its own compatriots in the Savona Division. Crüwell, who was searching for his Panzergruppe, came across the Italian armour and hastened it on its way back to Sidi Rezegh. The great dash was over. Almost a complete failure, it had seen loss of momentum, dispersal, disorder and dissipation. Far from ending the campaign at a single stroke, it had cost Rommel men and panzers he could ill afford, to add to the losses he had suffered during *Totensonntag*. According to von Mellenthin: 'The Afrika Korps had accomplished nothing on the frontier and was only a fraction of the magnificent force which had entered the battle on the 18th.'[35] Westphal echoes this: 'The two Afrika Korps divisions returned from their fruitless raid in such poor shape that they were unable to tip the balance in our favour.'[36]

If the dash had been successful it would have been the high point of Rommel's career; as it turned out, it was the lowest. It ended with the loss of a divisional general and the farce of his picnic hamper. Von Ravenstein had gone ahead of his division and ran into a NZ battalion near Pt 175. He was taken into custody, pretended to be a certain Schmidt but then admitted to his correct identity, and was passed down the line. The picnic hamper found in his staff car and containing a box of Crosse and Blackwell goodies was not passed down the line.

With his great ability to adjust, Rommel put all this behind him; not simply the day but every moment of it. As his son Manfred was to write later: 'He photographed only when advancing.'[37] He was returning to Sidi Rezegh, he was taking his Champions back to the cockpit. But he was returning to a different scenario from the one he had so recently left. The defeated and scattered XXX Corps had done a Phoenix; it had risen from the ashes of its burning cruisers, gathered together its bits and pieces, and added other bits to these. It was ready to return to the field. To mix metaphors a little, and to return to the less classical one used earlier, there is an adage among the cauliflower-ear fraternity which says that you must never turn your back on an opponent no matter how glazed his eyes may appear. On the contrary, that is the moment when you give him your biggest biff. There is nothing in Rommel's biography to suggest that he was ever inside a ring, but he was a fighting man and he should have known better than to leave the battlefield before administering the knock-out.

The three days of Rommel's absence had been vital ones for XXX Corps. Its strength had been restored to more than 100 armoured fighting vehicles fit for action. When he left on his dash its brigades had been shattered and their wrecked tanks were smoking all across the Sidi Rezegh valley. Now here were two of those brigades back in action: 22nd Armd Bde blocking the Trigh Capuzzo and preventing PZ15 from getting through, and 4th Armd Bde on the panzer division's flank and peppering its vehicles. To continue the metaphor, this ability of the British to get up from the floor and return for more, should have raised questions in Rommel's mind as to how much longer his own fast-tiring troops would be able to lift their arms to deliver a punch.

Alas, risen from the ashes they might have been, but better-educated as a result of the burning, the British tank commanders certainly weren't. The two brigades held up PZ15 until nightfall and then withdrew, of course, into laager, thus presenting the panzers with the freedom of the track. The astonished but grateful panzers accepted it and rolled on through the night and climbed the escarpment. PZ21 was to the east but was also headed for the Sidi Rezegh area. So too was Ariete. Pitt says that the New Zealanders on Sidi Rezegh were unaware of this growing danger, and that they spent this night gathering their dead and preparing to move into Tobruk.[38] That they should have been so ignorant of the danger they were in is scarcely credible. True, Scobie's earlier orders to Willison to be ready to move on 'Plonk' and 'Bondi' in association with the NZs suggests an optimistic view of their situation, but Scobie's later message (timed at 1645 hrs) contradicts his first. It stated quite clearly that the New Zealanders were expecting trouble. From where did this warning originate if not from them?

Break-Out D+7: on the TOBFORCE front

The morning which had opened with a general stand-to at 0545 hrs in the corridor and had been expected to bring attacks against both Duda and the perimeter saw nothing like that. Indeed, the only action was carried out by KDG patrols. Sergeant John in one car captured two truckloads of Germans and went on to take out a machine-gun nest and its crew in a wadi near Bir Belhamed. Fifteen minutes later, Sergeant Bristow and Corporal Bourhill ambushed two more trucks filled with German infantry. Lieutenant Richardson had a different type of patrol; he was detailed to escort General Scobie from the perimeter to meet the New Zealanders in the corridor.

If there was not much in the way of action there was quite a bit of friction, brought about by the previous night's division of command in the corridor and break-downs in communication. At 1130 hrs 70th Div received orders from XXX Corps to occupy the Bir, the northern part of Belhamed, from 1400 hrs in order to help the NZs. They ordered O'Carroll to send a squadron of tanks and 19th NZ Bn from Duda to seize the Bir. Unfortunately they sent the order via Nichols of the Essex and not through Willison. This was probably done because O'Carroll was in charge of all forces on Duda and 70th Div were using Essex to transmit messages to him. But this movement of tanks to Bir Belhamed affected the overall position inside the corridor and was therefore within Willison's province. Willison was being badgered by 70th Div to make an attack against both 'Walter' and 'Freddie' so that some of the strain building up on that side of the corridor against the New Zealanders could be eased. He had also been warned to stand by to meet an attack on El Duda. Given the size of his tank force the two tasks were scarcely compatible.

At 1055 hrs he was asked: 'When will the other party commence? (the attack on 'Walter') It is important not to delay too long.' Almost before he had time to reply 70th Div was assuming that as soon as the 'Trigh situation' (the threat to El Duda) was over, Zero would be ready for this northern party (the attack on 'Walter').

Willison gave the orders for the northern party at 1129 hrs. It was to be in three parts:

FREDDIE: S/L east and west track 2,500 yds south of FREDDIE.

1 Company 2nd Queen's to advance at Zero.

7RTR to advance at Zero + 10.

All artillery to fire on FREDDIE from Z-10 to Z+20

WALTER: S/L from rally after first phase.

Tanks and infantry cross S/L at Z+45.

Rally in area between Bardia Road and WALTER.

Artillery Z+50 to Z+60. 3 troops on WALTER, 1 on FREDDIE.

ROAD BLOCK S/L for tanks, the track north-east and south-west
    north of WALTER.

S/L for infantry = JACK

Artillery; 1RHA, 30 minutes on the road block.

The first phase got under way fifteen minutes later when 7RTR moved to its start-line, and it was shortly after this that O'Carroll received his orders through Nichols to attack Bir Belhamed. He decided to check the authenticity of these orders and asked the ACV, 'Is this okay?' Willison was so deeply involved in the northern action that this question had to be withheld until he had a free moment. As if one complication were not enough another had just arisen; 7RTR, who were forming up on their start-line, reported a group of enemy tanks to the east of 'Wolf'. Willison immediately warned O'Carroll and Brown that this might be the armoured attack which had been expected since the previous night. By now 7RTR's Matildas were being heavily shelled from the north-east and Willison ordered them to stop their attack and to withdraw the infantry.

It was into the minutes after Willison had called off the northern attack that O'Carroll came on to the air again and said that he had been asked to carry out two operations, the Bir Belhamed attack (by 70th Div) and the repelling of an attack on El Duda (by Willison). He could not do both. Which had priority? Willison was perplexed, he had not given an order for an attack on Bir Belhamed. Then O'Carroll's original questioning of the order from 70th Div was passed to him. He was furious. He snarled over the air to the unfortunate officer manning 70th Div wireless link: 'You are issuing instructions to my tanks on El Duda not through me. I cannot carry on a show unless orders are issued by me.' The reply came that the attack against Belhamed was extremely important and that the Commander (Scobie) insisted that both go on. Willison, good soldier that he was, calmed down immediately, but some damage was done, and it was later claimed (by Holden of 7RTR) that for a time 70th Div would only take messages from Windsor in the ACV. I was in the ACV during this period and was never aware of such a situation. Meanwhile Willison now had three problems with which he must deal:

(i) the raid on 'Freddie'

(ii) the attack on Bir Belhamed

(iii) the unidentified enemy columns south of El Duda.

Five minutes after the spat Willison was ordering 7RTR to commence the attack on 'Freddie', but warning Holden that no rear protection could now be offered. Holden replied that in that case he would have to deal with enemy infantry before he could begin the attack, and Willison agreed to this. Then Holden asked that the start of his attack be delayed as the threat to his supporting infantry was serious. Willison again agreed. During the next two hours the actions were so interwoven that they are best read in the form of selections from signals and crowded war diaries:

1415 hrs 7RTR rallied after driving enemy from flank of attack and are now advancing with infantry on FREDDIE.

1428 hrs Squadron of 4RTR set off for Belhamed taking NZ infantry to 430411 to join 4RTR on top of Belhamed.

1445 hrs FREDDIE strongly held. Infantry have been unable to get through the wire and are pinned down. Tanks unable to get through mines.

1502 hrs (from KDG) 2 enemy columns to the south have now joined up.

1511 hrs (from 7RTR) Infantry have many casualties.

1515 hrs (from 7RTR) Have only 2 'I' tanks and 2 lights still in action. 4 tanks on minefield. 1 knocked out and 1 cruiser blown up.

1516 hrs (from Willison) Clear off FREDDIE! Stand by! Do not go on to WALTER!

1525 hrs (Willison to 70th Div) Not going on with WALTER attack.

1532 hrs (from 1RTR) Enemy moving west. Our cruisers are going to assist 7RTR.

1602 hrs (from 7RTR) Infantry CO does not consider that he can withdraw his troops before dark.

1608 hrs (from 1RHA) CO reports his guns [supporting 7RTR] are red hot and the shells are having to be rammed in.

The infantry were the King's Own, and they were as usual in a very tight spot. They had crossed their start-line at 1415 hrs and were followed ten minutes later by five Matildas. Shelling was fairly heavy during the approach march and HQ Platoon tank on the right received a direct hit. The tanks caught up with and passed the infantry about 1,600 yards from the S/L but ran on to a minefield 700 yards south of 'Freddie'. Soon four tanks had been immobilised, two crewmen killed, three wounded and four were missing. Holden's tank was one of the casualties but he had managed to get out and climb on to another tank. When the King's Own reached the minefield they were without tank support. They came under heavy automatic and mortar fire and were finally stopped 300 yards short of the post. Captain Freeland ordered his reserve platoon to crawl up on his left flank but they were brought to a halt by fire coming from the right of 'Freddie'. The enemy's front seemed to be crescent-shaped so that the whole of the infantry company was under fire from the front and from both flanks. Freeland crawled to the tanks and asked them to try to get forward to cover another attempt by his men, but they managed to move only 50 more yards. He then found the FOO, Captain Turner, and asked him to get a concentration of fire put down over the post. Turner obliged, and although wounded in the shoulder, continued to fire his guns until his carrier was hit and its wireless set destroyed. Freeland then decided to try to pull his men out and asked the tanks to give them smoke cover. The tanks tried to do so but their canisters fell behind the enemy. Freeland and his men had no option other than to keep their heads down, squeeze themselves to the ground and pray for dark. At about 1800 hrs a brave KDG driver took his car out to them and brought out some of their wounded. By the time the rest of the company followed fifteen minutes later they had suffered 35 casualties.

While this action was being fought there was a development in the corridor which was to prove significant. Scobie ordered 16th Bde to move 2/13th on to El Duda as quickly as possible. Willison was given the news at 1705 hrs and again showed his appreciation of the fighting qualities of the Australians by his reaction. There was, however, the matter of getting them on to Duda. Willison asked Lindsay to come and see him, with the intention of giving the KDG Commander the task. When Lindsay arrived it was immediately obvious that he was not capable of doing anything. He was utterly exhausted. He was literally rocking on his feet. He was unable to follow Willison's words. Streams of caked blood ran from each ear and down the sides of his neck. There is only so much the human frame can take and his had taken it and more. As I remember that moment, de Winton volunteered to go and went to find transport. Lindsay was taken out of the action and sent into the perimeter to the fortress hospital. He was evacuated some days later so that his ear-drums could receive the treatment they needed. I was sorry for Lindsay, he had performed great deeds in his idiosyncratic way, but I was pleased for Maers. Premonitions can be soul-destroying.

Not long after this Willison was told that the NZs on Sidi Rezegh and Belhamed were running short of ammunition. Two destroyers had arrived in the harbour bringing 50 tons each; this had been unloaded and a convoy of 80 trucks was waiting inside the perimeter to take it through to them. Willison decided to use the Australians and KDGs to escort the convoy to El Duda. Then he met Scobie at Bridge Z, who told him that the NZs were down to 5 rounds per gun. Willison decided to go forward with the ammunition himself, but just before midnight he met XXX Corps' HQ which had come in via Duda. After discussing the situation he decided to send the convoy with a KDG escort, and the armoured cars managed to get it through to its destination. Alas, much of that ammunition was soon being used against TOBFORCE.

Lindsay was not the only Tobruk Tanks stalwart to depart the scene on this day. A bomb, though not of the aerial type, at last caught up with George Hynes. He was with Lieutenant Geddes of 1RTR when they saw the thing, Hynes picked it up. 'Christ!' he exclaimed, 'It's hot!' and he threw it away. He was too late; it exploded, wounding both men, Hynes so severely that his war was over. This meant that all three of the regiment's squadron commanders had become casualties in the corridor.

Break-Out D+7: on the Eighth Army front

The build-up and movement into position by the returning Axis forces continued but there was nothing in the way of major action during the day.

TWELVE

Break-Out D+8: on the TOBFORCE front

The morning began with an amusing interlude for the men in the corridor. The three HQs which had been to the east of Sidi Rezegh had grown tired of being harried by enemy columns and had decided to come inside the fortress. From midnight there had been a steady stream of B Echelon vehicles passing through Duda and going on into the town. It was very slow going along the now quite dreadful tracks and by 0630 hrs the traffic was halted nose to tail between the ridge and 'Tiger'. It was an inviting target and Böttcher and his guns seized on it. Their shells rained down, and the bottle-neck cleared as though by magic, to the great and naughty joy of the men in 'Tiger'.

There had not been much in the way of sleep for the ACV personnel because of this traffic and of midnight conferences and early-morning planning. The astonishing thing was how Willison stood up to it. He was twice as old as we were, he had been on his feet well after midnight, following a pretty hectic day, and yet he was back on them well before first light, spruce as ever and ready to go. At 0400 hrs he was issuing orders for an attack which the brigade had been asked to make on Dahar Adeimat Ridge, to the south of Sidi Rezegh. The brigade armour now stood at 26 Matildas, nine cruiser tanks, 20 light tanks and seventeen armoured cars, which was roughly half the force that had crossed the bridges nine days before. Considering the casualties suffered since then, these figures spoke highly of the work being done by his recovery and repair teams.

Willison decided to use the Matildas in this attack. The infantry was to be Antipodean, men of 19th NZ in the fore and the Australians of 2/13th on their left rear. A troop of anti-tank guns from 149 Battery was to accompany the NZs, and 1RHA gunners were to support the attack. The start-line was to be the Axis bypass. His plan of attack was interest-

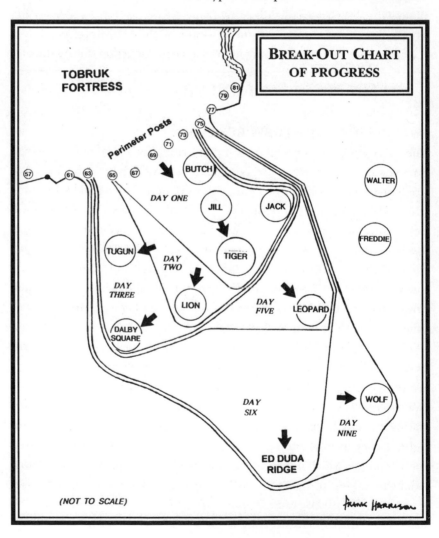

ing. When the ridge had been taken and the NZs established on a firm footing there, the Matildas were to wheel left and attack any troops between them and Sidi Rezegh. In other words, he was adopting Rommel's favourite hammer-and-anvil tactic, with Freyberg's men on Sidi Rezegh as the anvil. Unfortunately, a salvo of enemy shells fell among 2/13th before they had had time to dig in and casualties were suffered. This was worrying for more than the usual humanitarian reasons. Willison had been asked to be as sparing as he could with the battalion because of the special circumstances of its presence in the fortress and he was hyper conscious about it suffering casualties.

At 0740 hrs he went off in his car to find out for himself what the situation was on Belhamed. He reported back that it was no longer held by the NZs, but he was not completely correct in this – they still held Bir Belhamed. Zero Hour for the proposed attack was now postponed until the location of the NZ brigade could be verified. In the meantime 70th Div came up with yet another request, this time for an attack from 'Wolf' against Belhamed. There was a proviso: Willison should not commit 2/13th any more than was absolutely necessary. Then at 1046 hrs came the sudden end to all this talk about offensive movements. Willison was warned that the enemy might attack him 'today', and was ordered to maintain 'extreme vigilance'. He immediately ordered defensive positions to be taken up.

The panzers made their first appearance at 1140 hrs, an FOO reporting sixteen of them about 10,000 yards from El Duda. It was PZ15, which had come west along the Rezegh plain and was now turning north to attack Duda from the south-west. After capturing the ridge, its orders were to sweep on around the NZs on Bir Belhamed and isolate the whole of their division in the Sidi Rezegh pocket. Crüwell had wanted a direct attack on Sidi Rezegh but Rommel had vetoed this on the grounds that it would allow the NZs to escape into Tobruk. The second sighting was made by KDG patrols, which reported enemy panzers advancing on El Duda from the south. The third sighting was made by Willison himself. He had driven across to warn Nichols personally about the approaching tanks and on the return trip had decided to make a little recce of his own towards El Adem. He was on the lower escarpment when he suddenly saw panzers on the ridge above heading in the direction of El Duda. He raced back to warn the brigade. On his way he met Scobie, who was also out making a little recce. He told Scobie what he had seen, but Scobie had already heard about the approaching panzers. He now ordered Willison to deal with these, and departed quickly.

The panzer attack on El Duda

Willison raced back to El Duda where he ordered every tank he could find to start up and assemble on the ridge to meet the enemy. He then established his Battle HQ in a wireless truck on the slope of the Duda Sghifet which accorded a full view of the battlefield. His first message was to 70th Div, to be transmitted by them to Godwin-Austen and from him to HQ Eighth Army: 'Tobruk garrison is being attacked by a superior force of enemy tanks. Can an armoured division be sent to our assistance?' Some time later the answer filtered back down this route: 'Yes, but not today.'

By 1330 hrs panzers were coming up the Trigh Capuzzo in some numbers and then turning east in deployment. Two troops of Mk IVs came into action, firing their 75mm guns, and the battle was on. They were too far out of range for the British tanks but A/E and B/O Batteries had moved to the north of the escarpment with the former on the right and the latter on the left. They had four FOOs on the ridge: Captain Salt was north of the Axis bypass in his light tank and Captains Armitage, Goschen and Escher were south of him. Their guns engaged the enemy and knocked out the first panzer in this particular battle. At 1405 hrs a group of Mk IIIs came through the Mk IVs and echeloned outwards; they were firing the new 50mm guns but had come within range of the Matildas' 2pdrs and the British tanks were able to reply. Enemy tanks were now appearing on all sides and it seemed that El Duda was being deliberately isolated. Fifty approached from El Adem, six were to the south of Belhamed, another twenty were to the east, and sixteen in the north-east. It was noticed that their movements were hesitant, and the conjecture was that there were some very tired men inside those panzers.

Next came reports of concentrations of panzers and infantry in dead ground out of sight of Duda, and at the same time KDG, who were east of that position, came under attack. They were ordered to withdraw and 1RTR's guns were brought forward to cover this flank. This meant that the rest of the corridor had been stripped of its defensive armour except for the single tank which was serving as protection to Brigade Forward HQ.

At 1515 hrs Willison saw some 88mm guns being brought up alongside the enemy tanks and these were soon in action. Panzers had now reached to within 1,000 yards west of El Duda and lorried infantry were arriving from the direction of El Adem. The cruisers reported a considerable number of infantry at 433417 and Willison ordered 1RHA's guns to attack these. Shortly after this the enemy's plan of attack took shape when combinations of panzers and infantry moved from out of the dead ground and advanced against the Essex positions. This was the critical moment. Willison ordered every tank in the corridor to get up on to the ridge no matter what its condition, and then went out personally to position them. They came up with jammed turrets and broken guns, some crawling along. One or two tanks which were already there and had been knocked out earlier but whose guns were still capable of firing, were now manned. If it was to be a last stand, the Tobruk Tanks would make it together – win or perish, their Brigadier among them.

And that was the moment when the flank attack came in against 'Dalby Square'. It opened up with an artillery barrage and then sixty of the small Italian tanks approached the post followed by three companies of infantry. Here was an extension of the crisis; if 'Dalby Square' fell, this attack could be developed across the corridor to cut off El Duda. Willison detached six cruiser tanks from the main battle and sent them to intervene. He also ordered the single tank at Bde HQ to join them in a counter-attack. The Italian tanks were driven off and York and Lancs reported heavy casualties among the infantry that had accompanied them. Meanwhile an interesting three-way conversation was taking place between Willison on El Duda, Windsor on 'Tiger' in the ACV and GSO2 in Tobruk.

Willison: 'I think we are countering an armoured division. Our fellows are putting up a magnificent fight and are being well handled.'

GSO 2: 'From which direction is the attack?'

Willison: 'From the south-west.'

GSO 2: 'Is the battle on top of the escarpment or between the
    perimeter and the escarpment?'

Windsor: 'Still on top or I wouldn't be here.'

At 1655 hrs the enemy attempted to slip down the escarpment to attack
the corridor in flank, possibly in conjunction with the Italian attack.
There were several lame-duck British tanks to the north-west, disabled
but capable of putting up a fight. Willison ordered that these be manned.
Two of 7RTR's Matildas which were on their way back from the repair
shops joined them. As the panzers began their descent these crocks
opened fire and were supported by the RHA guns. Together they drove
back the enemy tanks. Then a group of about thirty panzers which were
on the north side of the Axis Road began to advance east against Duda.
Willison asked that every artillery piece that could range on these tanks
should do so. The panzers advanced behind a heavy protective barrage
and O'Carroll ordered his tanks forward to meet them. It was at this
moment when Captain Bennet, the liaison officer, arrived with news that
the NZs on Sidi Rezegh were also under attack. A major assault on the
whole of the Sidi Rezegh–Belhamed–El Duda pocket was under way.

As the light began to fail it became difficult to follow what was happening. At 1818 hrs enemy tanks and infantry came down the road from
the west and were engaged. They had brought anti-tank guns with them
and these began to knock the British tanks about a bit. By now the Matildas had been in action for five hours; they were outnumbered by three
or four to one but had as yet given up not an inch of ground. The KDG
Commander asked if, in view of the failing light, he could withdraw his
patrols which had been machine-gunning the enemy infantry and gun
crews. Willison agreed, but said, 'Keep them ready.' 'Any time, anywhere,' came the reply.

The panzers penetrate Duda's forward defence lines

Enemy tanks and infantry were now closing in on all sides. The panzers'
75mm guns were concentrating on the Essex FDLs and were causing
many casualties and gradually breaking down their defences. At 1700 hrs
they made the first breach, several panzers over-running a 149 anti-tank
section and B Coy's trenches. More infantry entered the breach and pen-

etrated the rear of A Coy's lines, taking prisoner most of the two Essex platoons manning that section. Some also came in from the south against D Coy's front but this incursion was halted. The rest of the panzers moved in for the kill. They were accompanied by more infantry and they pressed on until they reached almost to the RHA gun lines. The whole area under attack was being subjected to intense fire of every kind – mortar, artillery, tank and machine-gun. The light tank from which Captain Salt had been firing his guns was hit and he was killed. Then fifteen Matildas arrived on the scene and a tank battle took place. Soon, half the Matildas had been knocked out and the remainder were forced to withdraw. O'Carroll reported that enemy anti-tank guns were right up with the panzers and were knocking 4RTR about a bit, but he said that they had decided to stay and fight it out.

When Nichols reported his situation to be desperate he was not exaggerating. The Essex had lost all their anti-tank guns in the vicinity of the ridge, and were now without any external support. B Coy HQ and a small group of remnants were still holding out in some caves. C Coy held on to their position but there was no news of D Coy. The enemy had eighteen cruiser and seven light tanks inside Nichols' defences, and sufficient infantry to take complete possession whenever they felt so inclined. His only consolation was that at that time the German infantry were digging in around their panzers instead of doing this.

Willison had returned to the ACV on 'Tiger' when darkness fell. He was greeted by a shell which burst near his car and he was hit in the head by a bit of shrapnel, but it was not a serious injury. The gunfire was so intense that he was unable to hold a radio conversation and so he used the Black Watch RAP telephone line to explain the situation to Scobie, while at the same time having his head bandaged. Scobie ordered that the enemy tanks be driven off the Essex FDLs and the position be restored.

Willison reviewed the situation. His forward defence lines had been breached and enemy tanks were in among the Essex. But 19th NZ and 2/13th's lines were intact, 1RHA had a battery of guns right forward and there was a platoon of the NFs with its Vickers also on Duda. The important question was: did O'Carroll still have the strength to spearhead a counter-attack? He set off for Duda in a KDG armoured car, and called in on Lieutenant-Colonel Burrows, the CO of 2/13th Battalion. He told him: 'Two companies of New Zealanders will come under your command forthwith. When our tanks counter-attack you will go in with the bayonet and destroy his infantry. It is impossible to give a Zero Hour because the tanks are engaging the enemy and will have to win their fire-fight first. Your reaction must be immediate.' Then, over the car's radio, he asked O'Carroll, 'Are you still on the ridge?' O'Carroll told him: 'The position is still held. Approximately eighteen enemy tanks are on FDLs of left sector Essex. I have ordered a counter-attack to destroy them.' Willison replied, 'Magnificent work!'

At 2135 hrs an anxious Scobie spoke over the air to Willison again, and after being put in the picture said: 'The position must be held at all cost.' Willison: 'Our tanks are outnumbered ten to one but are clinging to the German armoured division and will cling to the last tank.' Scobie: 'Your message is appreciated. Use your infantry. Our tanks, however weak, are going in to the enemy. Good luck!'

Some time later the gallant Nichols contacted Willison. He had managed to extract the remains of his B Coy and a platoon of A Coy from among the Germans and had reformed them to the north of B Coy HQ. He told Willison that they were ready to take part in the counter-attack.

The retaking of El Duda
Meanwhile O'Carroll was in difficulties. At 2000 hrs his tanks had gone into a night formation. B Sqn under Major Patton was on the top of the escarpment, but he had several rickety tanks and would not be able to take part in the counter-attack. Major Pritchard's C Sqn was also on top of the ridge and was the logical one to use, but O'Carroll could not contact him. He asked Major Roberts, whose A Sqn was at the foot of the escarpment and covering the western flank, to check the position of the enemy tanks. Roberts tried to do so but failed to find them. At this point O'Carroll heard a commotion going on near his tank. He heard an Australian voice say: 'We found him sneaking about in our lines, the bastard. What's the use of walking him around in the dark? Why don't we just shoot the bastard?' There was a chorus of agreement and O'Carroll

jumped down to investigate. He discovered that the unfortunate 'bastard' was his missing squadron commander.[39] Poor Pritchard had been looking for his tanks in the dark and had been arrested as a suspicious person. O'Carroll rescued him and sent him to recce the enemy tanks. Pritchard could not find them either, but at that moment Armitage of the RHA came up to O'Carroll's tank and offered to show him where they were. The two men went out together, found the panzers, and O'Carroll returned to where Pritchard had assembled his tank commanders. Zero Hour for the counter-attack was imminent.

It has been generally accepted that O'Carroll gathered all his remaining tanks and sent them against the far more numerous enemy tanks in a last desperate shoulder-to-shoulder charge with all guns blazing. It sounds good, but is not correct. Pritchard lined up his half-dozen tanks and these alone made the charge. The other tanks on top of the ridge – Patton's cripples – only opened fire as the panicking panzers fled past them on their way off the ridge. Meanwhile the Australians coming up behind Pritchard got in among the enemy infantry and in moments it was all over. They had to be restrained from charging ahead, otherwise they might well have gone all the way to El Adem. Among the trophies of this night battle was an 88mm gun, taken with all its crew and with a live round still up the spout.

So ended eleven hours of dogged resistance. A panzer division had been taken on, held and finally driven away. PZ15's War Diary describes the night action: 'Our defensive positions were fought to a standstill one after the other by the English [sic] tanks and their weapons and ammunition destroyed. Battle Group I was overrun and most of it captured. Battle Group II had to abandon its positions, withdraw 1,000 metres west of El Duda and take up new defensive positions.' It went on to say that the strongest of Rommel's armoured formations was held on the western side of the Sidi Rezegh position for the better part of twenty-four hours. Moreover, it had happened in full view of Rommel, Crüwell and other senior staff who had taken stance on the southern escarpment at Bir Bu Creimisa to watch the attack go in.

It was a story in keeping with those of 14 April and 1 May, and how appropriate that the Australian infantrymen who had played such a key role on those dates should again be at the heart of the action alongside the tank men. It was also, of course, the story of a little more wasting away of the fast-declining Panzergruppe Afrika.

Break-Out D+8: on the Eighth Army front

Where was the British tank division which could not get to the corridor on that day? In short, trying but not too hard, to get to Pt 175 on the Rezegh escarpment. Bennet's information about the NZs on Sidi Rezegh being under heavy attack was incorrect, but they had been under pressure and had taken casualties. Freyberg was aware that PZ21 and other units were building up in his vicinity and wanted to get as good a grip on the escarpment as possible. He spent much of the day attempting to get the elements of XXX Corps which were south of him to come north and join him. The units in question were S. African 1st Brigade and the two British armoured brigades, 4th and 22nd. Pienaar had begun to emulate the Grand Old Duke of York, except that he failed even to reach the foot of the hill, never mind scale its heights. He certainly marched his men around and around but it was usually into or out of a huddle. Less than a week before, he had been close enough to the destruction of S. African 5th Brigade to feel the heat from that immolation and the experience seems to have dictated all his subsequent moves regardless of orders or appeals.

Gott did order an attack by the tanks towards Pt 175 in the afternoon, but this was brought to a rapid halt by the appearance of some enemy tanks, whereupon both sides spent the remainder of the day firing at each other from a range so extreme as to be a waste of ammunition. It appears that at last some common-sense caution was beginning to seep into the British armour commanders' tactical considerations. It was unfortunate that it should happen at the moment when a little rashness might have helped the New Zealanders. As it turned out, the only armoured force to get up on to the escarpment was Ariete; their commanders waved their berets at the men of 21st NZ as they approached them, and the NZs, thinking that their visitors, wearing black berets, were British tank men, ran out to join in the celebration. They were all captured. Buster Keaton, it seems, was still writing the script, but had changed sides.

As the day drew to its close the NZ positions reading from west to east were: 24th and 26th NZ Battalions were on the western end of the Sidi Rezegh escarpment; 18th and 20th NZ were five miles to the north on Belhamed; and 25th NZ was five miles to the east but also on the Rezegh escarpment. The nearest British armour was 4th Armd Bde which was some five miles to the south-east of 25th NZ and almost directly south across the airfield from Ariete. Pienaar's brigade was in laager some-where below the southern escarpment. The Axis positions reading in the same direction were: PZ15 on the southern escarpment to the south of 24th and 26th NZ; Böttcher's former Group (now the Mickl Group) far-ther to the east along the same escarpment; Ariete at Pt 175, and PZ21, now commanded by Böttcher, on the escarpment east of Ariete. It was a hodge-podge of a situation in which the British armour and infantry were separated from each other and in which the individual infantry battal-ions were each facing powerful enemy forces and had strong enemy forces on their western flank.. It was a situation made for exploitation by whichever Commander was quickest on his feet. Given the happenings of the past few days this was hardly likely to be General Norrie.

THIRTEEN

Break-Out D+9: on the TOBFORCE front

An enemy Order of the Day had been found during the recapture of the Essex position. It claimed that El Duda was very thinly held and must be retaken immediately. It was therefore expected that Rommel would renew his attempt to take the ridge and this expectation was confirmed in the early morning when fifty enemy tanks accompanied by infantry were seen approaching from the west. They were 4,000–5,000 yards west of Duda when the two artillery regiments, the guns of 1RHA and 104RHA, took them on. The tanks stopped immediately, and an hour later withdrew to the south-west. While this was happening Essex received a visit from G1 of 70th Div. He came to congratulate Nichols on his part in the previous night's battle and to inform him that command of all troops on El Duda now passed to him. This was customary when infantry, tanks and guns are operating together at a fixed site in a defensive situation, but it was also a diplomatic avoidance of a repeat of the row when 70th Div had gone over Willison's head to give orders to his subordinate. It should be stressed at this point that Willison and O'Carroll were the closest of friends and remained so.

A minor problem now arose but was solved almost as quickly. TOBFORCE had captured a large number of guns but the Commander Royal Artillery had no one to man them. O'Carroll mentioned this to Burrows, the Australian. He said he had men who could fire anything. He was told that there were four 75mm guns and plenty of solid-shot ammunition. He was invited to help himself and would he please use them as anti-tank guns on the north-east of the position. If he did so it would have been his final service for the garrison, because he was hit by shrapnel that day while speaking to Nichols and had to be evacuated from the corridor.

Willison now had an advance repair section and was getting the benefit of this, and of his retention of the battlefield. The previous day's tank and armoured car casualties were taken here for speedy repair, and when Willison asked at 1032 hrs 'Are any more tanks on the way?' he was told that three were coming up. On this morning the tank state and positions read:

On Duda were 20 'I' tanks (4RTR, thirteen; 7RTR, three; 44RTR, four); and three cruisers and three light tanks of 1RTR.

In a central position between 'Jill' and 'Tiger' were a troop of 1RTR's cruisers and all their light tanks, whose role was to protect the sides of the corridor.

Patrolling the corridor were two KDG troops of armoured cars numbering twelve in all, and five cars were in reserve behind 'Tiger'.

An outstanding feature of the battles in the corridor had been the recovery, repair and return to action of damaged armoured vehicles. This matched that of DAK, and there can be no higher compliment. One aspect of combat which helped towards this was the retention of the ground on which the actions were fought. At all times of the day and night single tanks could be seen trundling forward from the repair section in order to join their comrades.

After the big battle there was no resting in the corridor. Strengthening of the infantry posts went on all morning, new wire was put up and mines were brought out from Tobruk and sown around them. There was only one actual enemy attack, against 'Tugun', which the Beds and Herts dealt with, but there was the usual shelling, including air-bursts which were particularly unwelcome. A good deal of panzer movement to the south of Duda was observed but it was all at a distance. Three groups were seen on the move between 1530 and 1632 hrs, the last numbering about twenty AFVs which came from the south and then turned east and moved off along the Trigh Capuzzo. The slopes of Sidi Rezegh were reported as being like Hendon car park during an air show, but what was going on there was anything but festive. At 1745 hrs came a report that many of the vehicles on Sidi Rezegh were on fire and the most forward of TOBFORCE's tanks reported that a tank battle was going on there. Willison's order to 4RTR to pay particular attention to that flank was probably the most unnecessary order of the week.

Late that evening, some guns opened up on 'Jack', firing from a new position. When bearings were taken these showed that the offending guns were firing from the coast. Willison and Lieutenant-Colonel Williams had a conference and decided that this could be the softening-up process prior to an attack in that area. Williams ordered all guns in the corridor to be turned to face towards Tobruk until dawn, and Willison warned 1RTR and KDGs to be ready to counter-attack in the centre of the corridor should that be necessary. Both proved to be wise precautions. Meanwhile the fires on Sidi Rezegh had died down, leaving everybody in the corridor wondering what had taken place there and what state the NZs might be in. Then, at 1900 hrs, came a message asking for guides to take a convoy of ammunition to the NZs beyond El Duda, which indicated that they were still on at least a part of Belhamed, and that they had retained their fighting capability.

At some time during the day an organisational change took place. The objectives of the break-out having been achieved, command of all troops outside the perimeter less 32nd ATB (with 1RHA under command) reverted to the infantry brigade commanders. Responsibility for the area adjacent to the perimeter was invested in 16th Inf Bde, and the remainder of the corridor in 14th Bde. Adjustments were also made to the infantry positions in the corridor. Beds and Herts were ordered to move to the rear of Bir Belhamed and take up the task of protecting the south-eastern junction of the corridor with El Duda. Then, at 1530 hrs, York and Lancs were withdrawn from 'Dalby Square' and moved to the east, leaving only a dozen men and one officer behind to act as an outpost. Defence of the eastern side of the corridor and its link with Belhamed had suddenly taken precedence over that of the west.

Break-Out D+9: on the Eighth Army front

The burning vehicles on Sidi Rezegh belonged yet again to the Eighth Army, this time to its exposed New Zealand contingent. All day the NZs had watched for help to arrive either in the shape of British tanks or a S. African infantry brigade. It had not come. All afternoon they had been pounded by artillery of the Mickl Group, and then in the late afternoon the panzers of PZ15 moved in, smashing through 24th NZ Bn and scattering its personnel. Shortly afterwards, Mickl Group attacked and destroyed 26th NZ. By nightfall the whole of the Sidi Rezegh escarpment and airfield was back in Rommel's hands.

And while all this was taking place, where was the armoured division that Freyberg had called for until he was hoarse? It was no longer in existence as a division. Scott-Cockburn's fighting was over; he had handed what tanks of his Yeomanry brigade still survived to Gatehouse and had followed Davey to Cairo. Gatehouse now had a composite brigade of some 120 cruiser tanks, so it was still a force to be reckoned with. Unfortunately, by now it had also become a very cautious brigade. Norrie ordered it to combine with the South Africans to drive Ariete from Pt 175 and then to join Freyberg's men. Given the disparity in number and quality of tanks, Gatehouse should have been able to brush aside Ariete with ease. He failed to do so. His brigade wasted the day in a half-hearted attempt to come to grips with the Italian armour, and then retired for the night to the south of Pt 175 and far from the beleaguered New Zealanders.

As for the South African Infantry Brigade, Norrie went personally to 'ginger them up'. It was not a happy experience. He found himself at the head of the brigade, acting as carrot to an unwilling donkey. All afternoon he led it in a crawl, looking over his shoulder to see if he was still being followed and sometimes finding that he was not. It was a ridiculous position for a corps commander to put himself into, and one wonders how long Montgomery would have suffered it, or would have tolerated Pienaar's prevarication. Nor was the tardiness of the approach its only fault. Instead of taking the direct route across the airfield to Pt 175, Norrie led it on a looping route which eventually brought the South Africans to Bir Sciafsciuf well to the east of the Trig point. This put Ariete and PZ21 between them and the New Zealanders. It was almost dark by the time this brigade arrived at Bir Sciafsciuf. Pienaar made a slight probe forward which resulted in a few casualties and the brigade promptly went into laager. It was as well it did so. Had it tried to reach Freyberg it would have had to drive through both PZ21 and Ariete, and if it had achieved this miracle, it would have needed another miracle of resurrection to have found friends waiting there. Apart from a handful of HQ personnel, the NZs, who had waited and watched for support through three long days, had all been either killed or marched away into captivity.

Leadership on the British side was very culpable that day. Norrie wasn't only weak, his actions were faulty; his choice of destination put the troops he was leading beyond any possibility of helping Freyberg and his choice of route allowed Pienaar, a glutton in his devouring of time, a whole day to chew on whose every moment was crucial to Freyberg's men. Nor did Gatehouse shine; this was one time when risks should have been taken, but the hammerings the British armour had suffered were at last beginning to sear the reckless spirit it had previously shown. There were faults at higher level too; there is no sense, in the happenings of that day, of a firm hand at the centre of British activity. The only firmness lay in the insistence that Freyberg should remain in what was fast becoming an exposed position, and with a much weakened force. This requirement held credence only if he had armoured and other support. If that could not be guaranteed, he was only there to be destroyed.

A major difference between the tactics used by Rommel and those used by the British commanders becomes apparent when the movements of these few days are considered. The British seemed incapable of making up their minds as to what type of battle they wanted to fight, dithering between the positional and the mobile. This owed much to the arrangement of their forces into two clearly defined roles. Rommel was never less than certain about this. He would throw together into an active and unified whole whatever troops and commanders were immediately available to him for whatever task faced him. If a locality had to be defended (as at Hafid) he would ensure that it would become a 'killing' defence. But he would take his Panzergruppe wherever there was an enemy formation waiting to be destroyed regardless of the name or the topography of the location. The old canard on which the British soldier had been fed – that the German soldier was hidebound and little more than an automaton serving rigid masters – died for ever under Rommel's leadership. There were no disparate elements and no immutably fixed roles when he was on the scene; there were bodies to be fitted into the exigencies of the moment, and even when defending, he quite naturally took the aggressor's role.

There is a sense of Greek tragedy about the situation which unfolded remorselessly around those heights during the two days, with the New Zealanders doomed to destruction while the British commanders stood in the wings, dreaming dreams which lacked any possibility of fulfilment, making promises which could not be kept, and (presumably) wringing their hands when the destruction took place. A New Zealander on Sidi Rezegh on that day had every right to consider himself a sacrifice to self-interest, caution, weak leadership and poor tactics.

Break-Out D+10: on the TOBFORCE front

Action began early in the corridor on this first day of the Christmas month, with reports coming into the ACV during the night that sounds of men digging could be heard in the neighbourhood of 'Jill'. When Willison stepped outside to greet the dawn he found himself in the middle of what he later described as 'a real fireworks display'. He hurtled back into the ACV and to its microphone. Both KDGs and 1RTR were brought into action. As the light became clearer it was seen that about 130 German infantry armed with machine pistols, two anti-tank guns and two flame-throwers were attempting to seize 'Jill'. Had they managed to do this they would have been astride the main track leading from the bridges to El Duda. They were unlucky. The guns which had been turned around the previous evening rained shells on them. There was a short sharp battle in which the German were caught between the Leicesters and the machine-guns of the NFs firing from 'Jack', and the guns of 1RTR and KDG. The little battle was over quickly and left 26 Germans dead and 47, including two officers, taken prisoner. One of the latter, a major, carried the plan for this attack. It was to come in from the Tobruk–Bardia road to the north-east. There were two parts to it: ZUG A (against 'Jack') and ZUG B (infiltration between 'Jack' and 'Butch' to cut the corridor at 'Jill'). The ZUG A force had been shot up by the Leicesters and its remnants had been chased away by the KDGs. The ZUG B force had been wiped out by 1RTR.

The threat to 'Leopard'

(NB. At this point the actions being fought by TOBFORCE and Eighth Army converged and so they are presented together.)

The loss of NZ 6th Bde had forced Godwin-Austen into considering the hitherto unthinkable: the withdrawal of NZ 4th Brigade from Belhamed into the fortress. He was too late. Neumann-Silkow was on the move before dawn and at 0600 hrs his panzers supported by elements of Süm-mermann's division crashed through 20th NZ's lines. Freyberg withdrew with 4th Bde HQ to the east, where he was told that 4th Armd Bde was coming to cover his withdrawal. Had he been a cynical man he might have smiled a little at that news, but come they did at last. Drew, the first CO of the Tobruk Tanks, took 5RTR straight across the direct route from the south to the Rezegh escarpment while under fire from both Mickl Group and Ariete. He lost several tanks while doing so but pressed on in a gallant charge. He then provided a protective screen for Freyberg and his surviving men while they retired from the scene and the battle. The performance of the NZ Div had been notable. It had taken the frontier posts, advanced to Sidi Rezegh during the critical stage of the early battles, had taken the Rezegh positions and had held on to these under great pressure for days. Now for most of the New Zealanders the battle was over. At 1010 hrs 70th Div intercepted Freyberg's last message to Godwin-Austen: 'We hung on in the hope that South Africans would attack and recapture Pt 175 and Sidi Rezegh before dawn today without which our position untenable. Enemy has attacked and [captured] our HQ, half our artillery and divided our forces in two.'

The enemy's recapture of the Rezegh heights now made the junction between those NZ troops who were still on Belhamed and the British troops on El Duda, the critical focus, both of enemy action and defensive purpose. The NZs were now in jeopardy, and could expect to become Rommel's next target for destruction. When Willison was advised of the loss of the Rezegh position at 0935 hrs he must have blessed his previous night's decision to transfer the Beds and Herts from the western side of the corridor into 'Leopard' on the eastern side. All companies had arrived in this new position by 0200 hrs and had begun to consolidate at once, their first task being to complete the laying of a minefield along the eastern side of the corridor at the foot of the Belhamed escarpment. They had been in position for only a few hours when they heard sounds of battle coming from the direction of Belhamed. Soon, personnel from 18th NZ who had been to the west of 20th NZ fell back from much of Belhamed and began to filter into the Beds and Herts' lines. The first NZs came through at about 0730 hrs in vehicles. They brought news that the NZ brigade was being badly cut up. As others fell back, the Beds and Herts' position became a rallying point. Into it came twelve 25pdrs and a troop of Breda guns with their crews, and these were used in a rapid reinforcement of that sector of the position that was in direct line with the approach from Belhamed. Rapid re-organisation took place. A company of the Australians' 2/13th moved in, and the survivors of 18th NZ joined them here. Beds and Herts' A Coy's front was extended so that it now took in the line of the track on to the Belhamed escarpment. Everybody was now standing to, expecting at any moment to see panzers descending from Belhamed to attack them. The moments passed ... became an hour ... two hours. The panzers did not arrive; indeed, the sounds of battle died away. By 1445 hrs the position had been stabilised with 18th NZ and its support still holding the edge of the escarpment to the east of Beds and Herts' A Coy. At 1449 hrs the ubiquitous Loder-Symonds arrived with his B/O Battery. He took the surviving NZ guns under his wing and they stood firm alongside the NZs. The SITREP drafted by Beds and Herts at 1515 hrs gave an analysis of the situation on this side of the corridor:

(a) Position held is organised for all-round defence both for each company and for the battalion as a whole.

(b) Anti-tank defence is strong = 10 x 2pdrs and continuous a/t minefield extended along whole northern front.

(c) 18 NZs in position edge of escarpment preventing observation of battalion area.

BUT:

(a) Area dominated by Belhamed feature [Bir Belhamed].

(b) NZs are tired.

(c) NZs only holding small area of escarpment.

THEREFORE:

(a) Essential that NZ area should be as strong as possible.

(b) If enemy advances on Belhamed feature and occupies it both NZ area and this battalion area would be untenable.

The misapprehended order

At 1645 Beds and Herts were told by 14th Bde that they should be pre-pared to withdraw from 'Leopard' during that night to a position in the rear of 'Tiger'. At 1730 hrs Major Stephenson, the acting CO, held a con-ference to discuss the arrangements for this. Then at 1800 hrs the order was cancelled, and he was told to consolidate on his present position. The background to this order and counter-order has relevance, since it has led to a mistaken but generally accepted notion which has appeared in most of the accounts of this part of the desert campaign.

When the news of the loss of most of Belhamed and of Freyberg's depar-ture from the scene reached Tobruk, a crisis conference was held there. Scobie was ordered to take all the New Zealand troops under command and to be prepared to withdraw from El Duda. This last part of the order was transmitted down the line and Willison was instructed to use his brigade to cover a withdrawal which would take all the troops in the corridor back inside the perimeter. The powers that be were once again reacting to Rom-mel, rather than making policy; they were seeing their immediate salvation in a speedy return of their western wing to siege conditions.

The men who had won the corridor and its posts would have none of it. The order was taken to O'Carroll by armoured car, and he spoke to

Nichols about it. The two agreed that they would not contemplate leaving a position for which their men had fought and died: 'We felt that we didn't intend to have captured and held against all counter-attacks what we had, for nothing.' Similar statements were reaching Scobie from other units in the corridor. Willison informed him of the reluctance of his brigade to give up the ground for which they had fought so hard. He was confident that it could be held; at his disposal at the time were 91 anti-tank guns, five batteries of 25pdrs, three companies of heavy machine-guns and the AFVs of 32nd ATB, now numbering 36 'I' tanks, twelve cruiser tanks, thirteen light tanks and eight armoured cars, a not inconsiderable force at this stage of affairs.

The orders were withdrawn; there was no return into the fortress as historians claim. Apart from the loss of 'Dalby Square' (see below), at no time from the beginning of the break-out until the final link-up of TOB-FORCE and Eighth Army did the former quit one inch of the corridor it had created at such cost.

The attack on 'Leopard'

On the far (and enemy) side of Belhamed the infantry of PZ15 was given the task of clearing the northern part of that area and was told that all resistance there must be removed. An order issued by DAK at this time stressed the importance of Belhamed to the Germans: 'It has become clear since the loss of Belhamed, how extraordinarily important the possession of this place really is. For since Belhamed was occupied by the English [sic] there has been no connection with the group in El Adem except by dangerous and difficult routes.'

In the late evening an attacking force was sent against 'Leopard'. It was made up of infantry but included anti-tank, artillery and Pioneer elements. A and C Coys, Beds and Herts, both saw the attacks coming in, and also reported enemy tanks on their northern front. By 1822 hrs the two companies were under panzer and infantry attack. The NZs were also being attacked from the north-west, but B Coy, Beds and Herts, which was in an isolated position, was taking the brunt of the attack. At 1925 hrs, a D Coy platoon was sent in to help but failed to get through to them, and the telephone line to B Coy was cut. Within the hour men from this company began to fall back into D Coy and Bn HQ lines, and they brought word that B Coy had been overrun. The situation as then seen by the regiment's analyst was:

(a) B Coy position in enemy hands.

(b) The enemy attack has been held in front of A Coy and to the left rear of NZs.

(c) The enemy now in a position to exploit his attack on B Coy by taking Battalion HQ and attacking C Coy from the rear or avoiding C Coy altogether.

A plan of defence was drafted to meet the developing threat to the whole position. The enemy salient which had formed as a result of the loss of B Coy's position was to be sealed off by an anti-tank minefield. This would consist of a single line of Italian box-mines, spaced every four yards. C Coy less a platoon was to move 150 yards to the north-east of Bn HQ, thus commanding the re-entrance to the rear of the B Coy position. The remaining platoon was to remain on the original C Coy position to protect its two anti-tank guns. If the enemy made no further advance from the captured B Coy positions during the night, all available weapons would open fire on that area at first light.

Stealthily, within a hundred yards of the enemy, the mines were laid, the movements of men carried out. Then, perhaps, the defenders of 'Leopard' slept a little, but they were up and watching well before dawn.

In the meantime Tobruk had lost two of its original stalwarts. Captains Goschen and Escher of the RHA, who had been at the heart of so much of the action during the siege, and often at its sharpest edge, were wounded and evacuated. The brave but unfortunate Goschen was drowned when the ship taking him to Alexandria (probably the *Chakdina*) was sunk *en route*. Several more Tobruk stalwarts were to be lost in this sad way before Christmas.

This is a day which stands out in the memory. I was taking a spell outside the ACV in the 'Jack'–'Jill' area when I was approached by a padre from 14th Inf Bde. He handed me several small squares of white cloth, each about the size of a handkerchief, and asked if I would search around for the German dead left from the morning attack and when I found one, would I cover the man's face. He wandered away on his search and I began mine. I found several bodies and did as he asked. I didn't understand why he wanted this; perhaps it was a symbol of the closing of the light, perhaps it was simply to keep flies from what moisture still remained there. As for how I felt about it, sufficient to say that words like 'decimated' and 'wiped out' come easily from the tongue or pen, but that every battlefield death comes much less easily – it has been violent as well as untimely.

FOURTEEN

Break-Out D+11: on the TOBFORCE front

When that first streak of light in the east brought the new day to the Beds and Herts, it allowed them a view of their opponents and to make estimates of their numbers. They put these at 400 men in the old B Coy position and another 1,200 in front of A Coy, between the line of the Axis Road and the western edge of the escarpment. These were men of the Kolbeck Battalion of 90LT, among whom were 'Africans released from prison' – former German members of the French Foreign Legion. As arranged on the previous night, all weapons, including some Polish guns which had arrived in the early hours, were brought to bear on these enemy troops in order to frustrate any planned dawn attack by them. This barrage brought a quick result. Kolbeck had been reinforced by two panzer units and part of Anti-Tank Regt 605, but when the Poles knocked-out one of his panzers the others departed quickly, and his anti-tank guns were soon silenced by extremely accurate fire from the defenders of 'Leopard'`s Breda guns. The situation now looked a little more promising for the latter; their minefield had not been penetrated, the enemy facing A Coy had been caught in enfilade fire and were also overlooked by the NZ troops. The enemy in the former B Coy position were on a forward slope of which both C Coy and Bn HQ (which was now a fighting unit) had excellent observation. The fire being brought down on these exposed enemy positions by all arms was reported to be devastating. By 0720 hrs the enemy had had enough and began to withdraw. They tried to cover their movements by putting down smoke on A Coy's position but this was ineffective. Then they attempted to reform in dead ground, but that area was immediately shelled and mortared. It was all too much for Kolbeck's men and they withdrew completely. In a moment of impudent bravado, two of the battalion's carriers chased after them; it proved to be imprudent bravado, they forgot their own mines and one of the carriers went up in smoke.

This little battle for 'Leopard' had put O'Carroll in a quandary. Should he send tanks to help there (which would weaken the El Duda position that might also come under attack at any moment) or must he let the defenders of the post fight on without armour? He had Major Pritchard with twelve tanks situated 3,000 yards from Belhamed; Captains Kendall and Gardner with thirteen tanks on top of Duda, and Major Roberts with four tanks in reserve. He decided that he should send help and ordered Pritchard to move his left troop to the north where it could watch 'Wolf', and to advance his right troop and engage eight Mk IIIs, which had appeared south of Belhamed and were advancing on 'Leopard'. Roberts was to move directly east as a demonstration. Poor Pritchard! As he approached to help the Beds and Herts he was fired on by them, then lost two of his tanks on their minefield. This, following his experience at the hands of the Australians, must have made him wonder just who were his enemies. However, he was able to report that the enemy were withdrawing from 'Leopard', and then to open fire on a considerable number of enemy infantry who were trying to escape across the minefield, causing these to hurry back into captivity.

During the remainder of the day the El Duda position was gradually extended to the south until the Trigh Capuzzo was brought within range of TOBFORCE guns, and late in the evening, XIII Corps (which was still inside the fortress) gave 70th Div instructions for its part in yet another attack then being planned by Eighth Army. TOBFORCE, acting as its northern arm, was to advance west from El Duda along the edge of the first escarpment. It was surprising, and pleasing, to learn that Eighth Army had recovered its aggressive tendencies and was not already on its way helter-skelter to the frontier, but the proposal required that Scobie find yet more infantry from his fast-dwindling force. The only way he could do this was to thin out his perimeter defences still more. He did so, extending the Polish line until they and the Czech Battalion held half the

perimeter. This released 1st DLI and 4th Border Regt for whatever purpose Eighth Army might have in mind.

Break-Out D+11: on the Eighth Army front

Rommel had won yet another victory at Sidi Rezegh and one feels that had
he ever become a member of the British peerage that name would have
been chosen to embellish his nobility. He was now presented with several
alternatives. He could allow his troops to rest and renew (and his men were
in desperate need of this); he could finish off this pestiferous XXX Corps
by turning on 4th Armd Bde and S. African 1st Inf Bde and destroying
them beyond resurrection; or he could launch another attack on TOB-
FORCE. Godwin-Austen must have expected the last of these, hence his
orders of the previous day for TOBFORCE to abandon its corridor.

Yet one can imagine how these options were treated by this man
whose actions were so often instinctive. Rest his troops while they still
had breath within their chests and panzer tracks that would turn? Never!
Waste time and precious fuel chasing what was left of XXX Corps into
the desert? No! Let them be picked up at leisure. Have another go at this
extremely tough Tobruk nut? Yes, but with another option at the same
time. When his staff heard of this other, chosen, option they must have
blanched. Part of DAK would have another try to reduce the corridor by
attacking TOBFORCE, but the rest would make a second dash for the
frontier. They would relieve his troops at Bardia and Halfaya, and cut off
whatever remained of Eighth Army in Cyrenaica .

Crüwell, who favoured an all-out attack on TOBFORCE, wrote his condemnation of the idea: 'We must not repeat the error of giving up to the
enemy a battlefield on which the Afrika Korps has won a victory and
undertaking another operation some distance away, instead of destroying
the enemy utterly.'[40] It was to no avail; it is testament to Rommel's domination of such men that his will prevailed. He would attack El Duda and
he would send a strong force east. For this last foray he created two battle
groups, one from each of the panzer divisions, but without any internal
panzer elements. The first, Group Geisler, would advance along the Via
Balbia. It was ordered to gain the Sollum positions and the territory on
both sides of the Via Balbia, and to act as convoy protection for transport

supplying the Sollum front. The second, Group Knabe, would advance along the Trigh Capuzzo with similar tasks. Both groups would be under the command of Neumann-Silkow, who would follow with panzer support. Ariete and Trieste Motorised Division would go part of the way and guard the rear flanks of the two columns. The advance would begin at first light of 3 December. As for the attack on El Duda, this would be in traditional pincer form: one claw consisting of elements of the panzer divisions with Italian support would advance from the west; the other, Sümmermann's 90LT, would attack from north and east. As for the remnant of XXX Corps, his two reconnaissance battalions would move into the El Gobi area to check on what these bits and pieces might be up to.

Here then was yet another exercise in dispersal and one which would have turned the British Commanders green with envy. It placed fresh burdens on men who were far from fresh themselves. Worse, it echoed the error of his first dash to the frontier by allowing Eighth Army yet another breathing space in which to carry out a second programme of reorganisation and reinforcement. Liddell Hart describes his surprise on going through Rommel's papers, to find that such a thruster had been so thoughtful and that his audacity was so shrewdly calculated.[41] It is a description that hardly describes the thruster of 2 December. Meanwhile, Auchinleck had arrived at Fort Maddalena and was to remain in the field in an advisory capacity for the remainder of 'Crusader'. Renewal and reinforcement of Eighth Army presently in the field of action was accompanied by the building up of a force well to the south of Sidi Rezegh. A bumping-forward exercise took place which sent S. African 2nd Div to the frontier; which, in turn, sent Indian 4th Div into Cyrenaica. Other units coming forward included the divisional artillery of recently arrived 1st Armd Div and an armoured car regiment. Ritchie's intention was to shift the emphasis of attack to the El Adem area, thus endangering all the Axis troops east of this bottle-neck. The orders that 70th Div now gave to Willison formed the northern arm of this operation.

Break-Out D+12: on the TOBFORCE front

Willison was called into the fortress by Scobie to discuss the prospective attack westward. He was informed that his brigade's task was to capture

'Plonk' and also to advance west along the top and foot of the El Adem escarpment. He found these orders puzzling and said so – if he advanced along the top of the escarpment, all the posts below it would fall, including 'Plonk'. He had in mind the heavy casualties TOBFORCE had already suffered and was not happy about incurring more in an unnecessary exercise. Scobie told him that this was how XIII Corps wanted it to be done, and once again Willison, the good soldier, accepted his role.

For the various units in the corridor 3 December was a day of mixed fortunes. For the KDGs it was marked by two treats. One was a complete day of rest for the whole squadron for the first time since they had crossed the bridges thirteen days before. These had been days of unceasing patrolling punctuated by episodes of often frightening action. They needed the rest. The second treat was a special delivery of beer and cigarettes from the NAAFI. For 4RTR on Duda it was not such a happy day. It began well, with three Matildas coming forward from the workshops, bringing the tank state to 28 runners. The crews spent the morning watching large quantities of enemy traffic travel from east to west along the Trigh Capuzzo and speculating on what that presaged. One of the regiment's officers, Captain Redhead, was sent out in a light tank to destroy several 105mm guns which had been abandoned during the flight from Duda. On his return he reported the presence of more abandoned guns farther to the south. He was warned by Essex personnel to keep away from these because they were in a minefield and the enemy had a good line of fire on it from the southern escarpment, but the temptation proved too strong and Redhead set out to destroy this second batch. His crew returned on foot after dark. The brave but foolish Redhead had been killed as he baled out of his burning tank on the minefield. For 1RTR it was a quiet day, with one of its patrols reaching five miles outside the corridor. Other patrols, however, reported the enemy still present on all sides.

For the men of the Beds and Herts, the day brought a shared, if hidden, chuckle. They were visited by the Commander of 14th Inf Bde. He was examining a captured automatic pistol in the Battalion Post when it went off, narrowly missing their acting CO, Major Stephenson. For Lieutenant Lloyd, who had been left behind with a dozen men to hold 'Dalby

Square', there was to be no chuckling – at last light the night before, he had come under heavy fire and 4RTR on Duda had reported that a tremendous barrage was falling on his post. At 1700 hrs he and his men were reported missing by his parent battalion. Nor were these the only casualties suffered by the York and Lancs that day; those on the east side spent much of it under artillery fire, and lost three men dead from this and nine others wounded. The British guns were by no means silent either; E Troop fired off 150 rounds at the motor traffic which 4RTR were watching.

For the powers that be it was a day of preparation for the coming attack along the escarpment and against 'Plonk'. The Border Regt was ordered to relieve the Australian battalion on El Duda, and it moved its men on to the ridge at 2030 hrs. The Australians, in turn, relieved 1st DLI in the southern section of the perimeter line, which allowed the latter to come into reserve at the northern end of the corridor, ready to take part in the attack being planned.

Break-Out D+12: on the Eighth Army front

On the German side of the great divide it was not a happy day for the men whom Rommel had chased off to the frontier. Geisler and Knabe had got away to an early start but neither had reached his target. They were spotted from the air and preparations were made to give them a warm welcome. The armoured cars of Central Indian Horse tempted Geisler's column on to NZ 5th Brigade's Maoris, who took some revenge for what had happened to their kin on Sidi Rezegh by wiping out Motor Cycle Bn 15. Knabe ran on to the guns of 31FGR of the newly formed Goldforce Group, and could get no further forward than Sidi Azeiz. Both columns were being subjected to heavy air attacks, and Neumann-Silkow eventually withdrew them from action to await the promised armoured support. It never came. The second dash to the wire had been as fruitless as the first, and yet another exercise in debilitation.

Meanwhile an ominous little action was taking place against the Italians at El Gobi, who were being fired upon by yet another British division's guns. Gatehouse's composite armoured brigade had taken stance across the El Adem–El Gobi track, cutting off the strong-point which had so frustrated 22nd Armd Bde on the first day of the November battles, and it was now under attack by Indian 11th Bde. The Indian 4th Div had arrived back in the Western Desert, scene of its great triumph of the preceding year, and was making its presence felt.

Break-Out D+13: on the TOBFORCE front –
Rommel's last attacks on El Duda

The movements ordered on the previous day had been completed, Fourth Borderers were now on Duda, and had set up their HQ at 42574101; A Coy at 42694101; B Coy at 42614108; C Coy at 42654105; D Coy at 42594099. 18th NZ covered their left flank at the edge of the Belhamed position, and Nichols' Essex were on its right flank. However, it was not an ideal placing of troops; 1RHA officers reported that some miscalculation had left a gap between the Borderers' positions and that of the NZs.

At 0700 hrs Rommel began what was to prove his last attempt to sever the corridor by sending panzers and infantry in a pincer attack against El Duda. The first claw was a thrust from the west against the Essex position, the infantry working their way forward along several wadis. The second

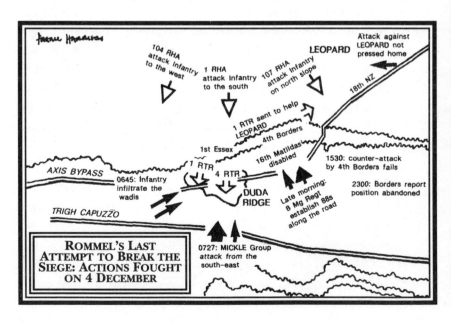

claw came in from the south-west. O'Carroll's tanks were soon fully committed and a squadron of cruisers was sent from the corridor to help them. The British guns also came into action, 107RHA attacking the infantry on the north slope of the escarpment, and 104RHA those to the south. This combined fire from infantry, tanks and artillery proved too much for the attackers and they melted away down the wadis from which they had emerged. By mid-morning this particular attack was over.

Shortly afterwards there came a second attack, this time against 'Leopard'. Cruiser tanks were sent across from Duda to help, but the attack was not pressed home. Then, at about midday, Rommel's troops did succeed in making a serious intrusion into the Duda position. Mickl Group managed to bring forward several anti-tank guns, including some 88mms. They got in under the noses of 4th Borderers and established themselves in the area 42804099–42704095, thereby almost facing the gap between the Borderers and the NZs which the gunners had identified and reported earlier. Their presence was discovered in the worst possible way. At noon O'Carroll sent out a patrol of Matildas; they were to make contact with the NZs and then return along the top of the escarpment, taking on any enemy they met *en route*. It appeared to be a routine task, but proved anything but that. The tanks completed the first part of their mission, but on their return leg they ran into Mickl's ambush and lost two of their number. There had been no report from 14th Bde about the presence of this enemy element, which included a sizeable infantry component as well as 75mm and 88mm guns, and the first O'Carroll knew about it was when one of the ubiquitous artillery FOOs, who seemed to regard the battlefield as their private estate, arrived in a truck at his HQ. He told O'Carroll that the enemy was astride the Axis Road just south of Duda and suggested an immediate attack before they had time to establish themselves there. Although he still lacked anything in the way of firm information or direct orders from the infantry brigade which was holding this sector, Willison took it upon himself to send in his tanks. The FOO concerned, directed artillery fire on to the area and then in went the Matildas. It was the same old story so far as the 88mm was concerned; before the tanks got to within firing range, three out of the five had been knocked out.

Suddenly, Willison had a crisis on his hands. By 1430 hrs six Matildas had fallen to these guns. By 1505 hrs the number had risen to ten tanks put out of action. O'Carroll was not prepared to send in any more without infantry cover. A counter-attack was called for but the Borderers – who had been the guilty party in the first place – were slow to their start-line and their C Coy made little progress before being driven to ground. Two more tanks were lost during this little episode. The gap between the Borderers and the NZs was finally closed at 1630 hrs when B Coy was moved into it, but at last light the enemy was still holding its position across the road from Duda.

Throughout this battle Willison had had the usual support from 1RHA. Its A/E Battery fired 1,200 rounds, but while doing so lost the services of one of its FOOs. He was Lieutenant Morrison, who had been fortunate on a previous occasion when the shell which hit his light tank failed to explode. This time the one that found him did, and he suffered shrapnel wounds which ended his participation in the battle.

Rommel now held a significant advantage over the troops on El Duda, although he does not appear to have realised this. That night, O'Carroll made his dispositions with the expectation that Rommel would attempt to exploit the advantage at first light. All the tanks that were running, and some which weren't but could still fire their guns, were sent to the crest of the ridge. Six Matildas went to the Essex positions and seven to face east with the Borderers. At the foot of the hill he had the crocks and two cruisers standing off to the north: three facing east, four facing west and five in reserve. During the night four more tanks came up from the workshops and the crocks were withdrawn and sent back to the repair section.

For 4RTR it was a night of brooding and of waiting for another fraught day. Following the loss of Redhead the previous day, Captain Kendall, Lieutenant Colliver, Sergeant Stringer, Lance-Corporal Meagher and Troopers Higgins, Norman and Wakefield had all been killed, and three others wounded by guns which should never have been allowed to get within such close range. O'Carroll's comment was particularly bitter: 'Had the Borderers maintained even watching patrols the enemy could never have reached the road without ample warning being given.' In fairness, it has to be added that the Borderers had spent much of the previous night on the move; had not had time to familiarise themselves with their new surroundings, and had come forward with attack rather than defence in their minds. It is possible that they did not appreciate the fragility of the El Duda position.

Break-Out D+13: on the Eighth Army front

It is somewhat ironic that this first really successful intrusion into the corridor, made by the Mickl Group, had not been made with the intention of destroying the corridor. That morning, Rommel had been presented with the bill for the victories he had been enjoying during the last days of November. He was given statistics of German losses in the battle to date and they did not make happy reading: almost 4,000 of his men had become casualties; 142 of his tanks had been destroyed; his artillery had lost eight 88mm guns, 34 anti-tank guns, ten heavy guns, seven medium guns, 24 field guns and 60 mortars.[42] His victories had indeed been Pyrrhic; the dogged and persistent resistance he had encountered during them, and the constant resurrection of seemingly defeated opponents was finally producing the attritional effects on which Auchinleck was now counting.

While he was suffering the impact of these statistics, Rommel's confidence received further knocks. There was the repulse of his latest attacks on the corridor. The two columns he had sent to the frontier were stalled there and were asking for armoured help which he did not have available. Reports were coming in of attacks by 'Jock Columns' on his convoys using the Trigh Capuzzo. He was told that the Axis base at El Gobi was being attacked by a British division that was completely new to him. He realised that Auchinleck was shifting the emphasis of battle from Sidi Rezegh to the El Adem–El Gobi area, and that this threatened those of his troops who were to the north and east of this region. This new emphasis had to be countered. He ordered Crüwell to attack the British force which was threatening the El Gobi redoubt. He recalled Neumann-Silkow's two groups from the frontier, a tacit surrender of his units still in existence there. He began to evacuate the Italian Bologna Division and 90LT (given its new title the previous day) from the investing posts on the Bardia side of the Tobruk perimeter and to move them west towards Gazala, to be preserved for another day. To get there, however, they had to pass along the Axis Road which was now under threat from a TOBFORCE that could sally from El Duda at any moment and block it. The enemy guns which had been giving O'Carroll's Matildas such a torrid time had been sent forward to prevent TOBFORCE doing this. Mickl's role in making the penetration had been one of aggressive defence and not of assault.

Break-Out D+14: on the TOBFORCE front

The worried Commanders of TOBFORCE knew little of Rommel's dilemma as they prepared for what they expected to be a hard day. O'Carroll wanted back every one of his disabled tanks and he also wanted to capture or destroy the guns which had done the disabling. Plans were made for an early morning assault on these, with the NZs attacking from Belhamed and the Borderers from El Duda. The Borderers were ordered to carry out the requisite reconnaissance patrols during the night. They did so, and one of these returned at 0200 hrs with surprising news – the enemy had disappeared from the left flank of the battalion. Nichols sent out a patrol and they not only brought back confirmation of the enemy group's departure but also the even more surprising news that the Germans had abandoned the gun position with such haste that they had left their wounded and even some of their guns behind, a sure sign that they were suffering severe psychological weariness.

Willison was asked by 70th Div to confirm that the enemy was withdrawing from the El Duda locality. He sent out a KDG patrol, but this was less fortunate than the foot patrols. It came under fire, one car was lost on a minefield and a second had a shell penetrate its rear door. But the patrol was able to confirm that the enemy who had been such a serious threat the previous evening had indeed departed the scene. Nor were they the only enemy troops who were on the move towards Gazala. During the night, an OP which 1RHA had set up on the ridge alerted Chestnut and E Troops to the fact that considerable east-to-west movement of traffic was taking place along the Trigh Capuzzo. The gunners got up early and were ready at their guns when daylight exposed a mass of enemy vehicles streaming westwards on the Axis Road. They spent the next two hours firing on some 1,000 vehicles which risked the dash through that bottle-neck.

As the day's dramatic events unfolded, patrols began to probe in all directions from the corridor. Many met resistance, but on the eastern side, a Polish officer who went out with an anti-tank group reported that he had driven as far as the Bardia Road and had found that the road block, 'Freddie' and 'Walter', which had so recently cost the garrison dear, had all been abandoned. For the first time in many months the way from Tobruk to the east was clear and open. A day which had begun with tension because of the artillery threat to Duda now became heady with the excitement of impending victory. It ended with 4RTR receiving the order to support an advance to the west of El Adem. Holden's Matildas would remain on El Duda as reserve to 1RTR, whose cruiser tanks would take over the positions which the resolute 4RTR had won and held on El Duda.

Break-Out D+14: on the Eighth Army front

Rommel might be withdrawing to the west but he was not quite finished. He had sent Crüwell to attack and destroy the British force at El Gobi. Meanwhile a clash of views had taken place between Ritchie and Norrie over the role of the armoured brigade *vis-à-vis* the Neumann-Silkow groups, and it had resulted in this brigade retiring to the east of El Gobi so that it could cover any movement by these two groups. As a result, when Crüwell arrived at El Gobi with the intention of taking them on and destroying them, he found only the unsupported infantry of Indian 11th Bde awaiting him. His panzers mauled the brigade, but were not able to finish it off, nor did Crüwell follow up this effort. This failure raises questions about the General's mental and physical state after so many days of unremitting conflict and manoeuvre, not to mention that of his men in their panzers. Indeed, the ones who came out of the day with most credit were the same Italians who had successfully held off the charge made by 22nd Armd Bde two weeks before, and who had now also managed to resist Indian 11th Bde.

Break-Out D+15: on the TOBFORCE front – The breaking of the siege

This, at last, was the day for spreading wings. 'Freddie', 'Walter' and the road block were all occupied by men of 70th Div without a shot being fired. Brown sent out his cruisers to beat up any enemy they might find to the south and east of El Duda. For the first time in many months they were free to operate in their intended roles and away they went, and did not return until last light. The KDGs were out too; Lieutenant Richardson took his armoured car east, where he came upon a NZ field hospital which had been taken and held by the Italians. He reported Sidi Rezegh clear of the enemy and found himself shaking hands with men of the 11th Hussars among the burned-out wrecks of that tank Golgotha. Among these he discovered Lieutenant Franks' armoured car. By the strangest coincidence, we in the ACV were just receiving news from another KDG patrol that Lieutenant Franks, minus an arm but otherwise all right, had been discovered in a captured German field hospital. Loder-Symonds also took wing. He met that other redoubtable gunner, Brigadier Jock Campbell, VC, by the mosque at Sidi Rezegh, but on this occasion, Campbell was able to take the time to chat.[43]

The Matildas stayed at home. Holden had only four tanks fit for action. O'Carroll had eleven runners left. He was ordered by Willison to withdraw to the north to lick his wounds. 'There is a good deal of licking to be done,' he replied. Alas, there was yet more to come; Captain McGeogh and Corporal Jones were both killed by shelling that night. As for Willison's HQ personnel, one thing became apparent during the planning of the advance on El Adem and this was that he intended to be in on it personally. That was only fair; if any man, apart from his friend O'Carroll, deserved to take the first objective after the siege was broken it was Willison, who had strong views regarding the raising of the siege. At one point during the recent strains and stresses he had snarled to the occupants of the ACV: 'I'll shoot the next man I hear say that Tobruk has been relieved. It was the Eighth Army that was relieved and it was the men from Tobruk who relieved it.'

Break-Out D+15: on the Eighth Army front

This great day for the defenders of Tobruk and its corridor was anything but great for Rommel. On the previous evening he had met the Italian

Colonel Montezemelo to discuss the question of supplies. The Colonel gave him statistics of the losses in tonnage that had been suffered on their crossing to Libya during November. They were horrific. Not only had 60 per cent of these gone to a watery grave, but the loss of so many cargo ships had created a shipping crisis. There could be nothing in the way of substantial supplies before the new year. While TOBFORCE and Eighth Army had been battling in the corridor and across the desert, the Royal Navy and the Air Force had been waging an equally influential war of attrition across the Mediterranean. The consequences of this, and of his own debilitating mistakes (which included the failure to seize the British supply dumps during his first dash to the wire), could no longer be shrugged off. Unless Crüwell could manage a quick victory at El Gobi and then capture one of the British FMCs, there would be no option other than to retire westwards.

He did not get either outcome. Crüwell attacked 22nd Guards Bde but made little progress against it. Then in quick succession Rommel lost two men on whom he had come to rely. Neumann-Silkow was severely wounded while standing in the turret of his command tank at El Gobi. He was taken to hospital where he died two days later.[44] Sümmermann followed him into a grave at Derna three days later, victim of an RAF fighter. By then, Rommel had departed this particular field of battle. He would return. There would be many, many more bones over which to clamber before he finally quit Africa, but that is not part of this story.

FIFTEEN

The end of the Break-Out: the capture of El Adem

Rommel now accepted that he must withdraw to the west. It must have been a bitter decision, not least because it meant that he would have to abandon men to whom he had made a promise, the brave Bach at Halfaya and Schmitt at Bardia.[45] It also meant giving up any hope of taking Tobruk in the immediate future. But he did have a last tactical card to play. He ordered DAK to hold back the forces now pressing in on all sides against El Gobi, so that he could withdraw the remainder of the

Axis forces first to Gazala, and then to safety beyond the salt flats at Fort Agheila. DAK did not let him down. Its men held XXX Corps at bay throughout one vital day, and in so doing they also did Willison a favour. Ritchie decided to let his other Corps, XIII, make the advance on El Adem rather than the by now hesitant XXX Corps, and this slipped the fiery commander of 32nd ATB from the leash.

Scobie decided on a night attack in the hope of catching the enemy abed. At 2030 hrs on 7 December 1st DLI moved through the Essex lines and took the Axis Road west; C Coy on the right, A Coy on the left and B and C Coys in the rear. Their objective was Pt 159, which they were to seize and consolidate so that the Borderers could then exploit towards Pt 162. Observation on the previous day had reported the Italians to be constructing a position at Pt 159 and that they were wiring and probably also mining the area. Since it was to be a surprise attack, no vehicles would take part in the initial phase. The infantry would go in, and the tanks would wait near by until called into action. In spite of this precaution, surprise was not achieved. No doubt these were jittery nights for a retreating enemy, and as the DLIs neared their objective they ran into defensive fire. It was especially strong on the left flank and A Coy were brought to a halt. C Coy did a little better and managed to get among some of the defensive sangars. The tanks were then called in. They skirted the position in order to avoid mines and then went in from the rear. As they did so, the DLIs put in a 'magnificent bayonet charge' and stormed into the front of the post. C Coy then got to its feet and charged from the rear and the post fell under this combined attack, 150 men of the Pavia Division being taken prisoner. There was a bonus to the attack; on their way to take part in it the tanks had overrun and seized a battery of four 75mm guns. The Borderers now came through and resumed their advance to Pt 162. Luckier – and perhaps a little quieter in their advance – they really did find the occupants abed, actually in their sleeping-bags. They went into an altogether different type of bag.

Next day, the Borderers, with 7RTR's Matildas in support, moved on to El Adem airfield, the former hub of Axis activity. It was as simple as that; there was no resistance, but a fratricidal battle almost ensued. Willi-

son had sent his cruisers on to the airfield and was following in their dust.
Brown's tanks were advancing at speed along the Axis Road when he saw
tanks and infantry on the airfield. The cruisers battened down, and prepared to attack what they took to be the enemy. Fortunately, Holden had
informed Willison that the airfield was already his and the Brigadier was
able to cool the situation. He had been pursuing the cruisers in the ACV,
which was travelling even faster than it had done on the retreat from El
Agheila in the previous March. He had his head out of the roof window.
At one moment he was shouting that the cloud of dust which had
appeared along the escarpment to the south-east of the airfield must be
Jock Campbell, and that he bloody well wasn't going to race us on to the
airfield, in the next he was ducking back into the vehicle to order its driver to get a move on for God's sake. We were taking turns to stick our
heads out of the rear-roof window, enjoying our share of this little triumph over the Eighth Army. The vehicle rocketed on through the
smoke of burning aircraft which had so recently damaged our days and
nights, and then we were there, at the buildings which had so recently
housed Westphal and Rommel's HQ. Shortly afterwards along came
O'Carroll with his regiment of Matildas, and with their arrival Willison
had his whole brigade on the airfield, well before anyone else arrived.
The entry in 4RTR's diary of that day complains that when the regiment
arrived on the airfield it found its Brigade HQ already in occupation
there.

That was that – or almost. Eighth Army came up and we went a little
way with them. On 12 December we were in the Acroma region when we
were buzzed by enemy planes. It was an unpleasant and unexpected surprise. Later that day we caught up with our KDG patrol, who had as usual
been probing ahead of us. We stopped for a chat and a report. Neither
were happy. They too had had visitors from aloft, and one of their cars
had been singled out for attention. George Maers had been killed while
seated at his set. The lads who had been with him knew that he had been
a personal friend and tried to console me by telling me that it had been
'instant' ... that he had hardly been marked, only a tiny hole behind his
ear ... that they had covered his desert grave with stones, so that the
piards could not get at him.

PART THREE:
ROMMEL DURING 1941
An Appraisal

Rommel: the myth

'In contrast to their own defeats of the last few months and the inadequacies of the men who commanded them, stood the successes attend-
ing the efficiency and co-ordination of the Afrika Korps under their
now-legendary commander, Rommel – all of which the fighting troops of
the Eighth Army had closely observed, and with which they had been
only too closely involved. And they wished that they were commanded by
such as Rommel, and controlled by as efficient an organisation as that
under which the Afrika Korps had won such conspicuous success.'[1]

So wrote Barrie Pitt of the situation at the time of the first battle of
Alamein. Anyone who was serving in the Desert Army at that time would
echo these sentiments. Rommel had by this time acquired mythical status, more so perhaps among his opponents than with his own men. Was
this reputation deserved or did it arise purely from comparison with the
inefficient, occasionally brave but more often stupid – and rarely inspir-
ing – leadership under which the British and Commonwealth soldiers
suffered and died in that theatre of war?

Rommel the General

Rommel's strategy during the second half of 1941 was direct and simple.
He would eliminate the obstacle which Tobruk presented to his progress
eastward. Next he would destroy the enemy forces ranged against him in
the western desert, advance into Egypt and take the Canal Zone and its
cities. He would then fulfil his role in Hitler's *Plan Orient* by taking the
Caucasus. His tactics were also direct and uncomplicated. The initiative
must never be surrendered: 'Let it be clear, there is no such thing as a
direction front, but only a direction enemy.'[2] Whenever and wherever
possible he would concentrate the fire power of his panzers, artillery and
bombers in mobile battles, combining and restructuring these elements

into cohesive Battle Groups to suit the situations whose developments he would himself control. Although he might be compelled by circumstance to establish static positions, these must be anvils against which the hammer blows of his mobile forces would crush the enemy at the chosen moment. Every defensive action must be aggressive, the aim being the weakening of the attacking force as a prelude to counter-attack.

For these tactics to succeed he needed a combination of fire-power and mobility, of sufficient intensity as to overwhelm his opponents at the chosen point of attack, plus the ability to bring this combination to that point at the moment of his choosing. He needed responsive subordinates both at the sharp end, and at the supply and recovery side of battle. He needed committed leadership in battle, and troops who would accept and follow that leadership. Rommel had all of these things, but not in unlimited quantity; indeed, in the later part of 1941 he was often at a numerical disadvantage in the three elements of battle: men, guns and armour. It was therefore essential that he make quality in every aspect of battle count over quantity. Nothing should be squandered in the way of *matériel* or man-power. It was also essential that he make the correct decision in those moments when a commander tells himself 'one last heave will do the trick', while knowing that if the heave were to fail, the trick would be trumped. Most of all, of course, he needed the personal qualities of leadership: intelligence, a recognisable integrity, physical and mental courage, ruthlessness, determination and charisma.

The myth has it that he possessed these qualities in abundance, that he was superior in tactical thinking and practical delivery to anyone on the opposing side, and that as a military leader he was so superior to his opposite numbers that had they simply exchanged roles he would still have successfully dominated the battlefields of the western desert. It was the man, who won the battles, rather than his troops. This myth can be tested in the six major battles of 1941, three of which he launched, and three to which he had to react.

(i) Rommel's attack in Cyrenaica in January 1941

Rommel was not to know the weak state of the enemy when he launched his initial 'reconnaissance in force' which was to take him all the way to the Egyptian frontier, but as soon as it became apparent to him he took every advantage of it while the British were still off balance. He formed three battle groups and sent them in enveloping movements which he himself controlled from the air. When the important desert cross-roads at Mechili fell into his hands, he immediately formed an *ad hoc* group under Oberstleutnant Ponath and sent it ahead of the rest of the Afrika Korps to Derna, where it captured Generals O'Connor and Neame. By this time the German troops were scattered over a huge expanse of territory, but it is evident from Ponath's diary and the account written by Rommel's aide Heinz Schmidt, that Rommel was the dynamic that galvanised the dispersed and tiring troops, gathered them together and drove them onwards to the Egyptian frontier. The British soldiers who had been so rudely treated were not aware at the time of who was dealing out this treatment, but soldiers are quick to learn such things and to discuss them with one another. A new and very threatening physical power had arrived on their scene and in their lives – a German general, and his name was Rommel. The myth was in embryo.

(ii) Rommel's Easter attack on Tobruk

This attack was launched without proper reconnaissance; on the basis of poor intelligence, using tired infantry as its sharp point, and before the troops to be engaged were fully *in situ* or ready for action. The tactical failures to extend the base of his penetration, or to support the advance of his panzers with infantry and artillery, were primary causes of its defeat and must be laid at his door. So too must his under-estimation of the calibre of his opponents. It was not recognised at the time that Rommel had presided over the first defeat to be suffered by German arms during the Second World War. Perhaps if British military intelligence had been more alert and had made this known to the ordinary British soldier in the Middle East the myth might have become still-born. Perhaps not; the soldier of whatever nation has an eager and huge appetite for myth, and a need for the heroic and the hero.

(iii) Rommel's May Day attack on Tobruk

The May Day attack was begun at a time when the arrival of PZ15 was imminent. This division's 150 or so panzers would have made a great difference to the outcome of these battles, and Rommel was at fault in not waiting for them. His timetable for the capture of the town and harbour showed an optimistic expectancy which did not allow for the resisting capabilities of his opponents, and suggests that he had learned little from his Easter experiences. As for his tactics, his penetration of the defences was good, he established a strong force of panzers and infantry inside the perimeter ready to advance on the town, but from then on Morshead's tactics were superior. Rommel sent his panzers in to a minefield which should have been discovered and neutralised by his panzergrenadiers before the armour rolled forward. This doomed the assault, and resulted in a second defeat for him. Morshead's mine-field and artillery placements prevented the full exploitation of the penetration, and his counter-attacks caused Rommel's assault to degenerate from attack on the fortress as a whole into defence of the sector that had been seized. On this occasion Rommel did manage to widen the base of his penetration, but the resistance offered by the men in the posts adjacent to the break-in zone, together with the bravery of the men manning the anti-tank guns and British tanks, prevented it from becoming the launch-pad for an alternative thrust. While Rommel did manage to create a salient in the defensive perimeter, this became as much a liability as it was an asset. Rommel was forced to man it with large numbers of crack troops, and these became virtual hostages to the sharp-shooting Australians, who made it a very dangerous place in which to try to exist.

There is little in either the Easter or the May Day battles to support the myth of a master tactician or a brilliant commander. There is much to suggest the commander who was too impatient by far, and perhaps too careless with the lives of his men.

(iv) Rommel during 'Brevity' (15–18 May)

Rommel's reaction to this attack by 7th Armd and 22nd Guards Brigades on the frontier posts and by the British armoured and infantry brigades on Halfaya Pass was instantaneous, mainly because he had brought his own armour away from Tobruk and had it in readiness to meet any such movement at the frontier. The British tanks were soon driven back across the wire, and although Halfaya Pass had fallen to them it was recovered within two weeks. The psychological impact upon the British and Commonwealth forces of this defeat and of the man who had brought it about can be imagined. When the British tanks had crossed the frontier only six months previously they had gone from victory to victory against the Italians. The rank and file must have expected that the same thing was about to happen again, or why, they might ask, was the attack being made at all? When the attacking troops came streaming back within a couple of days with their tails between their legs, those expectations took a severe blow. Rommel's reputation soared in inverse proportion to the fall in confidence of the ordinary British soldier in his own leaders. He had now defeated the British armour in two mobile battles; he had become the fearsome figure who came storming out of the desert with his panzers' guns blazing. 'Where', the British soldier began to ask, 'is our Rommel?'

(v) Rommel during 'Battleaxe' (15–17 June)

Rommel's defeat of his enemy in Operation 'Battleaxe' confirmed this reputation. He had used the experience of 'Brevity' to prepare for the next British attack which fizzled out in bloody frustration against his defensive positions at Hafid Ridge and Halfaya Pass. When, at a critical moment in the struggle, he switched his armour in a movement which threatened the British rear, the British armour had no option other than retreat. Once again the survivors went streaming back across the wire, but this time they left behind a great number of their tanks and men, and they were far from happy. As he left yet another battlefield in a hurry, the British soldier gave no consideration to the unreliability of the Crusader tanks, or to the superiority of the 88mm gun during the aggressive defence of the positions under attack, or to the elementary mistakes made by his own commanders. Rommel had done it again, it was as simple as that. Wavell, the former hero, had now lost out to him three times in a row and was obviously no match for him. But who on the British side was? The Rommel myth was in full and summer flower after this engagement and deservedly so, for in 'Battleaxe' the man had shown himself to be master of his opponents whatever the form of battle.

(vi) Rommel during 'Crusader' (18 November–9 December)

There has been much discussion of Rommel's behaviour during the first days of this, the largest British operation in the western desert to date. Two criticisms are levelled against him:

(a) that he was so thrown off balance by the advance of the two British corps, which he had earlier refused to accept as a possibility, that he absented himself from the early stages of the battle and gave Crüwell free rein with the Afrika Korps..

(b) that instead of concentrating his attention on the advancing Eighth Army, he remained at his HQ at Gambut determined to launch an attack on Tobruk from there.

The main reason advanced to explain these aberrations is that he was obsessed with capturing Tobruk to the exclusion of rational thought, and that this compulsion would not allow him psychologically to accept the fact of the arrival of Eighth Army in force across the frontier. The word 'myopic' is used to describe his condition at this time.[3] There is the account of his throwing aerial maps to the ground without looking at them because they showed a situation that he refused even to consider. It has also been said that the scales only fell from his eyes when he heard of a broadcast made by the BBC announcing that a full-scale attack was in progress in Libya.[4]

If these criticisms are true; if he deliberately discounted the arrival of an enemy army on his front lawn because he was obsessed with the carrying out of a cherished project in his backyard, the accusations are serious enough to have blighted any general's subsequent reputation, but can they be substantiated?

Influences on Rommel's thinking at the start of 'Crusader'

Four influences must have been making themselves felt in Rommel's thinking at that time, and each was indeed related to the fortress. The first was the change in emphasis of Hitler's approach to the Middle East conflict in the summer of the siege and of the attack on Russia. The taking of Tobruk would allow Panzergruppe Afrika to advance towards the Caucasus and complete its role in Hitler's *Plan Orient*. The knowledge that he had Hitler's support in a third attempt to reduce the fortress must have been a major influence. Secondly, was his awareness of the great benefit that the fall of Tobruk would bring in the way of relieving one of his greatest concerns – the shortage of supplies. The RAF and the Royal Navy were playing havoc with his sea lines of communication. At the end of July, the *Preussen* was sunk off Pantelleria and down with her went 6,000 tons of ammunition, 1,000 tons of petrol, 1,000 tons of food, 300 lorries and 200 men.[5] Ten Axis ships had been sunk during September and seven in October; indeed, von Mellenthin said that of 50,000 tons of supplies sent in October only 18,500 tons arrived.[6] He claimed that it was the sinking of supply ships that had caused Rommel to postpone his attack until November. Yet inside the fortress lay all that Rommel needed to take him to Cairo if only he could lay hands on it. Without it he could not sustain any action for long.

The third, a strategic influence, was the knowledge that if Tobruk did not fall to him before the next British attack on the frontier, he would find himself fighting on two fronts. Westphal said later that faced with the problem of the two fronts, Rommel was doubtful if they could be held, and so he concentrated all the force he could muster for an assault on Tobruk.

Each of these influences carried military justification. A fourth influence may well have been a personal, and less justifiable imperative. Rommel had planned every stage of the imminent attack on the port himself, and had overseen the training of the men who were to make it. It was the first military operation that he had planned in such detail, and it was in direct contrast to his previous history of success through intuitive and instantaneous action or reaction. There must have been a great compulsion to see it through to an end which would have proved his mastery in static as well as mobile battle. However, if it did indeed exist, this was a compulsion that he should have resisted.

Yet to what extent did any compulsion regarding Tobruk dictate his thinking? Despite the references to myopia and scales over the eyes, the acid test of Rommel's intentions must lie in the orders he had given to his two panzer divisions. It will be remembered that PZ15 had been detailed to make the attack on Tobruk, but had also been placed on 24-hour notice to go to the assistance of PZ21 should this be required. It is therefore in the movements of PZ15 after the arrival of Eighth Army in Cyrenaica in November that the answer to the question of Rommel's reaction to the British incursion lies. On the morning of 19 November, not much more than 24 hours after Eighth Army crossed the wire, Rommel sent Crüwell with elements of PZ21 to attack the British armour *and at the same time, moved PZ15 from north of the Via Balbia to south of Gambut.* This last can be seen as a half-way transfer of PZ15 from its intended role in the attack on Tobruk to a quite different role in support of PZ21. Thus Rommel was keeping open the option of an attack on Tobruk while he watched the developments on the frontier. At 1145 hrs PZ15 was given orders to concentrate with PZ21 that evening against the British armour. This killed off the attack on Tobruk because there was no way in which PZ15 could, within the space of two days, march in search of the enemy armour, engage and destroy this, and return fit enough to spearhead an attack on the fortress. This release of PZ15 from its Tobruk commitment took place more than 24 hours before the BBC broadcast, and it thus becomes nonsense for historians to claim that Alvar Liddel (or whoever made the broadcast) removed the scales from Rommel's eyes.

Rommel's awareness of British planning and intentions

A counter argument can be offered to show that Rommel never had scales over his eyes, but was well aware of the coming offensive. Hoyt says that Colonel Fellows, the US Military Attaché in Cairo, was privy to all British military intentions and planning; was transmitting regular distillations of these to Washington, and was using a code which had been broken by the Germans. Rommel was receiving daily copies of this distillation. Hoyt says: 'It was as if Rommel was being briefed every day or two by a British operations staff officer', and claims that by the autumn of 1941 Rommel was well aware of whatever the British were planning.[7] At the time, Major Revetria, the Italian Head of Intelligence, was convinced that an attack was about to be launched by Eighth Army, and von Mellenthin, Rommel's Intelligence Officer, went out of his way to disabuse him of the notion. On 11 November he told the Italian liaison officer: 'Major Revetria is much too nervous. Tell him not to worry because the British won't attack.' Von Mellenthin was to write later: 'Actually, we were very perturbed at the possibility of a British offensive and Rommel took competent measures to meet it.'[8] The inference must be that far from being deceived by the British or blind to their intentions, Rommel was well aware of what they intended but was up to his old game of deceiving his (nominal only) Italian superior.

Rommel's preparations immediately before 'Crusader'

The 'competent measures' taken by Rommel had two purposes: the stiffening of his defences along the frontier against any attack by Eighth Army, and the preparation for his own intended attack upon Tobruk. Von Mellenthin tells us that Rommel estimated that it would take three days for any British attack across the frontier seriously to interfere with a German attack on the fortress, and says: 'In the meantime we hoped to capture the fortress.'[9] It was with these estimates in mind that Rommel had taken the measures referred to.

In defence, Savona Infantry Division, stiffened by German elements, was entrenched in a fixed defensive line along the frontier zone. Hauptmann Bach was commanding the forbidding defensive positions at Halfaya Pass. Both were considered to be capable of holding out for three weeks if that should prove necessary. In close support was PZ21, directed by Crüwell from his HQ at Bardia, and von Wechmar's Reconnaissance Regiments were patrolling the wider desert flank to the south and east. The Italian armoured and motorised elements of Panzergruppe Afrika were in defensive positions covering the southern approaches from the desert – Ariete at Gambut, and Trieste at Bir Hacheim.

For the attack on Tobruk, Rommel's HQ was at Gambut, and PZ15 was on the coast to the north-east of the fortress in readiness for the move to its start-line. Sümmermann's Div zvB Afrika had replaced the Italians in the posts from which the infantry's share in the attack would be made. Panzer crews and infantry had undergone specialised and associated training. No less than three Italian divisions, Brescia, Bologna and Pavia, were investing the fortress under the command of Italian General Navarini whose HQ was at El Adem. In so far as was possible, Rommel was well prepared positionally for his twin objectives, and his men were at a peak in their training.

To sum up. Rommel was on the point of launching an attack on Tobruk which he was confident would solve the problem of supplies, and which he expected to be over within two days. With the danger of finding himself fighting on two fronts thus eliminated, he would be able to direct all his attention and destructive capability against any Eighth Army incursion which might be made while he was taking Tobruk. His troops were ideally placed to fulfil these objectives. It is arguable that in these circumstances his best strategy on hearing that the British armour was once again in the field was that which he then exercised – to hold on to the Tobruk option for as long as he could, while at the same time watching to see how the situation developed along the frontier. This reaction can hardly be described as 'myopic'.

Criticisms of his remaining at Gambut ignore the fact of two fronts, and that the Tobruk garrison had the capability of exploiting this situation whenever it decided to emerge and threaten his rear lines of communication. Westphal has something to say about this, too. 'There is no doubt that it was only the immediate presence of the German Commander at the Tobruk front that enabled the daily recurring crises to be surmounted.'[10] It was hardly coincidence that when 7th Armoured Brigade launched its drive from Sidi Rezegh towards El Duda, who should appear on the scene at this critical moment but Rommel himself, bringing with him the 88mm guns that killed off the drive.

Rommel's tactics during 'Crusader'

Rommel re-entered the tactical scene on the evening of 20 November, when he recalled Crüwell's panzers to the Sidi Rezegh area. With the return of the panzer divisions under way, he turned his attention to the Tobruk front. Willison had brought his tanks and infantry of 70th Div out beyond the perimeter and was advancing slowly towards El Duda. Meanwhile 6RTR had moved forward from Sidi Rezegh and was heading towards the fortress. Rommel quickly spotted the danger in this link-up and intervened personally against 6RTR, and then against Willison's tanks. Lewin quotes Kriebel's account of how his commander had 'scraped together all the reserves of Div zbV Afrika, Army Artillery, anti-aircraft artillery and all the signals personnel he could lay hands on and ordered Reconnaissance Unit 3 to move up by forced marches. At the head of these troops he halted the enemy by mid-day.'[11] As mentioned earlier in this account of the break-out, his intervention against 6RTR resulted in the destruction of this battalion of cruiser tanks, but his intervention against TOBFORCE did not play as significant a role as Kriebel (and others) claim. The failure of Eighth Army to reach the area of El Duda on that day brought Willison's advance to a halt, not Rommel.

At midday of the 22nd, Rommel sent PZ21 against the British armour on the Rezegh airfield, destroyed much of it and drove away what was left. This was but a prelude to the destruction of S. African 5th Bde on the next day. Rommel's plan for this action differed from what actually took place. He had intended trapping the remnant of the British armour between DAK (the hammer from the north) and Ariete (the anvil in the south). Crüwell varied the plan, so that DAK made a destructive sweep to the south through a mass of soft-topped vehicles, collected Ariete, and then turned a full circle and drove back to the north, right over and through the S. African brigade. But this was a Pyrrhic victory, in a continuing battle which was now becoming as much a war of attrition as a series of victories. It is arguable that Rommel's hammer-and-anvil plan for this action would have been less self-destructive than Crüwell's steam-roller tactics. It would at the very least have divided the attention of S. African 5th Bde, and caused its artillery to be looking both ways.

Rommel's dash to the frontier
So far then, Rommel had dealt successfully with the foolishly dispersed British armoured units. Now he was about to make a judgement which will be argued over whenever the war in the western desert is discussed. The situation, so far as he knew it, was that the major part of XXX Corps had been destroyed; the break-out from Tobruk had come to a halt, leaving TOBFORCE exposed in a narrow corridor, and XIII Corps was in the frontier region and waiting to be trapped against the wire and his frontier posts. He now had several options open to him :
  (i) To attack Tobruk. The artillery and tanks which had resisted his previous attacks on the fortress were now tied up in the corridor,

as were many of the garrison's infantry battalions, leaving the perimeter defence line greatly undermanned.

(ii) To attack TOBFORCE in the corridor before it had time to disengage and re-organise itself inside the perimeter. The destruction of Willison's troops would have allowed him free entry into the town.

(iii) To search out and destroy the scattered remnants of the British armoured brigades before they had time to recover and rebuild their strength.

(iv) To find and capture the huge supply dumps which Eighth Army had brought forward into Cyrenaica. This would have brought what remained of Eighth Army inside Cyrenaica to its knees.

(v) To launch a sweeping attack into the rear of Eighth Army, destroying its lines of communication and supply, and driving XIII Corps against the anvil of his frontier posts, where it would be destroyed.

He chose the last option and led the attack personally. There was tactical merit in the decision but it required close supervision which he was unable to give. His widely dispersed units lost the power of concentration, communications broke down, and he was completely out of touch with what was going on during the 24 hours when he was stranded on the wrong side of the wire. The decision also required better appreciation of the actual situation on the ground than his mistaken understanding of XIII Corps' position. In the end, the dash proved a fatal mistake. He achieved little of what he sought, lost much that he could little afford, and eventually lost control of the sweep and almost of the whole battle. Only the resolute action of Colonel Westphal in recalling von Ravenstein saved the Axis position around Tobruk. Rommel led back a dispirited and tired DAK, leaving his troops on the frontier to their fate. It was only a matter of time after that until the moment when the decline in his supplies of *matériel* and men dictated withdrawal to the west. There was much more fighting to come and other victories, particularly against Freyberg's New Zealanders on the Sidi Rezegh–Belhamed ridges, but on 8 December he was finally forced to quit the battlefield.

Rommel's last tactical decisions in 1941 were devoted to getting the Axis forces out of Cyrenaica without incurring too great a loss. He was

310

successful in this, partly because of his own efforts and partly because of the lack of aggression in what should have been a pursuing force. His tired troops were able to retreat without any of the headlong dash for safety which accompanied the retreats of his opponents.

Taken as a whole, then, Rommel's tactics during this, the biggest desert battle to date, resulted in a mixed bag of outcomes. The success of *Totensonntag* was offset by the failure of the dash to the wire; the recapture of the Sidi Rezegh escarpments and airfield by the failure to destroy TOBFORCE; the scattering of XXX Corps by the failure to contain XIII Corps. Most telling, in an extended battle which was fast becoming a war of attrition, his tactics caused unnecessary loss of both men and *matériel* on an unsupportable scale. On the positive side, he was often outnumbered in the aggregate but made a nonsense of this disadvantage by his mastery of manoeuvre. If it were to be argued that too often Rommel was only saved by the skin of his 88mm guns' ferocious teeth, it should be remembered that he was the man who moulded those teeth. Rommel's one undeniable tactical success was his introduction of the combination of tank and anti-tank gunfire against any enemy units that might be foolish enough to be lured into ambush against them – alas, in the battles of 1941 these were far too many.

Rommel's relationship with his allies

It should be borne in mind that Rommel had at his disposal, if not actually under his command, a considerable number of Italian troops, including armour, infantry and artillery. Time and again he appears to have been frustrated by Italian commanders who were less dynamic than himself, but by a blend of goading, persuasion, intimidation, and blatant ignoring of their requests he usually got what he wanted. Yet he was prepared to give the ordinary Italian soldier more credit than most of those engaged in that field of conflict. Schmidt says that Rommel was never tactless with his allies, nor overbearing, and he watched the relationship on a daily basis. He tells for example, how Rommel went out of his way to praise the men who were building the Axis Road, and how the recipients beamed at the compliment.[12] This little action must be compared with that concerning the guns which Rommel discovered in Bardia in the autumn of 1941. These had been left behind in the previous December when the port had been captured by O'Connor, and they had been rusting away ever since. Rommel immediately ordered that they be renovated and put to use in the defensive line which he was then creating along the frontier. Italian General Gariboldi forbade such use, saying that the guns were Italian property and must be used only by Italians. Rommel was not prepared to be put off and ignored the prohibition.[13] When Bastico, Gariboldi's replacement, together with others high in command, tried to persuade Rommel not to retire from the Gazala Line after the relief of Tobruk, we are told that Rommel simply shouted them down and carried on as he had always intended.[14]

It is perhaps fair to say that Rommel received a better performance from the Italian troops than Italian generals had before his arrival on the scene.

Summary

There is nothing mythological about Rommel's leadership of Afrika Korps during 1941. There is evidence of personal and psychological bravery, but evidence also of recklessness, impatience, and a stubborn nature. There is evidence of great drive and single-mindedness, but also of ruthless ambition and refusal to conform to anything other than his own will. Tactical successes were matched by tactical failures. Victories were diluted by a draining away of men, machines and supplies in achieving them. Although he had his opponents reeling on many occasions, he was never able to strike the knock-out blow. In a final analysis of Rommel's performance during 1941 it has to be said that the year ended in the temporary destruction of what had been a supremely efficient fighting force through too much having been demanded of it by its commander.

Why then the myth? Four reasons are offered:

(i) German propaganda

It suited Goebbels to have a hero to describe to the German nation (just as it had also suited the British Ministry of Information to have Wavell for a hero in the previous year). The German propaganda broadcasts in English did not go unheard in the western desert, indeed they became a source of amusement; the Rats of Tobruk taking their name from German broadcasts heard during the siege, and converting the sneer into an honour. But as the Allied soldier listened to the praises of Rommel he nodded in agreement. His experiences at the hands of Rommel gave legitimacy to the extravagances. Rommel didn't need a Goebbels to tell him how good a general he was.[15]

(ii) Rommel's reputation among his own men

The verses of a popular song of the first World War ended:

> *'If you want to find the Sergeant Major I know where he is...*
> *he's miles and miles and miles behind the line.'*

This was a gripe common also to the men of the Second World War. The sergeant major of the song was simply a symbol for the higher rankers. Soldiers who operate at the sharp edge of conflict are hypersensitive towards those who dictate from a distance. Rommel could never be accused of this; on the contrary he led from the front. Several times in France and Libya he had escaped death by inches. His men knew him, they saw him enduring the same conditions as they suffered but without making the complaints they made. He might burst in on them at any moment and curse and chase them onwards and they might silently curse back, but they remembered that he had been there, and insisted that their leaders be there too. As von Mellenthin says: 'The men knew that Rommel was the last man Rommel spared; they saw him in their midst and they felt "this is our leader".'[16] They did not need Goebbels to tell them; they saw Rommel work himself into physical collapse, but return to action. They watched him eat the food they ate, and live the way they lived. They saw how his spirit retained its initial purity of determination despite the ravages of jaundice. They *knew* that he was a great leader in battle, and that he belonged to them.

The pity is, that he appears to have seen them only as means to an end. Reading his papers, one cannot escape this feeling, and it was echoed by Heinz Schmidt, the man who was probably closest of all to him in 1941: '... but Rommel never became really intimate with anyone',[17] and 'It was months before he called me anything but the formal Leutnant, and only after he had decided that I was more than a necessary additional limb did he address me by name, bother to find out my age, whether I was married ... or indeed, even to think of me other than as something that filled a uniform or answered a command',[18] and '... and Rommel, supremely practical, hard, indifferent to the personal problems of others, concerned with personalities only in so far as they affected his military aims'.[19] These are chilling comments. They find some support from Barker: 'In Germany however, Rommel is less popular, for the men of the Afrika Korps knew him as an ambitious and ruthless driver, a hard man who placed more reliance on the whip than on the carrot.'[20] Yet awe takes root more easily in the soil of isolation and 'apartness' on the one hand, and a little fear on the other. Rommel was feared, respected and held in awe by the men he led and the men he fought. The myth was shared by both sides in that desert conflict.

(iii) Rommel's perceived successes

Rommel's first advance from El Agheila came as a great shock to the Middle East system. His subsequent victories during 'Brevity' and 'Battleaxe' were clear-cut and undeniable. His two defeats at Tobruk did not receive the attention they should have had because of what was happening in Greece. His overall defeat during 'Crusader' was masked by his many successes during that series of battles: his destruction of the South African and New Zealand brigades and much of XXX Corps, and also by the fact that he had withdrawn with the Afrika Korps intact, if badly bruised. He had not suffered a single major defeat during the year in which he first arrived in Africa.

Those who had fought against him in these battles knew this, and were not fooled into over-optimism when he withdrew in December. They realised that it was only a question of time before he would be back harassing them again. A perverse pride in this, by now mythological, enemy leader grew among those who had fought against him and had survived. If one has to be defeated then let it be by a super-general, not by some run-of-the-mill operator, and Rommel was *the best*. For so long as they might live, desert war veterans would remember that they had fought against Rommel; it allowed them to take a little reflected glory from the man.

(iv) The ordinary British soldier's comparison of his own leaders with Rommel

The soldier of whatever nation needs a mythological figure as a leader. The British and Commonwealth soldier in the Middle East during early 1941 was already manufacturing his own mythology about 'Red' O'Connor, when that fine general was captured, and by whom? None other than Rommel. The daring of Rommel's dashes through the desert had much of the O'Connor pattern, and won at first a grudging, then a wholehearted admiration among the men who suffered from them. But it was in comparison with the failings of a succession of British commanders that Rommel's mythical status was confirmed. Rommel was seen by the Eighth Army soldier as a winner, whereas his own leaders were all proven losers. Of the senior officers in the field only Campbell (who was killed in his prime), and the colonials, Morshead and Freyberg, were admired. The Auk was respected as a distant figure. The remainder were neither admired nor respected. Gott's reputation survived surprisingly well for one who had commanded during all three of Eighth Army's excursions over the frontier in late 1941 yet had no clear-cut success to his name. Beresford-Peirse and Creagh (one of the heroes of Wavell's push) shared the disaster and ignominy of 'Battleaxe 'and departed the scene. The commanders of the 'Crusade' operation too often gave the impression of being men without a notion of what to do next, other than have a discussion and agree to disagree. Nor was there a single one in the field who could enforce a policy. Cunningham was out of his depth in the desert and cracked under the strain. Ritchie was an over-promoted commander who could not command; Godwin-Austen was too cautious and Norrie had neither the requisite dash nor drive (both eventually asked to be relieved of their commands, in contrast to Rommel's commanders who died in their posts). Scott-Cockburn presided over the destruction of 22nd Armoured Bde and retired to the Delta. Not one of them seemed able to put together a battle properly and to fight it to a finish. This list of failures was to continue until the arrival of an egotist whose ambition matched that of Rommel, who was every bit as ruthless, and who was able to transpose into ultimate success the numerical superiority in arms which almost all his predecessors had also possessed but of which they had failed to take proper advantage.

So far as the ordinary soldier was concerned, all these commanders seemed to do was to present their armies, brigades and battalions in rotation for Rommel ritually to slaughter. There were rarely any victories to savour and those which did happen were all too soon overtaken by inevitable defeat and hurried retreat. Equally inevitable was the dawning realisation that their leaders were simply not sufficiently intelligent, nor good enough soldiers to match Rommel. In the British soldier's mythologising of the German commander lay evidence of his growing contempt for his own commanders at all levels, and there were sound reasons for this contempt. If ever there were grounds for indictment of the social engineering that produced (and produces) Britain's military leaders, they lie in the war cemeteries of the western desert, to which the inadequacies of their commanders condemned them.

The young and impressionable desert soldier was able to embrace the Rommel myth as part of his existence. The General imposed himself upon the Australian, British and New Zealand soldier who fought against him no less than he did upon the German soldier under his command. Each of the former would have given much to have had the man as *their* commander (in the case of the Australian and New Zealander, alongside Morshead and Freyberg of course). The British soldier survivors of those bloody days in the desert probably thank God now that he wasn't.

Rommel the menace
Why should this closing remark have been made? It is the role of the military leader to become a menace to his opponents. Rommel more than fulfilled that role; he was a menace to every soldier who opposed him, be they tank men, gunners, front-line infantry or B Echelon drivers. All were at risk from the man's sweeping attacks and concentrations of fire-power and from his use of air power. But it was not only the British and Commonwealth soldier who suffered at his hands; Rommel was a menace also to the German and Italian soldier of whatever rank, *en masse* and individually.

Those closest to this man who insisted on being at the very sharpest edge, were most at risk: his Signals Officer was killed in France, his dispatch rider was killed and his driver wounded in the early days in Libya, his Adjutant was wounded in France and died in Libya (see below). There is a litany of senior officers who fought and died under his command. First among these was also the first commander of PZ15, von Prittwitz, and he was killed before his division had even arrived in Africa. Upbraided by Rommel, he rushed headlong into an ambush and paid the price. He was soon followed by the heroic Ponath, who had already given his all in the advance on Tobruk only to find that Rommel wanted even more. He paid with his life, along with so many of his panzergrenadiers and panzer crews, in the Easter attack which had been neither thought out nor properly reconnoitred. Next to suffer were the men of the Faltenbacher Battalion who took part in the May Day attack; this resulted in more than 1,200 German casualties for the gain of a salient which then became another source of death and injury. Then came the unnecessary and futile dream-trip across the wire which attracted the attention of the RAF and ended with Rommel's driver becoming one of seventy casualties.

In the 'Crusader' battles there was the dash to the frontier which brought the death of the brave Colonel Stephan, Commander of PZR5, and the ruination of DAK. Von Mellenthin's assessment of this was: 'Afrika Korps had accomplished nothing on the frontier and was only a fraction of the magnificent force which had entered battle on the 18th.'[21] There was the second (aborted) trip to the frontier and the death of Neumann-Silkow, Commander of PZ15; which was quickly followed by the death of Sümmermann, Commander of 90LT, near Derna. The list grew in the following year and reflected Rommel's insistence that his Generals should be front-line men: von Bismarck, CO PZ21, killed; Stumme, Rommel's temporary replacement, dead of a heart attack in battle. Vaerst, CO PZ15; Nehring, CO DAK; Gause, Chief of Staff; Westphal, Operations Officer and Kleeman, Commander of 90LT, all wounded. Von Ravenstein, CO PZ21; Schmitt, in command at Bardia; Crüwell, CO DAK; von Thoma, his successor, and Major Bach of Halfaya fame, all captured. Perhaps the supreme example of this, almost wilful sacrifice of willing war-horses, was the unfortunate Major Schraepler, Rommel's Adjutant. Seriously wounded when standing at Rommel's side during the crossing of the Meuse, he rejoined him in the desert, led Ariete in a vain effort to repair some of the damage done on 14 April, led the break-in group which penetrated the defences on 29 April, and – with an irony which seems symbolically apposite to the point being made – was crushed to death under the wheels of Rommel's own Mammoth. And what sympathy and recognition was given to the faithful-unto-death Schraepler by his commander? A single line written almost as an after-thought to Frau Rommel: 'PS. I don't think I've told you yet that Schrae-pler met with a fatal accident.'[22]

This was indeed a 'hard' man.

But it was the footslogger who suffered most. Indeed, the real hero of the western desert was not a general of any persuasion, he was the ordi-nary soldier on each side of the confrontation – Australian and Italian; German and Briton; New Zealander, Pole and Indian, whose courage, perseverance, ability to survive extremes of terrain, temperature and the elements, and whose willingness to pay in blood for the blunders of his superiors, won whatever victories there were to be had in that benighted land.

Rommel the writer

No appraisal of Rommel would be complete without reference to his writings and a consideration of what, if any, influence this activity may have had upon the decisions which he made as Commander of the Afrika Korps. He had already tasted success in this field with the publication of his work *Infanterie Greift An* (*The Infantry Attacks*), a study based on his experiences during the First World War. By the time of 'Crusader' this work, helped no doubt by his victories in France and Libya, was achiev-ing best-seller status in Germany. On 10 October 1941, only one month before the beginning of that operation, he wrote to Frau Rommel: 'I received the grand news from Voggenreiter (his publisher) yesterday that Royalties for the large edition (50,000) will not be less than 25,000 marks ... that's something worthwhile ....'[23] His son Manfred wrote later: 'My father planned from the start of operations to write a book about his new experiences and publish it after the war. He dictated them (his notes) or gave them for typing only to my mother and one of his ADCs, Oberleutnant Schmidt.'[24] Schmidt had something to say about this side of Rommel: 'Every wish and every order given by the General had to be accurately recorded in writing, and there were endless memoranda on exact times, names, localities, unit strengths and so on.'[25] Rommel also wrote to his wife every day and she was under instructions to preserve his letters, which often carried more military than personal information. When for some reason he was not able to write to her, the faithful Schaepler did so, and he also referred to military matters. After the war the Rommel family asked the foremost British military historian, Basil Liddell Hart, to edit those papers which had survived Rommel's death and the searches of the Gestapo, and there was sufficient material for Liddell Hart to produce *The Rommel Papers*, a detailed account of most of the actions fought by Rommel.

The historian may decry the notion that during every action in which Rommel played a part he was thinking of how it would later appear in print, yet how else is one able to reconcile these quotations, and Rommel's insistence on the recording of the most minute detail? Only a writer knows the compulsion that keeps him/her at the word-processor day after day into eternity, often without ever seeing a word in print. Rommel had the added compulsion to better a best-seller. His book on the First World War was written by a lower-grade infantry officer and concerned that branch of the Services only. His book on the Second World War would be written by a General and would cover all aspects of warfare, especially victory (his own) by *Blitzkrieg*. It is a pity it was denied to the world; it would perhaps have been one of the greatest military histories ever written, and what a compulsion that thought must have generated in this thorn in the flesh of the German military hierarchy. Can we be sure that he was able to compartmentalise his thoughts so that this hope would not intrude on the more urgent matter of the relevance and priority of his next blow against the enemy.

EPILOGUE

THE TWO DIVISIONS

Australian 9th Infantry Division

After taking a rest in the Delta and then doing garrison duties in Syria, 9th Div returned to combat at El Alamein. Its battalions announced their return by the destruction of the Italian Sabratha Division, and then took part in the fighting around Tel el Eisa. During the final El Alamein battle the division fought fiercely on the seaward flank of Montgomery's attack, and played a crucial role in his ultimate victory.

It then left the Middle East, and after spending some leave in Australia, went to New Guinea, where its 20th Bde formed the initial wave in the sea landings at Lae. The full division took part in the successful, but bloody attacks on Finschaven, and Sattelberg on the Huon Peninsula in New Guinea. Then it sailed to Borneo where it took part in the fighting at Brunei Bay, with 26th Bde landing and capturing Tarakan Island. Although serving in an autonomous role under Blamey, it came under the over-all direction of General MacArthur. This was not an entirely happy relationship, that General suffering the usual complaint of Second World War American Generals in wanting all victories to be first of all in his name, and then in the name of the United States. But the Australians were able to maintain the integrity of their division, and while fighting in an environment that could not have been more different from that of Tobruk, enhanced the great reputation which they had won there. This was epitomised in the winning of the Victoria Cross by Sergeant Tom Derrick, at Sattelberg. The Commander of the Tobruk garrison, Lieutenant-General Morshead, was appointed Commander of Australian I Corps during the Borneo campaign. Both he and the division finally went home to rest on their laurels and these were many.

British 70th Division

Less fortunate was the British 70th Division. It left the Middle East after its return to the Delta from Tobruk and sailed to India, where it served under the Eastern Army as part of IV Corps. During the latter half of 1942 a good deal of popular disaffection arose, caused by the political situation in the sub-continent, and the division was used to patrol affected areas. The nature of this work meant that action was limited to small units rather than divisional operations. When the division was sent to Burma it probably expected and hoped that it would revert to its proper role of a fighting division, but covetous eyes were fixed upon its parts. The Chindits' leader, General Wingate, was building up forces for his forthcoming second expedition into the heart of Burma and he laid claim to the brigades for use as long-range penetration columns. Auchinleck protested furiously to Churchill, who was in Canada at the time, but Auchinleck had fallen from favour while the piratical Wingate's aggressive nature appealed to Churchill's current whimsy. Wingate, who was in Canada with Churchill, got what he wanted. The division ceased to exist as such and was never reformed. Major General Symes, who commanded it at the time, appears to have accepted the break-up without a fight and was appointed Wingate's second in command.

TABLE 6

The personnel and structure of the three original brigades was changed, to become:

14th Brigade (Brig Brodie)	16th Brigade (Brig Fergusson)	23rd Brigade (Brig Perowne)
2nd Black Watch	1st Queen's Royals	2nd Duke of Wellington's
1st Beds and Herts	2nd Leicesters	4th Borderers
2nd York and Lancs	51st Field Regt RA	1st Essex
7th Leicesters	45th Recce	

It will be noted that 2nd King's Own, 2nd Queen's Royal Regt and 1st DLI were no longer with the brigades, and that 51FRG, the artillery regiment which had fought so well against Rommel's tanks during Rommel's May Day attacks, had been converted to two infantry columns. Fergusson and Brodie's brigades both took part in Operation 'Thursday', the second Chindit expedition. Fergusson's men marched overland through 600 miles of most difficult country, established the defensive position 'Aberdeen' from 20 March onwards, and then set out in columns to engage the enemy. Brodie brought his brigade into 'Aberdeen' in gliders three days later. Thereafter both brigades fought various actions against the Japanese and suffered severe casualties. Fergusson brought out his exhausted 16th Bde by air at the beginning of May following the death of Wingate in a plane crash. According to Fergusson his brigade had done a lot of trudging and pioneering, without much honour and glory; but his men had put their best into it. It had also, of course, suffered many casualties.

Brodie's 14th Brigade suffered the misfortune of having to co-operate with the American General Stilwell after the death of Wingate. This man's less than generous treatment of his British allies and troops has become notorious; sufficient to say that he too climbed over many bones in order to win his four stars, not a few of which belonged to British Chindits. The brigade fought a last successful action that August, capturing a hill ringed with mortars and machine guns. It then flew out from Burma.

The third of 70th Div's brigades, Perowne's 23rd, was also trained to serve as a Long-Range Penetration Brigade, but did not become part of the Chindit expedition. It was attached to Stopford's XXXIII Corps in the latter's drive to retake Kohima and operated successfully as a penetration column against the Japanese communication lines between the Chindwin and that area.

Thus, 70th Div's only coherent action was its heroic seizing and holding of the Tobruk corridor. This fine and well-experienced division was allowed to be broken up and, it might be argued, wasted in the jungle of Burma. It is perhaps an added irony that it ended its life fighting in the Forgotten Army, because if ever a division's achievements have gone unheralded or have been erroneously chronicled this was the one. In his work *The Life and Death of the Afrika Korps*, Ronald Lewin gives the breakout just nine lines in the 37 pages he devoted to 'Crusader'. Barrie Pitt, in *The Crucible of War 2*, is slightly more generous, but gives little credit to the hard fighting that went on over those desperate days, or to the crucial importance that lay in the creation of the corridor and then the capture and retention of El Duda. Several historians commit errors in their reporting of the break-out: Barnett's comment in *Desert Generals* that Rommel stopped the break-out using a scratch force; this has been dealt with in PART TWO of this work. Several writers echo this. Paul Carrell, for example, in *The Foxes of the Desert*, has the sortie by the Tobruk garrison on the 21st being repulsed, and a subsequent effort being more successful until Recce3 closes the gap. In his work *Blood Tears and Folly* Len Deighton never mentions the break-out or 70th Div, but has Black Watch taking part in the fighting on the Sidi Rezegh airfield. It has also become received (and incorrect) wisdom that after the loss of Belhamed by the New Zealanders the division withdrew back inside the perimeter. Perhaps most undeserved of all are the comments and quotations given by Paul Freyberg in his biography of his father. After having TOBFORCE break out from the perimeter on 26 November when it fact it did so on the 21st; and claiming that two companies of 19th NZ Bat attacked El Duda on the 27th, whereas TOBFORCE had captured it on the previous day and were waiting there to greet the NZs, he quotes his father as saying that the Tobruk garrison had failed to come out as had been planned, because of the condition that the New Zealanders must first be on El Duda. This suggestion of a failure by TOBFORCE through timidity is unfair on two counts. First, the condition to which he refers was not set by either Scobie or Willison, but had been the original and sensible requirement when TOBFORCE was expected to meet the South Africans there. There would have been little sense in TOBFORCE making a sortie with no one on the escarpment to meet them. Secondly, at the time of the supposed complaint Willison's men had been holding the corridor they had seized, for days, without any external help, and throughout those days he had been champing at the bit to make the attack on El Duda, finally doing so as soon as he was allowed to. There is worse: Freyberg has his father saying that the active role was temporarily handed over to Tobruk, as if TOBFORCE had been in some subsidiary and non-active role, whereas my account of the break-out in Part Two demonstrates that there was never a time after it came over the bridges when TOBFORCE was not pursuing an active and independent role. The most unkind cut though, has his father saying: 'During the night Tobruk reported that they had come out eight miles – felt inclined to send a reply that NZ Division had come out 308 miles.' So they had, but TOB-FORCE's eight miles had taken it through a ring of heavily mined and fortified defence posts manned by the best of Rommel's infantry, and at no little cost to the men making that journey. The comment was unworthy of Freyberg, and much out of character. On the whole then, 70th Div's contribution to the eventual success of 'Crusader' has been given little, scant, and often mistaken recognition by the men who have written the history of the Western Desert campaigns.

One cannot escape the feeling that had this been anything other than an ordinary British division the world would have heard much more about its bravery and its accomplishments than has been the case, nor would anyone have dared to propose that it be broken up. But it was a division without glamour, formed from a variety of county and regional regiments, and therefore dispensable. To one division then, the fame and glory ... to the other, the jungle version of the knacker's yard, and ultimate oblivion. It hardly seems fair, hence this History.

THE FOUR SIGNALMEN

We rode the rails, as Charlie had in his Canadian boyhood, but these were the rails taking us from Habata to Alexandria and Christmas. It was terribly cold and we tore boards from the walls of the wagon and built a fire in the middle of its iron floor. We sang the songs of Crosby, and of Flanagan and Allan, of George Formby, but more often we sang the esoteric and richly imaginative ballads of the fighting soldier. We were the Rats of Tobruk triumphant. We had beaten Rommel. We were kngs of the desert.

Alas, our reign did not last for long. Six months later, Charlie, Jim and I were behind barbed-wire and Louis had disappeared from our lives in the same way in which he had first appeared in them ... silently, perhaps with an apologetic murmur, he drifted away like the sands of a light khamsin.

We became separated. Charlie was found lying dead, early one morning beside an open latrine in a POW camp in Italy. He was suffering from dysentery and had dragged himself out for a last time. It was perhaps as well. Back home his wife had been hurrying down a London street with their child in her arms. The flying bomb fell and nothing was found of either of them. All the leading players of that sunny day's ceremony in long ago Thursley were gone – padre, partners and procreated. It were as if it had never happened.

Jim and I met up occasionally after the war as civilians. One day in the fifties I received a letter from his aged mother telling me that he was ill with flu. I drove over to Manchester that night only to find that I was too late; it had been a virulent form of leukemia, not flu. She said that he had been asking for me, if she had been able to find and use a telephone I would have got there in time, but she was of that generation which did not use telephones.

Memories.

Bones.

ROMMEL

Rommel, the Commander

Rommel won his heart's desire in June 1942, when the South African General Klopper surrendered Tobruk and handed over its garrison after a battle lasting little more than twenty-four hours. That the defences were no longer so strong nor the defenders as resolute as they had been during the siege, does not lessen his achievement. It was to prove the pinnacle of his success as a Field Commander, however. From then on, there was little for him to celebrate.

He led his exhausted men to the gateway of the Nile Delta and found it barred against him. Beset by problems of supply, suffering attrition from a series of attacks launched by Auchinleck, and almost immobilised by health problems, he made one last effort to break through to Alexandria. It foundered under the concentrated British guns on Alam Halfa. Three weeks later he reported sick and returned to Germany, where he went into hospital at Zemmering. Meanwhile, his nemesis had arrived in Africa. A cautious and rigid commander had taken over Eighth Army. Against Rommel's charismatic leadership; instinctive military flair, fluidity in action and utter determination, Montgomery would pit numerical superiority in arms; exact tactical calculation; logistic and communicative competence, and an equal determination.

On 24 October Hitler telephoned Rommel in hospital, told him there was bad news from Africa, and asked him to go back and resume command. He did so. Handicapped by a desperate shortage of petrol, he was unable to resist Montgomery's continuous onslaught, and defeat became inevitable. Rommel now showed himself to be a master of retreat. He turned what had begun as a rout into an orderly retreat, and withdrew the bulk of his army, never allowing it to be outflanked or drawn into a major action which he could not have won. He took his troops all the way back to the Mareth Line, and with his southern flank thus protected, turned on the Americans at Kasserine Pass. It was his last victory in Africa. He made a final attack on the Eighth Army positions at Medenine and was driven off. Then he returned to Germany and to hospital.

When the Italian Government surrendered to the Allies in the summer of 1943, Hitler sent him into Italy at the head of Army Group B, and during those critical days he tightened the German grip on this southern front. He was then sent to inspect the coastal defences in western Europe and found them to be almost non-existent. He threw himself into the task of creating a defensive barrier along the coast of France, and in January 1944 he was appointed Commander-in-Chief of the German armies in the west. The invasion brought him face-to-face with Montgomery again, but his generalship was constrained by constant interference from OKW and ultimately, by Hitler. On 17 July 1944 he was at the front when his luck finally ran out. The car in which he was travelling from General Dietrich's HQ was strafed and he suffered a fractured skull and injuries to his left eye and his mouth. He lay unconscious on the road before being taken to hospital near St-Germain. On 8 August he insisted on returning to his home in Herrlingen because he did not wish to fall into enemy hands. It would have been far better had he done so.

Rommel and Hitler

Rommel was brought into high command by Hitler. He was exactly what Hitler wanted: a non-political general, free from the taint of the military establishment, who through his battle-worthiness and victories, was able to be presented to the German people as a brave and obedient soldier hero. For his part, Rommel saw Hitler as the man who had brought Germany out of chaos and who had re-established the German nation as the powerful entity at the heart of Europe. It began as a partnership of mutual attraction, and ended with Rommel carrying a revolver when he went for his daily walk because he feared that Hitler had ordered his death.

The beginning of Rommel's loss of faith in Hitler can be timed exactly. With the battle of El Alamein lost, it fell to Rommel to get his troops out of Africa in such condition as would conserve them for action in Europe. He ordered the withdrawal to begin, and reported this to Hitler. At 1330 hrs on 3 November 1942 he was ordered not to yield a yard of ground and to show his troops no other road except to victory or death. This splendid army which had given its all to the German cause was to be sacrificed in a propaganda exercise by his political master. Although he was stunned by the order, he was prepared to obey, but the decision was taken out of his hands by Montgomery, who broke through the Axis lines. From that moment, Rommel saw a different Hitler from the one he had so admired.

His disillusionment grew during a meeting between the two later that month, when Hitler, in front of staff officers, called him a defeatist and said that his men were cowards. When Rommel asked would he rather lose Tripoli or the Afrika Korps, Hitler shouted that the Afrika Korps was dispensable. There followed two meetings in 1943, at one of which Hitler told Rommel that if the German people were incapable of winning the war they could rot. By this time Rommel was also becoming aware of the atrocities being perpetrated by Himmler's SS, but when this highly moral soldier protested to Hitler about SS excesses in Italy he was told that it was not his business. Early in 1944 he decided that the Hitler régime must be brought to an end if anything of the Germany he loved was to be saved. He thought that the movement to replace Hitler must come on the western front, through a *rapprochement* with the Allied commanders, and began to sound out other German military men, using his Chief of Staff, General Speidel, as an emissary.

There was a last meeting between Rommel, von Rundstedt and Hitler in June 1944, at which both generals tried to make Hitler realise the gravity of the situation – and failed; Rommel dared to ask Hitler how he imagined the war could be won. Von Runstedt was replaced by Field Marshal von Kluge whose first act was to censure Rommel's handling of the battle in France. Rommel reacted vigorously with an analysis of the battle and a condemnation of the interference by OKW (and, by implication, of Hitler). He sent a copy of this to Hitler at the beginning of July, and followed, it with a last letter on 15 July in which he said that the unequal struggle in the west was reaching its end. These reminders that Hitler's tactical errors were about to result in catastrophe must have caused the final breach between them and from then on his life was in jeopardy. Then came the air attack. Three days after this, von Stauffenberg left his satchel containing a bomb at Hitler's conference table, and in the purge that followed General Beck, the former Chief of the General Staff, and twelve other generals were tortured, tried and executed. General Speidel was among those arrested and questioned. Rommel's African past caught up with him here; one of the members of the military tribunal which tried Speidel was Kircheim, whom Rommel had sent home from Africa 'on his camel'.

Rommel now knew that it was only a question of time before they came for him. On 7 October 1944 he was ordered by Field Marshal Keitel to go to Berlin and refused to do so, suspecting that he would be killed *en route*. Two days later Generals Burgdorf and Maisel arrived at his home. After spending an hour with them, Rommel emerged to tell his wife that he was either to take poison immediately or face a People's Court. He departed in the car in which they had arrived. A few hundred yards down the road Maisel got out. Ten minutes later, Rommel was dead. Frau Rommel later told how, when she saw him, he had a look of contempt on his face.

There followed the cynicism of telegrams of sympathy from Hitler, Göring, Goebbels and Ribbentrop, a State Funeral at Ulm, and the offer of a monument, which Frau Rommel spurned. Erwin Rommel had given everything he had to the German nation. He deserved better than the miserable end it gave him in return.

NOTES

Where no reference number has been given, the information has come from the War Diary of the unit concerned.

PART ONE

1. Schmidt, p. 78.
2. A field regiment had a component of 24 guns. There were three batteries, each of eight guns. Each battery was divided into two troops of four guns.
3. *Portées* were trucks whose backs had been cut away so that the 2pdrs mounted on them could go into action without having to be unloaded. This saved time and allowed greater mobility.
4. Major-General R. Leakey: personal account told to the author.
5. Major-General A. Lascelles: personal account told to the author.
6. Agar-Hamilton and Turner.
7. John Cross, an RAF ground gunner in 6 Squadron, 'won' the clock which had served this rudimentary control room. He took it back to England, had it mounted in the hub of a Hurricane propeller, and subsequently presented it to the squadron.
8. The urgency is shown in item 7 of Order 2 promulgated by 14Lt AA on 6 April: 'A mobile striking force will be ready to move off motorised at 15 minutes warning and will consist of:
Command O.C. Town Duties
Notts Yeomanry 5 officers and 120 men
39th Lt AA 2 officers, 45 men and 5 Bredas
Royal Navy 2 officers and 50 men
57 Battery will have sufficient officers and men with as many 75mm guns or larger as may be found and made serviceable to move up to the perimeter fence, place and time to be made known later.'
In other words, men from the AA defences and the Naval Shore Party were to be ready to drop everything and rush to defend the town itself or help plug any gap which may have been forced in the outer defences.

9. The three field regiments were all Territorial Regiments: 104RHA were the Essex Yeomanry; 107RHA were the Notts Hussars; 51FRG were the Westmorland and Cumberland Yeomanry.
10. For example, 39LAA were firing eleven Bredas in the vicinity of King's Cross, where they were defending field gun positions.
11. No description of the artillery of Tobruk would be complete without mention of RSM Clarke, RA, and also of the Bush Artillery. The Italians had removed the sights from their guns before surrendering. Clarke collected some Italian howitzers and fitted them with sights which he made himself. They were brought into use, and were known as Mr Clarke's guns. RSM Clarke did not survive the break-out. *RA Commemoration Book*, Bell, 1950, p 183. The Bush Artillery also consisted of captured Italian guns. They were fired by Australian infantrymen who didn't bother about sights but simply squinted along the barrel and shouted 'Let 'er go, Mate!' Personal recollection of the author.
12. The RAF can claim to have fired the first shots and scored the first small victories of the siege. On 9 April at 1100 hrs a heavy raid developed over the fortress. Squadron Leader Murray raced to the airfield with three pilots. Within ten minutes they were aloft and engaging the enemy aircraft. Pilot Officer Goodman brought down the first enemy plane to fall over Tobruk – an Me 110. Later that same day Goodman had to crash land but survived the incident. 73 Squadron War Diary.
13. Willison, p. 41.
14. One entry in 3rd Armd Bde's Diary of 1 May reads: '1040 hrs R13 being attacked by 25 tanks on north side. B Sqn 1RTR sent to intercept them.' This represented a four-way series of communication:
(i) from the infantry in Post R13 to 9th

Div HQ
(ii) from 9th Div HQ to 3rd Armd Bde
(iii) from 3rd Armd Bde to HQ 1RTR
(iv) from HQ 1RTR to B Sqn 1RTR.

15. Bergot, p. 75

16. Barker, p. 28, attributes the remark to Rommel; Bergot, p. 75, attributes it to von Prittwitz.

17. Obertleutnant Ponath, extract from his personal diary, found on his body after the battle of 14 April.

18. Behrendt, p. 69.

19. Schmidt, p. 11.

20. Barker, p. 30.

21. MG2 was the sister battalion to Ponath's MG8 in Panzergrenadier Regt 104.

22. Schmidt, p. 44.

23. Citation in the *London Gazette*, Friday 4 July 1941.

24. Captain Goschen had been using this house previously.

25. The RHA War Diary later commented on the neat way in which lifted mines had been stacked by the German Pioneers.

26. *RA Commemoration Book 1939–1945*, p. 185.

27. Major General R. A. Leakey, unpublished memoirs (lent to the author), p. 77. Apparently Mulligan was able to fire more accurately when he had a cigarette in his mouth, hence Leakey's ignoring of the prohibition against smoking inside the turret. Leakey later met the man who suffered the emergency amputation walking about on crutches in a hospital in the Middle East.

28. Battery Sergeant-Major Batten (known as 'Jean' after the famous aviatrix) received the DCM for this action.

29. Liddell Hart, p. 126.

30. Heckman, p. 77. Schraepler had been with Rommel in France and had been wounded then. Within two weeks he was back in action, but in the meantime his successor had been killed '*within a yard of me*', according to Rommel's letter to his wife (letter from Manfred Rommel to Liddell Hart boxed under 9/24/24 Liddell Hart Centre, King's College).

31. Letter from Rommel to Lucy Rommel, dated 15 April 1941, Liddell Hart Centre.

32. Pitt, p. 10.

33. Heckmann, p. 109, says there were 35 Italian and German batteries concentrated opposite Ras El Medauur.

34. *The Halder War Diary*, p. 374.

35. Ibid., p. 359. Halder wrote: 'Rommel makes preposterous demands. His wishes can be satisfied only in so far as preparations for BARBAROSSA permit.'

36. Schmidt, p. 38.

37. Liddell Hart, p. 132.

38. Irving, p. 94. Irving says that by 0900 hrs, Pt 209 had been taken from the rear and the main attempt to drive north-east towards Tobruk began. It was in fact taken at 2130 hrs on the previous evening and the drive began at 0800 hrs.

39. Report by Brigade Major (later Major-General) A. J. Lascelles entitled 'Third Armoured Brigade in Tobruk', filed under WO/169/1278, Public Record Office, Kew.

40. Armitage had escaped the net at Mechili. He found his way back across the frontier and then returned to his regiment in Tobruk by sea. He ended the war as a Brigadier.

41. Wilmot.

42. Heckman, p. 116.

43. Lavarack lost command of CYRCOM and was downgraded to command of 7th Australian Division.

44. Liddell Hart, p. 133.

45. Quartermaster's Report, 'The Siege of Tobruk, April to June 1941', PRO, filed under CAB 106/838.

46. Heckstall-Smith, p. 124.

47. Pitt, p. 11.

48. Heckstall-Smith, p. 73.

49. Ibid., p. 91.

50. Captain Seebohm was Rommel's ears in the desert. His 3rd Radio Intercept Coy brought radio interception to a fine art and Rommel placed great store by him. Unfortunately for Rommel, Seebohm was killed through the stupidity of a senior German officer.

51. Churchill, p. 221.

52. At about this time, Leakey's brother, Sergeant N. G. Leakey of the King's African Rifles, was winning a posthumous VC at the crossing of the River Billate in Abyssinia.

53. See Smithers, *Rude Mechanicals*, for details of British tanks, their production, and their weaknesses.

54. Warner, p. 186.

55. General Bayerlein, letter filed under CAB 106/763 at PRO.

56. Churchill, p. 220.

57. Ibid., p. 304.
58. Heckman, p. 130.
59. Colonel N. Berry, OBE, was Chief Mechanical Engineer for XIII Corps in 1941. He said that the Crusader had a 12-cylinder 400hp aero engine of 1915 design vintage. In the desert it needed a cooling arrangement. One was designed which involved two water-pumps driven by a chain from the crankshaft. The design took no account of the dust raised by a tank on the move. This collected on the chain which then stretched and began to jump the crankshaft driving-sprocket. Changing the sprocket was a 3-day job. Also, the water-pumps could not take the heat and sprang leaks. There were no facilities in Egypt to manufacture a new design. At a vital time in the 'Crusader' battle 200 Crusaders were under repair in the workshops. Quoted by Warner, pp. 178–9.
60. Behrendt, p. 86.
61. Schmidt, p. 64.
62. Major-General Lascelles in a post-war letter to the author.
63. The Medical Orderly was wounded during the Corridor battles, insisted in staying in action and was subsequently killed there. For Maers' fate see p. (**PAGE No TO GO IN**)
64. Wilmot, p. 200.
65. Pitt, p. 20.
66. This was Leakey's last action at Tobruk. He was taken, against his will, from a perimeter post to a ship in the harbour, so that he could attend a Staff Course in Cairo. He survived the war and the Korean War, and ended his career as Major General.

PART TWO

1. Australian newspapers had been carrying stories of how their men in Tobruk were degenerating into military gypsies, and must be brought out before the process became irreversible.
2. Willison, p. 100.
3. Wilmot, p. 288.
4. *Tobruk House News*: Official Journal of the Victoria Branch ROTA, August, 1989.
5. Silvertop, then commanding 3RTR, was killed at St Anthonis in Holland during Operation 'Market Garden', September 1944.
6. Halder, p. 454. Halder told Gause in July 1941: 'Rommel's character defects make him extremely hard to get along with, but no one cares to come out in open opposition because of his brutality.'
7. Agar-Hamilton, pp. 69–70.
8. Willison, p. 12.
9. Pitt, p. 27.
10. Lewin, p. 78.
11. Hoyt, p. 197.
12. Von Mellenthin, p. 57.
13. Ibid., p. 57.
14. Connell, p. 336.
15. The 'Jumping Jack' was a German mine, about the size of a large jam jar. It had an inner container which was thrown into the air when any of the mine's three prongs or an attached trip-wire was triggered. Once in the air, another charge blasted 140 solid steel balls in all directions.
16. Kippenberger, p. 81.
17. Lewin, p. 81.
18. Heckman, p. 187.
19. Pipe Major Roy had escaped from captivity in Greece before going to Tobruk. 'The Piper of Tobruk' was published in *The Scottish Record* before it was known who the piper was. He survived his wounds.
20. Walter Benzie survived the break-out but was killed fighting a lone battle against several panzers during the retreat to El Alamein.
21. Agar-Hamilton, p. 199.
22. Barnett, p. 101.
23. Major Fenski did not have long to savour his triumph, being killed on the following day.
24. Barclay, p. 62.
25. Carrell, p. 78; Agar-Hamilton, pp. 255–6.
26. Von Mellenthin, p. 72.
27. Barker, p. 59.
28. Von Mellenthin, p. 72. Irving, p. 141, says that the two Field Maintenance Centres (FMCs) were set up under Rommel's nose before the battle began. This was not so. XXX Corps Admin Instruction No 2. reads: 'On D Day 2 FMCs will be established ref 1.250000, 62 FMC 459341, 63 FMC 455325.' All the advancing A Echelons crossed the wire carrying three days' supplies.
29. Among Rommel memorabilia held at the Liddell Hart Centre and boxed under 9/24/20 is a map drawn by Rommel

some time after 'Crusader' in which he shows Sidi Omar to have been in Axis hands at that time.

30. Agar-Hamilton, p. 308.
31. Masters, pp. 116–17.
32. Barclay, pp. 63–4.
33. This photograph was published in *The London Illustrated News* on 27 December 1941. Years later it came into the writer's possession but sadly he was just off camera.
34. Barclay, p. 62.
35. Von Mellenthin, p. 77
36. Westphal, p. 109.
37. Page 2 of a letter from Manfred Rommel to Liddell Hart, filed under 9/24/24, PRO.
38. Pitt, pp. 126–7.
39. Lieutenant-Colonel O'Carroll, 'Operations Report', 4RTR Records, Tank Museum, Bovington, p.2.
40. Humble, pp. 168–9.
41. Liddell Hart, Introductory proof for *Rommel Papers* dated 2 October 1952, p. 3, Liddell Hart Centre for Military Archives.
42. Pitt, p. 142.
43. Neither man survived the war. Campbell was killed soon after 'Crusader' when the truck in which he was being driven (by Roy Farren) turned over. Loder-Symonds, then a Brigadier, was killed in Italy.
44. The panzer in which Neumann-Silkow received his mortal wound probably bore the divisional crest – an ace of spades.
45. Schmitt and Bach both put up stiff resistance before being forced to surrender. Bach died while a prisoner of war.

PART THREE
1. Pitt, p. 303.
2. Schmidt, p. 78.
3. Lewin, p. 85
4. Pitt, p. 64.
5. Carrell, p. 106.
6. Von Mellenthin, p. 55.
7. Hoyt, p. 197.
8. Von Mellenthin, p. 57.
9. Ibid., p. 58.
10. Westphal, p. 116.
11. Lewin, p. 59.
12. Schmidt, p. 83.
13. Tute, p. 25.
14. Lewin, p. 115.
15. Rommel remained a hero to the German nation even after his death. The author remembers a banner headline seen in a German newspaper on the day the news of Rommel's death was given to the German people: 'Our Erwin is dead'. There was of course no mention that he had been done to death by the state machine. The heroic myth was thus perpetuated in German folklore.
16. Von Mellenthin, p. 46.
17. Schmidt, p. 85.
18. Ibid., p. 88.
19. Ibid., p. 92.
20. Barker, p. 64.
21. Von Mellenthin, p. 77.
22. Liddell Hart, p. 176.
23. Letter from Rommel to Lucy Rommel dated 10 October 1941, quoted by Liddell Hart, p. 151.
24. Page 1 of letter from Manfred Rommel to Liddell Hart, filed under 9/24/24 at the Liddell Hart Centre.
25. Schmidt, p. 72.

APPENDICES

APPENDIX 1
ORDER OF BATTLE: TOBRUK FORTRESS, 5 APRIL 1941

Commands and Staff.

Fortress Commander:Major-General L. J. Morshead

General Staff

GSO1: Colonel C. E. M. Lloyd

GSO2: Major T. W. White

Quartermaster-General: Colonel A. P. O. White (later Colonel B. W. Culver)

QMG Staff: Major N. G. Dodds and Major R. J. Barham

Administration Services: Colonel H. G. Furnell; Lieutenant-Colonel A. L. Noton

Commander Royal Artillery: Brigadier L. F. Thompson (later Brigadier P. Myburgh)

Brigade Major: Major J. C. Smith

Commander 4th AA Brigade: Brigadier J. N. Slater (later Brigadier Muirhead)

Brigade Major: Major K. W. L. Roberts

Royal Australian Engineers Colonel J. Mann

Royal Australian Signals: Lieutenant-Colonel D. N. Vernon

Australian Army Service Corps: Lieutenant-Colonel J. A. Watson

CO 3rd Armd Bde: Lieutenant-Colonel H. Drew (later Davey, Keller and Willison)

Brigade Major: Major A. J. Lascelles (later Uniacke, Silvertop and Windsor)

CO Aust 18th Inf Bde: Brigadier G. F. Wootton

Brigade Major: Major T. J. Daly

CO Aust 20th Inf Bde: Brigadier J. J. Murray

Brigade Major: Major L. H. Allen

CO Aust 24th Inf Bde: Brigadier A. H. L. Godfrey

Brigade Major: Major R. W. Ogle

CO Aust 26th Inf Bde: Brigadier R. W. Tovell

Brigade Major: Major F. W. Speed

Senior Naval Officer: Captain A. L. Pollard

Naval Officer in Command: Commander Smith, RN

Liaison Officer: Lieutenant-Commander A. H. Green, RN

CO 258 Wing: Wing Commander Johnson

CO 73 Squadron: Squadron Leader Murray

CO 6 Squadron: Squadron Leader Weld

RAF Liaison Officer: Squadron Leader E. R. Black

CO Tobruk Sub-Area: Colonel T. P. Cook

Note that decorations are not given here, in order to avoid confusion with decorations awarded subsequent to the siege.

APPENDIX 2
TOBRUK: THE ROLL CALL OF REGIMENTS

Australian Troops
9th Division
HQ Signals and Intelligence Services
20th Infantry Brigade
HQ and Signal Section
2/13th Bn*
2/15th Bn
2/17th Bn
20th Anti-tank Coy
24th Infantry Brigade
HQ and Signal Section
2/28th Bn
2/32nd Bn
2/43rd Bn
24th Anti-tank Coy
26th Infantry Brigade
HQ and Signal Section
2/23rd Bn
2/24th Bn
2/48th Bn
26th Anti-tank Coy
18th Infantry Brigade (attached)
HQ and Signal Section
2/9th Bn
2/10th Bn
2/12th Bn
16th Anti-tank Company
Royal Aust Engineers
HQ
2/3rd, 2/4th, 2/7th, 2/13th Field
  Companies
2/4th Field Park Company
2/1st Pioneer Battalion
Royal Aust Artillery
2/12th Field Regiment
3rd Anti-tank Regiment
8th Light Anti-Aircraft Regiment
Aust Army Service Corps
HQ
9th Div Supply Column
9th Div Ammunition Column
9th Div Petrol Column
7th Div Supply Column

Composite Company AASC (in the
  Red Line)
Aust Army Medical Corps
4th General Hospital
2/2nd Casualty Clearing Station
2/3rd, 2/5th, 2/8th, 2/11th Field
  Ambulances
Bacterial Laboratory, Ophthalmic
  and Stores Units
Other Australian Troops
2/4th Field Hygiene
4AOD
9th Div Provost Company
Div Postal, Salvage and Employment
  Units

British Troops
3rd Armoured Brigade (32nd Army
  Tank Brigade)
HQ and Signal Section
1st Royal Tank Regiment
4th Royal Tank Regiment
D Sqn, 7th Royal Tank Regiment
1st King's Dragoon Guards
3rd Queen's Own Hussars
Heavy Machine-Gunners
1st Royal Northumberland Fusiliers
Royal Artillery
HQ and Signal Section
51st Field Regiment and 144 (SSY)
  Field Regiment
1st, 104th, 107th Royal Horse Artillery
3rd Royal Horse Artillery and 149
  Anti-tank Regiment)
4th Durham Survey Section
4th Anti-Aircraft Brigade
HQ and Signal Section
51st Heavy AA Regiment 152, 153,
  235 Batteries. 192 Indep. HAA
13th Light AA Regiment 37, 38, 1 Batteries
14th Light AA Regiment 39, 40, 57
  Batteries

Notts Yeomanry 206 and 530 Coastal
  Batteries
Royal Engineers
551st Army Troops Company
295th Army Field Company
4th Field Squadron. 2/12/54 Field
  Coys
143rd Field Park Company 219 F Park
  Coy
Royal Army Service Corps
5th, 14th, 15th, 346th MT Companies
Line of Communications Company
51st and 307th Companies, Section
  51 Heavy AA Regiment
VRD, MTSD, Bulk Storage, Butchery,
  Bakery Units
Royal Ordnance Corps 503th AOW,
  Port Workshop Detachment, AOD,
  AAD

70th Infantry Division (replacing Australian 9th Division)
14th Infantry Brigade
HQ and Signal Section
2nd Bn Black Watch
1st Bn Beds and Herts Regiment
2nd Bn York and Lancs Regiment
16th Infantry Brigade
HQ and Signal Section
2nd Bn King's Own Royal Regiment
2nd Bn Leicestershire Regiment
2nd Bn Queen's Regiment
23rd Infantry Brigade
HQ and Signal Section
1st Bn Durham Light Infantry
4th Bn Border Regiment
1st Bn Essex Regiment

Indian Army
18th Cavalry Regiment

Royal Navy
Inshore Squadron

Royal Air Force
235 Wing HQ
6 Squadron (Lysanders)
73 Squadron (Hurricanes)
Ground Crew Rear Party

Polish Troops
1st Carpathian Brigade/Polish
  Artillery Regiment

Czechoslovak Army
One Battalion

Other detachments
Army Post Office, Army Stationery
  Unit,
POW Cage and Transit Camp Units
Y Docks, Tug and Crew, Z Tug and
  Lighter Units
1st, 2nd, 4th Libyan Pioneer Battal-
  ions

NB. The Third Hussars Regiment was
present in the early days of the siege
but most of their troops were withdrawn and fought in Greece. Some
remained and served with HQ
Tobruk Tanks; Captain George Hope,
for example, served as Staff Captain
in that brigade.

The King's Dragoon Guards were
present during the early part of the
siege and served as infantry for some
time before being withdrawn, leaving
behind their C Squadron.

Elements of both 5th and 6th RTR
were present in the early days but
were soon withdrawn to join their
regiments elsewhere.

APPENDIX 3
TOBRUK: THE ACCOUNT RENDERED

Army Casualties (April to October)*

FORCES	KILLED	WOUNDED	MISSING	TOTAL
Australian	744	1,974	476	3,194
British	88	406	15	509
Indian	1	25	–	26
Polish	22	82	3	107
Totals	855	2,487	494	3,836

70th Div casualties including those incurred in the break-out**
138 officers and 1,815 Other Ranks (categories not available) 2,153
Combined total 5,989

Royal Navy, Royal Aust Navy and Merchant Navy*

	KILLED / MISSING	WOUNDED	TOTAL
RN and RAN	469	186	655
Merchant Navy	70	55	125
Total	539	241	780

Royal Air Force

Casualty List not available, but ten pilots and six ground crew are buried at Tobruk, and there were the six including the padre who were shot down in the harbour.

Total casualties
6,791

HM ships sunk: 2 destroyers, 3 sloops, 7 anti-submarine and minesweepers, 7 store carriers and schooners, 6 A Lighters, 1 fast minelayer: total 26

HM ships damaged: 7 destroyers, 1 sloop, 11 anti-submarine and mine-sweepers, 3 gunboats, 1 schooner: total 23

Merchant Navy ships sunk: 6 plus 1 schooner total 7

Merchant Navy ships damaged: 6 total 6

Sunk or damaged by enemy action total 62

*Playfair
**70th Div War Diary
***Cunningham, p. 472

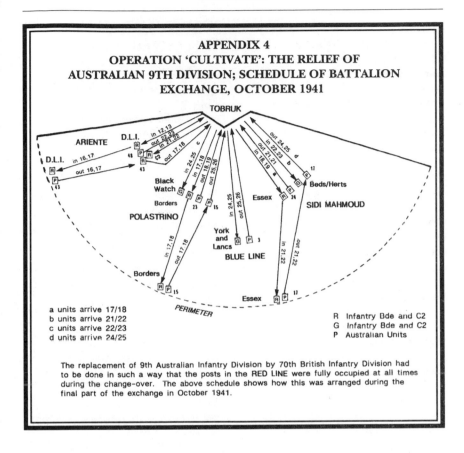

APPENDIX 4
OPERATION 'CULTIVATE': THE RELIEF OF AUSTRALIAN 9TH DIVISION; SCHEDULE OF BATTALION EXCHANGE, OCTOBER 1941

a units arrive 17/18
b units arrive 21/22
c units arrive 22/23
d units arrive 24/25

R Infantry Bde and C2
G Infantry Bde and C2
P Australian Units

The replacement of 9th Australian Infantry Division by 70th British Infantry Division had to be done in such a way that the posts in the RED LINE were fully occupied at all times during the change-over. The above schedule shows how this was arranged during the final part of the exchange in October 1941.

APPENDIX 5
BRITISH MILITARY FORMATIONS IN THE WESTERN DESERT (1941) AND THE ABBREVIATIONS USED IN THE TEXT TO DENOTE THEM

The Hierarchy:

Army; Corps; Division (Div); Brigade (Bde); Battalion (Bn); Company (Coy); Platoon (Plat)

Eighth Army had two corps, each of which had two divisions; each division had three brigades of three battalions; each battalion had three companies of three or four platoons.

NB: These were standard components, but there were variants according to circumstances.

XIII Corps comprised Indian 4th Div; NZ 2nd Div; 1st Army Tank Bde; plus supporting arms

Indian 4th Div comprised Indian 5th, 7th, 11th Bdes; plus supporting arms

NZ 2nd Div (2NZ) comprised NZ 4th, 5th, 6th Bdes plus supporting arms

1st Army Tank Bde comprised 42nd, 44th Tank Bns, equipped with Infantry Tanks (Matildas or Valentines)

XXX Corps comprised: 7th Armd Div; 22nd Guards Motorised Bde; S. African 1st Div

7th Armd Div comprised: 4th, 7th, 22nd Armd Bdes; 7th Support Group; plus supporting arms

4th Armd Bde comprised: 8th Hussars (8HUS); 3rd Bn Royal Tanks (3RTR); 5th Bn Royal Tanks (5RTR)

7th Armd Bde comprised: 6th Bn Royal Tanks (6RTR); 2nd Bn Royal Tanks (2RTR); 7th Hussars (7HUS)

22nd Armd Bde comprised: 2nd Bn Royal Gloucester Hussars (2HUS); 3rd, 4th Bns County of London Yeomanry (3YEO)

S. African 1st Div comprised: S. African 1st, 5th Bdes; a machine-gun bn; three reconnaissance squadrons

7th Support Group comprised: 2nd Bn Rifle Bde; 60 Field Regt RA; 3rd RHA (anti-tank guns)

NB. Supporting arms included artillery, reconnaissance units and engineers. Parent Units are shown in bold type.

The Tobruk Garrison Units (excluding ancillary units listed in Appendix 2)

Australian 9th Div: 20th, 24th, 26th Bdes; 18th Bde (attached)

20th Bde: 2/13th, 2/15th, 2/17th Bns

24th Bde: 2/28th, 2/32nd, 2/43rd Bns

26th Bde: 2/23rd, 2/24th, 2/48th Bns

18th Bde : 2/9th, 2/10th, 2/12th Bns

British 70th Div: 14th, 16th, 23rd Inf Bdes

14th Inf Bde: 2nd Bn Black Watch; 1st Bn Beds and Herts; 2nd Bn York and Lancs

16th Inf Bde: 2nd Bn King's Own; 2nd Bn Leicesters; 2nd Bn Queen's Own

23rd Inf Bde: 1st Bn Durham Light Inf; 4th Bn Border Regt; 1st Bn Essex Regt

Until 19 September **3rd Armd Bde:** elements of 3rd, 4th, 5th Royal Tank Regt; 3rd Hussars; King's Dragoon Guards (KDG) during part of the siege; 1RTR (less A Sqn); D Sqn 7RTR; C Sqn KDG during the entire siege

From 19 September **32nd Army Tank Bde:** 1RTR (less A Sqn); D Sqn 7RTR; all of 4RTR, C Sqn KDG

4th Anti-Aircraft Bde: 13th, 14th Lt AA Regts (shown as 13LAA, etc.); Aust 8th Lt AA Regt; 51st Heavy AA Regt (shown as 51HAA)

13th, 14th Lt AA Regts: 39, 40, 57 Light Batteries (shown as 39LAA, etc.)

51st Heavy AA Regt: 152, 153, 235 Heavy AA Batteries (shown as 152HAA, etc.)

Field Guns: 1st, 3rd, 104th, 107th Royal Horse Artillery Regts (shown as 1RHA, etc.); 51st Field Regt (51FRG); Aust 3rd Anti-Tank Regt (shown as 3AA-T)

Notts Yeomanry: 206, 530 Batteries, defending the coastline

APPENDIX 6
AXIS MILITARY FORMATIONS IN THE WESTERN DESERT IN 1941 AND THE ABBREVIATIONS USED TO DENOTE THEM

The Hierarchy

Panzergruppe Afrika comprised two Corps whose components varied:

(1) **Deutsches Afrika Korps (DAK)**: 5th Light Div; 15th Panzer Div (PZ15); Div zbV Afrika; Corpo d'Armata XX1

NB. 5th Light became 21st Panzer Division (PZ21) in August 1941; Div zbV Afrika became 90th Light Div (90LTD) in November 1941

PZ15: Panzer Regt 8 (PZR8); 15th Rifle Regt (RR15); Reconnaissance Bn 33 (RB33) plus divisional artillery and Engineers

PZ21: Panzer Regt 5 (PZR5); 104 Rifle Regt (RR104); Recce Bn 3 (RB3) plus divisional artillery and Engineers

90LTD: Infantry Regt 155 (INR155); Afrika Regt 361 (AFR361); Sonderverband 288 (S288); Recce Bn 580 (RB580)

Corpo d'Armata XX1 (Italian): Bologna Div; Brescia Div; Pavia Div; Savona Div; Trento Div; Artillery Group Böttcher (Böttcher)

(2) **Corpo d'Armata di Manovra:** Ariete Armoured Div (Ariete); Trieste Motorised Division Trieste)

Ariete: 132 Armd Regt; 8th Bersaglieri Regt; 132 Artillery Regt

Trieste; 65th Inf Regt; 66th Inf Regt, 9th Bersaglieri Regt plus supporting arms

NB. Rommel was prone to form *ad hoc* Battle Groups from whatever sources were immediately available (e.g., the Stephan Group)

Other abbreviations used in text

ACV	Armoured Command Vehicle
AFV	Armoured fighting vehicle
CO	Commanding Officer
FOO	Forward Observation Officer
OP	Observation Point/Post
DR	Dispatch Rider
WT	Wireless communication in Morse Code
RT	Oral communication by wireless

BIBLIOGRAPHY

SOURCES AND THEIR LOCATIONS

Public Record Office, Kew
WO201/2270 Order of Battle, Tobruk Fortress, April–June 1941
WO201/2275 List of Units, Siege of Tobruk, June–October 1941
CAB106/838 Quartermaster's Report, Siege of Tobruk, April–June 1941
CAB106/372 Visit to Tobruk by Lt-Col J. S. Wheeton, RA, August 1941
CAB106/513 Copy of letter concerning events February–April 1941
WO201/362/3 Report on the 'Crusader' Battles
CAB106/630 Report by CRA on operations at Tobruk, April–November 1941
CAB106/812 Notes on the Siege (Royal Horse Artillery)
CAB44/93 The Ellenberger Report, Relief of Tobruk
WO201/631 Eighth Army Situation Reports, November 1941.
CAB106/715 S. African 1st Brigade, 1941 Action (with maps)
CAB106/736 Letter from General Bayerlein on tank tactics 1941–3
WO208/1558 Weekly Review of Situation
CAB105/8 Signals from GHQ Middle East 1941
WO234 North African and Mediterranean Maps (Map Room)
MPHH/678 Various diagrams and sketches drawn by Aust 9th Div surveyors; locations of field guns, Tobruk 1941 (Map Room)

War Diaries
WO201/353 Aust 9th Div 1941
WO169/1278 3rd Armd Bde
WO169/1303 32nd Army Tank Bde
WO169/1409 1st Royal Tank Regt
WO169/1413 4th Royal Tank Regt
WO169/1417 7th Royal Tank Regt
WO169/1384 King's Dragoon Guards
CAB106/812 1st Royal Horse Arty
WO169/2385 104th Royal Horse Arty
WO169/1435 107th Royal Horse Arty
WO169/1454 51st Field Regt RA
WO169/1599 152nd Heavy AA Regt
WO169/1600 153rd Heavy AA Regt
WO169/1612 235th Heavy AA Regt
WO169/1371 Counter-Battery, RA
WO177/417 70th Div Medical Reports
WO169/1705 4th Border Regt
WO169/1707 2nd Black Watch
WO169/1717 1st Essex Regt
WO169/1737 1st Northumb Fusiliers
WO169/1713 1st Durham Light Inf
WO169/1738 2nd Queen's Regt
WO169/1736 2nd Leicestershires
WO169/1731 2nd King's Own Regt
WO169/1704 1st Beds and Herts Regt
WO169/1215; WO169/1216 70th Inf Div
Filed under AIR
RAF 258 Wing
Microfilm 6, 73 Sqns RAF

Liddell Hart Centre for Military Archives, King's College, London
General Siegfried Westphal *German Generals* (proof copy)
Editorial papers and correspondence between Liddell Hart, Manfred Rommel and General Fritz Bayerlein in connection with the publishing of the *Rommel Papers*
Other correspondence between Liddell Hart and Manfred Rommel
Memorabilia, including maps drawn by Erwin Rommel

Imperial War Museum, London
War Diaries (stored in the Documents Department)
Deutsches Afrika Korps
5th Light Division
15th Panzer Division
21st Panzer Division
90th Light Division
Photographs: Middle East 1941, Filed under 'E' Category

Tank Museum, Bovington
Brigadier O'Carroll Report on the El Duda Operations (boxed as 4RTR); Map of the tank locations on El Duda (boxed as 4RTR); Report on the action in which Captain Gardner won the VC
1st, 4th, 7th Royal Tank Regt Memorabilia
Photographs

Royal Vorps of Signals Museum
Photograph of 32nd Army Tank Brigade HQ in the Tobruk Corridor (in the ACV Room)

PUBLISHED SOURCES
Agar-Hamilton, J. A., and Turner, L. C. F. *The Sidi Rezegh Battles 1941*, OUP, 1957

Barclay, Brigadier C. N. *The History of the Northumberland Fusiliers*, William Clowes, 1951
Barker, A. J. *Afrika Korps*, Bison, 1978
Barnett, Corelli *Desert Generals*, Pan, 1962
Behrendt, H. O. *Rommel's Intelligence in the Desert Campaign*, Kimber, 1985
Bekker, Cajus. *The Luftwaffe War Diaries*, Macdonald, 1966
Belchem, D. *All in the Day's March*, Collins, 1978
Bergot, Erwan. *The Afrika Korps*, tr. Richard Barry, Wingate, 1976
Bowyer, Chad. *Men of the Desert Air Force*, Kimber, 1984
Burdick, Charles, and Jacobson, Hans Adolf. *The Halder War Diaries 1939–1942*, Presidio Press, 1988
Carrell, Paul. *The Foxes of the Desert*, (tr. Mervin Savill), Dutton, New York, 1961
Carver, General Sir Michael. *Tobruk and El Alamein*, Batsford, 1964
Churchill, Winston S. *The Second World War*, vol. III, Cassell, 1960
Cunningham, Admiral. *A Sailor's Odyssey*, Hutchinson
Deighton, Len. *Blitzkrieg*, Cape, 1979
Douglas, Keith. *Collected Poems*, Faber
Forty, George. *Afrika Korps at War*, Allen, 1978
Freyberg, Paul. *Bernard Freyberg, VC*, Hodder & Stoughton, 1991
Hall, Timothy. *Tobruk 1941, The Desert Siege*, Methuen, 1984
Hargest, Brigadier James. *Farewell Campo 12*, Michael Joseph, 1945; Morely edn, 1973
Heckmann, Wolf. *Rommel's War in Africa*, tr. Stephen Seago, Doubleday, New York, 1981
Heckstall-Smith, A. *Tobruk*, Blond, 1959
Hoyt, Edwin P. *Hitler's War*, Robert Hale, 1989

Humble, Richard. *Crusader*, Leo Cooper, 1987

Irving, David. *The Trail of the Fox*, Dutton, New York, 1977

Jackson, W. G. F. *North Africa Campaign 1940 to 1943*, Batsford,

Kesselring, Field Marshal. *Memoirs*, Kimber

Kippenberger, Sir Howard. *Infantry Brigadier*, OUP, 1949

Lewin, Ronald. *The Life and Death of the Afrika Korps*, Batsford, 1977

– *Rommel as Military Commander*, Batsford, 1968

Liddell Hart, Sir Basil. *History of the Second World War*, Cassell

– ed. *Rommel Papers*, Collins, 1953

Masters, David. *With Pennants Flying*, Eyre and Spottiswoode, 1943

McGuirk, Dal. *Rommel's Army in Africa*, Stanley Paul, 1987

Mellenthin, Major-General von. *Panzer Battles*, Cassell, 1955

Mitchem, Samuel W. Jnr. *Triumphant Fox*, Stein/Day, New York, 1982

Montgomery, Field Marshal the Viscount. *Memoirs*, Collins, 1958

Murphy, W. E. *The Relief of Tobruk*, Official History (for the Department of Internal Affairs), Wellington, NZ, 1961

Pitt, Barrie. *Churchill and his Generals*, Sidgwick and Jackson, 1981

– *The Crucible of War 2. Auchinleck's Command*, Papermac edn, 1986

Playfair, Major-General I. S. O. *History of the Second World War*, vol. III, HMSO, 1960

Quarrie, Bruce. *Panzers in the Desert*, Stephens, 1978

Rankin, Kenneth. *Top Hats in Tobruk*, Rankin, 1983

Ritchie, Henry S. *The Fusing of the Ploughshare*, Ritchie, 1987

Roberts, Major-General P. *From The Desert to the Baltic*, Kimber, 1987

Schmidt, Heinz W. *With Rommel in the Desert*, Harrap, 1951

Slessor, Kenneth. *The War Diaries of Kenneth Slessor*, Slessor, 1985

Smithers, A. J. *Rude Mechanicals*, Leo Cooper, 1978

Strawson, John. *The Battle For North Africa*, Batsford, 1969

Tute, Warren. *The North African War*, Two Continents, New York, 1976

Warner, Philip. *Alamein*, Kimber, 1979

Willison, Brigadier A. *Relief of Tobruk*, Leagrave Press

Wilmot, Chester. *Tobruk*, Angus and Robertson, 1945

Yndrich, Y. *Fortress Tobruk*, Ernest Benn, 1951

Young, Desmond. *Rommel, the Desert Fox*, Collins, 1950

Royal Artillery. *Commemoration Book 1939–1945*, Bell and Sons, 1950

New Zealand Army Board. *Return to the Attack. New Zealand Division In Action*

ROTSA Association. Victoria Branch. *Tobruk House News*, August, 1989

INDEX

Military formations are shown under national listings. German names ignore the 'von'. Names appearing in the bibliography have not been included. Parental units are shown in brackets.